The Emergence of Whitehead's Metaphysics

SUNY Series in Philosophy

ROBERT C. NEVILLE, EDITOR

The Emergence
of
Whitehead's Metaphysics
1925–1929

Lewis S. Ford

Old Dominion University

STATE UNIVERSITY OF NEW YORK PRESS
ALBANY

Published by
State University of New York Press, Albany

© 1984 State University of New York

Printed in the United States of America

For information, address State University of New York
Press, State University Plaza, Albany, N.Y., 12246

Library of Congress Cataloging in Publication Data

Ford, Lewis S.
    The emergence of Whitehead's metaphysics, 1925-1929.

    (SUNY series in philosophy)
    Includes indexes.
    1. Whitehead, Alfred North, 1861-1947. I. Title.
II. Series.
B1674.W354F67 1984   110'.92'4   83-18206
ISBN 0-87395-856-X
ISBN 0-87395-857-8 (pbk.)

10 9 8 7 6 5 4 3 2 1

To William A. Christian and Ivor Leclerc
Pioneers in the Interpretation of
Whitehead's Systematic Philosophy
This Study of his Pre-Systematic Philosophy
Is Dedicated

Contents

Preface

THIS study has its origin in work undertaken while on a National Endowment for the Humanities Senior Fellowship in 1973–74, when I became convinced that Whitehead's novel conception of the atomicity of time became the means whereby he was able to harvest a lifetime of philosophical reflection. But the book received its strongest impetus in May, 1976, when I set out to learn just what the "slight expansions" were that Whitehead made to his Lowell Lectures of 1925. They were precisely those passages in *Science and the Modern World* pertaining to the atomicity of time. I began to suspect—rightly, I think—that the Lowell Lectures, taken by themselves, present quite a different philosophical outlook from the later parts of the book. Thus we have the phenomenon of a book written for the most part from one perspective, but proposing to be read from quite another on the basis of later additions. This phenomenon, as we shall see, is duplicated in *Process and Reality*.

It is a confusing business, especially if we also include the twists and turns of Whitehead's philosophizing in between. Endeavors to piece together Whitehead's later writings so as to form one coherent whole frequently end up harmonizing disparate ideas and interpreting suggestive and incomplete ideas from the earlier writings in terms of a rather narrow canon of Whiteheadian insights, usually drawn from the later stages of *Process and Reality*. This book is a plea for a different interpretive strategy. It attempts to determine the chronological order of Whitehead's writings from *Science and the Modern World* to *Process and Reality*, so far as this can be ascertained, and then to interpret each unit in terms of its own concepts and those of previous units, excluding any ideas found only in writings still to come. Instead of our unit of interpretation being very broad (all of Whitehead's writings, or those since 1925), I have endeavored to isolate the narrowest meaningful unit, and to show the interpretation which arises from that.

This study will probably disturb prevailing interpretations of Whitehead's philosophy less than might be imagined, for the interpretations have largely been based on what I call in chapter 9 "the final revisions" of *Process and Reality*. The texts I am principally concerned with are either ignored or reinterpreted in the light of those final revisions. That final philosophy is the *position* we are primarily interested in, since all the others are only preliminary. Yet the history of Whitehead's emerging philosophy also deserves attention: *how did he come* to hold that position? This is a tale of high philosophical adventure, a true adventure of ideas. The very idiosyncrasies of Whitehead's books give us some valuable clues about the surprising twists and turns his reflections led to. I have sought to chart these unanticipated insights as accurately as possible, showing how they contributed to his final position.

Most philosophers, in endeavoring to present their ideas in the most systematic and rigorous form possible, eliminate all traces which would suggest how they arrived at them. Whitehead has left his scaffolding standing. It may obscure the systematic presentation but it certainly aids the study of his creativity. While this is particularly a study of Whitehead, from 1925 to 1929, it can also serve as an example of philosophical creativity generally.

Two studies pertinent to this undertaking have preceded this one: Victor Lowe's "The Development of Whitehead's Philosophy" [1] and Nathaniel Lawrence's *Whitehead's Philosophical Development*.[2] The scope of Lowe's undertaking differs markedly from mine. His covers the entire span of Whitehead's published writings, from 1898 to 1941, whereas mine covers only four years. The real difference, however, lies in our varying estimate of the degree of continuity or discontinuity in Whitehead's development. Do his writings suggest one coherent outlook, such that his development is the continuous unfolding of what was already implicated in his early writings? Or do his writings show unexpected discontinuities, where Whitehead changes his mind and adopts positions which seriously call into question earlier claims? I suspect the truth lies somewhere between, but Lowe and I have adopted opposed methodologies designed to expose these continuities and discontinuities. Despite these differences in approach, Lowe has been most helpful to my investigations in making some student notes of Whitehead's Harvard lectures available to me, for which I am very grateful.

Nathaniel Lawrence's study, like that of George Hélal,[3] is in many ways the complement of my undertaking, exploring the development of the philosophy of nature prior to *Science and the Modern World*. Where there is overlap, however, our approaches are quite different, as Lawrence treats the books from *Science and the Modern World* up to (but not including) *Process and Reality* as forming one undifferentiated whole. For the earlier period of the philosophy of nature I suspect that many of his individual insights are correct, because this period probably gives more appearance of tight uniformity than close inspection of the texts warrants. His general thesis (and Hélal's) that epistemological difficulties and tensions in the philosophy of nature led Whitehead to shift over to a different, more metaphysical approach, is contrary to mine, principally because it assumes that *Science and the Modern World* presents a unified perspective. If, as I contend, there is an earlier metaphysics continuous with the philosophy of nature, the urge to metaphysical generalization would be sufficient to account for any movement from the earlier books, while temporal atomicity would be the impetus that transformed this first metaphysics into something quite different.

In the main this book is a detailed study of the metaphysical ideas of *Science and the Modern World* and *Religion in the Making*, together with a study of those materials (mostly unpublished) which serve as the sources for our knowledge of Whitehead's position just prior to the composition of *Process and Reality*. I deem such a study to be prerequisite for a detailed history of Whitehead's philosophy in *Process and Reality*. Since otherwise most readers might find the present book unsatisfying, I have included a preliminary sketch of *Process and Reality* in chapters 8 and 9. Without these two chapters, they would not find the Whitehead they knew, nor would they see how Whitehead was able to get his final position from the thought of 1926–27. Furthermore, there is a natural completion and closure to his metaphysics in *Process and Reality* that we cannot claim for any position before this. But I must stress the provisional and partial character of these final chapters. The compositional history of *Process and Reality* is so complex, and so poorly understood at present, that it does not yet warrant definitive examination. The concluding summary (chapter 10) presenting the main findings apart from their justification may provide a convenient overview and preliminary orientation.

Chapter 10 has been placed last in order to follow the justifications upon which its conclusions are based, but many readers will find it best to read chapter 10 first. With this summary orientation in hand, it may also be desirable to skip chapters 3 and 7 on first reading.

So that the order of composition of *Process and Reality* may be seen at a glance, the letters **A** through **M** are used in the table of contents and in the text. Capital letters are used now so that in a more definitive analysis of *Process and Reality* lower-case letters can be used. Letters rather than numbers are used so that subsequently a passage may be cited in a way that indicates its stratum (e.g., PR 157C).

Many persons have had a hand in this enterprise, but I must acknowledge a special debt of gratitude to Professor Walter Maner of Old Dominion University, who designed and monitored the computer program used to organize and store thousands of individual notes about Whitehead's compositional history. The readers of the press provided invaluable suggestions, particularly the only one known to me by name, David Ray Griffin. Without his proposal there would probably not be a concluding summary, while the enlarged analytical index he provided the corrected edition of *Process and Reality* has proved to be an essential tool for compositional analysis. Jennifer Hamlin von der Luft, a Haverford undergraduate at the time she participated in one of my summer workshops in June, 1980, has edited the William Ernest Hocking notes published as Appendix 1. Appendix 2 is here reprinted by permission of the Harvard University Philosophy Department. Appendix 3 is reprinted by permission of Mrs. George Burch, the Harvard Archives, and Dean Dwight C. Stewart. Appendix 4 is reprinted by permission of Professor Paul Weiss. Appendix 5 is reprinted by permission of Professor Edwin L. Marvin. Appendix 6 has the permission of Victor Lowe and the University of Edinburgh. George L. Kline and Harry K. Jones have provided many helpful suggestions and stylistic corrections.

October 16, 1982
Old Dominion University
Norfolk, Virginia 23508

NOTES

1. Pp. 15–124 in *The Philosophy of Alfred North Whitehead*, ed. Paul Arthur Schilpp (New York: Library of Living Philosophers, Inc., 1941), reprinted in Victor Lowe, *Understanding Whitehead* (Baltimore: The Johns Hopkins Press, 1962), pp. 123–296.
2. Berkeley: University of California Press, 1956.
3. *La philosophie comme panphysique: La philosophie des sciences de A. N. Whitehead*, Montreal: Bellarmin, 1979.

A Note on References

REFERENCES to Alfred North Whitehead's major books will be by standardized abbreviations, as follows. For convenience, *Process and Reality* will be cited according to the corrected edition edited by David Ray Griffin and Donald W. Sherburne (New York: Free Press, 1978), and two (RM and SMW) will be cited according to their respective paperbound editions. For the conversion of these citations to the other standard editions indicated below, please consult the final citation index. *Process and Reality* is often cited according to section markings, which are constant for both editions. Thus, e.g., PR II.1.7 signifies *Process and Reality*, Part II, chapter 1, section 7.

AE   *The Aims of Education*. New York: Macmillan, 1929.

AI   *Adventures of Ideas*. New York: Macmillan, 1933.

CN   *The Concept of Nature*. Cambridge: Cambridge University Press, 1920.

ESP   *Essays on Science and Philosophy*. New York: The Philosophical Library, 1947.

FR   *The Function of Reason*. Princeton: Princeton University Press, 1929.

IS   *Interpretation of Science*. Ed. A. H. Johnson, Indianapolis: Bobbs-Merrill, 1961.

PNK   *An Enquiry Concerning the Principles of Natural Knowledge*. Cambridge: Cambridge University Press (1919), second edition, 1924.

PR   *Process and Reality*. New York: (Macmillan, 1929), corrected edition, The Free Press, 1978.

R   *The Principle of Relativity*. Cambridge: Cambridge University Press, 1922.

RM   *Religion in the Making*. New York: (Macmillan, 1926), Meridian Edition.

S   *Symbolism, Its Meaning and Effect*. New York: Macmillan, 1927.

SMW   *Science and the Modern World*. New York: (Macmillan, second edition, 1926), The Free Press, 1967.

ONE

The Composition of *Science and the Modern World*

MOST readers have found a vast difference between Whitehead's earlier works in the philosophy of nature, published 1919–1922, and his later metaphysical writings, starting with *Science and the Modern* (1925). Why should this be so? The shift in outlook has been variously explained. Nathaniel Lawrence sees Whitehead's later philosophy as gradually emerging out of the tensions and conflicts already inherent in the "idealist" and "realist" strands of his epistemological reflections in the philosophy of nature, conflicts Whitehead was not able to resolve to his own satisfaction until *Process and Reality*. [1]

In contrast, Ivor Leclerc questions whether such epistemological conflicts existed in Whitehead's philosophy of nature, and suggests that the different positions he later espouses are due to the different problems he encounters. After 1924, Whitehead explicitly broadens the scope of his endeavor to include metaphysics, which had been rigorously excluded heretofore. In August 1924, in the preface to the second edition of *The Principles of Natural Knowledge*, Whitehead wrote that he hoped "in the immediate future to embody the standpoint of these volumes in a more complete metaphysical study" (PNK ix). This occasioned preoccupation with a different set of problems, those posed by Plato, Aristotle, Descartes, Hume, and Kant, rather than those posed by the breakup of the Newtonian world-scheme, or by the polemic against scientific materialism. This shift in concern, Leclerc contends, led Whitehead to readapt his constructs of "events" and "objects" to a new situation.[2] But a shift in concern alone need not have brought the far-ranging transformation of philosophical issues that Whitehead's investigations into metaphysics propose. On the basis of his philosophy of nature, one would have anticipated some sort of "scientific philosophy" closer in orientation to Bertrand Russell's, for example. What actually emerged, however, was something quite different.

We propose a third explanation. The distinctive features of Whitehead's later thought arise not out of epistemological conflicts inherent in the earlier philosophy of nature, nor from the mere shift to metaphysical questions, but from difficulties arising out of his initial metaphysical view. The emergence of Whitehead's metaphysics can be found in the successive revisions Whitehead made of this initial sketch which had been designed as a metaphysics appropriate to his philosophy of nature.

This explanation assumes, as the others do not, that there is a genuine metaphysics of the philosophy of nature, a metaphysics belonging to the earlier philosophy. Both Lawrence and Leclerc assume that the shift to the later philosophy coincides with the shift to metaphysics. For the distinctive features of Whitehead's later philosophy are already present in his first metaphysical writing, *Science and the Modern World*. Ordinarily, in interpreting a philosophical work, we assume it to be written from a single, consistent standpoint. Nearly all commentators, therefore, have assigned *Science and the Modern World* as a whole to Whitehead's later philosophy, and frame their explanations of the shift accordingly. However, this book has a complex history of composition. If we rigorously attend to the *original* layer it contains, we do not find certain basic features characteristic of the later philosophy, except possibly pansubjectivity in a qualified sense. The original Lowell Lectures, delivered in February 1925, constitute Whitehead's first metaphysical synthesis, an extension of his earlier philosophy of nature into metaphysics, quite unlike the developments which were to follow.

1. BASIC CHARACTERISTICS OF THE LATER PHILOSOPHY

To make this thesis more precise, we must describe the three basic characteristic features of Whitehead's later philosophy which particularly mark this shift: temporal atomicity, pansubjectivity, and theism.

(1) *Temporal atomicity*. Unlike the actualities of traditional philosophies, Whitehead's fundamental actualities are not enduring substances but events. Like Democritus and his modern followers, however, he takes these fundamental actualities to be atomic, that is, incapable of subdivision into smaller entities that are equally actual. Just as an elementary particle is incapable of reduction to any "more

elementary" particles (although it is extensive and hence "mathematically divisible"), so an elementary event or "actual occasion" cannot be subdivided into any subevents which are themselves as fully actual and determinate as actual occasions.

While pansubjectivity and theism are topics outside the purview of the philosophy of nature, this doctrine of temporal atomicity directly contravenes Whitehead's earlier emphasis upon temporal continuity. "The continuity of nature is the continuity of events . . . every event contains other events as parts of itself [and] every event is a part of other events" (CN 76).

(2) *Pansubjectivity.* As a direct consequence of this temporal atomicity, the only present immediacy each of us has direct access to is our own momentary subjectivity. All other events, even those ingredient in our present apprehension, must already be past to be experienced. Thus the subjective/objective distinction becomes a temporal one: the subjective factors of experience refer to one's own present immediacy, while the objective factors refer to those past events ingredient in this immediacy. Since every event was once present, it must have enjoyed its own present immediacy, and the only language at our disposal which can appropriately describe this present immediacy is that used to describe our own subjectivity, suitably purged of all anthropomorphism.

Once the subjective/objective distinction is freed from any necessary correlation with the mental/physical distinction, the latter can take on a new dimension of meaning. Whitehead interprets the physical in terms of repetition of the past, while the mental applies to the origin of novelty. There is much more origination of novelty in the world than just in the animal mind. Living cells, for instance, exemplify it. While all occasions in their own present immediacy are equally subjective, there are degrees of mentality commensurate with their origination of novelty.

Unlike that sort of panpsychism which ascribes degrees of awareness or consciousness to all actualities, Whitehead ascribes consciousness only to those few complex occasions of high mentality capable of sustaining intellectual feelings. There are no degrees of awareness below this threshold, so the scope of consciousness in Whitehead is not much different from that of ordinary theory. Subjectivity, mentality, and consciousness, however, must be sharply distinguished for the later Whitehead, since he is a pansubjectivist.

(3) *Theism.* Whitehead's theism was never merely conventional, for he would never countenance the idea of God as transcendent creator of the world. When first introduced, God is conceived as the

principle of limitation ordering the world; later in *Process and Reality* God is also ascribed a consequent nature. None of this appears in the earlier philosophy of nature. We should not expect it in the earlier books, as outside their purview, but Whitehead's reticence in the metaphysics of the Lowell Lectures is more striking. This metaphysical sketch, taken at face value, constructs a tidy naturalism, although Whitehead does not remark upon that fact. God's existence and nature were not introduced as essential features of his metaphysics until after the shift.[3]

With these three distinctive features in hand, it becomes possible for us to specify more precisely when the shift between the earlier and the later philosophies of Whitehead took place. Since temporal atomicity is first emphatically espoused in *Science and the Modern World*, many readers have rather naturally supposed the shift to have taken place prior to its composition, perhaps in 1924, the "silent" period during which Whitehead published little. Compositional analysis, however, suggests the shift came *during* the writing of that book, and Whitehead did not go back and revise what he had already written to make it conform to his newly revised outlook.

The eight Lowell Lectures of February 1925 form the core of *Science and the Modern World*. He wrote them after coming to Harvard the previous September, at the rate of one lecture a week. The lectures "with some slight expansion" were "printed as delivered," with the addition of two lectures he had delivered elsewhere and two fresh chapters on "Abstraction" and "God" (SMW viii).

Now it is possible to isolate at least three passages that were added to the Lowell Lectures. In itself this could be unremarkable, but it so happens that both Whitehead's temporal atomicity and his philosophical theism first make their appearance here. Moreover, there are passages in the original Lowell Lectures which stand in considerable tension to these additions. Thus it appears that Whitehead's basic shift took place between the original Lowell Lectures in February and the completion of the book in June 1925.

Had Whitehead confined his later views to the two "metaphysical" chapters on "Abstraction" and "God," it would have been considerably easier for readers to recognize the shift in point of view within *Science and the Modern World*. But we ordinarily expect a book to reflect a coherent perspective, so we do not anticipate such shifts. The shift was made all the more difficult to discern in that these three additions give the earlier material the coloring of the later philosophy.

Thus, let us first detail the four compositional layers of *Science and the Modern World*, as a necessary basis for the analysis of the doctrines of these compositional layers in succeeding chapters. Then we shall conclude this chapter with a study of endurance and vibration, because this particular topic nicely illustrates the differing doctrines of the two main layers of this book.

2. THE FOUR LAYERS OF SCIENCE AND THE MODERN WORLD

(1) The eight Lowell Lectures, delivered in February 1925, form the core of the book. They comprise nine of the chapters: 1, 3, 4, 5, 6, 7, 8, 9, 13. (One lecture, we are told in the preface, was subdivided into two chapters, 7 and 8.) The Lowell Lectures were designed to give a history of modern science to recent times, together with a critique of "scientific materialism." Whitehead also gave a positive alternative in brief sketches included in most lectures. If this was not the "more complete metaphysical study" of the foundations of his philosophy of nature which Whitehead had promised (PNK ix), it was a preliminary study thereto. At any rate, these brief sketches are all that we have of Whitehead's first metaphysical sketch, drafted in fundamental continuity with the earlier philosophy of nature. The adoption of temporal atomism marked a fundamental reorientation in his metaphysical thinking.

(2) Chapters 2 and 12 were occasional lectures delivered elsewhere (SMW viii). They can be classed with the thought of the Lowell Lectures.

Chapter 2, "Mathematics as an Element in the History of Thought," was delivered as a lecture before the Mathematical Society of Brown University. Because its subject-matter is predominantly mathematical, this lecture is difficult to relate to Whitehead's metaphysical views. What slight clues we have point towards the earlier period. Towards the end of this lecture, the paradoxes and perplexities of the quantum theory are introduced (SMW 34f). After sketching his own alternative, Whitehead concludes: "It seems, therefore, that the hypothesis of essentially vibratory existence is the most hopeful way of explaining the paradox of the discontinuous orbit" (SMW 36). To be sure, this might be taken to refer to the atomistic theory of vibration introduced in the final paragraphs which were added to chapter 8 on "The Quantum Theory" (see 3[c] below), but more probably refers to the "general theory of the vibration of primates" (SMW 135) included within the original Lowell Lecture.

One possible addition of six paragraphs may have been made to chapter 2. If so, it was made in conjunction with the chapter on "Abstraction," and will be evaluated with respect to that final layer. In that case Whitehead composed chapter 2 from the standpoint of the Lowell Lectures, revising them later from his newly discovered standpoint by the insertion of this fresh material.

Chapter 12, "Religion and Science," formed an address delivered at the Phillips Brooks House at Harvard. Because it comes immediately after the chapter on "God," we would naturally expect the same theistic perspective to prevail. Then it would be strange that chapter 12 nowhere forthrightly affirms God's existence as in chapter 11. But here Whitehead's philosophical shift must be taken into account. While the later Whitehead is emphatically theistic, the earlier Whitehead is implicitly nontheistic. I say "implicitly," because he was exceedingly reticent about declaring himself in these matters, but the Lowell Lectures are quite consistent with a thorough-going naturalism. Whitehead rejected the notion of a transcendent creator, and did not embrace theism until the concept of God could be disentangled from that notion.

Thus, the issue to be determined is the temporal relationship between "Religion and Science" and the adoption of temporal atomism. According to the *Harvard Crimson* for the next day, this lecture was presented on Sunday, April 5, 1925.[4] Two days later Whitehead first announced his discovery of temporal atomicity to his classes at Harvard, as something brand new, as something he had not espoused even two weeks before.[5] It is highly unlikely that he had yet thought through its implications for theism. His particular understanding of God, moreover, is closely connected with his analysis of "Abstraction," and Whitehead first mentions the theme of "Abstraction" in his classroom lectures for May 1925.

For these reasons I conclude that "Religion and Science" belongs with his earlier, nontheistic period. The extremely high estimate of religion in this lecture takes on added poignancy when we realize it was penned by a (possibly reluctant?) nontheist. Consider these words: "It is the one element in human experience which persistently shows an upward trend. It fades and then recurs. But when it renews its force, it recurs with an added richness and purity of content. The fact of the religious vision, and its history of persistent expansion, is our one ground for optimism. Apart from it, human life is a flash of occasional enjoyments lighting up a mass of pain and misery, a bagatelle of transient experience" (SMW 192). To be sure, these words could be interpreted in terms of some nontheistic religious stance, such as Buddhism. Whitehead, however, defines religion in terms of God in this same address: "Religion is the reaction of human nature to its search for God" (SMW 191). We shall examine this chapter later, along with the chapter on "God," in chapter 5.

(3) The first two layers belong to Whitehead's earlier philosophy, the last two to his later philosophy. The third layer consists of three passages which 'have been inserted into the texts of the original Lowell Lectures. Together they appear to comprise the "slight expansion" Whitehead mentions in his preface.

(a) The "Triple Envisagement" Addition. This insertion to Whitehead's chapter on "The Nineteenth Century" consists of the three paragraphs overlapping page 105, and beginning with the sentence: "The total temporal duration of such an event bearing an enduring pattern, constitutes its specious present" (SMW 104).

The text of this chapter reads quite smoothly with the omission of these three paragraphs. Thus the paragraph immediately following the intrusion begins: "The atomic material entities which are considered in physical science are merely these individual enduring entities . . ." (SMW 106). What do these material entities refer to? They do not refer to anything in the immediately preceding paragraph in the printed text (SMW 105f), which summarizes his immediate train of thought in terms of a triple envisagement, but refer to four paragraphs earlier, where Whitehead had been considering the extrinsic reality of "an enduring individual entity" (SMW 104). These two paragraphs originally followed one another, and Whitehead inserted a paragraph to explain his newly discovered theory of endurance based upon temporal atomicity, coupled with two paragraphs outlining a triple envisagement which anticipates some of the themes of the later chapters on "Abstraction" and "God." We suspect this passage was written after his introduction of temporal atomicity in the "Relativity" addition (to be considered next), but before he had decided to include his reflections on "Abstraction" and "God" in *Science and the Modern World*.

We shall consider this section, insofar as it pertains to endurance, in the next section, and insofar as it pertains to the triple envisagement, in chapter 5 on "God."

(b) The "Relativity" Addition. This is the most important of Whitehead's additions, for in it he introduces his reasons for temporal atomicity, which serves as the catalyst for the other shifts he introduces into his metaphysics.

We know from his preface that Whitehead subdivided his sixth Lowell Lecture on "Modern Thought" into two separate chapters on

"Relativity" and "The Quantum Theory." Together these two chapters comprise some 32 pages in the second edition, whereas the other Lowell Lectures average 25 or 26 pages, the longest being the first, which runs just 4 lines over 27 pages. Hence we may anticipate that some 5 to 7 pages were added to the sixth lecture. Moreover, if the bulk were added at the end of the section on "Relativity," no awkward transition would be required, since "The Quantum Theory" could form a new chapter.

If we consider chapters 7 and 8 together, then the first paragraph of chapter 8 ("The Quantum Theory") follows quite naturally from the paragraph of chapter 7 beginning: "It only remains to add that Einstein would probably reject the theory of multiple space-time systems which I have been expounding to you" (SMW 122). Whitehead had been discussing the Michelson-Morley experiment and presenting the theory of relativity (in his own terms) as an advance on Newton. In this brief concluding paragraph he alludes to some of the differences of interpretation he has with Einstein, differences articulated in his book, *The Principle of Relativity* (1922), not mentioned here by name. The first paragraph of chapter 8 immediately picks up the theme, and it can be easily read as a transitional paragraph from the earlier discussion of the principles of relativity to the second topic of his Lowell Lecture, the quantum theory.

The last ten paragraphs of the chapter on "Relativity," beginning with "The theory of the relationship between events at which we have now arrived . . ." (SMW 122), thus constitutes this second addition. While the preceding discussion of relativity theory is carried forward in the next chapter, none of the topics of this insertion are alluded to, such as the theory of external and internal relations, the atomicity of temporalization, the inconsistencies of Kant's analysis of extension, and the present validity of Zeno's paradoxes.

Temporal atomicity, however, powerfully crystalizes several lines of argument present in the original Lowell Lectures. For one thing, it enables Whitehead to clarify the relation between an event and an act of prehension. They are identified in the Lowell Lectures, but this is an uneasy identification. Some events are far too long, for the repeated reiteration of pattern within an enduring event suggests that it has several acts of prehensive unification, not just one (SMW 104). Since events as such can be of any length whatsoever, some might be far too brief for a prehensive act.

Also, temporal atomicity allows for the unification of process and prehension. If we conceive of a continuously unfolding nature, each prehensive unity might be thought of as an instantaneous unity of some slice of nature. Each prehensive unity would be naturally internally related to the whole of nature simultaneous with itself at that instant. If that were the case, there could be no "process" of unification. Such a process must be temporally thick and closed upon itself to make room for the activity of unification.

We shall examine the nature of Whitehead's argument for temporal atomicity in chapter 3. Its ramifications are far-reaching, and will concern us in later chapters as well as in the concluding section of this chapter.

(c) "The Quantum Theory" Addition. Here Whitehead briefly sketches, in an afterthought to this chapter, an alternative solution based on his newly-discovered temporal atomicity. This we take to be the last four or five paragraphs of chapter 8. It is clearly dependent on the "Relativity" addition, as Whitehead explicitly notes. In the preceding paragraphs he had been intent upon giving a theory of the apparently discontinuous character of electrons (generalized as "Primary organisms" or "primates") in terms of vibratory patterns. Then he adds: "The theory of a primate or a vibratory pattern given above, together with the distinction between temporality and extensiveness in [the addition to] the previous chapter, yields exactly this result" (SMW 135). There follows an alternative theory of vibration, couched in terms of successive atomic durations, as required by the theory of temporal atomicity.

The last four paragraphs initiated by the sentence just quoted belong to this addition, but it is less certain whether the immediately preceding paragraph does or does not. We incline to the view that it does, because otherwise it would be the final paragraph of this chapter, unless Whitehead had discarded his original ending. This seems not to have been his usual practice, as we shall see. That paragraph is better understood as a transitional paragraph introducing the new theory than as the final paragraph of the chapter without the addition. On the other hand, *its* predecessor makes a satisfactory terminus to the chapter, and could well have been its original ending.

(4) Finally, after these three additions, we come to the last layer of the book, chapters 10 ("Abstraction") and 11 ("God"). Unlike much of Whitehead's literary production, they were not first delivered as lectures, but written especially for *Science and the Modern World*. They represent his first systematic effort to articulate his revised metaphysics, as modified under the impact of temporal atomicity.

As the "Triple Envisagement" addition adumbrates several key themes in these chapters, Whitehead may have composed that addition before firmly deciding to incorporate "Abstraction" and "God" within the book. These final chapters not only presuppose the shift, but the three additions as well.

These chapters alone use what becomes Whitehead's standard technical term, "actual occasion." The rest of the book, including the additions, uses "event," although rarely it uses "occasion" in a nontechnical sense, without suggesting its atomicity. Surprisingly enough, "actual occasion" is introduced quite casually, even though it is his standard term throughout these two chapters. This is very much like Plato's casual introduction of the Forms in the *Euthyphro*. In both cases every one is presumed to be already familiar with the terms.

Besides these two chapters (to be considered in detail later), we should examine one possible addition which would belong to this final layer. In his occasional lecture on mathematics (chapter 2), mathematics is described as "a resolute attempt to go the whole way in the direction of complete analysis, so as to separate the elements of mere matter of fact from the purely abstract conditions which they exemplify" (SMW 24). The next six paragraphs may have been added as a meditation in the light of the chapter on "Abstraction" concerning this theme. The predominantly historical thematic of the lecture is picked up seven paragraphs later with the observation that "Pythagoras was the first man who had any grasp of the full sweep of this general principle" (SMW 27). "This general principle" appears to refer to the very sophisticated logical harmony involved in the unity of an occasion, which is the ostensible referent in the immediately preceding paragraph, but it may refer back to the careful description of mathematics enunciated seven paragraphs before. Textual considerations alone are insufficient to determine the matter.

There is reason to believe, however, that these six paragraphs are in fact a reflection, from a mathematical perspective, of the metaphysical enterprise Whitehead undertakes in "Abstraction." He comments at the end of "Abstraction" : "The idea [concerning the nature of mathematics], ascribed to Pythagoras, has been amplified, and put forward as the first chapter in metaphysics" (SMW 172). This suggests the following order: first, that definition of the nature of mathematics is directly ascribed to Pythagoras; second, the chapter on "Abstraction" is composed applying that idea to metaphysics; third, a meditation on that definition in the light of "Abstraction" is inserted into the earlier lecture.

Whitehead's use of "occasion" and "occasion of experience" in these six paragraphs is most provocative. As we have noted, he generally uses "event" throughout the Lowell Lectures, while only the two metaphysical chapters use "actual occasion." Presumably Whitehead has "actual occasion" in mind, but wishes to avoid this particular technical term as inappropriate for a preliminary discussion such as this.

"Mathematics as an Element in the History of Thought" was delivered at Brown in April, 1925.[6] Substantially the same lecture was given in New York City May 15 or 16, and Whitehead appears to have repeated its salient points to his Harvard class.[7] William Ernest Hocking's notes do not indicate that those six paragraphs were discussed as part of the lecture. To be sure, any one taking notes omits a lot, or Whitehead could have simply omitted these ideas in his abbreviated presentation. But Whitehead had just been lecturing on the very topics which are to be found in the chapter on "Abstraction" both before and after this isolated lecture on mathematics. If he had composed these six paragraphs as part of his public lecture, or particularly if he had inserted them in his public lecture as an afterthought growing out of his preoccupation just then with the themes of "Abstraction," we could expect him to dwell precisely on that material during his class presentation.

Thus this additional evidence tends to indicate that while the mathematics lecture as a whole is independent of those metaphysical features marking Whitehead's shift, those six paragraphs were added later, probably in conjunction with the chapter on "Abstraction." They form an addition consequent upon that chapter, and not a precondition to the metaphysical chapters. Hence this addition is not classed with the three additions which effected the shift itself.

If the foregoing compositional analysis is correct, all the passages explicitly espousing temporal atomicity and theism were added to the original Lowell Lectures. This alone is not sufficient to demonstrate any shift in Whitehead's outlook, however. It is conceivable that he already had these ideas in mind, yet had no opportunity to develop them. Moreover, much that he writes about "events" in the Lowell Lectures makes as much, if not better, sense when interpreted in terms of the atomic actual occasions Whitehead later explicitly introduces. But as we will show, there are other passages in the Lowell Lectures which cannot be so interpreted, and which are at odds with any theory of temporal atomicity. We shall proceed, therefore, on the assumption that *Science and the Modern World* is composed of various layers best interpreted from diverse perspectives.

A book of this sort calls for a different hermeneutical strategy than most. The strategy is quite different for a systematic account than for a genetic analysis. In a systematic account the interpreter strives for maximum coherence of argument, utilizing whatever evidence he can find. Disparate materials are assembled to fit one total scheme. For this purpose it is desirable to find the maximum systematic meaning in each passage, one which will be both appropriate for the text and consonant with the elaborated complex meaning of the whole. In a genetic interpretation, however, the levels of allowable meaning are stratified, and a given text is interpreted in terms of the context of meaning for that stratum. We endeavor to find that meaning appropriate to the text consonant with that particular stratum (and with earlier strata insofar as they are still affirmed). No text should be interpreted in terms which exceed that which is explicitly warrantable for that particular stage of the thinker's development.

The genetic principle of interpretation demands considerable discipline on our part, since we customarily approach the text with systematic concerns in mind. Moreover, Whitehead's language is frequently proleptic, leaping ahead of itself. Metaphysical terms, however much stabilized as technicalities, "remain metaphors mutely appealing for an imaginative leap" (PR 4). His language is always straining beyond itself, trying to express the vision Whitehead barely saw and could not fully grasp. His thought has its own entelechy, so that frequently intuitions expressed in earlier works only find their full justification in later ones. The best example of this would be the highly personalistic language about God's care for the world in *Religion in the Making*, which only finally makes full sense in terms of the conceptual tools he devised for the consequent nature of God developed in *Process and Reality*.

We shall attempt, as much as possible, to interpret such language primarily in terms of those concepts at Whitehead's disposal at the time it was articulated. We will not always succeed. Whitehead's reasoning is sometimes elliptical, dependent upon intermediate inferences of which he was not always fully aware. Sometimes these suppressed premises or arguments or distinctions come to light in his later work, but sometimes not, as in the case with many of his statements in the final chapters of *Process and Reality* and *Adventures of Ideas*. Because many of these cryptic assertions become powerfully illuminating when supplied with the necessary intermediate steps, the imaginative systematician is encouraged to hope that the rest will ultimately yield to rational justification. So it may be the case with the earlier works. They may be intelligible only in terms of suppressed considerations, first supplied in the later books. But so far as it will be possible, we shall endeavor to interpret these texts solely in the light of the arguments developed at the time. In this way contrasting positions can be dramatized, making it possible to trace the stages of Whitehead's development.

3. ENDURANCE AND VIBRATION

Before examining the individual layers separately, we shall examine the question of endurance and vibration in *Science and the Modern World*, because this theme shows quite clearly the tensions and conflicts existing among the layers.

In Whitehead's final theory, actual occasions come into being and perish, but do not change (PR 35). "The fundamental meaning of the notion of 'change' is 'the difference between actual occasions comprised in some determinate event' " (PR 73 and 80). As with change, so endurance. An 'enduring object' is that common element remaining the same for several successive occasions.

Events and occasions are here sharply distinguished. An actual occasion is the atomic unit of temporal realization. An occasion may be divided coordinately, but such parts lack full actuality of the occasion. On the other hand, an event is any spatiotemporal volume, large or small. An event many include many occasions or fragments of several occasions, or simply be part of one occasion. An occasion, in contrast, is a definite ontological unit of becoming, a single con-crescence or process of actualization. With respect to actualities, "an actual occasion is the limiting type of an event with only one member" (PR 78).

These distinctions were not explicitly elaborated when the term "actual occasion" was introduced in the final stratum of *Science and the Modern World*, but Whitehead's usage follows these distinctions. Whenever the ontological unit of prehensive unification is referred to, "actual occasion" is used in the chapters on "Abstraction" and "God." In contrast to the rest of the book, "event" is rarely employed. It is either used non-technically, as in "the general course of events" (SMW 161), or in contexts referring both to individual occasions and to groups of occasions forming larger events (SMW 158f, 177).

"Actual occasion" becomes a feature of Whitehead's technical vocabulary when he first finds it necessary to distinguish atomic units of temporal realization from events, which retain their divisi-bility. Previously, it is true, he had spoken of the "prehensive occasion" (SMW 71), and such an event would be an occasion in which the fullest concreteness would be achieved. Hence it would be appropriately called "actual" (cf. SMW 158). But no such technical terminology was ever suggested in the Lowell Lectures, let alone stabilized. "Prehensive occasions" are just events like any others.

In one case, in the chapter on "Abstraction," the event in nature is regarded as merely the objective aspect of an actual occasion: "So far I have merely been considering an actual occasion on the side of its full concreteness. It is this side of the occasion in virtue of which it is an event in nature. But a natural event, in this sense of the term, is only an abstraction from a complete actual occasion. A complete occasion includes that which in cognitive experience takes the form of memory, anticipation, imagination, and thought" (SMW 170).

It is the ascription of these inner aspects to spatiotemporal volumes which marks the difference between *Science and the Modern World* and Whitehead's earlier books. In the philosophy of nature, events were described solely in terms of that which was perceived or prehended; here events are described (in the Lowell Lectures) as activities of prehension. "Thus, concrete fact is process. Its primary analysis is into underlying activity of prehension, and into realized prehensive events. Each event is an individual matter of fact issuing from an individualization of the substrate activity" (SMW 70). Viewed internally, "space-time is nothing else than a system of pulling together of assemblages into unities. But the word *event* just means one of these spatiotemporal unities" (SMW 72; cf, 93). For these reasons, and since, for the Lowell Lectures, "the event is the unit of things real" (SMW 152), it is very easy to suppose that the word "event" here is simply an earlier term for "actual occasion," used to signify actual occasions before Whitehead coined the term, simply inherited from his earlier distinction between "events" and "objects" in the philosophy of nature.

Under this supposition, when Whitehead became increasingly aware of the need to distinguish his earlier purely objective approach from his growing concentration upon internal concerns, he would have coined the term "actual occasion." This language could have been suggested by the fact that such an event was the occasion or opportunity for prehensive unity. In the Lowell Lectures he had already spoken of the "prehensive occasion," although as yet nontechnically, and it would only take time before he could adopt "occasion" as his characteristic term.

The difficulty with the supposition is that there are uses of "event" in the Lowell Lectures for an enduring object. The possibility of using "event" in this meaning presupposes notions of continuity and divisibility which directly contravene the atomicity assigned to actual occasions. Here terms are less important than the absence of temporal atomicity from Whitehead's analysis of endurance.

"Endurance is the retention through time of an achievement of value" (SMW 194). This understanding of endurance is common to all strata of *Science and the Modern World*. What differs is whether the enduring object is characteristic of the event as a whole, simply reiterated in each of its parts (subevents), or whether it is the repetition of the common characteristic in successive occasions. In the early theory endurance is conceived primarily in terms of a single total event: ". . . endurance is not primarily the property of enduring beyond itself, but of enduring within itself. I mean that endurance is the property of finding its pattern reproduced in the temporal parts of the total event. It is in this sense that a total event carries an enduring pattern" (SMW 152).

The enduring characteristic is thus conceived as a continuous property of the event, applicable to all of its sub-divisions. "We can give a precise definition of endurance in this way: Let an event A be pervaded by an enduring structural pattern. Then A can be exhaustively subdivided into a temporal succession of events. Let B be any part of A, which is obtained by picking out any one of the events belonging to a series which thus subdivides A. Then the enduring pattern is a pattern of aspects within the complete pattern prehended into the unity of any temporal slice of A, such as B. For example a molecule is a pattern exhibited in an event of one minute, and of any second of that minute" (SMW 108; cf. 119f). Also any fraction of that second whatsoever, since Whitehead as the inventor of the method of extensive abstraction had a very lively awareness of the unrestricted scope of meaning to be assigned to *any* part. Here there is no suggestion that there is any lowest bound below which the pattern cannot be displayed. This pattern, which is "reproduced in each temporal slice of [the event's] history," is the "enduring object" (SMW 119, cf. 120, 94).

From a traditional standpoint, the enduring object is the primary reality, and the subevents are merely artificial ways of dividing the one event. To be sure, they "reproduce" the common pattern, but merely because it is all-pervasive. Sometimes Whitehead appears to share this perspective, but he is also fascinated by the role these partial events can play in providing the basis for "the property which we may call indifferently *retention, endurance* or *reiteration*. . . . The reiteration of a particular shape (or formation) of value within an event occurs when the event as a whole repeats some shape which is also exhibited by each one of a succession of its parts. Thus however you analyze the event according to the flux of its parts through time, there is the same thing-for-its-own-sake standing before you. Thus the event, in its own intrinsic reality, mirrors in itself, as derived from its own parts, aspects of the same patterned value as it realizes in its complete self. It thus realizes itself under the guise of an enduring individual entity, with a life history contained within itself" (SMW 104). Thus it is the total enduring event which realizes itself, not the individual events which then jointly constitute the enduring object.

Yet the passage is ambiguous, for it may mean that the parts are merely arbitrary subdivisions of a total event exhibiting the same enduring pattern, or that the partial events produce this pattern, which is then ascribed to the whole. Whitehead seizes upon this latter meaning in order to insert his "Triple Envisagement" addition. The first paragraph of this addition is inserted to explain endurance now in terms of his new theory of temporal atomism, and it is probably inserted at this point to capitalize upon the ambiguity just noted. Because of it, there could be an apparently smooth transition, but the presuppositions of the bridging paragraphs are quite distinct. In the first, "*however* you analyze the event according to the flux of its parts through time" (SMW 104, italics added), the pattern remains the same and is exhibited in each of the parts. Now, however, Whitehead introduces the notion of the event's specious present, such that it is "within this specious present [that] the event realizes itself as a totality" (SMW 104). It comes into being as a single actuality, in conformity with the later atomistic theory.

To effect the transition, Whitehead has to force the temporal span of what is referred to as the total event into very narrow quarters. In the original lecture he is intent upon explaining endurance, and the event could be of any length. A few pages later, in the same lecture (but after the insertion), he can use the endurance of a molecule throughout a minute as his illustration (SMW 108), and there is no reason why we could not conceive of the endurance of the Egyptian Sphinx since its construction as such an event. Now, however, we are told that "the *total* temporal duration of *such an event* bearing an enduring pattern, constitutes its specious present" (SMW 104, italics added), which is extremely brief. The word "duration," which ordinarily signifies something enduring a while, was technically introduced by Whitehead for a very short temporal expanse approaching instantaneousness, in order to explain simultaneity (CN 56f). In the addition to the chapter on "Relativity," "duration" is regularly used for atomic temporalization. "Time is sheer succession of epochal durations" (SMW 125). The theory expressed in this first paragraph of the "Triple Envisagement" addition, trying to explain endurance in terms of temporal atomicity, is clearly transitional, because it reflects neither the assumed continuous endurance of the pattern as in the original lecture, nor the later theory in which endurance applies only to the common characteristic of many successive actual occasions. In this first paragraph he is trying to explain what he conceives to be the enduring pattern of a single occasion.

According to the later theory, endurance and prehensive unification are contradictory attributes, since prehensive unification can only apply to individual actual occasions, and endurances to the succession of many occasions. At the time of the Lowell Lectures, however, Whitehead had only the single concept of "event" to cover both cases. Moreover, he believed that no difficulty was involved in conceiving both prehensive unification and the enduring object in similar terms. Thus he could say that "an event is the grasping into unity of a pattern of aspects" and refer to this same pattern as enduring: "If the pattern endures throughout the successive parts of the event, and also exhibits itself in the whole, so that the event is the life history of the pattern, then in virtue of that enduring pattern the event gains in external effectiveness. For its own effectiveness is reinforced by the analogous aspects of all its successive parts" (SMW 119).

This thesis could then be summarized: "Endurance means that a pattern which is exhibited in the prehension of one event is also exhibited in the prehension of those of its parts which are discriminated by a certain rule" (SMW 119f). This sentence can be easily misunderstood if we try to interpret it purely systematically in terms of *Process and Reality*. Then the event becomes a single actual occasion, and the parts various genetic phases with their multiplicity of prehensions. We have to remember, however, that this passage was written before Whitehead anticipated temporal atomicity, let alone thought about genetic division. Also, the term "prehension" has not yet acquired the primary connotation of being the taking account of single datum. That first develops with the differentiation between prehension and concrescence, such that a concrescence is the growing together of many prehensions into one. In *Science and the Modern World*, prehension primarily means prehensive unification, the grasping together of aspects from all events into the unit of the single present event.

The combination of prehension and endurance is not so strange if we bear in mind that the notion of an activity of unification was not yet very developed. "Prehensive unification" in these lectures appears to mean little more than its synonym "prehensive unity." It has exactly the same force as "synthesis" in Kant's "synthesis of the manifold of intuition." Whitehead conceives of prehension as a state of relatedness between the objective aspects of all other events and the prehending event. Since changes in the environment are negligible with respect to a given enduring object, the prehension or mutual relatedness of the whole can be reflected in the prehension of each part. Thus "that which endures . . . is not self-sufficient. The aspects of all things enter into its very nature. It is only itself as drawing together into its own limitation the larger whole in which it finds itself" (SMW 94).

Despite this, however, there was a subtle tendency upon White-head's part to conceive of prehension as more than just synthesis, as involving successive acts of unification. Then the total event becomes exhibited in the successive subevents, and the subevents, as individual acts of unification, have a stronger ontological foundation than the overall event. Yet the single concept of event, signifying any spatiotemporal volume, however large or small, and his predilections for extensive continuity prevent Whitehead from acting on the strength of this tendency. Once temporal atomicity is discovered, however, the picture is immediately clarified: the individual acts of prehensive unification are then understood as atomic occasions, while enduring events refer to groups of contiguous occasions.

The theory of endurance for the Lowell Lectures, as we have presented it, is incomplete. It could be assumed that each pattern reiterates the same pattern throughout the event, just as on the materialist assumption there is undifferentiated sameness throughout the life of an elementary particle. Whitehead recognized that there can be differences among the parts of an event, although at first he was content to describe these in merely spatial terms. "It is not true that any part of the whole event will yield the same pattern as does the whole. For example, consider the total bodily pattern exhibited in the life of a human body during one minute. One of the thumbs during the same minute is part of the whole event. But the pattern of this part is the pattern of the thumb, and is not the pattern of the whole body" (SMW 120).

In the sixth Lowell Lecture, after describing the quantum theory, Whitehead was ready to introduce temporal differences as well: "In the organic theory, a pattern need not endure in undifferentiated sameness through time. The pattern may be essentially one of aesthetic contrast. A tune is an example of such a pattern. Thus, the endurance of the pattern now means the reiteration of its succession of contrasts" (SMW 133).

This theory accepts temporal continuity, at least in the sense that any event can be temporally sub-divided into sub-events whose objective characteristics in succession exhibit the character of the whole. Here it is not argued that the parts have no determinate character in themselves, but are only phases in a single process of determination. The determinate parts can be individually objectified, and their succession exhibits the determinate character of the whole.

Whitehead had already accepted, possibly from Bergson, the notion that some events, at least, must have a minimum duration to be themselves. Thus, in his address to the Aristotelian Society in 1919 on "Time, Space, and Material," Whitehead tells us that "a molecule of iron and a tune both require a minimum time in which to express themselves" (IS 67). Such "nonuniform" objects, as he terms them, do not immediately induce him to adopt temporal atomicity. Events and the objects which characterize them are here contrasted, and what atomicity there is is ascribed to the objects. "The continuity of nature arises purely from the extensional properties of events. . . . The atomic properties of nature arise entirely from objects" (IS 67).

Whitehead foresees the importance which vibration will play in quantum theory, but does not suggest that temporalization is itself atomized. "Whenever nonuniform objects emerge, then time-minima become important in physics (i.e. *quanta* of time, in the modern nomenclature). The atomic property of objects and the nonuniformity of some types of objects are obviously the basis of the quantum properties of nature which are assuming such an important position in modern physics" (IS 68). Such vibrations are expressed in terms of a succession of several atomic objects characterizing some of the subdivisions of the continuously divisible total event.

The addition to the chapter on "The Quantum Theory," which we have previously isolated as not part of the original Lowell Lecture, introduces a drastic restructuring of this theory. Here Whitehead distinguishes between (atomic) temporality and (continuous) extensiveness. "The continuity of the complex of events arises from the relationships of extensiveness; whereas the temporality arises from the realization in a subject-event of a pattern which requires for its display that the whole of a duration be spatialized (i.e., arrested), as given by its aspects in the event. Thus, realization proceeds *via* a succession of epochal durations; and the continuous transition, i.e., the organic deformation, is within the duration which is already given. The vibratory organic deformation is in fact the reiteration of the pattern" (SMW 135f). The reiteration of the pattern in terms of successive determinate parts is retained for the event's objective display, but the event itself is conceived as an atomic unit of actualization. "One complete period defines the duration required for the complete pattern. Thus, the primate [roughly, the elementary particle] is realized atomically in a succession of durations, each duration to be measured from one maximum to another" (SMW 136).

This same theory of vibration underlies the initial paragraph of the "Triple Envisagement" addition discussed above. "One and the same pattern is realized in the total event, and is exhibited by each of these various parts through an aspect of each part grasped into the togetherness of the total event" (SMW 105). The successive parts now display the total pattern of this vibration, but they are all unified in a single prehensive unification, i.e. in a single occasion.

The theory of vibration expressed here and in the addition to the chapter on "The Quantum Theory" is not Whitehead's final one. Each vibration, measured from one maximum to another, constitutes here a single atomic event, while later Whitehead analyzed it in terms of two successive patterns, alternating with one another (PR 277–79). In part he wants to show how novelty (each occasion is different from its immediate predecessor and successor) and stability (each occasion is the same as every other one in this series) can be wedded together to achieve a modicum of intensity, but in part he was following the implications of his theory of change. Change is "the difference between actual occasions comprised in some determinate event" (PR 72). Since even a single vibration involves some change, this must be displayed in the difference between at least two occasions. At first Whitehead was willing to see the change involved within a vibratory event to apply to a single atomic occasion, but not later.

This discussion of endurance and vibration, together with the compositional analysis earlier in the chapter, indicates the shift that took place in Whitehead's metaphysics during the composition of *Science and the Modern World*. In order to gauge the extent of that shift, we need to know the character of his metaphysics beforehand, as it can be ascertained from the Lowell Lectures. That is the task of the next chapter.

NOTES

1. *Whitehead's Philosophical Development: A Critical History of the Background of* Process and Reality (Berkeley: University of California Press, 1956). In apparent independence from Lawrence (whom he never cites), Georges Hélal comes to strikingly similar conclusions in *La philosophie comme panphysique: La philosophie des sciences de A. N. Whitehead.* (Montreal: Bellarmin, 1979).

2. "Whitehead's Philosophy" (a critical examination of Lawrence's book), *Review of Metaphysics* 11 (1957–58), 68–93.

3. Many of his early English admirers, such as L. Susan Stebbing, were shocked by this turn of events, for they had supposed him to be a "tough-minded" empiricist who was done with religious views.

4. I am indebted to Professor John E. Skinner of the Episcopal Divinity School, Cambridge, Massachusetts, for this information.

5. See chapter 3, and Appendix 1, for details.

6. Victor Lowe, "Whitehead's Gifford Lectures," *The Southern Journal of Philosophy* 7/4 (1969–70), 331.

7. See Appendix 1 for the notes of Whitehead's Harvard Lectures of May 19, 1925.

TWO

The First Metaphysical Synthesis

BECAUSE *Science and the Modern World* has been widely regarded as all of one piece belonging to Whitehead's later period of philosophizing, it has ordinarily been seen as a convenient propaedeutic to *Process and Reality*, and its doctrines as very incomplete and embryonic versions of the later philosophy. If we focus on the Lowell Lectures, examining them strictly in their own terms, however, we find a metaphysics which is continuous with the earlier philosophy of nature. In August, 1924, Whitehead hoped shortly "to embody the standpoint of these volumes (CN and PNK) in a more complete metaphysical study" (PNK ix). These fragmentary sketches incorporated within the Lowell Lectures come closest to being that metaphysical study. They form Whitehead's first published metaphysical synthesis, and the one most continuous with the earlier books.

In the Lowell Lectures Whitehead was asked to depict the rise of the scientific world view since the seventeenth century. He not only did so, but challenged the scientific materialism underlying this development, proposing his own "philosophy of organism" as an alternative. Because of its direct confrontation with materialism, this "philosophy of organism" perhaps has more justification to the title than does his later philosophy.

1. THE PHILOSOPHY OF ORGANISM

The basic features of the philosophy of organism can be grouped around three topics, each replacing some aspect of that scientific materialism Whitehead found inadequate: (1) Simple location is replaced by prehensive unity. (2) Materialistic mechanism is transformed into "organic mechanism," involving the evolution of increasingly complex organisms. (3) Consciousness is reconceived, so that it is no longer an independent actuality but a function of bodily events. These three topics are closely interrelated, since the epistemological justification for prehensive relationships lies in conscious perception, yet this conscious activity must be explained naturalistically in terms of the evolution of organisms. Organic mechanism, on the other hand, with its stress on the internal relatedness of part to the whole environment it participates in, draws its strength from the more comprehensive theory of prehensive unity. At the same time it justifies the emergence of such complex organisms as will explain consciousness.

Because of this continuous dialectic with scientific materialism, Whitehead does not offer a single compact presentation of his philosophy of organism, but prefers to present it piecemeal as an alternative to that aspect of the dominant position he is attacking at the moment. Yet the passages presenting the alternative can be fairly easily isolated for our systematic study of these three topics.[1]

(1) *Prehension.* According to the dominant theory Whitehead challenges, nature is made of matter, by which he understands anything which has the property of simple location (SMW 49). "To say that a bit of matter has *simple location* means that, in expressing its spatio-temporal relation, it is adequate to state that it is where it is, in a definite region of space, and throughout a definite finite duration of time, apart from any essential reference of the relations of that bit of matter to other regions of space and to other durations of time" (SMW 58). That last qualification is the most important, for it is the claim of materialism that each particle is externally related to all others. In some sense, everything is simply located, and this gives an important truth. The problem is rather whether it tells the whole truth. Is an event merely located where it is most concretely actual? For Whitehead, simple location does define the locus of the event where it realizes just those qualitative characteristics it has. Simple location, however, abstracts from the event's complex interrelatedness with other events, and with the percipient event. Simple location applies basically to a partial abstraction. To regard this as fully concrete is to mistake the abstract for the concrete, and thus to commit the fallacy of misplaced concreteness (SMW 51, 58).

Philosophy's task is to criticize such abstractions, and particularly our modes of abstraction. In jarring us loose from the familiar abstractions we mistake for the concrete, it suggests alternatives to enliven our theorizing. In this way it can contribute essentially to the advance of civilization (SMW 59; cf. 18, 87, 142).

In his earlier philosophy of nature, Whitehead described events primarily in terms of extension, understood as the property of over-lappng or extending over (CN 58, 75; PNK 74f). An event extends over other events smaller than itself, and is extended over by others larger than itself. Two events, no matter how far apart they might be, are extended over by some third. Such extended events and objects (the characteristics of events) replace the trio of space, time, and matter, which were basic to scientific materialism. In terms of his 1906 memoir, "On Mathematical Concepts of the Material World," this is the advance from Concept I (describing the Newtonian world view) to Concept II (dispensing with matter, and describing everything in terms of points and instants). In the meantime Whitehead had learned of the fusion of space and time through work on relativity theory, and he had become suspicious of all talk of nature-at-an-instant. The method of extensive abstraction, whereby a series of events could be understood as a route of approximation to a point-instant, freed him from any necessity to treat these as ultimate constituents. Hence in Concept II, points and instants could be replaced by events in the philosophy of nature and in the Lowell Lectures.

Events understood entirely in terms of extension, however, need not entail any process, and Whitehead had come to the conclusion that process was fundamental, extension derivative (PNK 202). In the Lowell Lectures he contrasts these separative properties of ex-tension with the unitive properties of prehension (SMW 64). For unless an event can reach out and include within itself other events in some fashion, an event such as a percipient event would be condemned to the solipsism of its own experience (SMW 43f).

Here we have moved from Concept II to Concept V of the 1906 memoir. It defined points in terms of "projective points," the bundle of lines converging together. Now an event may be understood as "prehensive unity of volume" (SMW 64). It brings together the aggregate of contained parts that the separative character of space-time has held apart. But "each part is something from the standpoint of every other part [apparently even outside that given volume], and also from the same standpoint every other part is something in relation to it." Thus, the togetherness of the parts brings together this aspectival relatedness to all other events. "The prehensive unity of A is the prehension into unity of the aspects of all other volumes from the standpoint of A" (SMW 65).

Prehension is here merely conceived as the converse of extension. To be sure, extension is not merely separative; it unifies in that events are both extensively contiguous and overlapping. In the primary sense, however, that which is extended has part outside of part. For this reason, Leibniz argues, nothing simple can be extended, and extension must be the aggregation of simples. Prehension is the opposite of "part outside of part," since other events are really constitutive of the prehensive event. Extension can be interpreted strictly in terms of external relations, while a prehension is precisely a spatiotemporal internal relation. Prehensive unity is simply the unity of these internal relations to other events within a single event. Prehension is here synonymous with prehensive unity. Prehensive unity is a many-termed relation whereby many events are prehended into the one prehending event (A), something on the order of Kant's synthesis of the manifold of intuition. With respect to any one of these many prehended events (such as B), there is a special two-termed relationship of location. Thus the event is prehended at A with its mode of location at B, and "the aspect of B from A is the mode in which B enters into the composition of A" (SMW 65). "Accordingly, there is a prehension, *here* in this place, of things which have a reference to *other* places" (SMW 69).

This two-termed relationship of location in prehension requires the double role of eternal objects, possibly because eternal objects are not inalterably located in any one event. Events have fixed locations, from which they prehend and can be prehended, but eternal objects are not so fixed. The event is constituted by the eternal objects which characterize it, but such characterizations are only externally related to the event, and can equally well characterize other events. "The aboriginal data are the aspects of shapes, of sense-objects, and of other eternal objects whose self-identity is not dependent on the flux of things. Wherever such objects have ingression into the general flux, they interpret events, each to the other. They are here in the perceiver; but, as perceived by him, they convey for him something of the total flux which is beyond himself. The subject-object relation takes its origin in the double role of these eternal objects" (SMW 151; cf. 103).[2]

In the third lecture, Whitehead introduces sense-objects such as "green," the perceived characteristics ingredient in particular events (SMW 70f), generalizing them as eternal objects. This is a striking reversal of his conviction, just one year before, that such sense-objects were *not* 'eternal.' In a letter dated January 24, 1924, to Norman Kemp Smith commenting on his essay "Whitehead's Philosophy of Nature,"[3] he wrote: "The main point in your lecture with which I disagree was the statement that I considered 'objects' (and in particular 'sensa') as 'eternal.' I should not call them 'eternal' because (as stated in my Principles of Natural Knowledge) I do not consider them as 'in time' in the primary sense of the phrase. I should call an unending event eternal."[4]

Kemp Smith's is a carefully crafted and quite readable essay on the metaphysical implications of Whitehead's philosophy of nature. It eschews expository detail for commentary on philosophical import. Despite Whitehead's apparent charge, it nowhere speaks of "eternal objects." Nevertheless, Kemp Smith's characterization of "objects" does give some basis for this charge, since he views them as involving "the notion of permanence in some form." He questions whether the melody of the nightingale persists, in the manner of an object, or whether it should not be classed with events. "Traditional physics will not countenance persistent melodies, but it does believe in . . . persistent electrons, atoms, and molecules." But Whitehead questions this idea of the persistence of the molecule which assumes that the pattern of iron is displayed in every instant of its existence (PNK 22f).

In his reply Whitehead is struggling against the misunderstanding that his "sense-objects" are "eternal" in the sense of being unending or everlasting. ("Eternal" has two radically different meanings, being that which fills all time [the everlasting] or which is utterly devoid of time [the timeless]. These two notions were conflated when classical theism synthesized the Hebraic and Greek understandings of God.) Since Whitehead's objects have no definite temporal origin or terminus, if they were persistent, they would be "eternal" in the sense of being unending. But they do not persist through time, since they "are not 'in time' in the primary sense of the phrase."

Some of Whitehead's other kinds of objects are persistent and recurrent, such as "perceptual objects" and "scientific objects." It is these which give rise to Kemp Smith's misunderstanding. Hence Whitehead sees the desirability of reclassifying his objects primarily in terms of their temporal relations to events. Those which are persistent and recurrent are now the "enduring objects;" those which "come" and "go" are the "eternal objects." The exchange with Kemp Smith may have suggested this term, once the more Greek meaning of "eternal" became dominant in Whitehead's thinking. A more neutral term, such as "timeless" or "atemporal object" might have been less confusing, although he may have chosen "eternal" for its connotation of uncreatedness.

His contrast between endurance and eternality is presented in a succinct and masterful way: "The mountain endures. But when after ages it has been worn away, it has gone. If a replica arises, it is yet a new mountain. A colour is eternal. It haunts time like a spirit. It comes and it goes. But where it comes, it is the same colour. It neither survives nor does it live. It appears when it is wanted. The mountain has to time and space a different relation from that which colour has" (SMW 86f). These "eternal objects of sense" are essentially unrelated to time, ingressing only insofar as they are instantiated in existent events, unlike enduring objects which sustain themselves in and through temporal events.

Yet while the atemporality of the eternal objects remains a constant feature of Whitehead's philosophy thereafter, eternal objects were not originally given the same scope as later. Initially they designated only the sense-objects. These characterized events in their actuality, and were features of their objective display. In the Lowell Lectures no eternal objects were experienced in the privacy of the occasion's own subjectivity, without being part of that occasion's final objectification, unless that subject were conscious. Nor were there any unrealized eternal objects. The whole topic of possibility and its influence upon actuality in general was not systematically considered in this philosophy of organism.

Although prehension, as effected by the double role of actualized eternal objects, appears to be formally conceived in terms of spatio-temporal relatedness, in practice Whitehead tends to restrict himself to a purely spatial relatedness within the simultaneous present. To be sure, it is axiomatic in *Process and Reality* that only past actual occasions are complete, and only complete entities can be prehended. But this doctrine depends upon a firm distinction between becoming as the process of determination, and being as the determinate outcome of this process, and that distinction in turn depends upon the doctrine of temporal atomicity, not yet endorsed. At this stage a more naive, commonsensical attitude prevails: only the present really is, for the past is no longer, and the future is not yet.

Unlike the later theory of asymmetrical relatedness, in which the prehender is internally related to the datum prehended, while the datum is merely externally related to the prehender, this theory of the Lowell Lectures appears to be the more usual doctrine of symmetrical or mutual internal relatedness. Here each term of the relation is internally related to the other. This claim may seem contravened by Whitehead's claim that *some* relations are asymmetrical: "the relatedness of an event are all internal relations, so far as concerns that event, though not necessarily so far as concerns the other relata. For example, the eternal objects, thus involved, are externally related to events" (SMW 122f). Eternal objects must be externally related in order to play their atemporal role. This reflection comes from the "Relativity" addition, and may not represent Whitehead's earlier thinking in the Lowell Lectures. Even if it did, it need not mean that he then held that any other relata were externally related to the event. The evidence appears to be the other way, that the other events internally related to the prehending event themselves incorporate that event into their own essences. There appears to be a mutual internal relatedness, and Whitehead never suggests otherwise in these lectures.

Thus, "every volume mirrors in itself every other volume in space" (SMW 65). With respect to the parts which form the prehensive unity of a volume we are told that "the parts form an ordered aggregate, in the sense that each part is something from the standpoint of every other part, and also from the same standpoint every other part is something in relation to it" (SMW 65). Nature is conceived as a complex of interlocking prehensive unifications (SMW 72). Whitehead's model is evidently a physical field, such as the field of electricity, in which each part simultaneously influences every other part. We might also think of the complex field of gravitational attraction. "The aspects [prehended] are aspects of other events as mutually modifying, each the others. In the pattern of aspects they stand in their pattern of mutual relatedness" (SMW 151).

If through prehension events mutually modify one another, prehension seems understood in terms of mutual internal relatedness. This mutual relatedness can best be understood if the differences in temporal modalities, which later play a large role, are abstracted from. If we think of prehension as (unconscious) perception in a rather naive way, we simultaneously perceive an event when it in turn "perceives" us. If prehension applies equally well to past and future events, Whitehead not yet having discerned crucial differences, then the quality of naive simultaneity would extend into those temporal domains as well.

Yet any theory of mutual internal relatedness would seem to pose difficulties. If some events are past and some are future, then the past events would have to be themselves indeterminate, awaiting determination from the future course of history, or future events already share the determinate character of the past imposed upon them. Neither seems congenial to Whitehead's process orientation, so that the mutual internal relatedness of prehension seems to be restricted to spatial connectedness in the present.

To get at Whitehead's meaning, however, we need to focus attention on the internal relations themselves, and not the supposed character of events so related. A future event, Whitehead argues, is constituted by its relatedness to the present, but it is not fully constituted thereby. If it were, it would already be presently actual, not merely future. When it becomes actual, then it will be constituted in part by this relation. The relation is simply the conditions which the present event imposes upon the future. Such a relation to a future event is not yet determined as to its further contingent aspects and only affects the present event by placing that event within the entire spatiotemporal continuum. Thus, a mutually internal relation with some future locus, already affected by the concreteness of the present, has the same character as an asymmetrical relation to that event once it becomes concretely actual. By either alternative, the present event is only externally related to the concreteness of the coming event.

Future events are thus not conceived as somehow already actual, but as loci within the spatiotemporal continuum which will be affected by the conditions which the present lays down on the future. This is borne out by the one passage in the Lowell Lectures which means to take account of the past and future generally: "An event has contemporaries. This means that an event mirrors within itself the modes of its contemporaries as a display of immediate achievement. An event has a past. This means that an event mirrors within itself the modes of its predecessors, as memories which are fused into its own content. An event has a future. This means that an event mirrors within itself such aspects as the future throws back on to the present, or, in other words, as the present has determined concerning the future. . . .[5] These conclusions are essential for any form of realism. For there is in the world for our cognisance, memory of the past, immediacy of realisation, and indication of things to come" (SMW 72f).[6]

In this passage, Whitehead uses Leibniz' metaphor of "mirroring" in all three temporal modes; elsewhere he introduces the three psychic concepts of memory, perception, and anticipation. These are the dominant terms of his second, and last, discussion of prehension in the Lowell Lectures (SMW 67–73). (Considering how important pre-hension was to become, it is surprising that Whitehead should pay such brief attention to it initially.) The first discussion had considered the separative and prehensive character of space-time (SMW 64–66).

It showed one root for the concept of prehension, the mathematical root. The second discussion shows the other, in terms of perception, or more precisely, the percipient event.

Since nature is that which is perceived, excluding the perceiver, it would seem at first glance that the philosophy of nature should exclude the percipient event as well. That, however, just increases the distance between the perceiver and nature. Is nature to be perceived from some absolute, perspectiveless, stance? To be truly perceived, nature must be perceived from a standpoint within nature. But if truly within nature, it would seem to be outside mind. That, precisely, is how Whitehead originally conceived the percipient event: "This event is not the mind, that is to say, not the percipient. It is that in nature from which the mind perceives" (CN 107). The percipient event, we see, is epistemically central to the philosophy of nature.

Suitably generalized, the percipient event as the prehending event is also basic to the first metaphysical synthesis.[7] The fact that "percipient event" does not refer to mind is underscored by inventing a neologism: "The word *perceive* is, in our common usage, shot through and through with the notion of cognitive apprehension. So is the word *apprehension*, even with the adjective *cognitive* omitted. I will use the word *prehension* for *uncognitive apprehension:* by this I mean *apprehension* whith may or may not be cognitive" (SMW 69). Thus, a percipient event, when clearly understood as devoid of mind, is identical with a prehending event, but Whitehead has now learned to apply this designation to all events.

If we consider a prehensive unity solely in terms of mathematical terms, we find that its own volume is constituted by its relationships to all other volumes. So likewise the perceptual field of the percipient event is constituted by its perceptions of all other things. There is a one-to-correlation between the two models, so that both are equally valid ways to arrive at the notion of "prehension."

The difficulty that Whitehead faces is how to get the interiority promised by prehension without mentality, which he does not yet see as all-pervasive, and hopes to explain by other means. The trouble is that experienced interiority is incurably subjective, and no other sense of interiority is fully convincing.

One reason for his restriction in practice to the present may be found in his primary reliance upon perception as the basis for the meaning of prehension. In terms of the distinction he would later draw in *Symbolism*, perception in the Lowell Lectures is understood solely in the mode of presentational immediacy. Whatever is perceived belongs to the same duration of simultaneity as the perceiver. In order to expand his purely spatial account to include the temporal dimensions of past and future, Whitehead relies upon two other psychic concepts, memory and anticipation. These are understood analogically with perception, such that remembering is prehending the past, and anticipating is prehending the future. But these are merely indicated, rather than being developed in detail.

In conclusion, we may say that prehension, as conceived in the Lowell Lectures, applies to all events without exception, but it is basically a many-one spatiotemporal relationship among simultaneous events by which these events are internally related to one another. It is not yet a causal connection between past and present. Prehension is here unification, prehending only events, no other kind of data. A prehension has no subject which is the prehender, let alone a subjective form. None of these features are present in the initial theory, and accrue at later stages. The term "prehension" remains but its meaning will be constantly extended and transformed. From simple spatiotemporal internal relatedness it will become the basic ingredient for the construction of an incredibly rich internal dynamic of subjective experience, capable of explaining both causation and the solidarity of things. We must constantly guard ourselves against the anachronism of importing these later meanings into earlier formulations.

(2) *Organic mechanism.*[8] Careless readers are apt to confuse organism, Whitehead's alternative to scientific materialism, with some form of vitalism. Vitalism assumes a materialistic mechanism for inanimate nature, but pleads for some vital activity of the whole in living bodies, despite the materialistic character of the parts so vitalistically organized. Whitehead rejects this as an unsatisfactory compromise. Vitalism is dualistic, and does not sufficiently criticize materialism (SMW 79). Any wholesale acceptance of scientific materialism as "the only rendering of the facts of nature," which is then mitigated by some overarching theory of whole, such as idealism in its several forms, is rejected (SMW 63f).

Whitehead aims to develop a theory of mechanism, in which the activity of the whole can be affected by the interaction of the parts. But this is not a *materialistic* mechanism, whose parts are simply located bits of matter externally related to one another. "The whole concept of materialism only applies to very abstract entities, the products of logical discernment. The concrete enduring entities are organisms, so that the plan of the *whole* influences the very characters of the various subordinate organisms which enter into it" (SMW 79). Part influences whole, yet the whole also organically influences part.

Since a component part is internally constituted, in part, by the plan of the whole, it may be expected to have different properties divorced from the whole. Scientific materialism assumes otherwise, and seeks to explain the activity of the whole from such isolated parts externally juxtaposed. Yet "an electron within a living body is different from an electron outside it, by reason of the plan of the body. The electron blindly runs either within or without the body; but it runs within the body in accordance with its character within the body" (SMW 79). Now "there is no need to construe the actions of each molecule in a living body by its exclusive particular reference to the pattern of the complete living organism" (SMW 149). The molecule will also exhibit behavior consonant with its behavior apart from the living organism, which it is the business of chemistry to discover. The molecules follow general laws in their behavior, "but the molecules differ in their intrinsic characters according to the general organic plans of the situations in which they find themselves" (SMW 80). This suggests the possible evolution of the laws of nature, a topic to which we shall return.

Organic mechanism remains a permanent fixture in Whitehead's philosophy. "The molecules within an animal body exhibit certain peculiarities of behavior not to be detected outside of an animal body" (PR 106). Scientific advance is affected by this factor, since similarities of behavior are easier to detect than "the more subtle procedure of noting the differences between behavior within and without the society (i.e., the larger organism), differences of behavior exhibited by occasions which also have close analogies to each other. The history of science is marked by the vehement, dogmatic denial of such differences, until they are found out" (PR 100).

Because of the constitutive importance of the whole to the part in a living organism, and because of the central role Whitehead sees as being played by internal relations in prehensive unity, every part is affected by the larger whole to which it belongs. Most generally, that larger whole is the individual's environment. For the maintenance of any individual, a favorable environment is necessary. The part cannot be an absolutely simple, atomic particle impervious to its surroundings, for the environment enters into its very makeup, and could adversely affect its continued survival (SMW 109).

This doctrine is also retained later: "Thus the given contributions of the environment must at least be permissive of the self-sustenance" of the enduring individual (PR 90; cf. 99, 204f; 206f (iii)). Organic mechanism continues to be affirmed, although in a much more subsidiary role than in the Lowell Lectures.

There are organisms of organisms (SMW 110), organisms within organisms, as biological organisms include the organisms of physics. Leibniz saw organisms within organisms *ad infinitum*, but Whitehead thinks it "very unlikely that there should be infinite regress in nature" (SMW 103). There is also "the evolution of (more) complex organisms from antecedent states of less complex organisms" (SMW 107).

The older scientific materialism is actually inconsistent with any thoroughgoing evolutionary philosophy. Its ultimate bits of matter are incapable of any evolution, and all evolutionary explanation must be understood in terms of more and more complex readjustment of these ultimate parts. There is no transformation of these parts as they enter into more complex wholes, nor do these wholes constitute genuine individuals whose parts are internally interconnected. "The doctrine thus cries aloud for a conception of organism as fundamental for nature. . . . The organism is a unit of emergent value, a real fusion of the characters of eternal objects, emerging for its own sake" (SMW 107).

In Whitehead's later theory the accent here will fall upon the emergence of more complex actual occasions. Their internal concrescence can be conceived as more or less complex according to the number and variety of the several prehensions they synthesize. Events, however, in the rudimentary theory of the Lowell Lectures, are all on a par with one another as prehensive unities. Secondly, once the ontological principle is more fully clarified, occasions are the only things of the natural world which are fully actual, all other entities, such as enduring patterns, enjoying only derivative existence dependent upon their instantiation in actual occasions. In the lectures, to be sure, "we must start with the event as the ultimate unit of natural occurrence" (SMW 103). But the complete internal interdependence of the events does not allow any of them to enjoy "substantial independence" (SMW 70). Despite the obvious affinities between prehensive unities and Leibniz's monads (SMW 155f), Whitehead's early philosophy is really more like Spinozistic monism, with only the total interlocking activity enjoying substantial independence. The relative independence assigned to actual occasions, whereby they are independent of their contemporaries and successors, although dependent upon their predecessors, had not yet been developed.

Since events are not fully actual, they do not take final precedence over the patterns they exemplify. They are merely the opportunities for their ingression, and these patterns express the true individuality and character of the events. "The organic starting point is from the analysis of process as the realisation of events disposed in an interlocked community. The event is the unit of things real. [However,] the emergent enduring pattern is the stabilisation of the emergent achievement so as to become a fact which retains its identity throughout the process. It will be noted that endurance is not primarily the property of enduring beyond itself, but of enduring within itself [i.e. within the event it characterizes]" (SMW 152). While events are basic, they are only arbitrary subdivisions of the spatiotemporal continuum, and enjoy little ontological pre-eminence in contrast with the enduring things of everyday life, which are so much more obvious candidates for an approximate substantial independence in the eyes of common sense shaped by centuries of Aristotelian belief.

At any rate, the focus of this theory of organic mechanism is upon the enduring objects and not the events. These are its organisms: "the enduring organisms are now the outcome of evolution; . . . beyond these organisms, there is nothing else that endures. On the materialistic theory, there is material—such as matter or electricity—which endures. On the organic theory, the only endurances are structures of activity, and the structures are evolved" (SMW 107f).

These enduring objects are capable of tremendous modulation. They are not merely the elementary particles of materialistic theory, capable only of undifferentiated endurance. In addition to such uniform objects (PNK 167–69), Whitehead recognizes non-uniform objects which require some quantum of time to manifest themselves. Each successive reiteration may only manifest part of the pattern, exemplified in its entirety in the whole duration of the event. Vibrations and rhythms have such dynamic patterns of change. These are capable of explaining life and (as Whitehead hopes) even subjectivity and consciousness. Events, *qua* events, are all the same kind of spatiotemporal prehensive unities of other events, but the enduring objects ingredient in these events are to account for the variety and complexity of nature.

Usually such evolution of more complex organisms involves the concatenation of simpler organisms, each more or less following the last of its own nature, within the life-history of some more inclusive organism. Yet Whitehead also speculates on the possibility of the evolution of the laws themselves. Here he is skeptical about induction's providing the basis for the most comprehensive generalizations: "The wider assumption of general laws holding for all cognisable occasions appears a very unsafe addendum to attach to this limited knowledge" (SMW 44). In organic mechanism, "the entities are in themselves . . . liable to modification by their environments. Accordingly, the assumption that no modifications of these laws have been observed to hold, is very unsafe. The physical entities may be modified in every essential way, so far as these laws are concerned. It is even possible that they may be developed into individualities of more fundamental types, with wider embodiment of envisagement. Such envisagement might reach to the attainment of the poising of alternative values with exercise of choice lying outside the physical laws, and expressible only in terms of purpose" (SMW 106). Under the right modification of physical laws, then, it appears that these individual physical objects may evolve into beings capable of subjective decision. Yet it is still the enduring object (rather than the event) that is supposed to have such subjectivity.

These comments suggest the possibility of a gradual modification of the laws of nature holding sway in our present cosmic epoch, for others will be dominant in a successor epoch. Yet if Whitehead seems here on the verge of developing such a theory of cosmic epochs, it does not extend to different space-times. The final stratum of *Science and the Modern World* presupposes the invariance of this space-time. Thus, while "the spatio-temporal continuum is the general system of relatedness of all possibilities, in so far as that system is limited by its relevance to the general fact of actuality," (SMW 162), that general fact of actuality limits it to three dimensions of space (SMW 161; cf. 165f); all of these references stem from the chapter on "Abstraction." Throughout *Science and the Modern World* Whitehead speaks only of the spatiotemporal continuum; it has not yet been generalized into the *n*-dimensional topological "space" underlying all geometrical particularizations in various cosmic epochs. For this concept Whitehead later introduces the term "extensive continuum." That term is used once in this book, to be sure, but from the context it is clear that it is merely synonymous with the spatiotemporal continuum (SMW 126).

Apart from the possible modification of the laws of nature, the emergence of higher organisms is dependent on the workings of organic mechanism. This, in turn, is founded upon prehensive unity, the fact that each event is decisively constituted by its environment, those surrounding events to which it is internally related. This prehensive relationship depends upon the reciprocity between the patterns which that event itself displays. They must be internally related. "Each event corresponds to two such patterns; namely, the pattern of aspects of other events which it grasps into its own unity, and the pattern of its aspects which other events severally grasp into their unities. . . . There is thus an intrinsic and an extrinsic reality of an event, namely, the event as in its own prehensions, and the event as in the prehension of other events" (SMW 103f).

This clarifies the relationship between extrinsic and intrinsic patterns. What is never clarified, however, and what may be a weakness in this early philosophy of organism, is the relationship between the extrinsic pattern and the enduring object an event exemplifies. The two concepts arise from very different trains of thought; the extrinsic pattern from his new-found theory of prehensive unity, designed as the converse of extensive relationships among events, while the enduring object emerges as the contrasting term to the eternal object in a temporal classification of the various objects of the philosophy of nature. One derives primarily from events, the other from objects, but here there is a problematic convergence. Is the extrinsic pattern the same as the enduring object, or different?

Let us suppose they are the same. After all, every event has some sort of objective display, which would be its extrinsic pattern. The enduring object it may exemplify could also claim to be that objective display. Then the question arises how that objective display is derived. Does it come from the event's prehensive unity of the pattern displayed by all others events in the world, or from the ingression of the enduring object it exemplifies? If formed by the pattern of the world intrinsically appropriated, then this would seem to be completely sufficient, and there would be no need for any influence from the enduring object. On the other hand, if it is constituted by the enduring object that event reiterates, then what influence, supposedly essentially constitutive, does the prehended external world have upon it? Each is completely determinative, and there is no reason to suppose these separate determinations would coincide.

Whitehead's later theory can resolve this difficulty. In the first place, mutual prehensions of simultaneous events are replaced by asymmetrical prehensions of past occasions. The present prehending subject is constituted by these past occasions, while they are independent from any supervening prehension. Secondly, the enduring object is successively instantiated in a series of dominant predecessors to the prehending occasion, which inherits its basic characteristics from these predecessors. Thus, the way the enduring object is ingredient in the occasion and the way the occasion prehends all other occasions is exactly the same. While the dominant predecessor exemplifying that enduring object exerts a massive impact upon the prehending occasion, it is also influenced in its outcome by other occasions prehended. The enduring object is merely a convenient partial abstraction, fully concretized by the occasion's rootage in the total environment to which it is internally related.

At this early state, however, prehensive unity and the ingredience of enduring objects are exclusive alternatives whose union has not been thought through. They were not clearly identified, but they could not be regarded as different.

Suppose the enduring object and the extrinsic pattern to be different. The event can only display one single objective appearance. Yet it receives this display from two exclusive and potentially conflicting sources. Further, organic mechanism presupposes that the part can be internally and essentially influenced by the larger organism to which it belongs, and by the surrounding environment. But there is nothing in the nature of the enduring object *per se* that requires this. All such modification is derived from the character of prehensive unity, which in this case would be quite extraneous to the enduring object. In fact, the enduring object could exhibit precisely that same sort of undifferentiated endurance impervious to the surrounding environment which Whitehead had rejected in the classic scientific concept of matter. Without some connection with prehensive unity, there is no reason for the enduring objects constituting organisms to evolve towards any more complex organisms by genuine emergence.

Nevertheless, a certain looseness between the prehensive unities of events and the enduring patterns of organisms was also quite helpful to Whitehead, particularly with respect to his most complex organisms. The mutual internal relatedness of prehensive unity logically leads to a complete determinism inimical to freedom and subjectivity. If organic influences upon the enduring patterns of organisms were not as complete as pure prehensive unity might require, there could be sufficient room for the growth of mentality and consciousness he assigns to bodily events.

(3) *Bodily events.* Under this heading we shall consider Whitehead's early theory of subjectivity, which is ascribed not to prehensive events but to highly complex enduring objects.

This theory will be quite strange for anyone schooled in terms of Whitehead's later theory of prehension. According to *Process and Reality* every prehension has both datum and subject, and this subject is simply the actuality in its own process of becoming whereby it unifies its many prehended data into one. Each actuality as presently concrescing enjoys its own subjective immediacy. This subjectivity ceases upon the attainment of final unity, whereby the occasion becomes an objective datum for supervening acts of prehension. This subjective unification by present occasions is inaccessible to us, since every determinate actuality must already be past and complete to be prehensible. Thus our *only* purchase upon the present unification of prehensions is our own immediate subjective experience, so purged of all anthropocentric particularity that it can apply to all actual entities. Thus, from the standpoint of Whitehead's final theory, the subject *is* nothing but prehensive unification. Moreover, the enduring object is merely that constellation of common objective factors transmitted through a series of occasions. As purely objective, it contains nothing subjective. Whitehead's early theory in the Lowell Lectures is nearly the reverse of this later theory.

The epochal theory of time, not yet entertained in February 1925, enabled Whitehead to differentiate more sharply between enduring objects and events. Since earlier events could be of any duration, an event could be co-extensive with the enduring object it characterized. Once the idea of extremely brief actual occasions dominated Whitehead's thinking, however, the enduring object could only be understood as the reiteration of the common characteristic exemplified by a whole series of occasions. This raised more sharply the question of the location of subjectivity. Does it belong to the individual occasion, or to the enduring object? Eventually it was ascribed to the occasion, although initially, as we shall see, he ascribed it to the enduring object even after the introduction of the epochal theory.

Far from being the pansubjectivist of his later theory, Whitehead in the Lowell Lectures espouses a more conventional theory. Mentality (not yet sharply distinguished from subjectivity) is only characteristic of more complex events. In his later theory Whitehead carefully distinguishes between subjectivity (ascribed equally to all actual entities in the immediacy of their own becoming), mentality (ascribed to them by degrees according to their complexity and capacity for originating novelty), and consciousness (ascribed only to very specific class of highly mental, actual entities, capable of enjoying intellectual feelings).[9] In the Lowell Lectures subjectivity, mentality, and consciousness are not sharply differentiated. Whitehead tends to consider them all in terms of conscious knowing, or cognizance. Events, as events, are all alike prehensive unities. But they are characterized by more and more complex enduring objects, up to and including those pervasive bodily patterns capable of sustaining our subjective psychological fields.

This is not to say that there are not important analogies between prehensive unification and subjective experience. Although prehension is derived from extension, it is also a generalization from perception, and epistemological considerations demand that perception be intelligible in terms of prehension. Since, however, Whitehead has no means as yet for distinguishing between progressively more complex stages of prehensive unification, all the differentiation must be made in terms of enduring characteristics.

Thus it is in terms of objects, rather than events, that the mental is distinguished from the physical. Whitehead uses the instance of mind-body interaction to illustrate organic mechanism at one point, using the term "plan" to indicate the complete objective element present: ". . . the mental states enter into the *plan* of the total [animal] organism and thus modify the plans of the successive subordinate organisms . . ." (SMW 79, my emphasis).

Because of this understanding of mind, the pattern characterizing the bodily event plays a central role in Whitehead's early theory. ". . . the body is the organism whose states regulate our cognisance of the world. . . . if this cognisance conveys knowledge of a transcendent world, it must be because the event which is bodily life unifies in itself aspects of the universe" (SMW 91f). As in the later theory, the body mediates our interaction with the entire world. At this earlier stage, however, the body need not be understood as a complex society of interacting actual occasions, but can be taken as a whole as a single bodily event, whose interiority is our own private psychological field.

Thus, in his earlier analysis of prehensive unity, Whitehead notes, "I have started from our own psychological field, as it stands for our cognition. I take it for what it claims to be: the self-knowledge of our bodily event. I mean the total event, and not the inspection of the details of the body. This self-knowledge discloses a prehensive unification of modal presences of entities beyond itself. I generalise by the use of the principle that this total bodily event is on the same level as all other events, except for an unusual complexity and stability of inherent pattern" (SMW 73). He accepts the principle of continuity of materialistic mechanism, that no arbitrary breaks should be introduced into nature, but notes that materialism cannot make sense of our immediate, subjective experience. If, rather, we start from immediate experience, as Whitehead advocates, than we are led to an organic conception of nature.

Prehensive unity is thus a generalization of perceptual synthesis, which in turn is understood as the interiority of the bodily event.

Within this general solution Whitehead confronts many subordinate problems: How are we to reconcile the unity of perceptual experience with the aggregate nature of the human body? In what is our subjectivity finally to be lodged? In one extended passage in the seventh Lowell Lecture on "Science and Philosophy" Whitehead addresses these problems (SMW 148–52). We shall not here detail his complex solution to the first problem, but his comments on subjectivity deserve comment.

In line with what he later says about symbolic reference, Whitehead notes the double role played by sense-objects in perception. They are both in the perceiver and yet disclose the flux of things beyond. "The subject-object relation takes its origin in the double role of these eternal objects. They are modifications of the subject, but only in their character of conveying aspects of other subjects in the community of the universe. Thus, no individual subject can have independent reality, since it is a prehension of limited aspects of subjects other than itself" (SMW 151).

Taken in isolation, this passage clearly exhibits the pansubjectivity of Whitehead's final theory. In the immediate context, however, he underscores the radically provisional character of this term "subject." It is a "bad term" for his meaning, largely because the subject-predicate mode of analysis dominates Descartes' description of subjective experience, which can then only be thought of as the private qualities inhering in experience the way attributes inhere in a substance.[10]

In order to avoid the solipsism to which the subject-predicate mode of analysis leads, and to emphasize the public nature of what is prehended, Whitehead declares: "The primary situation disclosed in cognitive experience is 'ego-object amid objects.' By this I mean that the primary fact is an impartial world transcending the 'here-now' which marks the ego-object, and transcending the 'now' which is the spatial world of simultaneous realization. . . . The ego-object, as consciousness here-now, is conscious of its experient essence as constituted by its internal relatedness to the world of realities, and to the world of ideas. But the ego-object, in being thus constituted, is within the world of realities, and exhibits itself as an organism requiring the ingression of ideas for the purpose of this status among realities" (SMW 151f).

"Ego-object" is a strange term, for it is intended to designate the subject as an object. This is wholly against the grain of our usual classificatory schemes which treat subject and object as exclusive opposites. Yet, it is in accord with a basic contrast between events and objects. Events in themselves, being purely spatiotemporal volumes, have no differentiating characteristics, so that we cannot differentiate subjectivity from non-subjectivity except in terms of objects. Subjectivity is a function of the organism in its most complex form, the ego-object. The subjective character of the event is to be understood in terms of ego-object it exemplifies. Although Whitehead is willing to identify consciousness with the ego-object, he is not yet ready to specify its nature. "This question of consciousness must be reserved for treatment on another occasion" (SMW 152).

The conceptuality of "ego-object" is in line with Whitehead's remarks about the "enduring pattern" of an event, and about the way in which the plan of the whole modifies the plan of the part, and vice versa, in organic mechanism. The "ego-object" can be conceived as the plan of the whole organism within a conscious being, although Whitehead here, for epistemological purposes, restricts it to mean the seat of individual experience.

As we have seen, prehension is a generalization of the extensional properties of the percipient event. It is the "here-now," the event within nature from which all other events are perceived. Yet that perceiving is more than a locus of extensional relations; there is also a conscious mind. In this sense Whitehead could speak of the percipient event as "the bodily life of the incarnate mind" (CN 107). If we consider the percipient event in relative abstraction from its prehensive role, concentrating on its role with respect to mentality and consciousness, it is most appropriately described as a "bodily event."

Likewise, the "ego-object" is the descendant to the "percipient object." This is what characterizes a given event as percipient: "The percipient event is discerned as the locus of a recognizable permanence which is the 'percipient object'" (PNK 83; cf. 13, 90f). But while the percipient event is within nature, as an event among other events, the percipient object is not (as mind). Whitehead acknowledges the difficulties in the notes to the second edition concerning the distinction between "the percipient object, which roughly speaking is an individual, as mental, [and] a percipient event which is the flux of experience of a living organism. But the percipient object is shadowy in this book and is clearly outside 'nature'" (PNK 202; cf. 195).

This may well account for its absence from *The Concept of Nature*. The "percipient object" does not reappear, but Whitehead tries his hand at the idea it embodies when he introduces the "ego-object" into his first metaphysical synthesis. Since percipience has now been generalized to all events, Whitehead must concentrate on those features more specifically objective; hence the change in terminology to "ego-object." [11]

Now we are in a position to determine in what sense, if any, Whitehead espouses pansubjectivity in the Lowell Lectures. The problem is a confusing one, both terminologically and conceptually. In any flat-out sense, in which he expressly ascribes subjectivity to each and every event, the answer must be no. Unlike the later theory of occasions, events are not natural unities, and can thus designate *any* volume of space-time, such as clouds, intergalactic spaces, or the American republic since its inception. In particular it could designate the event of the whole, to which Whitehead never ascribes subjectivity.

Whitehead definitely does attribute interiority to events: (a) " 'Value' is the word I use for the intrinsic reality of an event" (SMW 93). (b) This intrinsic reality is characterized by an intrinsic pattern, that "pattern of aspects of other events which it grasps into its own unity" (SMW 103). (c) Prehension is not simply internal relatedness, but must be conceived from the standpoint of one of the relata. What is this but to conceive of that relatum "from the inside"? This inner aspect of prehension is essential if the connection is to be made to perception. To this we might add Whitehead's recognition of natural continuity, explicable only if we begin with immediate experience, not with external materialist assumptions.

While it makes some sense to ascribe interiority to every event whatsoever, to claim every event has subjectivity is highly implausible. That move would be facilitated by the restriction of actuality to the natural unities which are occasions. But interiority also needs some sense of mentality to become fully subjective, and at this stage Whitehead is no panpsychist. We can distinguish at least three different senses for panpsychism: (a) all actualities have some degree of conscious awareness; (b) all actualities are minds (Leibniz); (c) all actualities have some degree of mentality. Only the third is applicable to the later Whitehead, understanding mentality in terms of novelty of response. In the Lowell Lectures, however, mind is not understood as a general feature of prehensive unification, but rather in terms of the pattern or plan of some very complex events. Mind is understood in terms of object, not event. Even later, in *Religion in the Making*, Whitehead distinguishes between two classes of occasions, only one of which is mental.

In his final Lowell Lecture, Whitehead recapitulates his doctrine by substituting *organism* for *matter*: "For this purpose, the mind involved in the materialist theory dissolves into a function of organism. The psychological field then exhibits what an event is in itself. Our bodily event is an unusually complex type of organism and consequently includes cognition. Further, space and time, in their most concrete signification, become the locus of events. An organism is the realization of a definite shape of value. The emergence of some actual value depends on limitation which excludes neutralizing cross-lights. Thus, an event is a matter of fact which by reason of its limitation is a value for itself; but by reason of its very nature it also requires the whole universe in order to be itself.

"Importance depends on endurance. Endurance is the retention through time of an achievement of value. What endures is identity of pattern, self-inherited. Endurance requires the favorable environment. The whole of science revolves round this question of enduring organisms" (SMW 194).

In this summary prehensive unity, organic mechanism, and conscious cognition are subtly intertwined. An organism depends upon prehensive unity for the close interrelatedness it has with its environment, which ultimately includes the entire universe. At the same time an organism is an enduring pattern, whose complex evolution allows for the emergence of consciousness. Our conscious experience is thus what an event characterized by such an unusually complex organic pattern is in itself.

Although Whitehead does not advertise the fact, the tight coherence of prehension, organic mechanism, and consciousness forms a very self-sufficient naturalism which has no need of the theistic hypothesis. It is a natural outgrowth of his philosophy of nature, and provides a suitable metaphysical framework for its doctrine of events (including percipient events) and objects.

Whitehead intended to make process basic in his metaphysics, replacing the extensionality of events, which had been basic to the earlier philosophy of nature. Even mind now becomes process. "For Berkeley's mind, I substitute a process of prehensive unification" (SMW 69).

Whitehead understands process not merely as temporal succession, but as the emergence of the new. For that reason a world of events, linked primarily by extensionality, would not require process. A fully determined world, such as Leibniz's, could be conceived as a world of events, but it would lack process.

Prehension was designed to incorporate process within the metaphysical system, but this is used in two ways: for prehensive unity and for prehensive unification. Prehensive unity, however, is coextensive with event; it *is* the event in its relatedness to all other events. Process is to be sought not in these events, but in that which brings them into being, the acts of prehensive unification: "A prehension is a process of unifying. Accordingly, nature is a process of expansive development, necessarily transitional from prehension to prehension. What is achieved is thereby passed beyond, but it is also retained as having aspects of itself present to prehensions which lie beyond it [objective immortality, before being so named]. Thus, nature is a structure of evolving processes. The reality is the process" (SMW 72).

Thus, process is the transition from event to event as involving a succession of prehensive unifications. Here process is understood as a pure transition among events, with no hint yet of any concrescence of feelings within an event. Prehension signifies that unifying activity whereby the multiplicity of the world is drawn into the event; it does not yet mean a specific feeling with its own single datum so characteristic of his later philosophy. As long as prehension means prehensive unification, we do not have an interaction of many prehensions within a single concrescence, a prehension of prehensions, so to speak.

While Whitehead intends in his way to introduce process into his metaphysics, it may be questioned whether this goal was fully achieved in the Lowell Lectures. A first problem concerns the locus of process. If space-time can be exhaustively analyzed in terms of events, and these are all prehensive unities, when and where does prehensive unification take place? In some form or other this question will trouble Whitehead throughout his philosophical career, finally taking the form of the relationship between genetic division and temporality. But here it is posed in a particularly acute form, because events have no interiors which might serve as the locus of their coming into being. What might serve as the interior of an event is simply another slightly smaller event.

Another problem really concerns a basic unclarity, arising from the lack of any precise correlation between events and their prehensive unifications. A process of unification would seem to establish a single unified (and hence undivided) event, yet any event is subdivisible into many smaller events. If each of these should have its own process of unification, does this mean they all make up the one larger one? Or that the larger event is now the outcome of many processes of unification? If so, how is unity finally achieved by this many? Also, prehensive unification is finally a bold generalization from perception, a momentary affair. Can prehensive unification retain its roots in this momentary experience if the event to which it is correlated lasts for ages such as an enduring rock?

Whatever may have been the way by which Whitehead came to affirm temporal atomicity, launching his philosophical career in a new direction, there is no denying that it enabled him to resolve these two problems inherent in his first metaphysical synthesis. Temporal atomicity holds that there is a natural class of events, called occasions, which are not physically divisible. An occasion could be set in precise one-to-one correlation with prehensive unification; all larger events, being made of many occasions, would be therefore brought into being by many prehensive unifications. Occasions, being indivisible, have interiors which could serve as the locus for prehensive unification.

This may resolve problems immediately at hand, but it will generate others to stimulate further philosophical inquiry. Meanwhile we need to examine the nature of the specific arguments which led Whitehead to espouse temporal atomicity in the next chapter. First let us consider some relevant materials from Appendix 1.

2. SUBJECTIVITY IN THE HARVARD LECTURES OF APRIL, 1925

The theory of subjectivity and consciousness in the Lowell Lectures is, of course, prior to Whitehead's discovery of the atomistic character of temporalization, and we might anticipate some modification of this theory, perhaps in the direction of pansubjectivity, as a result of that discovery. Some of the statements he makes to his Harvard students on April 7, 1925, the day he first introduced the epochal theory, suggest just that. Yet, on April 18 he has no difficulty in still talking positively about the "ego-object": "The ego-object is in a world of objects. The world of objects modifies the essence of each object in that world. *The ego object knows itself as* amid other objects" (see Appendix 1). This recalls the theory of the ego-object we have just encountered (SMW 151f), indicating that Whitehead still ascribes subjectivity to the enduring pattern of the bodily organism. Also, throughout his Harvard Lectures of April 1925 Whitehead retains the contrast between the event and the subject.

His initial comments on April 7 are nevertheless quite suggestive. First, under point 5 he remarks: "But here we bump up against the atomic view of things, also the subjective view. The subjective view has got to be expressed within the objective view. It is there—the psychological field. You have got to express the subject as one element in the universe [as there is] nothing apart from that universe."

Then follows a diagram of the present duration showing both the event (E) and the subject as ingredient in that duration, in mutual interaction. He comments: "A subject is a parallelogram in our myth, having divisibility and transitions within itself." How this is to be reconciled with atomicity is not yet worked out, but the occasion is accorded its temporal thickness. "The subject has to realize itself qua the influence of the past on it. Limitation." Two paragraphs later, under the diagram: "The event E, is within, enters into the essence of the subject, not as being merely the subject [object?] but as being itself. The subject is what that grasping-together is. I am the apprehension of that . . . The whole duration as realized for the subject."

He seems to be saying that the subject *is* the prehensive unification of the occasion. (The technical phraseology of the Lowell Lectures, "prehension" and "prehensive unity," appears to be largely avoided in his lectures to his Harvard classes.) But because the subject and the event are distinguished in his diagram, Whitehead probably means that the subject is only a selective appropriation of the prehensive unity which is the event itself. In any case, his initial remark in this quotation is quite unclear. Quite possibly William Ernest Hocking, who took these notes, confused "subject" and "object" here, so that Whitehead's meaning is that the event enters into the subject not merely as an objective representation but as part of its very being.

Thus it looks like Whitehead may have adopted a provisional theory of subjectivity which could serve as a rough transition to his later theory ascribing subjectivity to all actual occasions. In this provisional theory events and subjects are distinguished yet correlated in that each subject is a selective appropriation (or "abstraction") from the prehensive unification which was the event. This would be particularly the case if we think of the subjective mind as merely a part of the total bodily event.

The subject was viewed both as sharing in the temporal atomicity of the series of events, and as continuous. On April 9 three event-states of the subject are depicted in the diagram, and to the right Hocking reports Whitehead as saying: "Taking the subject as real is to take it atomically as having in itself the flux of time. . . . What the subject is for itself includes the present as issuing from the past. Internal relations with the past." Later in that same lecture he balances this atomicity with the "Continuity of the subject [as] inheriting a pattern. (2) [the present occasion of the self, so designated in the diagram] inherits from (1) the totality of the subject as being past.

The subject inherits its own unity, its own grasping-together, as the same process only with the aspect of being behind." [12]

Since the unity of this process of grasping-together is inherited, the atomic pulsations of prehensive unification can be reconceived, Whitehead apparently thinks, as a continuous process of grasping-together centered upon the prehending subject. Here he is sensitive to our common intuition of the continuity of the experiencing self, yet wishing to supplement it with incoming experiences understood epochally. He combines these two strands in terms of a formula written on the blackboard: "Every *enduring subject* inherits . . . itself under *the aspect of other circumstances*," commenting that the fact "that I am the same person as lectured to you last time" seems "portentous" to Whitehead.

In the next lecture, on April 11, Whitehead abandons any notion of the subject "standing behind" the event: "The ego of any entity is out of space. [It is] the monistic total[ity] as exhibiting itself in that individual activity of realization." Here, as in Kant, time is distinguished from space, so that space is simply the form of the outer intuition. In his final theory, the self, at least in the guise of the mental pole, is out of space-time: "Every actual entity is 'in time' as far as its physical pole is concerned, and is 'out of time' so far as its mental pole is concerned" (PR 248).

The principle of selectivity, which we have proposed for the mind's relation to the bodily event, is applied to the body's relationship to the external world in Whitehead's lecture for April 14: "The body is to be looked on as a method of keeping out [causal influences rather than as a method for] letting [them] in. It selects what aspects shall be considered." On the one hand, this hearkens back to a principle enunciated by Bergson, that we should begin with the retention of everything past, and then explain what has been excluded. For example, it is not remembering that needs to be explained, but forgetting.[13] On the other hand, it points forward to Whitehead's final theory of the body, that it acts as a simplifier and amplifier, conveying an edited version of transmuted, vivid sensa to perceptual awareness.

In his lecture on "Cognitive Experience" for April 28, 1925, Whitehead introduces two ideas we need to note. One is the principle of the translucence of cognizance (conscious knowing). By this principle an occasion inclusive of cognizance presupposes the same facts as the occasion exclusive of cognizance. Whitehead sees this as a way of resolving the long-standing conflict between idealism and realism. He regards the difference as primarily temperamental, depending on whether one was brought up in philosophy to be an Oxford idealist or a Cambridge realist. As long as one admits that cognizance does not alter the fact, it makes no difference whether we agree with the idealists that cognizance is an important factor in the universe, or with the realists that what is apprehended is not modified by cognizance.

Secondly, we are told that the self of cognizant occasions, or the cognizant self, must be discriminated from the self of the standpoint occasions, which appears to be identified with the experient self. This seems to be a development of his earlier distinction in his lecture of April 7 between the subject and the event. In this distinction we construed the event as a prehensive unity of internal relatedness with all other events, at least of those simultaneous with itself. Subjectivity, insofar as it is identified with consciousness, is still distinguished from the reiterations of prehensive unity, but now Whitehead is prepared to use the term "experient subject" for that prehensive unity, a usage which verges on pansubjectivity.

His major point in distinguishing the cognizant and the experient subject in this particular lecture seems to be to take account of the inconstant character of consciousness. The cognizant self is fitful and variable. In fact, if we take into account the phenomenon of sleeping and waking, there are many cognizant selves of one individual; one for each waking period. "In relation to endurance, the important self is the experient self." This is the self we generally have in mind. "The self which has endured since birth is not cognitive."

This interpretation of consciousness remains a permanent feature of Whitehead's theory: "Consciousness flickers; and even at its brightest, there is a small focal region of clear illumination, and a large penumbral region of experience which tells of intense experience in dim apprehension. The simplicity of clear consciousness is no measure of the complexity of complete experience. Also this character of our experience suggests that consciousness is the crown of experience, only occasionally attained, not its necessary base" (PR 267).

In the lecture of April 28 consciousness is described as "between an emergent entity and the composite potentiality from which it emerges." This looks like an ancestor of his final view, in which consciousness is the felt contrast between what is and what might be, between actuality and potentiality.

In all, while the Harvard lectures of April 1925 show some leanings towards the pansubjectivity characteristic of his mature theory, they exhibit an even greater continuity with the understanding of subjectivity in the Lowell Lectures. There consciousness was identified with the enduring patterns of highly evolved organisms.

"The idea of self, qua idea, is [an] enduring object as much as any," we are told in his lecture of May 7 (in the fifth specification of the essence of A). There are a few hints, however, which tentatively and subtly transform his position. Hocking reports that in Whitehead's lecture for May 12, he "holds that our experience of ourselves in the past is the same in principle as of anything else in the past. [There is a] *general publicity* of the past in every present occasion of concrete experience." This does not yet mean, as it will in Whitehead's later thinking, that pastness *per se* is identified with objectivity, presentness with subjectivity, but it is clearly a step in that direction.

The lecture of May 22, addressing the question, "How is abstraction possible," bears a great many similarities to the chapter on "Abstraction" added to *Science and the Modern World*. Internal and external relatedness, individual essences, relational essences, are all discussed. The symbolization for a complex eternal object of the form R (A, B, C) is displayed. "Every occasion is a synthesis of being and not being." In illustration of this statement Whitehead remarks "I am not in that chain [i.e. series of actual occasions?] but in this one." He immediately corrects himself: "I should not have said 'I'—I am not an eternal object." But if his own subjectivity is not an eternal object, and hence not part of an enduring pattern, as he had previously held, he does not yet tell us what it is.

Notes

1. The primary discussions of his own philosophy of organism can be found on pages 17f, 63–65f, 69–72f, 79f, 86f, 88–94, 103–104, 106–109, 119–20, 131–35, 148–52 and 194 in the Free Press edition. These correspond to pages 25–28, 93–96, 101–107, 115f, 126, 128–37, 150–59, 174–76, 190–96, 213–19, and 278 in the 1926 edition. Note that SMW 103f originally formed a continuous discussion with 106–109, interrupted now by three additional paragraphs concerning the triple envisagement.

2. Whitehead here uses the customary word "subject" in designating the perceiver but then immediately replaces it in the next paragraph with the concept of an "ego-object," for reasons we shall consider shortly.

3. Reprinted in *The Credibility of Divine Existence: The Collected Papers of Norman Kemp Smith,* edited by A. J. B. Porteous, R. C. Maclennan, and G. E. Davie (London: Macmillan, 1967), pp. 226–50.

4. "Unpublished Letter from Whitehead to Kemp Smith," *The Southern Journal of Philosophy* 7/4 (Winter, 1969–70), 339.

5. This theory of the future in terms of the conditions the present lays down upon it becomes a permanent feature of Whitehead's philosophy, to be developed in considerable detail in his chapter concerning the future (AI 246–54). There "the future is immanent in the present by reason of the fact that the present bears in its own essence the relationships which it will have to the future" (AI 250). See also Whitehead's lecture of April 30, 1925 in Appendix 1 for the theory of internal relatedness with respect to the future.

6. William P. Alston overlooks the distinctions here involved, whereby an occasion can be related to the abstract conditions it imposes on the future without being related to the particular contingent concretizations of those conditions, in "Internal Relatedness and Pluralism in Whitehead," *Review of Metaphysics* 5 (1952), 535–58, at 552f.

7. This transition from 'percipient event' to 'prehending event' is also depicted, in a somewhat different way, by Victor Lowe in *Understanding Whitehead* (Baltimore: The Johns Hopkins Press, 1962), p. 228.

8. The principal texts for organic mechanism are fairly compact: pages 79f, 103f, 106–109, 149f in the Free Press edition, and pages 115f, 150–52, 155–59, 214–16 in the 1926 edition.

9. I have spelled out these differences in greater detail in "Can Whitehead Provide for Real Subjective Agency? A Reply to Edward Pols' Critique," *The Modern Schoolman* 47 (1970), 209–225, at 216f and in the monograph I edited, *Two Process Philosophers* (American Academy of Religion, Studies in Religion, Number 5, 1973), 81f.

10. This critique is retained and developed in PR 157–160.

11. I have analyzed the one paragraph discussing the "ego-object" (SMW 151f) as part of the original Lowell Lectures, but it is also possible this paragraph was inserted later.

12. What is meant by the subject "being behind" is none too clear, especially as we are warned earlier in this lecture under point 3 that "the mind is not something standing behind events but something realized in events."

13. See, e.g., Henri Bergson, *The Creative Mind* (Totowa, New Jersey: Littlefield, Adams & Co., 1965), pp. 153ff.

THREE

The Emergence of Temporal Atomicity

READERS primarily interested in the broad sweep of Whitehead's development may choose to omit this chapter, turning directly to the two major systematic chapters of *Science and the Modern World*, both of which were worked out in terms of the new orientation. This chapter inquires more precisely how Whitehead discovered temporal atomism.[1] Earlier, in assuming definite events, Whitehead explicitly tells us that "this assumption must not be construed either as asserting an atomic structure of events, or as a denial of overlapping events" (PNK 74). Now these events are given an atomic structure in the added paragraphs we have considered. In the final two chapters on "Abstraction" and "God" Whitehead introduces a terminological distinction to clarify matters: these epochal units are distinguished from other events by being designated 'actual occasions.' Thus in the short space of four months, from the conclusion of the Lowell Lectures in early March to the submission of the completed manuscript to the publishers in late June, Whitehead not only changed his mind on the continuity or atomicity of events, but worked out some of its basic implications for his thought. Is it possible to determine the reasons for this shift?

Here our argument must be very tentative and conjectural, as we have only the written text to go by, as supplemented by the notes of his Harvard classes.[2] These may not contain all the reasons which influenced Whitehead, only those he thought might persuade others of his newly-found position. But we can assess the probabilities among these arguments. Here the text we must scrutinize is the addition to the chapter on "Relativity" which we have already isolated (SMW 122–27) for this is the one text which explicitly introduces temporal atomicity.

Our analysis hopes to illumine the last ten paragraphs of the "Relativity" chapter. Whether it will also illuminate Whitehead's theory of temporal atomicity is another matter. The central argument here is exceedingly complex and obscure, and was not repeated in later presentations. Historical rather than systematic concerns prompt our inquiry, since it was most probably this argument that persuaded Whitehead to adopt temporal atomism.

There are several arguments, and the final one from Zeno (SMW 126f) has proven the most durable. It is repeated later as Whitehead's chief justification for insisting that there is no continuity of becoming (PR 68f), even in the particular form of subdividing the moment of the beginning of a movement, and not the ending, as is the usual practice. But a comparison of the two texts will show that in *Process and Reality*, where Whitehead is directly considering arguments by Zeno, Whitehead's particular formulation is an adaptation of Zeno's argument.[3] In *Science and the Modern World* he merely alludes to Zeno for an argument that may have been Whitehead's own invention. At any rate, a close examination of Zeno's texts does not seem to have provoked the question of temporal atomicity. The passage in question has more the quality of an argument Whitehead could devise on the basis of past reflection on Zeno, given his newly discovered temporal atomism.

Zeno's paradoxes probably came to his attention in at least two ways: through his study of ancient Greek mathematics[4] and through his reading of Bergson's exposition.[5] It seems unlikely that James' discussion of Zeno played any role here, for Whitehead seems to have first become aware of his affinities with James on this point through later reading.[6]

The inconsistency Whitehead detects in the two passages from Kant's *Critique of Pure Reason* (A 162f and A 169f) probably caught his attention because of his heightened sensitivity with respect to the problem of temporal atomicity, rather than because it prompted any sort of solution, at least initially. Unlike the Zeno argument, this discussion is not repeated in his later works.

Whitehead's Harvard lectures in the spring of 1925 may serve as an independent means of verifying our suggestions concerning the impact of these arguments from Zeno and from Kant. (See Appendix 1.) The atomicity of temporalization was not considered prior to Whitehead's lecture of March 31, well after the Lowell Lectures were concluded. In that lecture Whitehead had been discussing the paradoxes and difficulties in our ordinary understanding of time introduced by modern relativity physics. But he notes that difficulties about time had already been with us, and discusses both of these two passages from Kant, as well as Zeno's argument, the latter in the form Whitehead considered most compelling: "How are you going to move forward into the future? How is process possible? If you conceive it under the guise of a temporal transition into the non-existent, you can't get going. There is nothing you can point to into which there is a transition, or is then and there created."

Yet while this same argument later becomes the systematic foundation for the epochal theory of becoming (PR 68f), there is little evidence here, with or without the further issues Kant raises, that it was sufficient to prompt such a conceptual breakthrough. At this time they seem to produce only preplexity. Whitehead is more sure that something is wrong with the traditional notions of time than he is about how to overcome these difficulties.

Apparently while at a loss how to resolve this issue of temporal atomicity and continuity, Whitehead explored what the philosophical masters of the past had said on the subject during his lectures of April 2 and 4. His lecture of April 2 includes an interesting idea on the present as the integration of past and future. In speaking of the "moment," which was his technical term for that which distinguishes past and future, he says that "it is that particular concrete relatedness of that past to that future. We do not deal with the past passively[?], but with past events in their relation to future events." This idea is not immediately picked up, however, for, as we shall see, his basic argument for temporal atomicity in *Science and the Modern World* hinges on the temporal thickness of the duration of simultaneity, without explicit reference to past or future.

On April 4 he remarks: "These are the elements of thought we have got to play with: [both in metaphysics and] also in science, continuity and atomicity [are] always haunting [us]. Under the influence of the quantum theory the atomic aspect has become more urgent than before." Yet no concrete solution is forthcoming. Perhaps Whitehead had it, and just did not get around to announcing it. In any case it bursts full-blown onto the scene in his lecture of April 7, 1925.

It is a well organized lecture, but Whitehead prefaces his comments with the confession that he is in "a state of muddle due to the state of the subject." "Science at present is asking for an atomic theory of time. Shall metaphysics say to science it can't have it? This is not the function of metaphysics. Can we find any ground for it? "

The theory that he develops in this lecture is complex, and best considered in the context of his theory of bodily event (chapter 2, section 3) which considers subjectivity in terms of an enduring object. Also, it does not help us to understand how Whitehead himself may have arrived at his newly found doctrine. But the doctrine itself is unmistakably announced. "The temporalization of extension [is achieved] via [the] realization of the potential. [It is] the individual-ization of *each* event into a peculiar togetherness. . . . An event as present is real for itself. It is this becoming real which is tempor-alization." "The reality is the realization of something as entering into its own being. The pulling together of a duration from its own viewpoint, i.e., as entering into its own essence." "Realization may require a minimum duration. . . . The becoming real is not the production via the parts of the duration, contradicting Kant. The transition is in the nature of what has become real, but it hasn't become real because of the transition."

1. THE EARLY ARGUMENT

In order to see how Whitehead himself might have arrived at the idea of temporal atomicity thus announced in his lecture of April 7, we should attend to a peculiar and obscure argument presented in the first four paragraphs of the addition to the "Relativity" chapter. It grows out of assumptions inherent in the Lowell Lectures and *The Concept of Nature,* and may well have been the source of Whitehead's shift. As a way of persuading the reader, it is not terribly successful; the Zeno argument fares better. Its very complexity and obscurity, however, suggest that this may indicate the route by which he discovered temporal atomicity, recording it primarily as the argument *he* found convincing, since it grew out of the presuppositions he was then espousing. If this is so, the passage will repay very close analysis. Let us proceed step by step:

(1) An event is what it is by virtue of its internal relatedness to all other events. This is what Whitehead means by saying that it is a prehensive unity of aspects of all other events. In the light of his developed theory, we are likely to misinterpret this claim by spec-ifying its open-ended meanings in ways foreign to this early theory, particularly in two ways:

(a) We are likely to ascribe subjectivity and perhaps even mentality to prehensive unification, whereas Whitehead means only to conceive of prehension as the obverse of extension. The philosophy of nature, which was restricted to a description of what is perceived, analyzed spatiotemporal relationships in terms of part/whole overlapping. Larger events partially or wholly included smaller events, both spatially and temporally. This relationship, by means of abstractive sets, could explain the points and instants of traditional physics, as well as describe the whole of the spatiotemporal continuum.

As traditionally conceived, however, these relationships were purely external to the bits of material which occupied this continuum. Such external relatedness led to the simple location theory of scientific materialism, which Whitehead opposed as giving no justification for induction. If events are simply located in space-time, then there is no way we can infer from one to the other, as Hume clearly saw. So Whitehead replaces this relationship with an internal relatedness intrinsic to the event in question. Pushing to the opposite extreme, Whitehead conceives of events as mirroring all other events (SMW 65), as prehended *here* with their mode of location *there* (SMW 70). Hence "space-time is nothing else that a system of pulling together of assemblages into unities" (SMW 72). In this theory as thus far developed in the Lowell Lectures, there is no need to introduce subjectivity and mentality. At this point prehension names the internal relation functioning as the spatiotemporal connection between events which constituted extension according to the theory he had already worked out in the philosophy of nature.

(b) An event is internally related to all other events. Although this would be taken to mean, in terms of his later theory, all other *past* events, here he apparently means primarily *present* events. According to the final theory, it is impossible to prehend present events, for they are causally independent of their contemporaries, and only those events which have already concresced are sufficiently determinate to be prehended. At this point, however, no identification between causation and prehension could yet have been made. Prehension is here understood in terms of a generalization from (unconscious) perception, because perception is the awareness or the cognition of the unification of one's internal relatedness to other events.

That which we perceive is simultaneous with us. Whitehead's analysis of the simultaneous duration in which the percipient event is cogredient survives in his final theory in terms of perception in the mode of presentational immediacy. Perception in the mode of causal efficacy first makes its appearance later when prehension comes to be conceived in terms of causation as well, and when Whitehead is faced with the problem of reconciling these two modes of perception. Earlier, when prehension was understood only as unconscious perception, the events thus prehended were conceived to be co-extensive with a present of simultaneity; at least temporal modalities were ignored (cf. SMW 69).

In itself, a prehension could connect past, present, or future events. Whitehead makes no explicit limitation to the present. Though the past and future are rarely mentioned in the Lowell Lectures, one passage is important. There we are told that an event not only has contemporaries, but a past. "This means that an event mirrors within itself the modes of its predecessors, as memories which are fused into its own content." It also has a future. "This means that an event mirrors within itself such aspects as the future throws back on to the present, or, in other words, as the present has determined concerning the future. Thus an event has anticipation. . . . These conclusions are essential for any form of realism. For there is in the world for our cognisance, memory of the past, immediacy of realisation, and indication of things to come" (SMW 72f). This theory of physical anticipation remains a constant in Whitehead's philosophy, to be worked out later in *Adventures of Ideas,* chapter 12.

Prehensions of the past and future pose difficulties because of the assumption, at this time, of mutual internal relatedness. For there to be symmetry, it is necessary for the relata to share the same degree of determinateness. This does not mean that the event as a whole is completely determinate just because one of its prehensions is. When a past event and a future event are mutually internally related, both events share a determinate bond, but while the past event is completely determinate in all its relations, the future event is incompletely determinate, awaiting its relations to events yet to be actualized. In this way the totality of space-time or nature can be "conceived as a complex of prehensive unifications. Space and time exhibit the general scheme of interlocked relations of these prehensions. You cannot tear any one of them out of its context. Yet each one of them within its context has all the reality that attaches to the whole complex. Conversely, the totality has the same reality as each prehension: for each prehension unifies the modalities to be ascribed, from its standpoint, to every part of the whole" (SMW 72).

As we have seen, the "Relativity" addition introduces one type of relational asymmetry. Events are internally related to eternal objects, but eternal objects are only externally related to events. At this early juncture, however, prehensions do not pertain to eternal objects. Prehension is still strictly a spatiotemporal relation between various events. "It has been usual, indeed, universal, to hold that spatiotemporal relationships are external. This doctrine is what is here being denied" (SMW 123). Such relations seem to be either mutually external or internal, and any possible asymmetry of relatedness for prehensions is not considered.

Focussing upon this text, William P. Alston has argued that Whitehead's doctrine of mutual internal relatedness contradicts his affirmation of pluralism.[7] But this argument ignores any development. Whitehead held to mutual internal relatedness and to pluralism, but not at the same time. Mutual internal relatedness implies monism, not pluralism, which was Whitehead's position in *Science and the Modern World.* "In the analogy with Spinoza, his one substance is for me the one underlying activity of realisation individualising itself in an interlocked plurality of modes. . . . [Even though each event is an individual fact,] individualisation does not mean substantial independence" (SMW 70; cf. 123). The modes are not independent in any sense, but are summations of their internal relatedness to one another. By the time Whitehead fully comes to appreciate the asymmetrical character of prehension and its application to the past, such that the past is independent from supervening actualizations, his philosophy has already become pluralistic. Mutually internal relations and monism go hand in hand, as do asymmetrical relations and qualified pluralism. At no time does Whitehead espouse the inconsistency Alston charges him with. On the other hand, however correct Leclerc's reply may be from a systematic standpoint, it is mistaken, we believe, in interpreting Whitehead's early theory of spatiotemporal relatedness in terms of the later, final theory of prehensions.[8] For the early view Alston correctly insists upon mutual internal relatedness.

(2) The second step is given in the second paragraph of the addition. "The conception of internal relatedness involves the analysis of the event into two factors, one the underlying substantial activity of individualisation, and the other complex of aspects . . . which are unified by this individualised activity" (SMW 123). This is the germ of his later distinction between the becoming of concrescence and the being of the satisfaction, but it is not a new idea in the Lowell Lectures. Whitehead had already written that process could be analyzed "into underlying activity of prehension, and into realised prehensive events" (SMW 70). As yet the distinction is little more than the old one between event and object, as applied to the activity of prehension. The only difference is that now Whitehead sees the object as characterizing a particular event as the result of its own prehensive activity.

If we may anticipate a bit, this distinction takes on added meaning in the light of the conclusion of the argument. (Though to be sure, this added meaning does not function in the argument.) If there is epochal becoming, such that the internal process is not publicly displayed via its successive divisible parts, then there is room for the subjective privacy of realization distinct from its objective display. We may distinguish between the privacy of realization and its objective outcome.

It may be in the light of increased sensitivity to this distinction that Whitehead's attention was drawn to these words of Descartes: "Hence the idea of the sun itself existing in the mind, not indeed formally, as it exists in the sky, but objectively, i.e., in the way in which objects are wont to exist in the mind; and this mode of being is truly much less perfect than that in which things exist outside the mind, but it is not on that account nothing, as I have already said." [9]

Descartes apparently makes use of this distinction in the Third Meditation, when he is intent upon arguing that the representative idea of perfection in us can only be caused by a being formally perfect, i.e. perfect in its own actuality. Usually the purely representative character of ideas objectively existing in the mind is intended in this distinction, but the particular expression of Descartes could well be understood in Whitehead's more realistic sense of objectification. He quotes the passage in Process and Reality, prefacing his quotation with the remark: "In his efforts to guard his representative 'ideas' from the fatal gap between mental symbol and actuality symbolized, he practically, in some sentences, expresses the doctrine of objectification here put forward" (PR 76). In any case, Descartes' formal/objective distinction, so interpreted, becomes a convenient way for Whitehead to distinguish between subjective becoming and objective being in his mature philosophy, and he quite frequently makes use of it. [10]

The third paragraph of this addition re-emphasizes the distinction between the individualized activity and its objective aspect, yet with an anticipation of the conclusion of this argument. Also he notes that "this exhibition of the actual universe as extensive and divisible has left out the distinction between space and time" (SMW 123). This overstates his case, for one aspect of time is just as extensive and divisible as space. By "time" here he means to restrict himself to temporal realization as processive and atomic, described in the next sentence as "the process of realisation, which is the adjustment of the synthetic activities by virtue of which the various events become their realized selves" (SMW 123). Here is the germ of self-actualization, as yet quite undeveloped.

(3) The fourth paragraph contains two further steps to this argument, the third explicitly, the fourth implicitly. The explicit claim, which we discuss here, is that an event is internally related to the

entire duration of simultaneity in which it lies. (In later language, not yet wholly appropriate, the event prehends all the events in its presented locus.) The opening sentence anticipates the conclusion that temporal realization, here described as "the adjustment of the process of synthetic realisation," does not have the continuity of "the spatio-temporal continuum of nature" (SMW 124). By "nature" Whitehead restricts himself to what is perceived, which appears against the background of a continuum, in some sense extensive. A few pages later Whitehead refers to the "extensive continuum" (SMW 126), but this appears to be merely a synonym for the spatiotemporal continuum. There is no doctrine of cosmic epochs as yet, and Whitehead takes the arbitrary three-dimensionality of space to apply to all events and occasions without exception. He does not yet need a more inclusive notion of continuum than the ordinary spatiotemporal one.

The second sentence does not immediately follow from this announcement, as it might appear on first glance, but introduces a subsidiary argument, needed by Whitehead only because of the complications introduced in the determination of simultaneity by relativity physics. Later on he remarks: ". . . this doctrine of the epochal character of time does not depend on the modern doctrine of relativity, and holds equally—and indeed, more simply—if this doctrine be abandoned" (SMW 126). He does, however, need the notion of a definite specification of simultaneity. Each meaning of simultaneity in relativity physics depends upon its inertial framework or "space-time system," which can be determined by any enduring object stationary in its own framework. Thus every inertial framework defines its own meaning of simultaneity, and hence Whitehead must so develop his argument as to meet the possible objection that it cannot adequately handle a plurality of definitions for simultaneity among contemporaries.[11] Only for this reason does Whitehead introduce the notion of "a group of linear serial processes" (SMW 124), since each constitutes a particular inertial framework with its own particular specification of simultaneity. The emphasis is upon the linearity of this series: no specification need be made yet whether the series is one continuous event or a succession of discrete occasions.

For our purposes we can largely ignore this special need imposed by relativity physics, and concentrate our attention upon the character of this *"presented locus,"* to use a later terminology and conceptuality. It is described as an "immediate presentation through the senses of an extended universe beyond ourselves and *simultaneous* with ourselves," which is then infinitely extended by our understanding to "what is *now immediately happening* in regions beyond the [conscious] cognisance of our senses," illustrated by the patterns displayed by the enduring objects ingredient in that duration of simultaneity (SMW 124, italics his).

Now, because Whitehead has repudiated simple location, such that everything which has its mode of location *there* is also prehended *here* in a prehensive unity, the patterns displayed by the enduring objects out there are internally related to the pattern now realised here. The display of this pattern "is the display of a pattern as inherent in an event, but also as exhibiting, [because internally related to,] a temporal slice of nature" (SMW 124). The denial of simple location thus requires that there be an extremely close correlation between each event and the duration of simultaneity it is ingredient in (cf. SMW 103).

(4) The next premise in Whitehead's argument remains implicit, probably because he had already been firmly convinced of its truth for several years, and felt it needed no defense from him now. This is the claim that a temporal slice of nature must be "thick" in order to be perceivable. Because of this temporal thickness Whitehead introduces the term "duration," although these durations do not last very long at all. They last no longer than a *specious present*. It is "the whole simultaneous occurrence of nature which is now for sense-awareness" (CN 53). Since we perceive the passage of nature, we do not perceive nature simply at successive instants. To perceive the transition of passage, we must be able at least to perceive together the difference between what happens first, and what happens afterwards. So Bergson argues, and Whitehead endorses these arguments (CN 53–57; cf. PNK 110–112). "There is no such thing as nature at an instant posited by sense-awareness" (CN 57). It is only a convenient fiction which can be obtained from perceivable durations by the method of extensive abstraction.

Although such durations (Bergson's *durée*?) have temporal thickness (CN 56), they are therefore not necessarily temporally atomic. Bergson always affirmed the continuity of duration while insisting upon its temporal thickness and irreducibility to instants. Temporal atomicity becomes a major difference between Bergson and the later Whitehead. The earlier Whitehead of the philosophy of nature, however, had been one with Bergson in stressing temporal continuity. "The continuity of nature is the continuity of events. . . . every event contains other events as parts of itself [and] every event is part of other events" (CN 76; cf. PNK 66).

As long as we are considering nature as perceived, and not the act of perception, the obvious continuity of nature can be maintained. Each act of perception grasps a certain segment of this continuous passage, but there is no reason in principle why another act of perception (by another) could not grasp a slightly different, overlapping segment. The possible segments so grasped could be continuously overlapping, although each would have its own temporal thickness. Thus that which is perceived (or prehended) can form a continuous passage. This Whitehead always maintained, even after the adoption of temporal atomicity for the acts of perception. It simply makes his later theory somewhat more complicated.

(5) Coupled with the third premise above that an event is internally related to its duration (itself an inference in part from the first premise that events are internally related), this fourth premise that the duration of simultaneity is temporally thick suggests not only that the percipient event, as cogredient in this duration, has temporal thickness, but also that it is temporally atomic. The key concept is clearly present: "The epochal duration is not realised *via* its *successive* divisible parts, but is given *with* its parts" (SMW 125, italics his). Every layer of this temporally thick duration is internally related to the pattern of the percipient event which realizes that pattern. Thus "the pattern is spatialised in a whole duration for the benefit of the event into whose essence the pattern enters" (SMW 124). The pattern is both "out there" and "in here." The pattern is that whole configuration displayed in the whole simultaneous duration, out where the pattern has its mode of location. But the pattern constitutes a prehensive unity "in here," in "the event into whose essence the pattern enters."

This same pattern is "spatialised" in that it is spread out as to its mode of location, and the word "spatialised" also carries with it Bergsonian overtones. Bergson had protested against the intellectual spatialization of things as the "simple location of instantaneous material configurations" (SMW 50; cf. 148). Whitehead agrees: passage cannot be "frozen" into a series of instants. But he is prepared to say that it can be "frozen" into a series of (temporally thick) durations. "Thus a duration is spatialised, and by 'spatialised' is meant that the duration is the field for the realised pattern constituting the character of the event. A duration, as the field of the pattern realised in the actualisation of one of its contained events, is an epoch, i.e., an arrest" (SMW 125).

This same meaning for "spatialised" reoccurs in Whitehead's summary of his position at the outset of the addition to the chapter on

"The Quantum Theory": "the continuity of the complex of events arises from the relationships of extensiveness; whereas the temporality arises from the realisation in a subject-event of a pattern which requires for its display that the whole of a duration be spatialised (i.e. arrested), as given by its aspects in the event" (SMW 135).

Because the pattern "out there" is also "in here" by an internal relatedness constitutive of the subject-event, "the event is part of the duration, i.e., is part of what is exhibited in the aspects inherent in itself; and conversely the duration is the whole of nature simultaneous with the event, in that sense of simultaneity. Thus an event in realising itself displays a pattern, and this pattern requires a definite duration determined by a definite meaning of simultaneity" (SMW 124).

Thus the event is as temporally thick as the duration it lies in, yet as an act of prehensive unification it is atomic and indivisible, since it is the single act drawing these diverse aspects together into one unity. That which is to be unified (i.e. nature as perceivable) can be continuous and divisible, but not its final unity. This distinction between the content and its unification is implicit in the second premise of Whitehead's argument, together with the possibility of affirming the obvious continuity of perceived nature along with the atomicity of temporal realization.

2. CRITICAL EVALUATION

By itself this argument is not fully conclusive, despite its enormous complexity. A persistent advocate of the continuous unfolding of realization could concede that each percipient event requires a temporally thick simultaneous duration to unify prehensively, but that the resultant pattern the event displays forms an instantaneous static immobility. In this case events would so overlap each other such that the patterns they display would constitute a continuous succession of instants. Such an instantaneous nature could never be prehended as such, it is true, for any prehensive unity must take in a whole duration of such instants. Yet events could still display themselves continuously in successive instants.

This dodge, however, is effectively answered by the Zeno-like argument Whitehead subsequently introduces, both here and in *Process and Reality*. It is a simpler and a more potent argument. The argument we have considered, however, is rooted more intimately in the problem Whitehead was wrestling with, and thus is more likely to have been the route by which he discovered temporal atomicity. Once his attention was directed towards it, the difficulties with Kant's discussion of time and the reflections on Zeno's paradoxes would have readily suggested themselves.

Temporal atomicity, in turn, powerfully crystallizes several lines of argument contained in the Lowell Lectures, and provokes further themes for Whitehead's exploration. It is the great catalyst for Whitehead's later philosophy. For one thing, it enables him to clarify the relation between an event and an act of prehension. These are identified in the Lowell Lectures, but it is an uneasy identification. Some events are far too long, for the repeated reiteration of pattern within some events suggests that it has several acts of prehensive unification, not just one (SMW 104). Whitehead had not yet faced up to the opposite difficulty, that there might be events which are shorter than the temporal thickness of a prehensive act.

Temporal atomicity also unified two strands of the Lowell Lectures which had persisted uneasily side-by-side: process and prehension. In an appended note to the second edition (August, 1924) of *An Enquiry Concerning the Principles of Natural Knowledge,* Whitehead remarks: "The book is dominated by the idea that the relation of extension has a unique preeminence and that everything can be got out of it . . . the true doctrine, that 'process' is the fundamental idea, was not in my mind with sufficient emphasis. Extension is derivative from process, and is required by it" (PNK 202). But for all the rhetorical emphasis upon process in the Lowell Lectures, it was difficult to reconcile this concept with the other great idea, prehensive unity.

If there were a continuous unfolding of nature, then each prehensive unity would be an instantaneous unification corresponding to the instant it unifies. Each prehensive unity would be mutually internally related to the whole of nature simultaneous with itself. If that were the case, there could be no "process" of unification, for each instant would be given successively as a correlation of unity and spatial diversity with respect to the same pattern. There could only be a process of prehensive unification if each such act were temporally thick. Each must have the temporal "space" to take that which was diverse and gradually reduce it to unity. The moments of diversity and unity must be temporally distinct (in some sense) for there to be a unification.

Further, if there were a continuous succession of instantaneous prehensive unities, the resulting philosophy would be quite deterministic. Since each prehensive act must be internally related to, and wholly constituted by, aspects of spatiotemporal events simultaneous with itself, there would be no room for any self-creation. We are not suggesting that Whitehead held any such view, only that it would be a possible outcome from his theory in the Lowell Lectures on matters he had not yet clarified. In the absence of such clarification, however, Whitehead was unable to exploit these aspects in his argument. Thus the Lowell Lectures remain silent on such topics as freedom and effective possibility. The latter becomes quite important in the later additions. Freedom and possibility are closely related, for the mark of a free being is its capacity to respond to possibility. Possibility is ineffective by itself and means nothing for a wholly determined being. Alternative possibility would be sheer illusion.

While temporal atomicity enabled Whitehead to tie together a number of loose ends in the Lowell Lectures, most notably the correlation of 'event' and 'prehensive unity,' the argument by which he most probably discovered temporal atomicity did not survive. That argument depends too heavily on the assumption of simultaneous perception (prehension). An event's inner contents (=perceptual data) are conceived to be derived from the world immediately simultaneous with itself. Once Whitehead works out his theory of causal efficacy, whereby the perceptual data are derived from the *past*, and are then projected on the present in terms of perception in the mode of presentational immediacy, that assumption becomes obsolete. When Whitehead returns to the theme of justifying temporal atomicity, the argument which probably gave it its birth is quietly abandoned.

NOTES

1. If temporal atomism is a mistaken or insufficiently qualified doctrine, then Whitehead may not have discovered anything. For Whitehead, however, it certainly functioned as a major discovery. It was unanticipated and yet had momentous consequences in transforming his philosophical outlook. In using the word "discovery" we shall primarily refer to this psychological meaning, leaving the question of truth open.

2. All of Whitehead's papers were burned at his request.

3. Commenting on his own Zeno-like argument, Whitehead remarks: "Zeno in his 'Arrow in Its Flight' seems to have had an obscure grasp of this argument" (PR 68). Richard Gale and V. C. Chappell think that Whitehead's reference should be to the Dichotomy argument. [Gale, "Has the Present Any Duration?" *Nous* 5

(1971), 39–47. Chappell, "Whitehead's Metaphysics," *Review of Metaphysics* 13 (1959), 289.] For my examination of this text, in response to Gale, see "The Duration of the Present," *Philosophy and Phenomenological Research* 35 (1975), 100–106.

4. Whitehead cites the study of Sir Thomas Little Heath, *Euclid in Greek* (Cambridge: The University Press, 1920), at SMW 127 n.1.

5. It was an old problem for Bergson, one he wrestled with in his doctoral dissertation. See Connor J. Chambers, "Zeno of Elea and Bergson's Neglected Thesis," *Journal of the History of Philosophy* 12/1 (January, 1974), 63–76.

6. See PR 68 n.4. Whitehead's attention to James' remarks about experience growing "literally by buds or drops of perception" (PR 68) was first drawn by its quotation in J. S. Bixler's *Religion in the Philosophy of William James* (Boston: Marshall Jones Company, 1926).

7. "Internal Relatedness and Pluralism, *Review of Metaphysics* 5, (1952), 535–58.

8. Ivor Leclerc, "Internal Relatedness in Whitehead: A Rejoinder," *Review of Metaphysics* 6 (1952–53), 297–99.

9. *The Philosophical Works of Descartes*, translated by Elizabeth S. Haldane and G. R. T. Ross, vol. 2 (Cambridge: University Press, 1911), p. 10, quoted by Whitehead in SMW, the additional note to chapter 4.

10. See e.g. PR 45, 83, 215, 219f.

11. For a discussion of the aspects of relativity physics needed to understand Whitehead on this point, see my article, "Is Process Theism Compatible with Relativity Theory?" *Journal of Religion* 48/2 (April, 1968), 124–35.

FOUR

The Chapter on "Abstraction"

ONE of the idiosyncrasies of *Science and the Modern World*, soon noticed by its early reviewers, is the disparity between the leisurely nature of the Lowell Lectures and the demanding character of the two chapters on "Abstraction" and "God," among the most difficult and technical essays in all of Whitehead's writings. They were not part of the original lectures, but written particularly for the book (SMW viii). The two chapters belong together, for the account of "limitation" in the chapter on "Abstraction" points ahead to the chapter on "God" (SMW 161). They are also afterthoughts. As we shall see in the next chapter, the "Triple Envisagement" addition (SMW 104–106), which presupposes the new epochal theory, was incorporated before the chapter on "God" was yet definitely planned.

These two metaphysical chapters were inserted between the seventh and eighth of the Lowell Lectures, presumably to allow the forward-looking "Requisites for Social Progress" to serve as the climax and conclusion of the book as of the lectures. The occasional address delivered April 5, 1925, in the Phillips Brooks House at Harvard, "Religion and Science," was then inserted after the chapter on "God" because of its natural affinity, although that address generally remains quite neutral concerning the existence of God.

While we now prize the two chapters for the wealth of insight they shed on Whitehead's emerging metaphysics, they do detract from the structural unity of the lectures. Perhaps mindful of this, Dean Willard Sperry of the Harvard Divinity School prevailed upon Whitehead not to make any similar expansions of the text of the second set of Lowell Lectures in 1926, published as *Religion in the Making*.[1]

"Abstraction" casually introduces us to "actual occasions" (SMW 158), a technical designation used extensively in these two chapters, but nowhere else. It seems to be used as a well-understood term, for the term is not carefully described at its initial appearance. Obviously, however, it refers to the individual epochal durations (SMW 125) which so revolutionized Whitehead's theory. The "Relativity" addition does not give these epochal durations any specific name, but one would be needed in order to distinguish them from ordinary "events," which are conceived as ever divisible into other events. According to William Ernest Hocking's notes, the term "actual occasion" was first used in Whitehead's lectures for April 30, 1925. While already a technical term, its precise meaning is not explained in that context either.

The chapter on "Abstraction," however, is not primarily about "actual occasions" but about the "eternal objects" which characterize them. Although the term is used technically in the Lowell Lectures, here it receives a much wider range of application, although these new meanings are by no means discontinuous with the old.

1. ETERNAL OBJECTS, IMMANENT AND TRANSCENDENT

As introduced in the Lowell Lectures, "eternal object" is used as a contrasting term to "enduring object." The "enduring object" persists through an event, characterizing not only the event as a whole but every subevent within that event (SMW 108). Initially Whitehead seems to have thought of an infinitely enduring object as eternal. In response to Norman Kemp Smith's essay on "Whitehead's Philosophy of Nature," he wrote on January 24, 1924:

> The main point in your lecture with which I disagreed was the statement that I considered 'objects' (and in particular 'sensa') as 'eternal'. I should not call them 'eternal' because (as stated in my Principles of Natural Knowledge) I do not consider them as 'in time' in the primary sense of the phrase. I should call an unending event eternal.[2]

An unending event is later called "everlasting," in contradistinction to what is eternal, or better, atemporal. In other words, rather than allow his original predilection determine for him the meaning of "eternal," he uses his understanding of sensa to redefine the term. This is certainly one meaning for eternal in contrast with what is temporal. Thus endurance and eternality are contrasted: "the mountain endures. But when after ages it has been worn away, it has gone. If a replica arises, it is yet a new mountain. A colour is eternal.

It haunts time like a spirit. It comes and it goes. But where it comes, it is the same colour. It neither survives nor does it live. It appears when it is wanted. The mountain has to time and space a different relation from that which colour has" (SMW 86f).

This difference between endurance and eternality allows Whitehead to simplify his classification of the types of objects. In the philosophy of nature he had distinguished between (i) sensa or sense-objects, (ii) perceptual objects, (iii) scientific objects, and (iv) percipient objects. Now by reference to their differing relationships to space-time, he could reclassify all the objects in the last three groups as enduring objects. In a sense "eternal object" simply becomes another name for the sense-object, stressing its atemporality. This atemporality is in no way altered by the theory of "Abstraction," but now the implications of atemporality are explored in order to see whether and what kinds of eternal objects there might be in addition to the examples of sensa.

The epochal theory of time gave a powerful incentive to this undertaking because it was capable of showing that an enduring object could be conceived as the repetition of an eternal object in successive occasions. It also strongly suggested a close correlation between a single occasion and the eternal object which characterized it. This was not possible in the earlier theory of continuously over-lapping events. On this earlier theory there was, to be sure, a correlation between an event and the enduring object which characterized it. But the enduring object could not characterize every contingent characteristic about that event, since it had precisely the same defects as the old substance theory. It could only characterize what endures within the event, not what changes.

Moreover, the earlier theory could not account for eternal objects. Eternal objects could not be conceived as instantaneous enduring objects, and not only because Whitehead distrusted the instant as conveying anything about concrete nature. An instantaneous enduring object would be precisely situated in space and time, contrary to the very atemporality of eternal objects. On the other hand, enduring objects could not be constructed by the reiteration of eternal objects. If events are continuously subdivisible, the reiteration of a pattern characterizing each member of a series of events, no matter how minute, could not constitute an enduring object, for it would always be possible to subdivide these minute events still further. These subevents could not all be characterized by the reiteration of the pattern, since there would now be more events than reiterations.

In general, we may say that the role of eternal objects in the Lowell Lectures was restricted to the extrinsic characteristics of events. To be sure, though we are told that value is the intrinsic reality of an event (SMW 93), we are not told very much about this intrinsic reality, even though this becomes the all-absorbing topic of his later metaphysics. Eternal objects play a much more powerful role after the discovery of temporal atomicity, because they can now characterize intrinsic as well as extrinsic characteristics.

More than anything else, temporal atomicity enabled Whitehead to explore the intrinsic dimension of events. As long as events are conceived as infinitely subdivisible, it is difficult to conceive of the "inside" of any event except in terms of the smaller events it includes. Then any intrinsic properties of the larger event are simply extrinsic properties of some smaller event. But if there is some minimum extension to the event, now properly called an occasion, below which it ceases to be actual, then the intrinsic properties of that occasion are no longer the extrinsic properties of any other actualities.

Whitehead does not talk much about possibilities in the Lowell Lectures, but there is a way of thinking about them as extrinsic properties: they can be conceived as the extrinsic characteristics of future events. As we have seen, each event is constituted out of its relations to all other events, past, present, and future. Yet with the shift caused by temporal atomicity, actual occasions are not influenced by future occasions which do not yet exist. Possibility is no longer understood in terms of the extrinsic character of future events but in terms of the intrinsic character of the occasion now coming into being.

The relation between the possible and the actual can be understood in terms of this contrast. Since the characteristics an occasion actualizes are its extrinsic features, unactualized possibilities can only constitute the purely intrinsic characteristics the occasion has which fail to be actualized. Some of these may be possibilities for the more distant future, but the most relevant concern the actualization of that particular occasion. Some are realized, others not. The actual can thus be seen to be a definite limitation upon the possible.

This expansion of the role of eternal objects as possibilities points not only to the particular limitations actual occasions impose but to the limitation a basic principle could introduce. To the trained imagination of the mathematician, the range of sheer possibility is infinite and highly various. For there to be a world at all, there must be some general order, and Whitehead sees this order as a limitation upon possibility.

In traditional teleological arguments, God is taken to be the creator of this order. Whitehead fights shy of any such affirmation. As in the Lowell Lectures and still affirmed in these chapters, the underlying activity, as modally expressed in the actual occasions, creates contingent order by bringing it into being. God here has no creative role, but can still function noncreatively as the source of the world's order as the external uncreated principle or reason for the general limitation upon possibility, such that only those possibilities conformable to the general order are actualizable. The ontological significance and the infinitude of possibility in terms of the eternal objects thus gives Whitehead the opportunity to introduce a role for God, expressly conceived as non-creative.

2. ANTICIPATIONS IN THE HARVARD LECTURES

While there is little hint of Whitehead's philosophical theism in his Harvard lectures, there are some anticipations of the theme of "Abstraction" (see Appendix 1). Internal relations were already mentioned on April 11, and insisted upon April 18: "The internal relation is the fundamental metaphysical idea." Further, that same day: "If you insist that all your universals are in the particular realized entities, you get into a muddle. Can't see how the world then is to get on to anything new." Assuming by universals he means eternal objects, their scope must be much broader than just the sense-objects which were present only as ingredient in events. This assumption is strengthened by his immediately following sentence: "But they are always in a general relation to what is real." It suggests "the indeterminate relatedness of each eternal object to occasions generally" (SMW 163), which is the standard doctrine of "Abstraction."

The lecture adds later: "As for the eternal objects, the relations they enter into are external. Hence logically antecedent to realization." Since eternal objects are already internally related to themselves, both external and internal relations pertain to them and the way is paved for the insight that the same relation can be both internal and external, depending upon which relatum is involved. This step is taken in "Abstraction" : "Accordingly the relationship between [an eternal object] A and [an actual occasion] a is external as regards A, and is internal as regards a" (SMW 160). Although this asymmetry of relationship is later applied to the relation between the individual and the relational essence of an eternal object, it is not generalized to apply to prehension generally in Science and the Modern World. The notion of any contrast between physical and conceptual prehensions is not yet entertained, for the relation between eternal objects and actual occasions was wholly explained in terms of ingression. Hence all prehensions are implicitly taken to be what is later called "physical," that is, pertaining to relations between occasions. We are told in his lecture of April 30, "In regard to internal relations we must admit an essential difference between past, present, and future. . . . We must have a universe in which there is room for freedom." The notes do not specify, however, what this difference consists in.

On May 5, Whitehead lists 3 "Antecedent sources of definiteness":

a. Systematic relations in a general scheme whereby a niche is provided.
b. In respect to this niche there is a *potentiality* arising from
c. A definite character of the individual embodiment of creative energy. This question of creative character is somewhat arbitrary.

This passage is sketchy and tantalizingly ambiguous, for we cannot be certain whether (b) was left incomplete, or meant to be completed by (c), nor whether (c) refers to eternal objects (as creative character) or to actual occasions (as individual embodiments).

The lecture for May 22 indicates the double character of the relatedness of eternal objects: "Any eternal object *a* has determinate relations to other eternal objects, and indeterminate relations to actuality. It doesn't lie in the nature of red whether a given bull somewhere in Massachusetts will see red tomorrow. Red may or may not have that relation and yet be the same thing."

Two principles are specified:

I. An entity cannot stand in external relations unless it is indeterminate in its relations to others which it is patience to.
II. An entity which stands in *internal* relations has no being as an entity *not* in these relations.

An eternal object *A* is analyzed in terms of:

1. Its *A*-ness [i.e., its individual essence]
2. Its determinate relations to every other eternal object
3. A as patient of relationships which may be realized.

Furthermore we learn that "Every occasion is a synthesis of being and not-being. Every eternal object which is synthesized qua being is also synthesized as not-being." Using the notation to be adopted in "Abstraction" for the relationship among eternal objects (SMW 164), Whitehead continues in this lecture: "R(A, B, C) is another more complex eternal object. . . . What is actual is an abstraction from the world of possibility. Every actual occasion synthesizes every eternal object, including the complex eternal objects, either as existing or as not existing. This is the reason why every actual occasion is a limitation."

The May 22 lecture was the last of the term in which Whitehead presented his own ideas, because for the final class on May 26 he reverted to a discussion of Newton's laws and Einstein's modifications of them. In these presentations, particularly the lecture of May 22, Whitehead touched on many of the themes of his chapter on "Abstraction," except for the analysis of abstractive hierarchies. We can see how May 1925 was a period of gestation for this chapter.

3. METAPHYSICAL CRITERIA, MODES OF INGRESSION, AND GRADES OF ENTRY

In the light of Whitehead's total achievement, we tend to interpret "Abstraction" as the first technical elaboration of a portion of his total metaphysics, that pertaining to eternal objects. If we restrict ourselves to the position he had then worked out for himself, however, these two chapters offer a fairly complete metaphysical analysis of the "alternative cosmological doctrine" (SMW 157) he had outlined in the Lowell Lectures, especially as seen in the light of the transformation introduced by the epochal theory of time. This theory of actual occasions could be analyzed in terms of three "formative elements," as he was later to call them (RM 88): eternal objects (to be considered in this chapter), creativity, and God, (to be considered in the next).

The criteria governing this metaphysical description are the (i) empirical and (ii) rational criteria expanded in the first chapter of *Process and Reality* in terms of adequacy and applicability to experience, on the one hand, and logical consistency and coherence on the other. The rational criterion is here expressed as that which forms "A basis for harmonizing our systematised accounts of various types of experience." An additional criterion is also stipulated: the justification for the metaphysical chapters is to be sought " (iii) in their success as providing the concepts in terms of which an epistemology can be framed" (SMW 158). The criterion is perhaps implicitly seen later to be an instance of adequacy, but here it is important as indicating a motive leading Whitehead from the philosophy of nature to metaphysics. For epistemology depends upon the perceiver, and it was precisely the perceiver which could not be accounted for in the earlier philosophy of the perceived.

The analysis of an actual occasion yields three factors: (1) the underlying substantial activity it instantiates, (2) the highly complex eternal object which characterizes it, and (3) the various individual essences of those eternal objects constituting that complex eternal object which are realized in the occasion's aesthetic synthesis (SMW 170). Whitehead undertakes this examination of actuality after the necessary concepts of finite and infinite abstractive hierarchies have been defined, but it is helpful to keep the three factors in mind as we first consider the analysis of the component eternal object.

The eternal object is analyzed in terms of "(i) its particular individuality [its individual essence] (ii) its general relationships to other eternal objects as apt for realisation in actual occasions [its relational essence], and (iii) the general principle which expresses its ingression in particular actual occasions" (SMW 159). The eternal object as realized in any one particular occasion is the way that particular eternal object is a component of the complex eternal object in its mode of ingression into that actual occasion. That mode of ingression pertains to the actual occasion, not to the essence of the eternal object. If it were to pertain to its essence that self-same eternal object could not characterize more than one actual occasion, and its universal function would be lost. Thus "in the essence of each eternal object there stands an indeterminateness which expresses its indifferent patience for any mode of ingression into any actual occasion" (SMW 171). This "indifferent patience," as the general principle for its ingression into any occasion, was already mentioned in his Harvard Lecture of May 22 as the third factor in the analysis of an eternal object.

The one complex eternal object characterizing the actual occasion embraces all the eternal objects, for every occasion "synthesises in itself every eternal object" (SMW 162). Thus each occasion is a particular mode of ingression for each eternal object. Naturally each mode of ingression will be different, but each depends upon the way the eternal objects are related among themselves apart from actual occasions. The relational essence of systematic mutual internal relatedness among the different sets of individual essences retains its own particular identity in these various modes of ingression, but it is only as so related that any individual essence could be actualized. In actualization the individual essence must be realized, but it can only be realized by means of its relational essence. The compatibility and incompatibility of these relationships dictate the possible modes of ingression which then specify the particular combination and order for a given mode of ingression.

This strict correlation of a "mode of ingression" with a particular actual occasion is gradually abandoned. Mode of ingression, when used later, refers less to any particular concretization as to general types of ingression. Thus Whitehead speaks of three "primary modes of ingression into actual entities" as ingredient in the datum of a physical feeling, the datum of a conceptual feeling, or in the subjective form of some feeling (PR 290f). (None of these distinctions apply in the present chapter on "Abstraction.") As we shall see, he abandons the attempt to describe actual occasions in terms of ingression. In its place he introduces the notion of standpoint and perspective, describing actual occasions in terms of the unification of their prehensions.

We are likely to assume that a mode of ingression specifies the way an eternal object is included as an effective element in the aesthetic synthesis of the occasion. Only these, we feel, are truly ingredient in the actuality. Since contradictories cannot be included in exactly the same sense, only a selection of them can finally be present in the actuality.

The revised theory of *Process and Reality* moves in this direction, holding that any one occasion prehends only a selection of the eternal objects, and that those that are purely irrelevant to it are not even given for its concrescence. God as the agency of relevance is required to connect eternal objects to the occasions (PR 31f). But the theory in "Abstraction" depends on a more primitive relationship, whereby all eternal objects are ingredient in all actual occasions. This means that "ingression" must take on a very broad meaning, and that those eternal objects which definitely characterize the occasion to the exclusion of others must be distinguished as a subset of all the ingredient objects. This subset is described in terms of grades of entry.

Grades of entry can vary from "the inclusion of the individual essence of A as an element in the aesthetic synthesis (in some grade of inclusion) to the lowest grade which is the exclusion of the individual essence of A as an element in the aesthetic synthesis." When the individual essence is excluded, that eternal object does not characterize the occasion, but is simply "an element in the systematic substratum of unfulfilled content" of that mode of ingression. Thus a mode of ingression, which is the specific relationship of all eternal objects with respect to that occasion, has both fulfilled and unfulfilled content (SMW 162). Thus eternal objects excluded from characterization are nevertheless "included" by their grades of entry. It would be less cumbersome to hold that earlier phases of concrescence can include eternal objects which are excluded from later phases, particularly the satisfaction, and that only those eternal objects included in the satisfaction characterize that occasion. At this stage in the development of his theory, however, Whitehead had no access to the notion of differentiated phases of concrescence.

We are likely to think of individual essences solely in terms of sensa or pure qualities, abstracted from all patterns (PR 114f). But the individual essence is simply an eternal object considered in itself, taken in its own uniqueness. An individual sensum has a relational essence in terms of its unchanging internal relatedness to all other sets of eternal objects. That sensum cannot be itself a component of any relational essence, but such a component, such as R(A,B,C), considered in itself, can be an individual essence. Thus every sensum can only be an individual essence, but not every individual essence is a sensum.

Each eternal object is related to every other eternal object in all possible ways. The "relationships of these objects among themselves are entirely unselective and are systematically complete. We are discussing possibility; so that every relationship which is possible is thereby in the realm of possibility" (SMW 164). Sets of such relations would be self-consistent, but not all these sets would be compossible, nor could all be jointly realized. We cannot think of the relation of an eternal object to an occasion as if it were an additional relation to its essence, for its relational essence would already include this possible relation. The relational essence is not the abstract generic aspect of all the modes of ingression of a given eternal object. Rather the modes of ingression are particular selections from the relational essence. "Thus actualisation is a selection among possibilities. More accurately, it is a selection issuing in a gradation of possibilities in respect to their realisation in that occasion" (SMW 159). The mode of ingression is the particular way in which the components of that relational essence have graded entry into that occasion. "The relationships of A to an actual occasion are simply how the eternal relationships of A to other eternal objects are graded as to their realisation in that occasion" (SMW 160).

In his later thought Whitehead abandons this theory of the degrees of inclusion of individual essences. Instead of "grades of entry" he depends upon the elimination of alternative possibilities by means of negative prehension (PR 23f, 41). Gradation then serves a different function. There is the gradation (PR 87) or "graduation of the relevance of eternal objects to the concrescent phases" of each occasion (PR 31). This gradation is implied in the initial subjective aim supplied by God, for in determining the best possibility for a nascent occasion God thereby determines how and to what extent the eternal objects in his primordial envisagement are relevant to that concrescence. Those which are utterly irrelevant are nonexistent for that occasion. Others of varying relevance are eliminated, at least for the final satisfaction.

In "Abstraction" the question of relevance or irrelevance does not come up, since all eternal objects ingress in all occasions, and the question of realization is handled differently in terms of fulfillment or lack of fulfillment, that is, in terms of inclusion or exclusion from the aesthetic synthesis. Whitehead also uses the language of *being* and *not-being*. Thus if the eternal object *A* as ingredient only in the lowest grade of entry, that of complete exclusion, then *A* is conceived of as not-being with respect to that particular occasion. If *A* is abstracted from all occasions, then *A* is conceived as *not-being* simpliciter.[3] " *'Being'* here means 'individually effective in the aesthetic synthesis' " (SMW 163). Since "there can be no occasion which includes *A* in all its determinate relationships" (SMW 163),[4] since some of these relationships are contraries, *A* is *not-being* with respect to the excluded relationships, while with respect to other relationships *A* is *being* for the occasion.

This thesis, that "every occasion is a synthesis of *being* and *not-being*" (SMW 163) with respect to those eternal objects which illustrate it, is so abstract as to need some specific exemplification. For example, let us consider a white sheet of paper. All sorts of excluded alternatives have *not-being* with respect to a white sheet of paper. It is not red. It is not liquid, nor dark, and neither loquacious nor flamboyant nor tragic. Since it is white, white has being with respect to it as a sheet of paper, but not with respect to other forms of paper, such as a bundle of newspaper or as a sheet of sandpaper, etc. Considering the relationships white has to other characteristics it might or might not possess, there are ways in which it is and is not white. Hence the actuality is a synthesis of *being* and *not-being* white.

4. THE REALM OF POSSIBILITY

From the discussion of the relation of possibilities to actualization, Whitehead turns to an analysis of the realm of possibility in itself. This analysis is governed by two concerns. Since each actual occasion is limited "by its internal relatedness to all other actual occasions" (SMW 163), Whitehead must explain how finite truth is possible. He rejects the claim of Absolute Idealism that nothing short of intrinsically interrelated whole will do as "palpably untrue" (SMW 163), and so must find some basis for external relatedness, which he does in a theory of the *Isolation of Eternal Objects* (SMW 165).

The second concern centers on the spatiotemporal continuum in which all occasions are embedded. This spatiotemporal continuum is not merely an abstract matrix according to which particular occasions can be located, but entails (implicitly, at least) the community of occasions whereby each is derived from the others. In terms like those of the Lowell Lectures, each occasion is the prehensive unity of all the others, each is a standpoint from which it perceives all other events. Instead of being a container in which possibilities are actualized, the spatio-temporal continuum is a general limitation upon the realm of possibility. Thus in the remainder of this discussion of the abstraction from actuality in the form of possibilities (and of the abstraction from general possibilities in terms of more specific ones) the realm of possibility must be conceived very broadly in terms of purely formal considerations, so that in the next chapter Whitehead can introduce those general limitations on possibility (such as the spatio-temporal continuum) which are required for actualizability. Hence we must consider here "the general nature of abstract possibility, as limited by the general character of the actual course of events" (SMW 163).

The analytical character of the realm of eternal objects means that the internal relatedness of any one object can be analyzed in terms of an indefinite number of subordinate relationships, each of which are perfectly definite and limited. Thus there would be a perfectly definite relationship R(A,B,C) having no other eternal objects as relata except A, B, and C. (That is, in terms of its individual essence. In terms of its relational essence, R(A,B,C) is itself related to all other eternal objects. Note that the more complex an eternal object is, the simpler and more restricted will be its relational essence. The simplest eternal objects, the sensa, have the most complex relational essences.) Since all eternal objects are internally related, the problem is to explain how such subordinate limited relationships are possible (SMW 164).

Basically, the eternal objects are "isolated" in the realm of possibility in so far as many eternal objects, differing among themselves in terms of their individual essences, may have a common relational essence. (Thus "blue" and "red" share, for most purposes, the same relational essence "color".) On this principle hinges the possibility of a 'variable' in logic such as "any" or "some." The specification of a particular variable is the specification of a common relational essence which many individual essences can exemplify. The relational essence is the way in which a set of eternal objects are internally related to other (sets of) eternal objects, but the individual essences within this set are only externally related to the common relational essence. This externality provides the freedom whereby finite truth is possible.

5. SHERBURNE'S ANALYSIS

This isolation of the eternal objects in possibility solves one problem with respect to the locus of unrealized possibilities for the world, but generates another in turn. As we have seen, Whitehead holds that all entities of whatever sort depend for their existence upon actualities, although this general Aristotelian principle is never explicitly stated with full rigor in *Science and the Modern World*. Since God is not yet conceived as the locus of unrealized possibilities, but only as a principle of limitation, incapable of prehending anything, we may wonder how actual occasions can harbour the unrealized possibilities they must if there are to be any. If they have no unactualized status at all, then they would have to emerge *ex nihilo*, violating the rational requirement of complete explanation. Moreover, the systematic mutual relatedness of all eternal objects would be violated by the temporal emergence of any one which did not already fit this scheme. The eternal objects must depend upon one or more of the actual occasions already in existence, so Whitehead proposes that they depend on them all. To involve one eternal object in the existence of an actuality is thereby to involve them all, since they are all systematically related.

Donald W. Sherburne sees a problem this approach could generate: "An eternal object is supposed to bestow or withhold a specific, precise form of definiteness, but how can this be if every eternal object drags along with it, so to speak, the whole choir of eternal objects in virtue of the fact that its relationships to other eternal objects are eternal objects?"[5] Whitehead countered this possible difficulty with his distinction between the complete ingression of all eternal objects and their selective, graded inclusion within the occasion's aesthetic synthesis. Yet we may then question how such selective inclusion is possible. Why are not all eternal objects ingredient in the occasion equally included? Here the distinction between the individual and the relational essence comes to our aid. It is the realization of an individual essence which constitutes the unique quality of a given actual occasion. That eternal object is internally related to all other objects, but only in terms of their relational essences, since many individual essences can share the same relational essence.

Sherburne uses this example: "The relational essence of turquoise blue vis-à-vis any four-sided plane figure is not unique to turquoise blue, but is the same as that of pea green or jet black. Thus the individual essence of turquoise blue is quite aloof from the relational essence of turquoise blue and can characterize the specific definiteness of a particular actual entity without involving necessarily the specific individual essence of any particular geometrical shape . . ." [6] Thus while the individual essence is intrinsically related to its own relational essence, that relational essence is only externally related to its particular quality, since it is related to other qualities of the same sort in precisely the same way. As Whitehead writes, "the relationships (as in possibility) do not involve the individual essences of the eternal objects; they involve *any* eternal objects as relata, subject to the proviso that these relata have the requisite relational essences" (SMW 165).

The external relatedness of the relational essences makes room for unrealized possibilities, for otherwise an unrealized possibility would have all the qualitative specificity we assign to actualities. Moreover, the components of relational essences form hierarchies, whereby the more specific are internally related to the more generic, but the more generic are only externally related to the more specific. Turquoise blue or pea green must be colors, but not every color is necessarily one of these shades. Every color is necessarily a quality, but not every quality must be a color.

This theory solves the problem posed by the finite realization of specific qualities, but at the expense of any real ontological foundation for *all* the eternal objects. To be sure, any one realized eternal object is related to all the others, but it turns out on closer inspection that it is only internally related to their relational essences, and these are merely externally related to their individual essences. Only full internal relatedness will be sufficient to provide those individual essences with an adequate ontological foundation. That qualities exist does not necessarily entail that colors are even possible, let alone such specific colors as turquoise blue.

The virtue of external relatedness is precisely that the existence of one entity does not entail the existence of any other entity. Complete internal relatedness of the eternal objects, without any qualification, would undercut any pluralism or freedom, but in its absence there is no way that the existence of one realized eternal object can insure the possibility of the rest. Whitehead must ultimately appeal beyond the systematic mutual relatedness of the eternal objects among themselves for an adequate ontological ground. This he finds later in the one nontemporal actual entity capable of envisaging all the eternal objects apart from temporal passage. Though the eternal objects may be partly externally related among themselves, they are all externally related to God; but God is internally related to them all, since they determine the character of his nontemporal envisagement. Thus the unsatisfactoriness of his early solution as to the locus of unrealized possibilities may have led Whitehead in later works to expand the role of God beyond being simply the abstract principle of limitation.

6. INDIVIDUAL AND RELATIONAL ESSENCES

It is worth examining how an individual essence may be related to its own specific relational essence. To be sure, blue is related to all other non-color eternal objects in exactly the same way any color is: to surface, to liquid, to powder, and to all the irrelevant objects such as flamboyance, recklessness, and credence. But blue is related to other colors in ways they are not related to one another. On the color spectrum blue is between green and purple while red or yellow is not. Moreover, though we imagine in terms of some common sensum, we conceive it in terms of a common relational essence appropriate for all the various shades of blue. Like other blues, turquoise blue is between green and purple, although it in turn has its own particular relationship among such blues as royal blue and blue violet.

Sensa are associated with particular relational essences, but the connection becomes more tenuous for more general relational essences. We sense turquoise blue as a definite quality. Color, however, is already too general for us to associate with it any sensum. It is purely a relational essence specifying how the various different color-sensa can relate to all the other eternal objects. Blue is ambiguous. On the one hand it can signify that common relational essence all the various shades of blue share, or it can signify some sensum. Yet one sensum blue cannot be both turquoise and blue violet. Oftentimes blue does signify some one blue sensum vaguely taken to represent all the specific blue sensa.

Because one specific sensum can be thus taken to represent the class, 'blue' sometimes functions both as this representative sensum and as the common relational essence of the class of all blues. In this particular instance, the relational essence of the class is externally related to that one particular individual essence. This external relatedness, however, need not be the basic relationship between relational and individual essences, for generals are always externally related to particulars.

Nevertheless, it may well be questioned whether a relational essence can ever specify anything other than a class of closely correlated individual essences. It is an old scholastic problem: can specification by ever more narrowly defined classes ultimately individuate? If the sensa constitute a genuine qualitative continuum, then the relational essence specifies a particular segment of that continuum which, however, is divisible within itself. Although we may not be able to discriminate them, there is an inexhaustible range of sensa within this continuum, all of which are turquoise blue. Most precisely, turquoise blue as a structural possibility can only represent this class, which is externally related to the individual essences of these several sensa it includes.

Here the difference between possibility and actuality comes to play, for possibility primarily pertains to the relational essences which direct the individual essences in their process of realization. A realized actuality exemplifies individual essences, but these are only externally related to their associated relational essences, which can only specify classes, never individuals.

Because the relational essence of any eternal object *A* considered as a possibility merely involves other eternal objects as bare relata abstracted from their individual essences, the general relationship of *A* may be divided into a multiplicity of finite relationships of *A*. This analytic character of the realm of eternal objects means that it can be consistently divided into the realm of actualizability and of unactualizability. This is "the general limitation of relationships, which reduces this general unlimited scheme to the four-dimensional spatiotemporal scheme. This spatiotemporal scheme is, so to speak, the greatest common measure of the schemes of relationship (as limited by actuality) inherent in all the eternal objects" (SMW 166). Since all actual occasions must exemplify this spatiotemporal continuum, only those eternal objects directly compatible with it could possibly ever be actualized.

7. ABSTRACTIVE HIERARCHIES

The analytic character of the eternal objects enables Whitehead to distinguish between actual occasions, formally considered, and ordinary eternal objects. This requires the elaborate logical machinery of infinite and finite abstractive hierarchies, for which the distinction between simple and complex eternal objects is introduced. Insofar as a given eternal object can be analyzed into components, it is complex; otherwise it is simple. Whitehead gives a particular sensum, "such as a definite shade of green," as his example of a simple eternal object (SMW 166). It may be doubted whether examples other than sensa can be given.

Except for this particular context, Whitehead does not employ the distinction between simple and complex eternal objects. Possibly he became sensitive to the problem of specifying a single definite sensum, if the sensa constitute a qualitative continuum, but in any case he came to recognize that sensa were also complex with respect to their relational essences. "In one sense, a sensum is simple, for its realization does not involve the concurrent realization of certain definite eternal objects, which are its definite simple components. But, in another sense, each sensum is complex; for it cannot be dissociated from its potentiality for ingression into *any* actual entity, and for its potentiality of contrasts and of patterned relationships with other eternal objects" (PR 114). While its individual essence may be the most simple, its relational essence is the most complex.

Abstractive hierarchies may be conceived approximately as pyramids springing from some base, which may contain any number of members, finite or infinite, but "the infinity of the number of the members of the base has nothing to do with the question as to whether the hierarchy be finite or infinite" (SMW 168). For consider the class of all sensa. This is a definite eternal object, and hence a finite abstractive hierarchy, yet its base contains the infinity of the various sensa. Each level of the pyramid is more complex than the one it builds upon. It consists of a more complex eternal object having the level it builds upon as its components. The number of levels determines whether a hierarchy is finite or infinite: "An abstractive hierarchy is called 'finite' if it stops at a finite grade of complexity. It is called 'infinite' if it includes members belonging respectively to all degrees of complexity" (SMW 168).

Whitehead offers this formal definition of an abstractive hierarchy:

An 'abstractive hierarchy based upon g,' where g is a group of simple eternal objects, is a set of eternal objects which satisfy the following conditions,

(i) the members of g belong to it, and are the only simple eternal objects in the hierarchy,

(ii) the components of any complex eternal object in the hierarchy are also members of the hierarchy, and

(iii) any set of eternal objects belonging to the hierarchy, whether differing among themselves as to grade, are jointly among the components or derivative components of at least one eternal object which also belongs to the hierarchy. (SMW 167f)

Finite hierarchies have a grade of maximum complexity, such that "a member of it is a component of no other eternal object belonging to any grade of the hierarchy" (SMW 168). According to these definitions George W. Roberts,[7] Richard M. Martin,[8] and Vernon M. Root have all argued, in apparent independence of one another, that finite abstractive hierarchies are impossible. Root puts the argument this way:

Assume a finite hierarchy. Consider the entire set of eternal objects which constitutes this hierarchy. Since an eternal object cannot be a component of itself, condition (iii) requires that there be still another eternal object in the hierarchy. But this is impossible on our hypothesis. Thus, as it stands, condition (iii) can be satisfied by infinite hierarchies only.[9]

If we attend to Whitehead's general usage in this passage, however, we may recognize that by a "set" he has in mind a distinct multiplicity, that is, a set having different members. Condition (iii), or the condition of connexity as Whitehead calls it, declares that whenever there is a multiplicity of eternal objects at any grade of an abstractive hierarchy, there must be at least one eternal object of a more complex nature unifying them. Thus Whitehead observes that the "grade of maximum complexity must possess only one member; for otherwise the condition of connexity would not be satisfied" (SMW 168). In other words, this maximum grade cannot constitute a set (i.e. a multiplicity), for then it would be subject to precisely the regress noted.

Why, then, was not the condition of connexity more simply framed? The qualification "whether all of the same grade or whether differing among themselves as to grade" was included with an eye towards fulfilling the other function of connexity, to insure that all successive grades of complexity would be included. Sometimes the members of higher grades must unify members of several lower grades. These members of various grades can be quite distinct from one another. There is no distinct multiplicity, however, between the more complex eternal object and any of its components. The components merely reduplicate some of the superior's aspects, and this is no distinct addition with respect to pure forms. Nothing is added to the concept of a pink, well-fed panther by conjoining to it the component property of being well-fed: the two together do not constitute a genuine multiplicity requiring any further unity. Since all the other eternal objects belonging to a given finite abstractive hierarchy must be components of that one member of maximum complexity, that member cannot form a multiplicity with any other members. In the absence of a distinct multiplicity, the regress Root fears is non-existent.[10]

The purely formal character of the definition of abstractive hierarchies masks the vast differences between finite and infinite ones. Finite hierarchies have a maximum grade of complexity with one member which is its "vertex." It is the one single complex eternal object which the hierarchy specifies, since all the other grades merely reduplicate its components. Since any complex eternal object is analyzable into simpler components, its complete analysis must result in a lowest grade of unanalyzable elements, i.e. simple eternal objects. Since many eternal objects (e.g. freedom, mastery, number, reciprocity) contain no sensa as components, there must be simple eternal objects other than sensa, though what these are prove to be difficult to specify. On the other hand, if infinite hierarchies correspond to actual occasions, formally considered, their simple eternal objects must include the sensa, at least in the case of sensible actualities.[11]

The existence of infinite abstractive hierarchies signifies "that it is impossible to complete the description of an actual occasion by means of concepts" (SMW 169f). A concept is the limited specification of a class, but the class may have many members. Moreover, even if only one member is so specified, its full individuality is not exhausted in that specification. An infinite hierarchy is an infinite formal specification, functioning analogously to Duns Scotus' haecceity or thisness. Whitehead, however, does not regard this infinite specification as individuation, at least not in the sense that the actuality of the individual has thus been captured:

> It is to be noted that in dealing with hierarchies we are entirely within the realm of possibility. Accordingly the eternal objects are devoid of real togetherness: they remain in their isolation. (SMW 169)

In Kant's language these isolated eternal objects are all predicates, and in terms of predicates there is no difference between a possible hundred dollars and an actual hundred dollars. The abstractive hierarchy is what the actual hundred dollars has in common with its own individual possibility.

In possibility there is an isolation of eternal objects, because their relationships are expressible without reference to their respective individual essences. In actuality, the individual essences ingredient in the associated abstractive hierarchy "achieve an aesthetic synthesis, productive of the occasion as an experience for its own sake. This associated hierarchy is the shape, or pattern, or form of the occasion in so far as the occasion is constituted of what enters into its full realisation" (SMW 170). This brief mention of "aesthetic synthesis" suggests that Whitehead is approaching pansubjectivity by conceiving of each occasion as an experience for itself. In the Lowell Lectures every event was conceived as prehending or unconsciously perceiving every other one. Here, however, the aesthetic synthesis, or synthesis of feeling, is not of the perceptions of other events but of the individual essences of those eternal objects which characterize them.

Moreover, "the 'aesthetic synthesis' is the 'experient synthesis' viewed as self-creative, under the limitations laid upon it by its internal relations to all other actual occasions" (SMW 163). It is self-creative as a mode of the underlying substantial activity, because the synthesis cannot be attributed to any other factor, since all other relevant factors are elements in this synthesis. This synthetic activity is the substantial activity "which is omitted in any analysis of the static factors [the eternal objects] in the metaphysical situation" (SMW 165).

This self-creative activity is not yet conceived as a growing together of many feelings into one, for there is as yet no clear meaning as to what is the many which goes into this synthesis. Is it the ingression of many simple eternal objects in terms of their individual essences? No attempt is made to relate the aesthetic synthesis, carefully worked out in terms of abstractive hierarchies and individual essences, to prehensive unity, which played such a central role in the Lowell Lectures. The asymmetry of internal and external relations, so carefully worked out with respect to the eternal objects, is not applied to (physical) prehensions. Perhaps because prehensive unity was conceived solely in termed of internal relatedness, it may be here seen as an external limitation upon the experient synthesis, rather than as the means whereby this is achieved. The Lowell Lectures had analyzed the prehensive relatedness of events with one another; this chapter on "Abstraction" adds the relatedness of eternal objects to one another and to actual occasions. It was probably not yet appreciated how much coherence could be gained by drawing these two analyses together. They are not immediately unified. Prehensive unity turns up in *Religion in the Making* in terms of "physical occasions," aesthetic synthesis in terms of "mental occasions."

8. THE SUPERJECT

The realized togetherness of individual essences which is actuality is "the achievement of an emergent value defined—or shaped—by the definite eternal relatedness in respect to which the real togetherness is achieved. Thus the eternal relatedness is the form . . . ; the emergent actual occasion is the *superject* of informed value; value, as abstracted from any particular superject, is the abstract matter . . . which is common to all actual occasions and the synthetic activity which prehends valueless possibility into superjicient informed value as the substantial activity" (SMW 165). This passage is notable for its introduction of emergent value and superject, and for its new use of the term "prehension."

Whitehead first considered value in his Lowell Lecture on "The Romantic Reaction," seeing it as absent from scientific materialism yet permeating the poetic view of nature. Since science can only observe the extrinsic reality of nature, Whitehead assigned value to its intrinsic reality (SMW 93). This intrinsic reality is "the event as in its own prehensions" in contrast to its extrinsic reality, "the event as in the prehension of other events" (SMW 103). This intrinsic reality is intensified in the process of evolving new organisms. "The organism is a unit of emergent value, a real fusion of the characters of eternal objects, emerging for its own sake" (SWM 107). Now this character of newly evolved organisms is generalized to apply to all actual occasions, conceived as the fusion of the individual essences mediated by the associated abstractive hierarchy. Emergent value is the fusion, the real togetherness of eternal objects, but it is also limitation, for the many possible ways in which they might be together is reduced to the one actual togetherness. "Restriction is the price of value" (SMW 178).

The term "superject" is also introduced in our passage, not to be used again until it emerges as a basic technical concept in *Process and Reality*. Here there is no explicit contrast between subject and superject, for the contrast between the becoming enacted and the being achieved has not yet been made. This particular contrast would strengthen the coherence of the theory presented in this chapter on "Abstraction," for it would show the exact relationship between the intrinsic "aesthetic synthesis" (as becoming) and the associated infinite abstractive hierarchy (the being which it becomes). This would convert the infinite hierarchy from just being a particularly complex kind of possibility, composed purely of eternal objects, into a past actuality which is a potential for supervening occasions.

While the subject-superject contrast is absent, we may speculate as to the intended meaning of superject from the etymology of subject. "Subject" is "that which lies under" other things, initially as the logical subject of predicates, then as the Cartesian subject of experiences. The "superject" would be "that which lies beyond" its component elements. It is the outcome of the synthetic activity combining "form" and "matter" into "superjicient informed value."

This synthetic activity "prehends valueless possibility," valueless because not yet actual. The phrase is an extension of the earlier usage of the Lowell Lectures, which reserved "prehension" exclusively for the interrelatedness between events (by extension, between actual occasions). "Prehension" here still means "to draw into unity," except that now it is possibilities rather than perceptions that are so unified. It is the relatedness of synthetic activity, which now in "Abstraction" applies to eternal objects. This extended meaning of prehension was used once before (SMW 163), and reappears in the three paragraphs devoted to mental activity at the close of the chapter (SMW 170–72).

Perhaps the least convincing aspect of Whitehead's argument in this analysis of the superject of informed value is the claim that the synthetic activity brings together form and matter. Yet, suitably revised, the theory is enormously suggestive, beyond anything Whitehead worked out in his mature theory. In the context of this chapter, the synthetic activity fuses together the individual essences of the complex forms; past actualities do not enter into the picture. Nevertheless, Whitehead wants to appeal to these past actualities in terms of value: ". . . value, as abstracted from any particular superject, is the abstract matter . . . which is common to all actual occasions" (SMW 165). Value may well be the intrinsic reality of each occasion, but it may be doubted that there is any abstract value-in-general. Value derives from those specific limitations and particular restrictions which abstract matter prescinds from.

When Whitehead introduces a theory whereby concrescing occasions are derived from past actualities, these past actualities severally contribute their particular achieved values to the new concrescence. In this sense they contribute matter for the form supplied by the subjective aim. Matter here refers to particular values as potentials, not to some indeterminate content. This specific sense of value, moreover, can be correlated with realized individual essences, for only in actuality is this achieved.

9. "Aesthetic Synthesis" and "Superject" in the Later Philosophy

The theory of the togetherness of individual essences in aesthetic synthesis is not clarified any further in this chapter. "This complete ingredience in an occasion, so as to yield the most complete fusion of individual essence with other eternal objects in the formation of the individual emergent occasion, is evidently of its own kind and cannot be defined in terms of anything else" (SMW 169). However, once prehension is generically analyzed in terms of an asymmetrical relation, internal to the prehender but external to the prehended, and this togetherness is seen as an instance of prehensive unity, then we may see the isolation of eternal objects to be their external relatedness to each other (with respect to individual essences) and their togetherness as the way their common prehender is internally related to them. Then "every meaning of 'together' is to be found in various stages of analysis of occasions of experience. No things are 'together' except in experience" (AI 304; cf. PR 189f), the basic doctrine of his later philosophy.

As we have seen, there is not yet in Whitehead's theorizing the rhythm of subjective becoming and objective being, such that 'aesthetic synthesis' can be understood as an activity of experiencing terminating in determinate unity. But the groundwork is laid for the distinction between a 'definite' unity as the interrelatedness of eternal objects (leaving their individual essences isolated) and 'determinate' unity as the fusion of these individual essences. In determinate unity the common unity is internally related to all the individual essences.

The distinction between definiteness and determinateness, not yet made in this chapter on "Abstraction," is later formally introduced in terms of "position," understood as "relative status in a nexus of actual entities" (PR 25). This masks the more fundamental fact of derivation, for in order to have any particular status among actual occasions, an occasion must be derived from at least some of them. A definite eternal object is atemporal and can be anywhere, whereas an actual occasion is rooted in some particular spatiotemporal situation. Only in that situation is its activity of aesthetic synthesis possible. Moreover, it can only be determinate as deriving its determinateness from other determinations. Determinateness is analyzed not only in terms of the "form" of its unity supplied by the novel eternal object of the subjective aim, but also in terms of the "matter" of past actual occasions.

With the advent of the becoming/being distinction, such that the becoming of an occasion is productive of its being (PR 23),[12] it later becomes possible for Whitehead to analyze the static factor of actuality in terms of the determinate superject. (The superject in "Abstraction" is not clearly static, because the dynamic and static factors of the aesthetic synthesis have not been sharply differentiated.) This determinate superject is rooted in its situation, yet like the eternal objects it has the potentiality for entering into supervening occasions, as required by later theories of derivation.

If the superject becomes the static factor of actuality it is no longer necessary to analyze this factor in terms of an infinite abstractive hierarchy which necessarily attaches to the occasion together with its complete fusion of individual essence (SMW 169). The determinate superject is still the fusion of individual essences, to be sure, but it derives these individual essences from past superjects, not from some infinite abstractive hierarchy. Abstractive hierarchies have only the definiteness of possibility, not the determinateness of actuality.

Once past actuality can be classified with possibility as differing kinds of potentials for actualization, it becomes no longer necessary to analyze the static factor prior to actualization in terms of possibility alone. Finite abstractive hierarchies are sufficient to account for possibility. The inexhaustibility of the description of an actual occasion pertains to its actuality, that is, to its determinateness, not to the definiteness of any supposedly infinite abstractive hierarchy. The determinateness of any actuality is ultimately inexhaustible because it is derived from prior determinateness, and that from still earlier determinateness, *ad infinitum*. Complex eternal objects are all that are needed to mediate this determinateness from one occasion to the other. Since the whole analysis of abstractive hierarchies is introduced in order to explain the formal aspect of actual occasions, it can be abandoned as soon as it is replaced by the concept of determinateness.

10. INCIPIENT PANPSYCHISM

One further topic is lightly touched upon in the last two or three paragraphs of this chapter. Because of Whitehead's commitment to epistemological elucidation as one of the criteria of metaphysical endeavour (SMW 158), the question of how we know finite abstractive hierarchies must be considered. Their ingredient in actual occasions is interpreted in terms of mental activity, taken as including memory, anticipation, imagination, and thought. "These elements in an experient occasion are also modes of inclusion of complex eternal objects in the synthetic prehension, as elements in the emergent value" (SMW 170). Here eternal objects are being prehended, which seems just one short step away from conceptual prehension. Yet we must be aware that "prehension" here has more the meaning of the later "concrescence," although emphasizing unity more than the process of unification. For "synthetic prehension" we might substitute "aesthetic synthesis." The elements represented by finite abstractive hierarchies, Whitehead realizes, must be included within the occasion, and the only other term he has for such inclusion is prehension. Its meaning has been widened to make room for eternal objects.

The distinction between finite and infinite abstractive hierarchies, designed to distinguish the clear conceptuality of eternal objects from the inexhaustibility of actual occasions, also enables Whitehead to distinguish between concepts and percepts on surer grounds than Hume's empirical division between vivid impressions and "faint copies." For Whitehead the difference lies in "abruptness": "By "abruptness" I mean that what is remembered, or anticipated, or imagined, or thought, is exhausted by a finite complex concept (SMW 171).

While in several respects Whitehead is broadly pansubjectivist throughout *Science and the Modern World*, it is only here that he broaches a panpsychist solution to the mind/body problem. (Because it is specifically with respect to mentality that he may change his position, we use "panpsychism" very strictly to refer only to mentality.) A dualist solution postulating two kinds of unrelated occasions, mental occasions and physical occasions, would clearly violate his criterion of coherence, now expressed as success in "forming a basis for harmonizing our systematic accounts of various types of experience" (SMW 158). A modified dualism might be more acceptable. On this view some natural events would have no mentality whatsoever (i.e. physical occasions by themselves), while others have mental occasions attached to them. The key consideration is whether any purely physical occasion can exist as a complete occasion by itself (See RM 113).

In this chapter Whitehead conceives of an occasion in terms of its full concreteness to be an event in nature, and his analysis has been heretofore devoted to its consideration. The focus of the essay has been largely on the extrinsic properties of an actual occasion. "But a natural event, in this sense of the term, is only an abstraction from a complete actual occasion. A complete actual occasion includes that which in cognition takes the form of memory, anticipation, imagination, and thought" (SMW 170). This does not say that only conscious occasions are complete, but that all complete occasions have features which in consciousness take the form of memory, etc. A panpsychist solution may have been encouraged by Whitehead's lively awareness that even the infinite abstractive hierarchy cannot capture the full actuality of the occasion, and that he could not express the togetherness of individual essence in any other terms than aesthetic synthesis.

Thus, he concludes in the penultimate paragraph, "an actual occasion is a prehension [concrescence] of one infinite hierarchy (its associated hierarchy) together with various finite hierarchies" (SMW 171). A very complicated conclusion to reach, but it is consonant with Whitehead's program of analyzing actual occasions as far as possible in terms of eternal objects. The execution of that program, however, suggested difficulties encouraging further explorations. In particular the aesthetic synthesis of abstractive hierarchies needed to be correlated with the generalized theory of perception developed in the Lowell Lectures. This in turn led much later (PR) to a theory of derivation and determinateness doing away with the machinery of abstractive hierarchies entirely. Secondly, mental activity needed to be more fully integrated with the aesthetic synthesis. How can the full concreteness of an occasion be regarded as less than the complete occasion if it can find no place for purely intrinsic features? This is ultimately resolved by conceiving the concreteness as the (superjective) outcome of concrescence, while understanding mental activity primarily in terms of concrescence.

In the mature theory the theory of abstractive hierarchies, with its distinction between simple and complex eternal objects, is largely abandoned, although it was an essential ingredient in the evolution of Whitehead's thought. The distinction between the individual and the relational essence of the eternal object is retained (e.g. PR 114f), although in a more subdued role.

If in fact it suggests that physical occasions could exist by themselves, *Religion In The Making* may retreat from the tentative exploratory panpsychism expressed here. The 1926 essay on "Time" is the first essay to clearly express that *every* actual occasion is a combination of a physical and a mental occasion.

11. Note on Pythagoreanism

In the final paragraph of this chapter, Whitehead notes that the metaphysical description of actual occasions in terms of eternal objects is based upon the nature of mathematics discussed in chapter two. Pure mathematics was there defined as "a resolute attempt to go the whole way in the direction of complete analysis, so as to separate the elements of mere matter of fact from the purely abstract conditions which they exemplify" (SMW 24). Surely this analysis of "Abstraction" examines the purely abstract conditions which actual occasions exemplify! Thus Whitehead can comment: "The idea, ascribed to Pythagoras, has been amplified, and put forward as the first chapter in metaphysics" to be followed by a second chapter on "God" (SMW 172).

Seen in light of the chapter on "Abstraction," the six paragraphs in chapter two just after the definition of mathematics and before the mention of Pythagoras (SMW 24–27) seem to be a definite expansion of the lecture on mathematics. In the opening paragraphs of his talk Whitehead appears to be leading up to the definition of pure mathematics cited above (SWM 24). It is the idea ascribed to Pythagoras (SMW 172), so the statement that "Pythagoras was the first man who had any grasp of the full sweep of this general principle" (SMW 27) has its referent in the definition of mathematics some seven paragraphs before. This seems more plausible than to assume that the referent for "this general principle" is to be found in the very sophisticated logical harmony involved in the unity of an occasion, which is the ostensible referent in the immediately preceding paragraph of the text as published.

These six paragraphs seem to be a meditation, from a mathematical perspective, on the metaphysical enterprise Whitehead undertakes in "Abstraction." It is the search for absolutely general conditions which are "expressible without reference to those particular relations or those particular relata which occur in that particular occasion of experience. . . . these conditions are perfectly general because they refer to no particular occasion, and to no particular entities (such as green, or blue, or trees) which enter into a variety of occasions, and to no particular relationships between such entities" (SMW 24f). These general conditions are the general patterns of relations within possibility, apparently having as relata eternal objects and actual occasions.

Whitehead's use of "occasion of experience" here is most provocative. His general usage throughout the Lowell Lectures is to "events," while the use of "actual occasion" is restricted to the two metaphysical chapters. Presumably Whitehead has "actual occasion" in mind, but wishes to avoid this technical term as inappropriate for this preliminary discussion, just as he substitutes "occasion of experience" much later in *Adventures of Ideas* for the technical terminology of *Process and Reality*.

Chapter 2, "Mathematics as an Element in the History of Thought," was delivered before the Mathematical Society of Brown University in April, 1925.[13] Substantially the same lecture was delivered in New York on May 15 or 16, 1925. From the notes which William Ernest Hocking took of Whitehead's lecture in class on May 19 (see Appendix 1), Whitehead appears to have repeated the salient points of that lecture. Hocking's notes are sketchy, but several reflect passages in chapter two. I quote from Hocking's notes with some bracketed comments:

Absent in N. Y. Saturday May 16

Reading a paper on [the] Hist[ory of] Mathematics. To be published.

Pythagoreanism.

Classifying on Aristotelian grounds tended in [the] Mid[dle] Ages to displace measuring. How much we might have learned had this not been so. ["If only the schoolmen had measured instead of classifying, how much they might have learnt! " (SMW 28).]

Modern mathematics shows the emergence of new formulae by further generalization. Relations of relations, etc., being equivalent to new niches.

In becoming abstract, trigonometry became useful. . . . ["Thus trigonometry became completely abstract; and in thus becoming abstract, it became useful" (SMW 31).]

Christianity was not the product of a happy epoch. It is only in a happy epoch that the age can undertake the revision of fundamental concepts. Then mathematics becomes relevant to philosophy, and you are very near a Platonic view of philosophy [cf SMW 33].

These brief notes contain nothing which cannot be derived from chapter two, in the general setting of Whitehead's lectures at Harvard during April and May, 1925, without the six paragraphs we have assigned to its later expansion. Now this may seem inconclusive, since any one taking notes omits a lot, and Whitehead could have touched upon those ideas very briefly. I take the omission very seriously, however, since Whitehead had been lecturing on the very topics which constitute the chapter on "Abstraction" just immediately before and after this lecture on mathematics. If he had composed these six paragraphs much earlier for his public lecture, or particularly if he had inserted them into his public lecture as an afterthought growing out of his preoccupation just then with the themes of "Abstraction," we could expect him to dwell precisely on that material during his lecture of May 19. The evidence suggests therefore that these six paragraphs were composed after May 19, probably in conjunction with the chapter on "Abstraction," to be inserted in an otherwise completed essay.

NOTES

1. A. H. Johnson, "Whitehead as Teacher and Philosopher," *Philosophy and Phenomenological Research* 29 (1968–69), 376, and republished in *Explorations in Whitehead's Philosophy*, ed. by Lewis S. Ford and George L. Kline (New York: Fordham University Press, 1983), at pp. 8f.

2. "Unpublished Letter from Whitehead to Kemp Smith," *The Southern Journal of Philosophy* 7/4 (Winter, 1969), 339.

3. In this particular passage (SMW 162), Whitehead speaks of "actual events," an uncharacteristic usage for this chapter, which speaks either of "events" or "actual occasions." Presumably an "actual event" would be an event containing one or more actual occasions.

4. Whitehead has not yet distinguished definiteness and determinateness (see PR 25). In the light of that later distinction, these would be *definite* relationships.

5. "Whitehead Without God," in *Process Philosophy and Christian Thought*, ed. Delwin Brown, Ralph E. James, Jr., and Gene Reeves (Indianapolis: Bobbs-Merrill, 1971), p. 327. My response to Sherburne is adapted from "An Appraisal of Whiteheadian Nontheism," *The Southern Journal of Philosophy* 15/1 (Spring, 1977), 41–49.

6. *Process Philosophy and Christian Thought*, p. 327.

7. "A Problem in Whitehead's Doctrine of Abstractive Hierarchies," *Philosophy and Phenomenological Research* 28 (1967–68), 437–9.

8. "On Whitehead's Concept of Abstractive Hierarchies," *Philosophy and Phenomenological Research* 20 (1959–60), 374–82; incorporated in chapter 5 of his *Whitehead's Categoreal Scheme and other Papers* (The Hague: Martinus Nijhoff, 1974).

9. "Eternal Objects, Attributes, and Relations in Whitehead's Philosophy," *Philosophy and Phenomenological Reserch* 14 (1953–54), 198f.

10. Here see my note, "On Some Difficulties with Whitehead's Definition of Abstractive Hierarchies," *Philosophy and Phenomenological Research* 30/3 (March, 1970), 453f.

11. In his later philosophy Whitehead recognizes several kinds of non-sensible actual entities: God, occasions constituting empty space, entirely living occasions, etc. Whether he restricted actual occasions to those which could be characterized by sensa in this chapter on "Abstraction" must remain an open question.

12. So Jorge Luis Nobo, "Whitehead's Principle of Process," *Process Studies* 4/4 (Winter, 1974), 275–84.

13. Victor Lowe, "Whitehead's Gifford Lectures," *The Southern Journal of Philosophy* 7/4 (1969–70) 331.

FIVE

The Chapter on "God"

IN the Lowell Lectures events are conceived to be parts or modes of one underlying substantial activity (SMW 70). That monism is retained in the present chapter on "God": "The general activity is not an entity in the sense in which occasions or eternal objects are entities. It is a general metaphysical character which underlies all occasions, in a particular mode for each occasion. There is nothing with which to compare it: it is Spinoza's one infinite substance" (SMW 177). In neither instance is that one underlying activity identified with God.

1. WHITEHEAD'S MONISM

There are perhaps two lines of thinking in Whitehead's earlier philosophy of nature that lead to this monism:

(1) In the early theory of events and objects, the event has minimal characteristics. It is a particular spatiotemporal volume, containing and contained in an infinity of other events. It can be of any size or duration whatsoever. As such it could be either actual or merely possible, or some mixture of the two, as the event which is the course of human civilization during this century. On the other hand, objects were even more abstract. Some events, at least, could be conceived as parts of actuality.

But Whitehead does not conceive of the actuality of which these events are parts simply as a more inclusive event. For the dynamism of events must be accounted for.

(2) Whitehead maintains that we not only experience parts of nature, we experience its unity, in terms of the creative advance of nature. In pre-relativity days, this creative advance was often con-

ceived to be a particular present event. "We habitually muddle together this creative advance, which we experience and know as the perpetual transition of nature into novelty, with the single-time series which we naturally employ for measure. The various time-series [here functioning similarly to events] each measure some aspect of the creative advance," and are thus aspects or parts of that advance, but it itself is "not properly serial at all" (CN 178). This creative advance provides the underlying substantial activity for the events.

As long as events were conceived purely in terms of extension, these two notions could not be fully integrated. As Whitehead remarks in the appended notes of 1924, "the true doctrine, that 'process' is the fundamental idea, was not in my mind with sufficient emphasis. Extension is derivative from process, and is required by it" (PNK 202).

The concept of prehension enables us to explain the extensiveness of events in terms of process. Instead of conceiving events as primarily constituted by those smaller events they include, Whitehead conceives of them as constituted by their (internal) relations to all other events. His familiarity with projective geometry enabled him to generalize the notion of a percipient event, so essential to his philosophy of nature, to apply to all events. These internal relations were simply conceived from the standpoint of one of the events they constituted. Thus every event, insofar as it was constituted by its prehensions, was analogous to the percipient events.

Although Whitehead pioneered the notion of asymmetrical relations, holding that events are internally related to eternal objects, while those eternal objects are only externally related to events, he does not extend this asymmetry to prehension in *Science and the Modern World*. That is a primary reason for his decision for monism in that work: "The conception of internal relatedness involves the analysis of the event into two factors, one the underlying substantial activity of individualisation, and the other the complex of aspects . . . which are unified by this individualised activity. In other words, the concept of internal relations requires the concept of substance as the activity synthesising the relationships into its emergent character" (SMW 123).

The particular argument stems from the second paragraph of the "Relativity" addition. It is a summary justification of the basic monism of the Lowell Lectures, which Whitehead continues to affirm even in the shift to temporal atomicity. Yet it exists in some tension with that novel factor. As Whitehead notes, this analysis in terms of internal relations has "left out the process of realisation" (SMW 123), but that does not mean that it is incompatible with it.

This is by no means self-evident, since in absolute idealism the affirmation of complete internal relatedness often led to the denial of real temporal advance. McTaggart, whom Whitehead knew intimately for many years at Cambridge, argued for the unreality of time. If an event is determinately constituted out of its relations with all other events, past, present, and future, these events as well should be conceived as completely determinate.

A clue as to the direction of Whitehead's thoughts may be found in the later essay on "Time" of 1926, which argues that actual occasions must be incomplete: "Time requires incompleteness. A mere system of mutually prehensive occasions is compatible with the concept of a static timeless world. Each occasion is temporal because it is incomplete. Nor is there any system of occasions which is complete; there is no one well-defined entity which is the actual world" (IS 242).

Whitehead's theory on this subject is first fully spelled out in *Adventures of Ideas*, chapter 12. It is more developed than his position of 1925 would have been, particularly with respect to the ontological principle, but we hold this to be a fairly constant feature in Whitehead's thought, such that attention to the later account can help us understand his earlier position.

Here we need only consider the relation of the present to the future. First of all, "the future certainly is something for the present. The most familiar habits of mankind witness to this fact. Legal contracts, social understandings of every type, ambitions, anxieties, railway time-tables, are futile gestures of consciousness apart from the fact that the present bears in its own realized constitution relationships to a future beyond itself. Cut away the future, and the present collapses, emptied of its proper content. Immediate existence requires the insertion of the future in the crannies of the present" (AI 246).

If this is so, views of the future as merely subjective projections of human consciousness will not do. On the other hand, the claim that the future is something for the present must be counter-balanced by the claims of the ontological principle. As with all things, the future must be grounded in the nature of actualities, and "there are no individual occasions belonging to the future. The present contains the utmost verge of such realized individuality." Therefore Whitehead concludes that "the whole doctrine of the future is to be understood in terms of the account of the process of self-completion of each individual actual occasion" (AI 247). The future must be understood as an aspect of the present.

The future is then identified with the conditions laid down by the present occasion to which all subsequent occasions must conform. "The future is immanent in the present by reason of the fact that the present bears in its own essence the relationships it will have to the future. It thereby includes in its essence the necessities to which the future must conform. The future is there in the present, as a general fact belonging to the nature of things" (AI 250). Thus how the future is immanent in the present is precisely the way in which the present will become immanent in these future occasions, when they come into being.

This relation is symmetrically internal, constitutive of both the present and the future. To be sure, the future occasion does not yet exist, but when it does, it will in part be constituted by its relation to that now present occasion. The relation itself is independent of the temporal modalities, being equally constitutive of both. But the relation's existence is grounded in the present occasion.

There are no future occasions. Another way of conceiving this is to say the future is incomplete; it does not yet have its full complement of internal relations. It is not yet internally related to those occasions which precede it, but which have not yet come into being. When its entire past, including these immediately past occasions, comes into being, then the occasion itself is ready to come into being through concrescence. Moreover, by its act of becoming, the occasion lays down its own conditions on the future, thus forging its own internal relations with those occasions to come after it.

Thus while each such relation is symmetrically internal, it is ontologically grounded in the occasion coming into being. Present/future relations themselves come into being as the present occasions do, in accordance with the creative advance of nature. Past occasions are not being affected, because all of their relations have already been forged.

Whitehead does not assert an asymmetry, as Charles Hartshorne does, such that while the temporal relation is internal with respect to the present, it is external with respect to the past, the past is merely externally related to the present. Hartshorne's analysis is not false, but we must recognize that it applies to the entirety of the present in contrast to the past. Strictly speaking, a part, i.e. the (objective) datum, of a physical prehension is equally constitutive of both occasions. What is not constitutive of the past occasion is the way in which the present occasion freely appropriates that datum in a novel synthesis laying down new conditions on the future. This is the contribution of the subjective forms.

This theory from *Adventures of Ideas* shows how a doctrine of mutual internal relatedness can be reconciled with a real temporal advance, as it is there expressed in pluralistic terms. But there is no difficulty recasting it in monistic terms. Internal relations are traditionally associated with monism, and Whitehead (in 1925) may have thought that his commitment to internal relations entailed monism. Moreover, his conception of the creative advance was holistic, since he appealed to our experience of that advance as evidence for our experience of the unity of nature.

Nevertheless, temporal atomization introduced pressures towards pluralism absent from the earlier doctrine of the Lowell Lectures. The present, precisely because it is where the creative advance is located, is the theatre for atomization. Atomization, moreover, concerns "the process of *realisation*, which is the adjustment of the synthetic *activities* by virtue of which the various events becomes their realised selves. This adjustment is thus the adjustment of the underlying active *substances* whereby these substances exhibit themselves as the individualisations or modes of Spinoza's one *substance*" (SMW 123f). I have italicized four terms to indicate Whitehead's own pluralistic emphases within an over-arching monism.

The trend is accentuated by Whitehead's renaming of the atomic events "actual occasions' in these two metaphysical chapters. Events can be past, present, or future, and the creative advance may be conceived as applying to the whole of which these are parts. But there are no actual occasions of the future; the possible is precisely that which is excluded. The process of realization can now be identified with the actualization of these atomic occasions.

Traditionally, actuality has been understood either in terms of intrinsic activity or in terms of concrete determinate fact. The first alternative was not yet open to Whitehead, since any activity would be part of the underlying substantial activity. He did understand the actual occasions as concrete determinate fact. Each actuality is a definite limitation of possibility. Anything actual is a restriction of the infinitude of alternatives to one definite outcome. As he later said, "The limitations are the opportunities. The essence of depth of actuality . . . is definiteness" (RM 109).

Now the question for Whitehead's metaphysics becomes: what shall be the fundamental ontological unit, substance or actuality? To be sure, substance and actuality were identical for Aristotle, but their traditional usages down through the history of philosophy have diverged. Whitehead often took "substance" to be classically defined by Descartes as that "which requires nothing but itself in order to exist" (RM 102). Since with Spinoza he understands all particular things to require one another, only the totality can meet this definition. Only the total universe, including God, should there be a God, requires nothing but itself in order to exist. Within this framework, actual occasions might be concrete, determinate facts, but not yet the fundamental ontological units. Despite all the pressures for pluralism, Whitehead seems to remain a monist throughout *Science and the Modern World.*

2. The Introduction of God

The first and only place in this book where the existence of God is affirmed as an integral part of Whitehead's philosophy is in the eleventh chapter entitled "God." Even in the next chapter on "Religion and Science" the reality of God is not affirmed, except possibly in the final paragraph.[1] That chapter focuses upon Whitehead's hopes for a reconciliation between science and religion, but makes no mention as to how his particular concept of God as the principle of limitation, articulated in the previous chapter, might aid in effecting this reconciliation.

To be sure, the topic he was asked to address by the Phillips Brooks House at Harvard was religion, not God. But then the topic he agreed to speak on for his second course of Lowell Lectures in 1926 was a development of the very same topic, which did not hinder him from talking about God extensively in *Religion in the Making.* The topic he agreed to speak on for that series was " 'Science and Religion,' i.e. on the scientific criticism of religion."[2] Quite possibly a shift in Whitehead's convictions about God might account for these two diverse treatments of "Science and Religion." The surmise is strengthened by the fact that the chapter on "Religion and Science," while it follows the chapter on "God" in the text, was most probably composed from the earlier point of view. The lecture was given in Peabody Hall on Sunday, April 5, 1925, at the 19th meeting of the Phillips Brooks lecture series.[3] Whitehead was just then on the verge of formulating his epochal theory of time, first presented in class that following week (See Appendix I), and most likely had not yet thought through its implications for theism. This discussion on "God," on the other hand, is closely connected with the analysis of "Abstraction," and Whitehead's first mention of the themes of "Abstraction" in his classroom lectures begins in May, 1925.

Still, it is a difficult question to determine what attitudes towards God Whitehead held before the discovery of the epochal theory. It could just be that he did not regard the question of God's nature and existence to be part of his lectures prior to May, 1925, despite his own private theistic leanings.[4] Then, when two additional "metaphysical" chapters were inserted into the book before publication probing these final truths, it would be appropriate to consider the role of God.

On the other hand, it has been said that Whitehead had earlier given up theology as a bad job, after having studied it privately during the 1890's.[5] Bertrand Russell reports: "Throughout the time that I knew him well—that is to say, roughly, from 1898 to 1912—he was very definitely and emphatically agnostic."[6] Then the philosophical reasoning growing out of the need for a principle of limitation to order the infinitude of the transcendent eternal objects may have converted this agnostic to theism. The words used to describe Aristotle, that "in his consideration of this metaphysical question [the existence and nature of God] he was entirely dispassionate" (SMW 173), might equally well be applied to Whitehead.

Frederic R. Crownfield sees a gradual increase in Whitehead's rationalism, based in part on his reading of Paul Sarpi's *History of the Council of Trent*, which he assumes was part of Whitehead's theological reading between 1891 and 1898.[7] Whitehead lists Sarpi's book in the preface to *Adventures of Ideas* as one which chiefly influenced his way of thinking. Earlier he quoted from the fourth book of Sarpi's *History* to the effect that the presiding Papal Legates ordered "that the Divines ought to confirm their opinions with the holy Scripture, Traditions of the Apostles, sacred and approved Councils, and by the Constitutions and Authorities of the holy Fathers; . . . This order did not please the Italian Divines; who said it was a novity and a condemning of School Divinity, which, in all difficulties, *useth reason* . . ." (SMW 9). Crownfield: "What dawned on Whitehead as a result of reading Sarpi was that the attitudes of both scientists and papal delegates exhibited the same spirit. In reaction to the excess of scholasticism, truth was to be arrived at not by an appeal to reason but to some supposedly objective authority. The scientist appealed to the hard facts given as revealed words. What Whitehead realized was that this attitude was ultimately disastrous for both."

Crownfield goes on to show how Whitehead's rationalism is connected with his rationalistic theism as manifest in *Religion in the Making*, but there is little here to help us determine when and why he became a theist. Rationalistic agnosticism is surely another plausible alternative.

I believe the actual situation to be more finely nuanced than any of these alternatives suggest, and wish to draw upon all of them somewhat. Whitehead was raised in an Anglican vicarage and studied at Sherbourne, a public school which had originated as a Benedictine monastery. While Whitehead was a student there, Sherbourne celebrated its thousandth anniversary. During his senior year he lived in what was thought to have been the abbot's cell, steeped in Anglican piety and tradition. As an undergraduate he talked openly and freely about his interest in religion, particularly with respect to foreign missions: "We may not know precisely what many of Jesus' sayings mean, but the commandment to go into all the world and preach the gospel is very clear." [8] Russell reports that "as a young man, he was almost converted to Roman Catholicism under the influence of Cardinal Newman." [9]

If in middle life he became—in Russell's words—"emphatically agnostic," this may have been more a rejection of Victorian theology and apologetics than of religion *per se*. He became convinced that that which is supremely worthy of worship could not be portrayed as an omnipotent tyrant, but that the quest of worship is not thereby gainsaid. The horror of the first world war, bringing with it the death of Whitehead's younger son Eric, in air combat over France in 1918, may well have intensified this interest in religion.[10] As Russell writes, "The pain of this loss had a great deal to do with turning his thoughts to philosophy and with causing him to seek ways of escaping from belief in a merely mechanistic universe." [11] This war also slaughtered many of England's young men, including those who had been promising students of Whitehead's at Cambridge and London, and destroyed the fond illusion of inevitable progress the Victorian era had cherished. Despite it all, Whitehead can affirm that "the fact of the religious vision, and its history of persistent expansion, is our one ground for optimism." This optimism is rooted, however, in a profound sense of the meaninglessness of existence otherwise. "Apart from it, human life is a flash of occasional enjoyments lighting up a mass of pain and misery, a bagatelle of transient experience" (SMW 192).

During the opening months of 1925 Whitehead may be seen as strongly endorsing the importance of the religious vision, hoping against hope that religion and science could be conciliated, yet rejecting all those concepts of God known to him. He could not simply affirm God's existence, for this would mean ascribing reality to some one of those traditional images he rejected, and he could not yet ascertain the proper concept which might correct those distortions. While perhaps more strongly persuaded of the reality of God, he was radically uncertain as to God's nature. In particular he would have rejected the concept of God as the transcendent creator of the world. If the world consists of events, that which brings these events into being would be their sole determiner, both for good and for evil.

Whitehead once told William Ernest Hocking: "I should never have included it [the concept of God], if it had not been strictly required for descriptive completeness. You must set all your essentials into the foundation. It's no use putting up a set of terms, and then remarking, 'Oh, by the by, I believe there's a God.'" [12] The concept of God is not required for the philosophy of the Lowell Lectures, and therefore its omission from them by itself tells us nothing of his personal beliefs. Yet a discrepancy between one of the Lowell Lectures and his additional chapter on "God" suggests that Whitehead did not then have any particular concept of God he was willing to espouse publicly.

In his lecture on "The Romantic Reaction," delivered in February, 1925, remarking about the appeal to some greater reality standing behind nature, variously called "The Absolute, Brahma[n], The Order of Heaven, God," Whitehead comments: "The delineation of final metaphysical truth is no part of this lecture. My point is that any summary conclusion jumping from our conviction of the existence of such order of nature to the easy assumption that there is an ultimate reality which, in some unexplained way, is to be appealed to for the removal of perplexity, constitutes the great refusal of rationality to assert its rights" (SMW 92). He recognizes: "In a sense, all explanation must end in an ultimate arbitrariness. My demand is, that the ultimate arbitrariness of matter of fact from which our formulation starts should disclose the same general principles of reality, which we dimly discern as stretching away into regions beyond our explicit powers of discernment" (SMW 92f).

Ultimately this requirement is met in *Process and Reality*. The metaphysical principles may or may not be ultimately arbitrary, but in any case God discloses these same general principles of reality: "God is not to be treated as an exception to all metaphysical principles, invoked to save their collapse. He is their chief exemplification" (PR 343).

In the meantime, however, the principle of limitation Whitehead identifies with God in June 1925 does not meet this requirement in any obvious way. God does not disclose the same general principles of reality as the actualities do. They are conceived as modes of the underlying substantial activity, while God is a principle, at best an attribute of this activity. Moreover, "God is the ultimate limitation, and His existence is the ultimate irrationality. For no reason can be given for just that limitation which it stands in His nature to impose" (SMW 178). Here there is no longer the vision of general principles being forever exemplified by entities fading off into the distance, for we are up against a basic irrationality. There is a kind of incipient existentialism here. God stands as an ultimate reality behind things providing a determination to things which cannot be achieved solely by exemplifying the general principles. "God is not concrete, but He is the ground for concrete actuality. No reason can be given for the nature of God, because that nature is the ground of rationality" (SMW 178).

We have come to the limit of rationality. "For there is a categorical limitation which does not spring from any metaphysical reason. There is a metaphysical need for a principle of determination, but there can be no metaphysical reason for what is determined. If there were such a reason, there would be no need for any further principle: for metaphysics would already have provided the determination. The general principle of empiricism depends upon the doctrine that there is a principle of concretion which is not discoverable by abstract reason" (SMW 178).

Whitehead never abandons his appeal to experience in metaphysics, for he does not believe that metaphysical claims can be settled on rationalistic grounds alone. God also continues as the ground for any "arbitrary" selection of general determinations. But whereas here God's determination is subordinate to, and in addition to, the general determination of apparently necessary metaphysical principles, later at least some of these principles seem to be grounded in God: "His conceptual actuality at once exemplifies and establishes the categoreal conditions" (PR 344).

It might be possible to somehow conceive of a way of harmonizing the two passages from *Science and the Modern World*, one from the lectures of February and other from the written additions of May and June 1925. Still, if Whitehead had even a rudimentary idea of God as an irrational principle of limitation, he would have expressed himself quite differently in the first passage. He then expressed deeply held convictions, but later was willing to proclaim his newly discovered concept of God even though it did not yet meet his own self-imposed criteria.

If, as the occasional lecture on "Religion and Science" shows, Whitehead was then very sympathetic to the claims of religion, we may wonder why the Lowell Lectures contain no theistic dimension. To be sure, this naturalistic system of evolving organisms has no obvious need for God, but ways might have been found. Perhaps the primary reason the concept was not introduced was that all of the alternatives that suggested themselves proved unsatisfactory.

A supernatural reality standing behind nature to produce the whole of this natural system, we have seen, violates Whitehead's sense of rationality (SMW 92). The Absolute, if so understood, is thereby rejected. Such a supernatural production of nature is of one piece with the bifurcation of nature into causal and apparent nature Whitehead had previously attacked, questioning the status of causal nature in our account of what is perceived (CN 31, 39).

While his system bears strong affinities with Spinozistic monism, he never identifies substantial activity (or its pluralistic successor creativity) with God. Whitehead criticizes this identification: God "has been conceived as the foundation of the metaphysical situation with its ultimate activity. If this conception be adhered to, there can be no alternative except to discern in Him the origin of all evil as well as of all good. He is then the supreme author of the play, and to Him must therefore be ascribed its shortcomings as well as its success" (SMW 179). Spinoza recognized this implication, and conceived of God as transcending the distinction between good and evil. Whitehead insists upon the goodness of God, and is much more willing to abandon traditional notions of divine infinity and power, although in early 1925 he did not see quite how this could be done.

Perhaps the most promising alternative within the organic mechanism of the Lowell Lectures would be a theory of interlocking organisms, each in turn including its subordinates. In organic mechanism, the parts influence the whole by their mechanical interaction with other parts, yet the whole organically influences the parts. In this hierarchy of organisms, each organism in turn functions as a part for a more inclusive organic whole. Then "God" would name the most inclusive whole. This organic whole could still be open to the future, insofar as the future is not yet actualized. We do not know whether Whitehead ever considered this alternative, but if so, it was probably rejected because then evil would be included *sim-*

pliciter within God. Whitehead did not introduce the consequent nature whereby God experiences the world until he had worked out a satisfactory theory of divine persuasion, by which the evil God prehends could be overcome by good.[13]

3. THE NATURE OF RELIGION

If the metaphysics of abstraction and concretion engendered by the discovery of the epochal theory of time first suggested to Whitehead a fruitful conception of God, then the lecture on "Religion and Science" delivered on April 5, 1925, can give us valuable insight into his final phase of wistful agnosticism. He notes that within the past few centuries, "there has been a gradual decay of religious influence in European civilization . . . Religion is tending to degenerate into a decent formula wherewith to embellish a comfortable life" (SMW 188). Nevertheless, in the long run, "it is the one element in human experience which persistently shows an upward trend. It fades and then recurs. But when it renews its force, it recurs with an added richness and purity of content" (SMW 192).

The conflict between science and religion has always been with us (SMW 182), and is to be expected: "Can you be surprised that, in the absence of a perfect and complete phrasing of the principles of science and of the principles of religion which apply to these specific cases, the accounts . . . from these divergent standpoints should involve discrepancies? It would be a miracle if it were not so" (SMW 185). Moreover, "a clash of doctrines is not a disaster— it is an opportunity" (SMW 186). Whitehead illustrates this by the discovery of argon, arising from the discrepancy in the amount of "nitrogen" obtained by using two different methods. (One was found to have argon mixed in with the nitrogen.) Analogously, isotopes were discovered. Propositions proposed are sweeping generalizations containing hidden limitations and qualifications which have yet to be discovered, often by the clash of opinions. "Religion will not regain its old power until it can face change in the same spirit as does science. Its principles may be eternal, but the expression of those principles requires continual development" (SMW 189).

Religion is correlated with God for Whitehead, even in texts where Whitehead cannot see his way clear to affirm God's existence. "Religion is the reaction of human nature to its search for God" (SMW 191). Since "the immediate reaction of human nature to the religious vision is worship" (SMW 192), "the power of God [the object of the religious vision] is the worship He inspires" (SMW 192). Whitehead accords great importance to religious vision, but at the same time finds a great hindrance in the particular image of God being proposed in the existing religious community, on two grounds: it stifles the adventure of inquiry, and it perpetuates an outworn psychology of tyranny.

"In an intellectual age there can be no active interest which puts aside all hope of a vision of the harmony of truth. To acquiesce in discrepancy is destructive of candour, and of moral cleanliness. It belongs to the self-respect of intellect to pursue every tangle of thought to its final unravelment" (SMW 185). The advance of science is thus an opportunity to discover how the claims of religion should be qualified, made more precise, and freed from irrelevant accretions. In this sense "the worship of God is not a rule of safety—it is an adventure of the spirit, a flight after the unattainable. The death of religion comes with the repression of the high hope of adventure" (SMW 192).

In summarizing these views, we see that Whitehead had a fairly definite idea as to what God was not. He was not (a) a radically transcendent reality arbitrarily disconnected from basic metaphysical principles, nor (b) an all-controlling power, responsible for evil as well as good, nor (c) a power operating in terms of force rather than in terms of persuasion. Presumably, however, he did not yet have a clear idea of what God was, definite enough to disentangle this divine concept from the erroneous elements in the traditional images of God known to him.

His description of the essential character of the religious spirit is an intuitive, proleptic statement of what he was searching for, deliberately couched in paradoxical terms. He did not yet have the conceptual warrants to justify these claims, but they serve as a lure towards which his thought moves. Let there be no mistake here, for it is not merely religion but God he is seeking to describe. "Religion is the vision of something" which can only be God. "God," however, is not named, to avoid misunderstanding. However much Whitehead might be persuaded as to the reality of God, any affirmation of his existence, if not coupled with any fairly precise account as to his nature, would simply mean the affirmation of one of the traditional images of God which he had rejected. This would simply mean the existence of a discarded idol, not of God.

The proleptic, intuitive ideal Whitehead was striving for may be appreciated by interpreting this statement of the religious vision within the context of Whitehead's total writings about God. As the transcendent concrescence of the unlimited wealth of pure potentiality

God stands behind the passing flux of the temporal world. By providing the initial aims for each concrescing occasion, he stands behind the world as (in one sense) its creator (PR 224, 348). Insofar as these initial aims for occasions are transformed into subjective aims within the actual occasions God is immanent in the world. Both in the primordial concrescence and in the on-going everlasting synthesis of the world God is something real, "and yet waiting to be realised" both in terms of later temporal actualization of God's aims, and in terms of the consequent synthesis of those finite actualizations. As envisaging the highest ideals for the world God is "something which is a remote possibility, and yet" in his present reality "the greatest of present facts." God "gives meaning to all that passes" in many ways, primarily in terms of initial aims, "and yet eludes apprehension" insofar as any comprehension falls short before his infinite mystery (SMW 191f). (These last words would have particular import for the author of "Religion and Science," if he were then unable to give his intuitions any precise conceptual articulation.)

4. The Triple Envisagement

Before writing the chapter on "God" in May or June, 1925, as part of a fresh articulation of his metaphysical vision, Whitehead inserted the "triple envisagement" addition, which has a particular bearing on our topic (SMW 104–106). As we have already seen in chapter one, Whitehead exploits an ambiguity concerning "the reiteration of a particular shape" in the previous paragraph from the Lowell Lectures to understand this reiteration in terms of his newly-discovered epochal theory of momentary occasions, then devotes two paragraphs to the three types of envisagement he discerns, before allowing the text to return to its original topic concerning "The Nineteenth Century."

Here Whitehead is addressing questions of final metaphysical truth, a topic he had avoided in the Lowell Lectures. But he had as yet not worked out the theory of "Abstraction" in detail, at least not with respect to the isolation and the togetherness of the eternal objects (SMW 164f). In the later theory of "Abstraction," they were isolated in the realm of ideal possibility, but actualized in terms of their temporal togetherness. The "triple envisagement" addition speaks of "a real togetherness of eternal objects, as envisaged in ideal situations . . . apart from any reality" (SMW 105). This rides rough-shod over Whitehead's careful distinction. These two passages can only be reconciled by supposing that he later changed his position and failed to revise the earlier statement.

Clearly in these two paragraphs the word "envisagement" is crucial, but its meaning is difficult to grasp. Aside from this passage and the very next paragraph, "envisagement" is mentioned in two successive contexts in the chapter on "God." There Whitehead speaks of the "abrupt synthesis of eternal objects" as "the 'graded envisagement' which each occasion prehends into its synthesis" (SMW 176). In the next paragraph he speaks of the "general metaphysical character which underlies all occasions" whose attributes are modal differentiation, eternal possibility, and God, as "the envisagement which enters into the synthesis" (SMW 177; cf. top 178). Since to envisage means to confront, face, what is envisaged is that which the occasion has before it to synthesize. To envisage is not to synthesize, to bring into prehensive unity, but to entertain as an ingredient for such prehension. What is envisaged is conceived apart from realization, and therefore is non-individualized, since realization means individualization.

"Envisagement" is not used in *Religion in the Making*, as far as can be ascertained, but it shows up again in *Process and Reality*, particularly in terms of God's primordial envisagement of all the eternal objects. Here "envisagement" has the additional meaning of conceptual realization in nontemporal concrescence. But for the world, and for God's total, everlasting concrescence, it is still an envisagement in the sense of something to be included in further actualization. After considering the alternative terms for God's activity, "conceptual prehension," "appetition," "intuition," and "vision," Whitehead concludes that " 'envisagement' is perhaps a safer term than 'vision' " (PR 33f). For God does confront the eternal objects as already interrelated in themselves.

"The underlying activity, as conceived apart from the fact of realisation, has three types of envisagement" (SMW 105). That is to say, the one substantial activity, considered apart from its individualization into particular actual occasions, has three types of elements which go into its formation. In *Religion in the Making* these types are called "formative elements" and we shall see that there is a one-to-one correlation between them and the three types of envisagement by means of the three attributes of the underlying substantial activity. Here Whitehead is taking the point of view of an actual occasion, and asking himself imaginatively what kinds of formative elements it must take into account to achieve its own prehensive unity. "These are: first, the envisagement of eternal objects; secondly the envisagement of possibilities of value in respect to the synthesis of eternal objects; and lastly, the envisagement of the actual matter of fact which must enter into the total situation which is achieveable by the addition of the future" (SMW 105). The nascent occasion confronts all eternal objects and all (past) actual occasions, but a third factor is also needed: the ordering of the eternal objects into ideal possibilities. Without this, there would be no striving after value. In abstraction from actuality, the eternal objects are divorced from value. Even the ordered ideal possibilities are valueless (SMW 165), for value lies in the actuality. There is no value until actualized, but there must be an ideal ordering of the eternal objects providing that which occasions should actualize.

So the occasion confronts, as that which it is to synthesize, eternal objects, an ideal ordering of those eternal objects, and actual occasions. The word "envisagement," however, not only means what the particular occasions confront, but what has been given a status so that it can be confronted. Thus the first two types of envisagement are features of an "underlying eternal energy." This eternal energy or activity is probably not to be identified with God, nor even with the whole of the underlying substantial activity. It seems to be this substantial activity, abstracted from all concrete temporalizations. Since in terms of the Spinozistic monism of *Science and the Modern World*, only the modes are individuals, Whitehead conceives of these envisagements as pervasive non-individualized structures (attributes) which all the modes participate in. The most appropriate analogy can be found in the three hypostases of Plotinus. Just as every individual soul participates in Mind *(Nous)* and to that extent enjoys mentality, so each occasion, insofar as we abstract from its particular temporal situation, participates in a nontemporal envisagement of eternal objects and also confronts all these eternal objects from its own particular vantage point.

Thus if we abstract from the particular temporal modes of this underlying activity, and consider just its nontemporal aspects, we have an "eternal activity"—eternal because unspecified as to when it happens, yet as an activity capable of (subjectively) entertaining the eternal objects.[14] There are two types of this non-individualized eternal activity: the envisagement of all eternal objects (which all actual occasions directly envisage) and the restriction of this plenitude by means of ideal possibilities of value.

It may be questioned whether Whitehead conceived of this second envisagement in terms of God. After all, he was simply analyzing the formative factors which any actual occasion must synthesize into prehensive unity. Furthermore, he does not here conceive of ideal possibilities as a restriction upon the unlimited realm of eternal objects. (Their plenitude is perhaps not yet seen as requiring any limitation.) But when, in working out the theory of "Abstraction," Whitehead discovers the need for a principle of limitation, this conception of "an envisagement of all values to be obtained by a real togetherness of eternal objects, as envisaged in ideal situations" (SMW 105) as a limitation on the eternal objects providing the ultimate source of order in the world can be a powerful reason for naming that principle of limitation "God." For it is God's traditional role to be cosmic orderer.

Although Whitehead makes no further use of the idea, this paragraph also contains the first incipient notion of something analogous to subjective aim. The question is not yet faced in its utmost severity, whereby some origin for the subjectivity of each occasion whatsoever must be found. At this point Whitehead has not yet affirmed the principle, found toward the end of his essay on "Abstraction," which ascribes some degree of mentality to every complete occasion, although possibly subjectivity (or interiority) is meant to be explained some other way (SMW 170). At any rate, this final paragraph of the "triple envisagement" addition conceives of an enduring subjectivity in terms of an enduring object.[15]

"The individual perception arising from enduring objects will vary in its individual depth and width according to the way in which the pattern dominates its own route" (SMW 105f). The complexity of the enduring object the route of occasions exemplifies remains Whitehead's reason for the complexity of occasions' feelings, but the perceptions arise from the occasions themselves, not as here, from the enduring objects themselves.

The individual perception "may represent the faintest ripple differentiating the general substrate energy, or, in the other extreme, it may rise to conscious thought, which includes poising before self-conscious judgment the abstract possibilities of value inherent in various situations of ideal togetherness" (SMW 106). Clearly Whitehead is considering the influence of the ideal possibilities for value of the second envisagement upon occasions, including occasions of human experience, which will later suggest God as the source for the initial subjective aim. Here we may note that conscious occasions contemplate a range of alternative ideal possibilities derived from the second envisagement, and this speaks powerfully for a concept of human freedom as a response to divine lures. If there is already continuity of subjectivity, that enduring subject can confront many alternatives at the outset. In Whitehead's later theory, however, in which the subjective aim derived from God provides the continuity of subjectivity whereby the process of unification is provided a goal towards which it is to move, there can be only one aim, even though it can be modified considerably during concrescence. There must be continuity of aim throughout the concrescence, for the process of unification is powerless to proceed in the absence of some direction. A multiplicity of alternatives would not give this singleness of aim.

Whitehead concludes this speculation with respect to physical activities exemplifying vibration and the principle of least action: "The intermediate cases will group round the individual perception as envisaging (without self-consciousness) that one immediate possibility of attainment which represents the closest analogy to its own immediate past, having regard to the actual aspects which are there for prehension" (SMW 106).[16] Although the language used here is close to later descriptions of subjective aim, its purpose is quite different, since the question of the origin of subjectivity has not yet been raised.

Although at the time Whitehead was probably simply analyzing three types of factors which confronted any occasion for synthesis, in retrospect the second envisagement contains many of the features he later associates with God. Its role in providing ideal possibilities for the actualization of value may well have inclined him to designate the principle of limitation he discovered as God.

5. THE PRINCIPLE OF LIMITATION

Ordinarily a general principle of limitation is a strange entity to call God. It was not destined to remain Whitehead's concept of God, and the more elaborate conception developed in his later theory bears greater affinities with traditional concepts of God. For the time being, however, it was a concept by means of which Whitehead could once again affirm theism. This God was not the omnipotent creator of all there is, ultimately responsible for the evil as well as the good. Rather, "if He be conceived as the supreme ground for limitation, it stands in His very nature to divide the Good from the Evil" (SMW 179). Nor is he obviously a power that acts by force rather than by persuasion. On the positive side, if limitation could be the means of generating possibilities for value, God could be fittingly conceived as such a limitation.

Possibly Whitehead came to affirm a metaphysical principle of limitation by something like these considerations:

(1) As we have seen, the study of "Abstraction" brought vividly to his attention the enormous multiplicity of eternal objects. In the Lowell Lectures the eternal object was scarcely more than another name for sensa, in contrast with the enduring object. Afterwards the immanent eternal objects assume transcendent roles, which greatly expanded their scope. In "Abstraction" Whitehead conceives these eternal objects as having simple and complex features, individual and relational essences, infinite and finite abstractive hierarchies. The vast multiplicity of unrealized possibility beckons to each occasion. Some sort of limitation marking boundaries upon this infinitude seems desirable, even necessary.

(2) Possibility requires more than just internal consistency and formal perfection. It also needs actualizability. To be actualizable, an eternal object must be capable of exemplifying that present actual occasion situated with respect to all other actual occasions within the same extensive continuum. This continuum did not present itself to Whitehead as a bare abstract matrix, but as arbitrarily restricted to three dimensions of space and one of time. "Accordingly the spatio-temporal relationship . . . is nothing else than a selective limitation within the general systematic relationships among eternal objects" (SMW 161). There must be some principle of limitation which limits actualizable eternal objects to those which fit the four-dimensional spatiotemporal continuum.

Granting that there is a metaphysical principle of limitation, why should we call this principle 'God'? Because it is a cosmic source of order in the universe. The time-honored teleological argument infers from the existence of order in the world to a divine orderer. If there is an antecedent limitation on possibilities, such that only those exhibiting some sort of cosmic order can ever be actualized, then that principle of limitation orders the world. It becomes the means whereby Whitehead could affirm God as a cosmic principle of order without committing himself to affirming the existence of a transcendent creator. Once that means was discovered, Whitehead had no compunctions against announcing his discovery publicly.

Later he was to abandon this particular argument for God's existence. The arbitrary features of the observable world, such as its particular dimensionality, the particular values of its basic forces, the periodic system of the chemical elements, can all be ascribed to the general features this cosmic epoch. "The arbitrary, as it were 'given,' elements in the laws of nature warn us that we are in a special cosmic epoch" (PR 91). There are as many possible cosmic epochs as there are possible variations of these features. Not all need be actualized, to be sure, but particular ones could evolve out of other particular ones. This was also Charles Sanders Peirce's solution: ". . . the only possible way of accounting for the laws of nature and for uniformity in general is to suppose them results of evolution." [17]

In the Lowell Lectures Whitehead had already called for "the evolution of laws of nature [as] concurrent with the evolution of enduring pattern" (SMW 107). Here his initial opposition to the irrationality of postulating God as creator or sustainer of the enduring stability of nature is striking. He recognizes that "all explanation must end in an ultimate arbitrariness." As examples he cites among other physical constants the dimensionality of space. "But the very nature of these entities, the very nature of their spatiality and temporality, should exhibit the arbitrariness of these conditions as *the outcome of a wider evolution* beyond nature itself, and within which nature is but a limited mode" (SMW 93, italics added).

This standard of rationality is relaxed considerably when God's existence is introduced as the "ultimate irrationality" (SMW 178). Yet we must note that the two concepts of God being considered are quite different. In the first instance, the God Whitehead rejected as violating the canons of rationality was the traditional God behind the scenes, the author of the play. The God he now affirms is not a creator, but simply a principle of limitation. This general attribute of the underlying substantial activity receives a provisional dispensation from the strict demands of rationality. This relaxation is merely provisional, however, for in *Process and Reality*, as we shall see, Whitehead takes care that "God is not to be treated as an exception to all metaphysical principles" (PR 343).

This principle of limitation clearly applies to at least the second way of limitation Whitehead introduces. "Restriction is the price of value. There cannot be value without antecedent standards of value, to discriminate the acceptance or rejection of what is before the envisaging mode of activity. Thus there is an antecedent limitation among values, introducing contraries, grades, and oppositions" (SMW 178).

To be sure, every actuality has value. In the Lowell Lectures Whitehead had already identified 'value' with the intrinsic reality of an event (SMW 93). This does not reduce value merely to the level of matter of fact. Were matter of fact devoid of value, there would be no contraries, oppositions, or comparisons of better or worse Whitehead finds objectively present in the world. Value is not something we arbitrarily impose upon the world; it derives from the intrinsic reality of each occasion. For the occasion to have value,

Whitehead argues in this passage, there must be antecedent standards of value. Here we may have another anticipation of the later doctrine of initial aim. The value which is the intrinsic reality of the occasion could derive in part from an antecedent standard of value, whether this standard be conceived as general (SMW) or as individualized for that particular occasion (PR). That antecedent standard (initial aim?) might also enable the concrescing occasion to discriminate what it accepts or rejects from the initial data it "envisages," i.e. has before it for possible inclusion within its concrescence. In this sense the concrescent occasion is "the envisaging mode of activity." From this theory the two steps required to develop the later theory of initial aim are the individualizing of the antecedent standard of value for each occasion, and the recognition that this individualized ideal serves as the origin of that occasion's subjectivity. Once those two steps are taken, the freedom of the occasion could be reconceived as the continuous modification of subjective aim, rather than as inhering in some antecedently existing subjectivity which then receives standards of value from God.

6. The Three Forms of Limitation

It is less clear how God as the principle of limitation applies to the first way of limitation Whitehead discerns. Here his account is extremely terse, even cryptic. We are given no explicit guidance as to how the principle of limitation applies in these instances. "This limitation takes three forms, (i) the special logical relations which all events must conform to, (ii) the selection of relationships to which the events do conform, and (iii) the particularity which infects the course even within those general relationships of logic and causation" (SMW 177). Does the principle of limitation apply to all of these forms of limitation, some of them, or to none of them?

Kenneth F. Thompson, Jr. offers an extended argument that all of these apply to God.[18] We briefly summarize: Whitehead's general method is to offer a minimal account of the metaphysical situation, such that there can be no metaphysical order apart from God as the ordering principle. Creativity and the eternal objects alone cannot account for the actual occasions, he argues, for "apart from God, the remaining formative elements would fail in their functions. There would be no creatures, since, apart from harmonius order, the perceptive fusion would be a confusion neutralizing achieved feeling" (RM 100).

As a systematic interpretation of what Whitehead should have meant by his principle of limitation, in conformity not only with *Religion in the Making*, but also with *Process and Reality*, this reading has much to commend itself. For in his mature theory Whitehead did seek to ground the metaphysical order in the primordial, nontemporal decision of God. "This ideal realization of potentialities in a primordial actual entity constitutes the metaphysical stability whereby the actual process exemplifies general principles of metaphysics" (PR 40; cf. 18f, 344). Yet we question whether this interpretation can be sustained for the initial introduction of the principle of limitation.

The key question is whether Whitehead initially conceives of any metaphysical order apart from God. He argues that "what is metaphysically indeterminate has nevertheless to be categorically determinate" (SMW 178). This does not mean that all metaphysical determination is provided by that which provides the categorical determination (God), but that there is further categorical determination *in addition to* the metaphysical determination. This metaphysical determination is only abstract and partial; of itself it is insufficient to provide for concrete reality. This is the basic argument for the irrationality of God's existence. If it were metaphysically rational as following from the metaphysical principles, then ultimately these principles would be sufficient conditions for concrete existence. Since the metaphysical principles alone cannot provide for concreteness, there must be a categorical limitation that cannot be derived from metaphysical principles. "If there were such a reason, there would be no need for any further principle: for metaphysics would already have the determination." Thus metaphysics already partly determines an order, but this order is abstract and incomplete, requiring in addition a principle of concretion. "The general principle of empiricism depends upon the doctrine that there is a principle of concretion which is not discoverable by abstract reason" (SMW 178).

If, as we interpret him, Whitehead in *Science and the Modern World* conceived of the principle of concretion as supplementing an incomplete metaphysical order, then the first two limitations are best interpreted as limitations of logic and causation applicable to that metaphysical order. Thus "the special logical relations which all events must conform to" refer to the eternal objects in their mutual internal relatedness as described in the analysis of the chapter on "Abstraction." In addition to all these possible relationships, there is "the selection of relationship to which the events do conform" in that each occasion is the togetherness of all other occasions (SMW 174). "Any one occasion *a* issues from other occasions which collectively form its past" (SMW 176). These are the relationships of causality occasions happen to conform to.

The third type of limitation is rather vaguely described as "the particularity which infects the course even within those general relationships of logic and causation," but it can be given rather precise illustration by reference to "those matter-of-fact determinations—such as the three dimensions of space, and the four dimensions of the spatio-temporal continuum—which are inherent in the actual course of events, but which present themselves as arbitrary in respect to a more abstract possibility" (SMW 161).

Reflection upon such general matter-of-fact limitations, limitations which are general to all occasions, may well have prompted Whitehead's meditation on the need for a principle of limitation. In the chapter on "God" Whitehead catalogues all these types of limitation without any prior consideration as to which are to be found to need God as an additional principle of concretion. He summarizes his argument as requiring that "the course of events should have developed amid an antecedent [general] limitation composed of conditions [of logic and causation], particularisation, and standards of value." Then he begins a new paragraph with the very next sentence: "Thus as a further element in the metaphysical situation, there is required a principle of limitation" (SMW 178). Does this principle refer back to all these types of limitation, or only to some?

If our argument above has been sound, the conditions of logic and causation need no further principle. And it would seem most natural to refer the principle of limitation simply to the last-named "standards of value." Then only the second way, introducing value, would require God. But there is also the third limitation of particularization beyond the conditions of logic and causation. Whether this applies to God might well have been left deliberately vague on Whitehead's part. On the other hand, these conditions of particularity, such as refer to the dimensionality of space-time, do not appear to be part of the generic metaphysical order and seem to require some general principle of limitation.

Whitehead finally grounded the arbitrariness of nature in a series of successive cosmic epochs. In each epoch such arbitrary laws, derived from past actualities, have a long-lasting but ultimately limited sway. An epoch emerges as a complex fusion of slowly evolving patterns inherited from one group of occasions to the next, coupled with constant input from God providing the best relevant alternative to the past each occasion inherits. In the overwhelming majority of instances, such initial aims would not deviate from the general patterns of nature for that epoch, but they *could*, if this were best for the occasion. Then, if these alternative possible patterns were massively actualized, one epoch could slowly evolve into another. The whole process primarily depends upon the creaturely responses of the occasions themselves, for the laws of nature merely articulate those patterns which happen to be massively adopted in a given epoch. But *some* input from God is also required. Hence Whitehead can write that "apart from some notion of imposed Law, the doctrine of immanence provides absolutely no reason why the universe should not be steadily relapsing into lawless chaos. In fact, the Universe, as understood in accordance with the doctrine of Immanence, should exhibit itself as including a stable actuality whose mutual implication with the remainder of things secures an inevitable trend toward order. The Platonic 'persuasion' is required" (AI 146f). Since his final solution to this difficult problem involves both the evolution of differing cosmic epochs and the role of God in supplying the ordering possibilities, notions not yet fully developed, or even anticipated, some uncertainty at this time is not to be wondered at.

In summary, we find the first two types of limitation, of logic and causation, belong to the metaphysical order. The third type of limitation, particularization, is assigned to God. God is also introduced as the principle of limitation restricting possibilities to those productive of value.

7. THE ONTOLOGICAL STATUS OF GOD

How is God as the principle of limitation to be understood within Whitehead's ontology? While affirming an underlying substantial activity both in the Lowell Lectures (e.g. SMW 70, 107) and in his later additions, he did not identify this activity with God, as Spinoza might have done, for then God would become the all-determiner. On the other hand, this was a general principle of limitation applying to all actual occasions, and hence could not simply be one mode among others of this underlying activity. Rather, it had to be a general attribute of the activity, since every mode was equally affected thereby. It is not the only attribute; Whitehead names a total of three: God as the principle of limitation, eternal possibility, and modal differentiation (SMW 177). As we shall see later, once Whitehead's philosophy is transposed on a more pluralistic basis, the first two become, with the underlying substantial activity, the three formative elements which jointly constitute the character of the actual temporal world (RM 88): God, the eternal objects, and creativity.

The theory of these three general attributes of the underlying substantial activity also provides an ontological basis, in terms of Whitehead's Spinozistic monism, for the three envisagements described in the "Triple Envisagement" addition (section 4). There we were concerned with what kinds of things an individual occasion envisages as there to be synthesized: (1) eternal objects, (2) "values to be obtained by a real togetherness of eternal objects, as envisaged in ideal situations," (3) "the actual matter of fact," i.e., the past actual occasions (SMW 105). The second envisagement corresponds to God, while the third leads to modal differentiation, once the shift in context is taken into account. Here Whitehead considers what the individual occasion envisages, there what the general properties of the underlying activity are. Because each occasion must take into account a different group of past actual occasions, each occasion is at least minimally different, and that ultimately produces the modal differentiation of the underlying activity.

Whitehead concludes his discussion of the principle of limitation with these words: "What further can be known about God must be sought in the region of particular experiences, and therefore rests on an empirical basis. In respect to the interpretation of these experiences, mankind have differed profoundly. He has been named respectively, Jehovah, Allah, Brahma[n], Father in Heaven, Order of Heaven, First Cause, Supreme Being, Chance. Each name corresponds to a system of thought derived from the experiences of those who have used it" (SMW 178f).[19] These few remarks generate the program for *Religion in the Making*. Since any further understanding of God rests upon mankind's interpretation of his religious experiences, it becomes necessary to survey reflectively the rational religions of the world (RM, chapters 1 & 2), restate the abstract understanding of God derived from the metaphysical view of the world (RM, chapter 3), and then show how this understanding can be supplemented by specific interpretations of religious experience (RM, chapter 4).

This practice of first stating the nature of God as implicated in the general metaphysical scheme, and then supplementing it with those insights derived from specific religious experience, is repeated both in *Process and Reality* (Pt. V) and in *Adventures of Ideas* (380f).

8. ABSTRACTION VS. CONCRETION

We would be doing Whitehead an injustice, however, were we to conclude this analysis of the chapter on "God" without discussing the other topics considered in this chapter besides God. Properly speaking, its primary topic is concretion, thus supplementing the other metaphysical chapter on abstraction. It is called "God" only because God is the principle of concretion, and the inclusion of God was a novel element in his philosophy.

The general principle of limitation is an "antecedent" limitation upon possibility prior to actualization. In addition "every actual occasion is a limitation imposed on possibility, . . . by virtue of this limitation the particular value of that shaped togetherness of things emerges . . . Actuality is through and through togetherness—togetherness of otherwise isolated eternal objects, and togetherness of all actual occasions." Actuality concerns "the concrete, i.e. that which has grown together" (SMW 174). From this consideration the word concrescence will later be coined for the process of growing together (AI 303). That word is not used yet, although "concretion" is. Although both terms refer to the process of rendering something concrete, "concrescence" when used carries the more precise additional meaning of many prehensions growing together into one.

Since each occasion is the togetherness both of the eternal objects and all the other actual occasions, the question arises as to just how these two types of entities are to be integrated within the occasion. In accordance with Whitehead's cherished ideal of coherence, each performs a necessary role for the other: "the entrant occasions lend their aspects to the [abstractive] hierarchies [of eternal objects] . . . and the hierarchies lend their forms to the occasions . . ." (SMW 175). This is the germ of the theory of perspectival elimination whereby an occasion is prehended only in terms of one of its aspects (PR 236), already outlined in the Lowell Lectures (SMW 65). We have also the theory that physical prehension is mediated by eternal objects, for the same eternal object can be ingredient both in the occasion prehended and in the prehending subject. By lending their aspects to their hierarchies, and thereby actualizing what was otherwise an unrealized eternal object, that "spatio-temporal modality" of the underlying activity, that past actual occasion, is thereby converted into a "categorical" determination. That is, it is no longer a conditional or potential determination of the supervening occasion, but has determined it to that extent. In like manner God renders what was metaphysically indeterminate categorically determinate (SMW 178), in that this divine determination must be included in the final determination of each occasion. By lending their forms to the occasions the hierarchies in turn "limit the entrant occasions to being entrant only under those forms" (SMW 175).

Even though Whitehead pioneered the notion of an asymmetrical relation, internal to one relatum but external to the other, with respect to the eternal objects (SMW 160), he retains the doctrine of the Lowell Lectures that every occasion is internally related to all the others, past, present, and future. This does not mean it is now internally related to the determinate actuality which some future occasion will in time become, but that it is internally related to what that future occasion now is abstractly: "The occasion a . . . holds within itself an indetermination in the form of a future, which has partial determination by reason of its inclusion in a and also has determinate spatio-temporal relatedness to a and to actual occasions of the past from a and of the present for a" (SMW 176).

Two sentences from the beginning of this paragraph hint at a possible shift in the understanding of prehension, although that term is here avoided. In the Lowell Lectures, prehension primarily means (unconscious) perception, ultimately deriving from "nature perceived" as the whole of nature in simultaneous duration with our perceiving, the primary topic of Whitehead's philsophy of nature. Now Whitehead writes: "Any one occasion a issues from other occasions which collectively form its *past*. It displays for itself other occasions which collectively form its *present*" (SMW 176). Once prehension is understood in terms of the way past occasions are constitutive of it, it becomes primarily a concept for causation, and only secondarily for perception. Also the notion of "display" becomes urgent, since Whitehead must explain how we appear to perceive nature simultaneous with ourselves, yet all that we are is derived from the past. He sketched just such a theory, introducing even the term "presentational immediacy" in his essay on "Time" delivered in September, 1926 (IS 244f), which was then fleshed out in the Barbour-Page Lectures on *Symbolism* the following spring.

Here the theory of "display" is explained in terms of the associated abstractive hierarchy: "It is in respect to its associated hierarchy, as displayed in this immediate present, that an occasion finds its own originality. It is that display which is its own contribution to the output of actuality" (SMW 176). Here the associated hierarchy is conceived as being objectified for the occasion such that it can be the means whereby its objects, clothed with aspects derived from past actual occasions, can "display" the present to the occasion. But the realization of that hierarchy is also its own original contribution, which becomes part of what it passes on to its successors. This is the germ of the theory that the satisfaction, subjectively felt, can be objectified as the superject for supervening occasions.

Following the procedure he adopted in "Abstraction," Whitehead first describes the occasion in its physical aspects alone,[20] then adds there a section (cf. SMW 170f), here a paragraph (SMW 176), discussing any additional mental aspects. Later in *Religion in the Making* and in "Time" (1926) this procedure is read into the occasions themselves, whereby for each (complete) occasion a "physical occasion" is superseded by a "mental occasion." These unrealized eternal objects require a reference to some actual occasion or other, which provides the means whereby there is a "graded envisagement" of these eternal objects. Apparently they are graded with respect to their relevance as alternatives to that which is experienced as fact. This requirement suggests the possibility of conceptual derivation, whereby (unrealized) eternal objects are derived from the past occasions prehended, although Whitehead allows for the possibility of future occasions: "This abrupt realisation requires *either* a reference of the basic objects of the finite hierarchy to determinate occasions other than *a* (as their situations, in past, present, future); *or* requires a realisation of these eternal objects in determinate relationships, but under the aspect of exemption from inclusion in the spatio-temporal scheme of relatedness between actual occasions" (SMW 176).

Actual occasions derive possibilities, including possibilities of value, not from God but from each other. God is not an actuality for this early theory, and only actualities are prehensible. God is not a mode of the underlying substantial activity which is peculiarly situated so as to be prehensible by all. Rather, God achieves a timeless antecedent ordering of the eternal objects with each other, an effect which is actualized by each actual occasion as it prehends its world. Since God's role is purely timeless, requiring no reaction from the world, he can be conceived as simply a principle. Moreover, were God to be conceived as a person within this early ontology, he would either be the underlying activity, and then the sole determiner, or he would be just one among the many modal actualities. God as the antecedent limitation on the world could only be a principle.

NOTES

1. If we find evidence for Whitehead's affirmation of God's existence only in the final paragraph of this address, it may be because this paragraph was added when the address was placed after the chapter on "God." The two previous paragraphs, articulating the

religious vision, without which life would be but "a bagatelle of transient experience" (SMW 192), make a fitting climax to the address.

2. Letter to his son, July 19, 1925, quoted by Victor Lowe in "Whitehead's Gifford Lectures," *Southern Journal of Philosophy* 7/4 (Winter, 1969–70), 331a.

3. *Harvard Crimson*, April 6, 1925.

4. Henry Nelson Wieman discerned such leanings already in Whitehead's philosophy of nature (PNK, CN). See his *Religious Experience and Scientific Method* (New York: Macmillan, 1926), pp. 176–84, especially 180f: ". . . his insistence that the event, rather than the object, is the basic fact of nature and that nature is marked by a 'creative advance' lends itself most readily to the religious interpretation."

5. *Dialogues of Alfred North Whitehead*, as recorded by Lucien Price (Boston: Little, Brown, 1954), p. 151.

6. Letter to Victor Lowe of September 26, 1959, as recorded in *Understanding Whitehead* (Baltimore: The Johns Hopkins Press, 1962), p. 232. See also Lowe, "A. N. W.: A Biographical Perspective," *Process Studies* 12/3 (Fall, 1982), 137–47.

7. "Whitehead: From Agnostic to Rationalist," *Journal of Religion* 57/4 (October 1977), 376–85, at 378f.

8. Victor Lowe, *Understanding Whitehead*, p. 231.

9. Bertrand Russell, *Portraits from Memory* (New York: Simon and Schuster, 1956), p. 96.

10. See the dedication to *Principles of Natural Knowledge*.

11. *Portraits from Memory*, p. 92.

12. *Alfred North Whitehead: Essays on His Philosophy*, ed. George L. Kline (Englewood Cliffs, N.J.: Prentice-Hall, 1963), p. 16.

13. For the overcoming of evil by conceptual supplementation, see pp. 299–304 of my essay, "Divine Persuasion and the Triumph of Good," in *Process Philosophy and Christian Thought*, ed. Delwin Brown, Ralph E. James, Jr., and Gene Reeves (Indianapolis: Bobbs-Merrill, 1971).

14. This meaning of "eternal activity" must be carefully distinguished from the mere atemporal objectivity of the eternal objects. It is the nontemporality I sought to specify in "The Non-Temporality of Whitehead's God," *International Philosophical Quarterly* 13/3 (September, 1973), 347–76.

15. See the theory of the Lowell Lectures analyzed above in chapter two in terms of "Bodily Events."

16. This sentence illustrates the fact that the early Whitehead, when confronted with the ambiguity of "prehension" as meaning

both unconscious perception and synthesis, favors the latter interpretation. The later Whitehead would speak of "individual prehension" and "concrescence," respectively. But the term "concrescence"
had not yet been coined.

17. From "The Architecture of Theories," *Collected Papers of Charles
Sanders Peirce*, ed. Charles Hartshorne and Paul Weiss, vol. 6 (Cambridge: Harvard University Press, 1935), p. 12.

18. *Whitehead's Philosophy of Religion* (The Hague: Mouton, 1971),
pp. 25–42, though with this caveat (p. 24, n. 26): "I am not certain
that the interpretation I make of these types of order is precisely
what Whitehead intends in this passage. His discussion of them is
extremely short and cryptic; their meaning is far from evident. But
he must mean something by these remarks. And the interpretation
I do make of them may be justified in terms of what he says elsewhere
in *Science and the Modern World* and *Religion in the Making*." My
alternative interpretation is offered in the same spirit of tentativeness.

19. "Chance" is not absent from this list; allowance is made for
an atheistic interpretation of this principle of limitation.

Two of the terms, Brahma and the Order of Heaven, were already
listed in an earlier designation of the ultimate (PR 92).

20. "Also for the present I am excluding cognitive experience"
(SMW 175).

SIX

Religion in the Making

ON July 19, 1925, Whitehead wrote his son North in England that he had agreed to give "another course of Lowell Lectures in Boston next year on 'Science and Religion,' i.e. on the scientific criticism of religion." [1] As *Religion in the Making* developed, however, the problem of the identification of God with the principle of limitation took precedence. His analysis of the principle of limitation had been purely metaphysical, and he questioned whether anything further about its nature could be determined metaphysically (SMW 178). There had been no exploration of man's religious experience, yet "God" is fundamentally a religious term. It signifies that which is supremely worthy of worship. Any justification of the identification of God with the principle of limitation required such an exploration.

This concern is reflected in the structure of *Religion in the Making.* First, the contribution religion can make to metaphysics is identified in terms of dogma, articulated in the development of rational religion. The meaning of this dogma is then criticized by means of a metaphysics of "ordinary experience" outlined in chapter 3, while the way in which dogma, so criticized, can supplement "ordinary metaphysics is explored in the final chapter.

We will first consider the nature of this metaphysics that Whitehead proposes in 1926, and then explore the way God and religious dogma are discussed in the light of this metaphysics. Here we must begin by taking cognizance of the one major shift he made from the first metaphysical sketch of *Science and the Modern World,* namely, the shift from monism to pluralism.

1. THE METAPHYSICS OF PLURALISM

As we have already seen, temporal atomization as such generates a pressure towards pluralism by accentuating present activities of realization, which Whitehead acknowledges by naming them "*actual occasions.*" Nevertheless, these actual occasions are merely modes of the underlying substantial activity.

A key factor preventing Whitehead from espousing pluralism, we suspect, is that it would entail postulating God as a separate actuality. He was not prepared to do so, as long as God could then be conceived as the external creator of the world. This philosophy does not reject all notions of creation, but the creation must be purely immanent, in terms of a "creative advance of nature," which bears many affinities with Bergson's creative evolution. To be sure, he eschews all reference to creativity in speaking of an underlying substantial activity, but it is very much like Bergson's *élan vital* having the events or actual occasions as its by-products. Except for the more dynamic notion of "activity," Whitehead relies here primarily on the conceptuality of Spinoza. Possibly he wished to avoid any suggestion that creativity could function as some external creator.

Whitehead opposes the idea of an external creator. He denies that the whole of religious experience, taken generally, contributes any evidence for "God in any sense transcendent or creative" (RM 84). Such an external creator would be very much like a causal nature behind the scenes brought in to explain apparent nature. Whitehead had rejected the idea of a causal nature in his rejection of the bifurcation of nature. "The easy assumption that there is an ultimate reality which, in some unexplained way, is to be appealed to for the removal of perplexity, constitutes the great refusal of rationality to assert its rights" (SMW 92). The notion of God as creator, entirely different from the world and known only as its creator, was just such an assumption. He would be exempt from the basic metaphysical principles, and hence rationally unintelligible.

On traditional assumptions, divine creation and human freedom were considered quite compatible. God is conceived as creating the underlying being of the world, and/or the being of each agent individually, who then is free to act. But Whitehead sees creation in process terms, primarily in the act of bringing novelty into being. Each event which comes into existence never existed before. If its creation is to be vested in some external creator, then not only do we have complete divine determinism, but "the evil of the world is in conformity with the nature of God" (RM 92).

For these reasons Whitehead conceives of whatever creative activity there is as wholly immanent within the process itself. As long as this activity was conceived as a single activity, its immanence could be preserved only by adopting a complete monism. If such an *élan vital* were coupled with a real plurality of actual occasions, that *élan vital* would become the one source of many actualities, and this could be explained only by assuming it to be their external creator.

In this philosophy pluralism was possible only if the *élan vital*, the creative advance of nature, could be pluralized. This Whitehead finally achieved in *Religion in the Making* by retaining the substance/ mode distinction, but thinking of it as applying to each individual actual occasion separately. Instead of there being one activity and many modes, for each occasion there is just one activity and one mode, the outcome of that activity. The mode is the creature, that one emergent fact, which is coupled with the creativity which produced it. But if the immanence of this creativity is to be preserved, it cannot be separated from the creature it creates. "There are not two actual entities, the creativity and the creature. There is only one entity which is the self-creating creature" (RM 99). The creativity must be conceived in terms of the occasion itself, "as the cause of itself, its own creative act" (RM 98).

Thus the reconciliation of creativity and the demands of pluralism can only be achieved by introducing this strange and novel concept of 'self-creation.' We must recognize Whitehead's venturesomeness in being willing to adopt such a daring concept. He could only fall back upon Spinoza's endorsement of "*causa sui*," used within a monistic context with no appreciation for the dynamics of creation. In his mature metaphysics this self-creation can be more fully supported, but at the time it was introduced, self-creation could only be a seminal idea, a programmatic slogan, provoking further reflection. To many it must have seemed quite queer, since creation was traditionally reserved for an uncreated creator creating *ex nihilo*. For such a creator to be self-created would be quite nonsensical.

The shift from monism to pluralism required a reconception of the three attributes of the underlying substantial activity: God, the eternal objects, and modal diversity. The last one is no longer an attribute of reality, since now the actual occasions are the final realities. Instead of an underlying substantial activity and three metaphysical attributes, Whitehead now has the temporal world of actual occasions with three formative elements which jointly constitute its character: creativity, the ideal entities, and God (RM 88).

In this new pluralistic vision actual occasions form the ontological foundation, and creativity assumes the status of a formative element. It is described as that "whereby the actual world has its character of temporal passage into novelty" (RM 88). Since God is nontemporal and unchanging, creativity is not ascribed to him; it is a formative element, not of God, but of the temporal world.

The eternal objects, now designated as 'ideal entities,' or 'forms,' are conceived exactly as they were in *Science and the Modern World.* Their derivative existential status is now differently explained, since they are no longer dependent upon the underlying substantial activity but upon the actual occasions. Initially the eternal objects were conceived to be ingredient in the underlying activity, and thence made available to the occasions, but now they are synthesized directly within each occasion in differing grades of relevance. To insure complete relatedness, so that each occasion might include any eternal object, Whitehead stipulates: "Each such instance [actual occasion] embraces the whole, omitting nothing, whether it be ideal form or actual fact" (RM 108).

The term "ideal entities" may have replaced "eternal objects" because the contrasting term, "enduring objects," was not needed. "Prehension" and "ingression" are also avoided, possibly because Whitehead was undecided whether these two concepts were utterly diverse (as in SMW), or whether they represented two modes of ingredience that could be distinguished in terms of physical and conceptual prehension (as in PR). For the latter work "ingression" is simply a convenient converse for conceptual prehension, no longer needed as such.

The shift to pluralism also focussed Whitehead's attention upon the nature of an actual occasion's internal process. As long as all activity was ascribed to an underlying substantial activity, occasions could be only prehensive unities, the passive by-products of this activity. Now if all creativity is to be vested in the occasions themselves, they must be active, with their own inner processes. But how to conceive this inner dynamic in a way consistent with temporal atomicity was a persistent problem which generated several provisional answers up to the final theory of concrescence in part III of *Process and Reality.* The metaphysics of *Religion in the Making* sketches the earliest of these attempted solutions.

Many process philosophers, following the lead of Charles Hartshorne, have abandoned any attempt to devise a theory of internal process for occasions on the grounds that any such theory would be ultimately inconsistent with temporal atomicity.[2] Whitehead, I contend, did find such a theory, but only after considerable searching which we need to trace. Other process philosophers have been spared this search because they have adopted in effect an alternative theory of becoming which identifies becoming and change.

In his mature philosophy Whitehead sharply distinguishes between becoming and change. Actual occasions become, but do not change (PR 73, 80). Change involves at least two successive occasions, for it is the measure of differences between them. "The fundamental meaning of the notion of 'change' is 'the difference between actual occasions comprised in some determinate event' " (PR 73). If becoming were then to be identified with change, then becoming would be external to each individual event. Each occasion could still be accorded its measure of creativity, however, by understanding this creativity as the additional determination which the occasion imposes upon the indeterminate situation it inherits. Thus in reaction to causal determinism, Hartshorne asserts that since all the past conditions impinging upon a given occasion do not completely determine it, there must be some modicum of additional determination which the occasion in its own creativity imposes upon itself. Then there is one single creative unification of all these causal factors that results in the new occasion. Reality thus comes into being by droplets, as each occasion succeeds each other. This perpetual change of occasions, each introducing its own creative novelty, is what is understood as becoming.

This solution was not adopted by Whitehead, who was seeking for some sort of dynamic activity intrinsic to each occasion. Hartshorne's solution also differs from the theory of *Religion in the Making*, for other reasons. In that early theory Whitehead makes one assumption Hartshorne avoids. He assumes that the past causal conditions are ingredient in the present occasions in a distinct phase. Whitehead has a two-step process: first the *ground*, the unity of past conditions, and then the creative addition, the *consequent*. The internal process is thus a transition (or supersession) from ground to consequent. In Whitehead's later theory this is a form of the internal supersession of determinate states excluded by temporal atomicity once that theory has been extended to include all acts of becoming (first in PR II.1; cf. PR 69). (This exclusion still permits the succession of genetic phases, since incomplete phases are indeterminate, having only imperfect unity.) In *Religion in the Making* and in the 1926 essay on "Time" Whitehead had not yet extended his argument about temporal atomicity to cover other acts of becoming. In particular it was not applied to the consequent, which was considered to be added somehow outside time.

In the chapter on "Abstraction," Whitehead had analyzed the character of a "natural event," recognizing that this was a convenient abstraction from a complete actual occasion (SMW 170). The successor term for "natural event" in *Religion in the Making* is "physical occasion." As before he holds: "The most complete concrete fact is dipolar, physical and mental" (RM 114). As Nathaniel Lawrence indicates, this is in sharp contrast to his philosophy of nature, where "the most concrete fact capable of separate discrimination is the [natural] event" (CN 189).[3] Yet it is difficult to determine whether Whitehead at this time intended to espouse panpsychism in the precise sense of holding that every concrete occasion would possess a mental occasion. It may be that Whitehead preferred not to declare himself either way and chose his words very carefully.

If every concrete occasion were dipolar, as panpsychism would require, why is the complex conceptuality of *Religion in the Making* retained? Why is not 'ground' simply identified with 'physical occasion' in all instances? (Relative to a mental occasion, to be sure, its physical occasion acts as its ground, but this would not be true of a physical occasion considered all by itself.) It might well be, however, that Whitehead has not yet made the connection between novelty and mentality that his later theory makes. While every concrete occasion would have some degree of mentality, if this is not identified with novelty, it must also have a consequent to insure the possibility of novelty, as required by the creative advance.

On the other hand, Whitehead does not clearly say that all concrete facts are dipolar, only those that are *most complete*. And it is only of those most complete occasions that "the proportion of importance, as shared between the two poles, may vary from negligibility to dominance of either pole" (RM 114). This would leave room for the possibility that some concrete facts are incomplete, lacking all mentality, though this claim is never explicitly made. If so, some actualities might be purely physical occasions, having ground and consequent, but no attached mental occasion. In general, purely mental occasions are not concrete, i.e. independently actual, since each "is derivative from its physical counterpart" (RM 99). (Whitehead holds his doctrine to be entirely neutral "on the existence of purely spiritual beings other than God" (RM 107). If such non-derivative mental occasions should exist, they would be concrete along with any pure physical occasions.)

If not all concrete occasions have mentality, then they require the polarity of ground and consequent, in order to provide for the creative advance of nature. Otherwise, from purely physical occasions there would be no way in which more complex occasions could evolve. The two-fold conceptuality of *Religion in the Making*, having both ground and consequent, physical and mental occasions, can most easily be explained on the grounds that not all concrete occasions are dipolar, although the opposite assumption is also quite possible.

Vibrations might be considered purely physical occasions which are fully explicable in terms of ground and consequent (RM 111f). In the metaphysical sketch of chapter 3, where Whitehead is intent upon enumerating all the furniture of the universe, including minds, the contrast between mental and physical occasions is discussed. In chapter 4, where Whitehead is primarily concerned about the necessity for God's existence as the ultimate source of the novel consequent, mental occasions are ignored. They could be metaphysically super-fluous, as there might have been a time in the history of the earth when only physical occasions existed. Nevertheless even such physical occasions would require God.

In *Religion in the Making*, Whitehead understands mentality primarily in terms of analyticity. Since the physical occasion is the synthesis of its entire world, the derivate mental occasion may be conceived as the analysis of this synthesis. It possesses an analytic power capable of raising features of that synthesis to a discriminate awareness. "Ideal forms thus synthesized into a mental occasion are termed concepts. Concepts meet blind experience with an analytic force. Their synthesis with physical occasion, as ground, is the perceptive analysis of the blind physical occasion . . ." (RM 113).

Here Whitehead's first theory of consciousness is introduced. "It has the character of being an analysis of physical experience by synthesis with the concepts involved in the mentality" (RM 114). This is close to the final theory he adopts, that consciousness is the way the contrast between a conceptual feeling (specifically, a prop-ositional feeling) and its appropriate physical feeling is felt, but there are several intermediate theories in terms of contrasts between af-firmative and negative conceptual feelings. Here Whitehead is some-what ambiguous, for "such consciousness is a mental occasion" (RM 114), and we may readily think of the mental occasion as composed solely of concepts. At least this is true of God, the only purely mental actuality we know to be existent. As long as it is possible to think of consciousness primarily in conceptual terms, then God as conscious could be conceived in exclusively conceptual terms as the highest instance of the mental occasion, singularly underived.

Following his earlier theory, Whitehead sees physical occasions as acts of blind perceptivity (RM 98); in the earlier language, as prehensive unities. Mental occasions are derivative from these physical occasions, being entirely concerned with their analysis and reconstitution. The Cartesian division into mind and bodies is explained by routes of occasions: those which exemplify the transmission from physical occasion to physical occasion form bits of matter, those emphasizing the transmission from mental occasion to mental occasion form bits of mind (RM 105).

This solution has two major consequences: (1) Since mental occasions are entirely dependent on physical occasions, there is an influence of the physical upon the mental, but there might be no corresponding influence of the mental on the physical. At this stage in his theory Whitehead runs the risk of epiphenomenalism, even though this is contrary to his own conviction (SMW 78), simply because the logic of the argument requires it. Later this epiphenomenalism is overcome by conceiving of mental activity not as a passive, derivative by-product of physical activity, but as a necessary ingredient in the development even of the physical synthesis of an occasion.

(2) While every complete actual occasion is dipolar, the physical component of each occasion seems to follow immediately upon its predecessor physical occasion. Thus, there is no temporal duration, at least none in "physical time," in which the mental occasion can occur. Later on in Whitehead's mature theory, this will mean that the internal process of an epochal occasion does not occur in "physical time."

2. RELIGION AND DOGMA

Now the metaphysics we have just sketched on the basis of the third chapter was not fully anticipated by Whitehead when he embarked on the study resulting in *Religion in the Making*. In particular he did not anticipate his critique of monism and thus did not expect any further development in his conception of God beyond what had already been achieved: that God was an attribute of the underlying substantial activity as the principle limiting indiscriminate pluralism to permit the concretion of actuality. "What further can be known about God must be sought in the region of particular experiences, and therefore rests on an empirical basis" (SMW 179).

Thus the program of *Religion in the Making* was to interrogate the religious experience of mankind to see what further could be said concerning the nature of God. Whitehead does not restrict himself to a particular religious tradition, such as Christianity, but means to take account of the full sweep of religious experience as it was then understood.

Some general descriptions of religion are offered: "Religion is what the individual does with his own solitariness" (RM 16). This has often been criticized as overemphasizing whatever practices a single individual might engage in to the neglect of the social dimensions of religion, but Whitehead is here concerned with the individual's own determination of his final beliefs, however much social reinforcement he may receive. "Everyone must do his own believing, as he must do his own dying," Luther once said, adding: "but that does not prevent us from shouting encouragement to one another." "Solitariness" does not mean solitude so much as individual appropriation, as another description indicates: "Religion is the art and theory of the internal life of man, so far as it depends on the man himself and on what is permanent in the nature of things" (RM 16). Such art and theory focuses one's life, ridding it of unwanted irrelevance, which is Whitehead's later general definition of "dirt" (AI 343). Thus "religion is [the] force of belief cleansing the inward parts" (RM 15).[4]

In speculating about the emergence of religion in human history, Whitehead considers four factors: ritual, emotion, belief, rationalization (RM 18). For our purposes, only the last two are important. Religious beliefs may have arisen in many different ways; it is their systematic coordination and mutual criticism which interests us: "Rational religion is religion whose beliefs and rituals have been reorganized with the aim of making it the central element in a coherent ordering of life" (RM 30). Such rational religion stands between abstract metaphysics and the special principles which apply to only some areas of life. On the one hand, religion bases itself upon a small selection of the common experiences of the race. On the other, it claims universal validity for its concepts. "The doctrines of rational religion aim at being that metaphysics which can be derived from the supernormal experience of mankind in its moments of finest insight" (RM 31). These doctrines Whitehead designates as dogmas, using this term positively, although aware of its pejorative connotations (RM 124).

This intimate relationship of dogma and metaphysics should alert us to the novelty of Whitehead's approach. In his system dogma is not to be defined as the official teaching of some church, nor as the systematic presentation of the truths of sacred scripture. Nor is dogma in some sense derived from revelation. A dogma is a particular kind of metaphysical statement. "The dogmas of religion are the attempts to formulate in precise terms the truths disclosed in the religious experience of mankind" (RM 57). As such, a dogma seeks metaphysical generality: "A dogma is the precise enunciation of a general truth, divested so far as possible from particular exemplification" (RM 122). However, its precise expression can never be final (RM 125).

Since "dogma" is customarily associated with theological statements, Whitehead may be understood to differ from the long-standing theological tradition which seeks to coordinate theology and philosophy by claiming some independent, supplementary role for theology. It is sometimes claimed that theology yields propositions that are inaccessible to rational assessment by philosophy (e.g., Thomism), or that particular truths about God's interaction with man are less abstract than those of philosophy,[5] or that theology is an existential illumination in fact for that which philosophy presents merely as possibility (e.g. Bultmann). For Whitehead both ordinary philosophical statements and dogmas are coordinated in terms of metaphysics, by which he means "the science which seeks to discover the general ideas which are indispensably relevant to the analysis of everything that happens" (RM 82n).

Dogmas differ from other metaphysical statements only in terms of the scope of their empirical warrant. Here we may distinguish between "ordinary" metaphysics and "religious" metaphysics. "Ordinary" metaphysics derives its support from the common, everyday experience of humanity, the kind that everyone can verify. The dogmas of "religious" experience are derived from the insights of human experience at its best. While the experiential warrant for such metaphysical statements is exceptional, their rational validity is not. They must be coordinated with ordinary metaphysical statements, mutually criticizing one another.

On the one hand, Whitehead is discounting any privileged status dogmas may claim, such as in terms of divine inspiration or revelation. On the other hand, he is not content to ground metaphysics solely in ordinary experience. The total range of human experience must be taken into account (cf. PR 337f) insofar as it can yield insight into the generic nature of the whole. Also, as Whitehead later speculates, the ordinary consciousness of today was once quite intermittent and exceptional among our remote ancestors. What is

exceptional in human experience today might become ordinary tomorrow. These exceptional experiences, if properly criticized, may
yield clues concerning the structure of reality in its most ultimate
reaches.

This general strategy of *Religion in the Making*, of supplementing
the metaphysics of ordinary experience (chapter 3) with a metaphysics
of religious experience (chapter 4), is continued in *Process and Reality*.
There the first four parts describe the metaphysics of ordinary experience, while Part V uses a common rational basis with the rest
of the book, but a different empirical basis: "Any cogency of argument
entirely depends upon elucidation of somewhat exceptional elements
in our conscious experience—those elements which may roughly be
classed together as religious and moral intuitions" (PR 343).[6]

The example of *Process and Reality*, however, is likely to be misleading. For Part V introduces a whole new temporal dimension to
God's being, his consequent nature, which is hardly anticipated in
the previous parts of the book. This is presented as a genuine
supplementation to the ordinary metaphysics, based on religious
experience. Originally Whitehead may have anticipated just such an
outcome for *Religion in the Making*, but as things developed, the
doctrine of God based on ordinary metaphysics and that based on
religious dogma agree in all important respects. While religious experience "contributes its own independent *evidence*, which metaphysics must take account of in framing its description" (RM 76,
italics added), it need not result in different conclusions. In *Religion
in the Making*, at least, both avenues of approach lead to the same
result, gained by mutual criticism of each other.

At first glance this congruence, if not virtual identification, of dogma
and metaphysics seems surprising, since the depictions of God as an
abstract, impersonal principle give way to a clear affirmation of God's
personal actuality in the latter chapters. We are likely to understand
this shift in terms of an increasing appropriation of Western religious
traditions. But in considering religious evidence Whitehead carefully
directs our attention to what is common to all the major traditions:
"Thus religious experience [as broadly conceived] cannot be taken
as contributing to metaphysics any direct evidence for a personal
God in any sense transcendent or creative" (RM 84; cf. 60).

Nor can we argue that the concept of God presented in chapter
3 is simply the impersonal principle of limitation, becoming personal
in the final chapter, either because God can be indifferently described
as either impersonal or personal, or because Whitehead now allows
for the supplementation of metaphysics by Western dogma. For while

most of the personal description of God is relegated to the final chapter, and a good many of Whitehead's statements about God in chapter 3 can be interpreted impersonally, not all of them can be. For example, he speaks of "the purpose of God" (RM 97), or of God's "harmony of apprehension" (RM 114), "apprehension" being a term otherwise carefully restricted to consciousness. Moreover, none of the statements in chapter 3 require a purely impersonal interpretation. I think we must conceive of the God of ordinary metaphysics as just as much a personal subjectivity as the God of religious dogma.

The hypothesis which may possibly explain the text proposes that Whitehead may have formulated the basic content of the first two lectures under the continued, perhaps still unexamined, assumption of the monism derived from *Science and the Modern World*, only shifting to a pluralist stance when he worked out the metaphysics of ordinary experience in some detail. In both periods he sees a congruence between metaphysics and the broad deliverances of religious experience, but the detailed contents of this congruence shifts.

In his monistic period, God is conceived as an impersonal attribute of the underlying substantial activity. Like metaphysics rational religion is "an endeavor to find something permanent and intelligible by which to interpret the confusion of immediate detail" (RM 47f). This it finds in a "formative principle" which has "a character of permanent rightness." "This religious experience does not include any direct intuition of a definite person, or individual" (RM 60), for that is only true of some traditions. "But there is a large consensus, on the part of those who have rationalized their outlook, in favour of the concept of a rightness in things, partially conformed to and partially disregarded" (RM 65). This, Whitehead is convinced, is his own principle of limitation proposed in *Science and the Modern World*, as adapted to the special world of values discerned by rational religion. Just as the principle of limitation determines the cosmological constants for the concretion of this actual world, so it also determines the worth or worthlessness of different ideals of conduct.

3. GOD AS A FORMATIVE ELEMENT

With the shift to pluralism, God as "formative principle" (RM 59), becomes one of the three "formative elements" of the temporal world, along with creativity and the realm of ideal entities (eternal objects). "Such formative elements are not themselves actual and passing; they are the factors which are either non-actual or non-temporal, disclosed in the analysis of what is both actual and temporal" (RM 87). The principle of limitation or concretion now becomes "the actual but non-temporal entity whereby the indetermination of mere creativity is transmuted into a determinate freedom" (RM 88).

There is clearly a shift from the monism of "the underlying substantial activity" and the impersonal principle of limitation of *Science and the Modern World* to the pluralism of "a multiplicity of occasions of actualization" (RM 88), analyzed in terms of three formative elements. It is more problematic, however, whether this shift took place *during* the composition of *Religion in the Making*. That hypothesis may best explain the contrast between the stress on an impersonal understanding of God in the first two chapters, and the willingness to speak of God as personal in the last two chapters, though conceivably other explanations might be found. Some may find this shift to pluralism in the midst of his writing rather sudden, but it is no more sudden than his espousal of theism in *Science and the Modern World*, or his later espousal of divine temporality in *Process and Reality*.

It may be questioned whether Whitehead would shift his stance on such a basic issue without revising what he had already written. If *Religion in the Making* were the only book in question, we could well wonder, but our evidence shows that Whitehead's thought underwent a comparable shift both in *Science and the Modern World* and in *Process and Reality*. Were Whitehead a professional philosopher, we might suppose his commitment to monism could be long-standing, but under the circumstances it seems Whitehead adopted monism as the only theory consistent with the event-theory of the Lowell Lectures, and these reasons now no longer held.

While God is now designated as an "actual entity," it would be a mistake to conceive of a general realm of all actual entities, exemplifying the metaphysical principles, to which God and all the actual occasions belong. The proper context here is the total world of the "epochal occasions." It is more accurate to think of God as one of its formative elements, more like creativity and the eternal objects. Nevertheless, God is the one formative element which is also actual. What does that mean in this context?

A physical occasion is described as "a complete concretion of physical relationships in the unity of a blind perceptivity" (RM 113). An actual occasion is what Whitehead once called a "prehensive unity" or "unification," the synthesis of all prehensive relations to other events to constitute the actuality of one event. With the advent of temporal atomism, emphasis was laid upon the *activity* of this synthesizing as marking how the occasion was actual. To be actual meant to engage in an activity of synthesizing.

Once monism is abandoned, God as principle of limitation loses the status of being one of the three attributes of the underlying substantial activity. Its status becomes distinctly problematic, since it is not a formative element in the sense in which creativity or the eternal objects might be. If it were to remain an abstract principle, it could only be regarded as a complex eternal object. (There would only be actualities or eternal objects, at least until the hybrid entity of propositions is invented.) In that case God would lose his distinctiveness, and particularly any sense in which God is something over against the realm of eternal objects as their final limitation, determining which of them can participate in concretion.

At this point Whitehead recognized that two kinds of active synthesis were possible. Along with the temporal syntheses of past actual occasions there could also be one actual synthesis of the entire realm of eternal objects, thereby determining them into possibilities for concretion, and grading them in terms of their relevance to the process of actualization. Such a synthesis would be as actual as the temporal syntheses, but would be unlike these actual occasions in being strictly nontemporal, since the eternal objects have no necessary relationship to their temporal instantiations. By this means God becomes the one nontemporal actual entity.

Since God is nontemporal as well as actual, he must be the synthesis of everything that is not temporal, thus, of all the ideal entities or eternal objects. "God, who is the ground antecedent to transition, must include all possibilities of physical value conceptually, thereby holding the ideal forms apart in equal conceptual realization of knowledge. Thus, as concepts, they are grasped together in the synthesis of omniscience" (RM 147).

While Whitehead is reticent about noting the difference, this is not quite the classical understanding of omniscience, which includes the knowledge of future contingents. His concept of God fashioned here in *Religion in the Making* breaks with the classical model of a wholly self-sufficient knower of the world that requires this knowledge of future contingents even though such knowledge is incompatible with creaturely freedom. Nevertheless Whitehead conceives of God as omniscient, as knowing (nontemporally) all possibilities, as well as knowing all actualities in terms of their atemporal forms. It is not clear how God would know which of these alternative forms will be actualized, but this may be a problem we raise by hindsight.

4. *RELIGION IN THE MAKING* AND THE CONSEQUENT NATURE OF GOD

This last paragraph betrays my assumption that in *Religion in the Making* Whitehead did not conceive God to have a consequent nature. Some careful scholars have found it this to be early.[7] For example, John Cobb writes: "Like most of the rest of the ideas about God in *Process and Reality*, it [the fourth phase whereby God's consequent experience returns to the world (PR 351)] was foreshadowed in *Religion in the Making*." For "after *Religion in the Making*, nothing really new is added to the doctrine of God."[8]

Our disagreement may be largely semantic. In *Religion in the Making* God is personal, conscious, dynamic, and possibly even receptive to the temporal world, features which in Whitehead's final vision can only be ascribed to the consequent nature. If it is this foreshadowing of the consequent nature that is meant, then the consequent nature is already present in *Religion in the Making*. I have in mind a much narrower specification for the consequent nature: the ascription of physical feeling to God, allowing for the temporal/nontemporal contrast of God's two natures. This is the precise conceptual means whereby Whitehead could render the vision of *Religion in the Making* more intelligible, but it was not discovered until much later.

The specific issue turns on the introduction of divine physical feeling. In the latter chapters of *Religion in the Making* Whitehead conceived of God, I propose, as the nontemporal synthesis of the infinitude of pure conceptual feeling. Yet this nontemporal synthesis was far more dynamic and far more inclusive of finite actuality than we usually suppose, for we have been subjected to the critique and limitation the primordial nature has received by being contrasted with the consequent nature. In emphasizing the dynamic character of divine temporality, the character of divine nontemporality has been reduced to that which is purely static.

Is dynamic nontemporality possible? Perhaps not by the standards of the final argument, just as a purely conceptual divine consciousness is not finally possible (PR 345). Yet what Whitehead holds to be finally impossible may well be his teaching along the way, and it is this matter of consciousness that may well have prompted the later discovery of the consequent nature. As I propose, from the third chapter of *Religion in the Making* on, God was conceived to be a synthesis of pure forms or a concrescence of purely conceptual feeling, while at the same time held to be fully conscious. That was possible in terms of Whitehead's various theories of consciousness, up to the penultimate one:[9] ". . . all forms of consciousness arise from ways of integration of propositional feelings with other feelings, either physical feelings [with respect to actual occasions] or conceptual feelings [with respect to God] " (PR 256). The ultimate theory, couched in terms of "intellectual feelings," excludes that last permissive clause: *all* conscious feelings, without exception, require synthesis with physical feeling (PR 266f). If so, any divine concrescence of purely conceptual feeling can only be unconscious. If God is to be conscious, he must have physical feeling, comprising a consequent nature. This development probably comes quite late in the composition of *Process and Reality*, and may be the last step taken before the presentation of the Gifford Lectures in June, 1928.[10]

This is one way we can explain why the consequent nature is only mentioned three times prior to the final ten pages of *Process and Reality* (PR 12f, 31, 32), after the exalted language of *Religion in the Making* describing God's involvement in the world. It could perhaps be explained another way: following the strategy of the earlier book, with its contrast between the metaphysics of ordinary experience (chapter 3) and the metaphysics of religious experience (chapter 4), Whitehead could have decided to concentrate solely on ordinary experience in the first four parts of *Process and Reality* requiring God only in his primordial nature, while reserving the metaphysics of religious experience to Part V, which introduces the consequent nature. Something like this seems to be his strategy in *Adventures of Ideas*. That religious metaphysics is reserved for the end may be inferred from a sentence already quoted to the effect that this final argument entirely depends upon elucidation of the religious elements in our experience (PR 343).

Such may well have been Whitehead's intention when he drafted the original Gifford lectures during the summer of 1927, for this sentence seems to be part of the draft. All of this is also consistent with a later introduction of the consequent nature. (The reason *Adventures of Ideas* has this particular structure can be explained another way: if Whitehead were dissatisfied with his own efforts at integrating the two natures, he may have chosen to deal with them separately.) What is not consistent in this interpretation, perhaps, is the way Whitehead refers to God in Parts I–IV: sometimes as "the primordial nature of God," sometimes as "the non-temporal actual entity" or as "the primordial actuality". The first would be most appropriate if a systematic contrast with the consequent nature were then part of Whitehead's conceptuality. The latter formulations would be most misleading, since they suggest an understanding of God devoid of any temporal or physical feelings. Since I take Whitehead originally to have conceived of God as a concrescence of pure conceptual feeling, such descriptions would be most appropriate, while the contrastive term, "primordial nature" could have been introduced along with the later discovery of the consequent nature. (All mention of either contrastive term, "primordial nature" or "consequent nature," outside Part V could well be later insertions into the text.)

The issue here may be a very narrow one, but it is hardly trivial, for it affects our interpretation of the composition of *Process and Reality*. For the rest of this chapter we shall be analyzing seven passages from *Religion in the Making* which seem to imply the presence of the consequent nature in Whitehead's thinking. I shall challenge that reading, not because it does not make sense of those passages, but because it does not make the best sense out of the composition of *Process and Reality*. There the consequent nature seems to arise out of problems Whitehead is then grappling with, not as something he brought with him from *Religion in the Making*. It may well be that some of these passages can be explained better in terms of a consequent nature; my only point will be that Whitehead did not need the conceptual device of divine physical feeling to say what he did here.

These are the principal passages intimating the presence of a consequent nature for God:

1. Since God is actual, He must include in himself a synthesis of the total universe. There is, therefore, in God's nature the aspect of the realm of forms as qualified by the world, and the aspect of the world as qualified by the forms. His completion, so that He is exempt from transition into something else, must mean that his nature remains self-consistent in relation to all change (RM 95f).

If God includes within himself a synthesis of the *total* universe, this seems to mean all actuality as well as all possibility. Moreover, if his primordial nature were "the aspect of the realm of forms as qualified by the world," then the consequent nature appears to be "the aspect of the world as qualified by the forms."

Yet the very next sentence of the quotation stresses God's unchangingness. This is essential for his argument that God is *necessarily* free from evil. He argues that evil is inherently unstable (RM 92–94). Then if God "is above change, He must be exempt from internal inconsistency which is the note of evil" (RM 95). Now some kinds of internal inconsistency are not necessarily evil, for instance, the successive experiencing of one thing and its contradictory. This is the sort of experience we would ascribe to the consequent nature. But since it involves internal inconsistency, it cannot pertain to the concept of God here portrayed.

The sort of unchangingness which Whitehead here ascribes to God, we believe, is the nontemporal synthesis of atemporal forms. This is different from the unchangingness we would ascribe to an enduring object such as a rock or to the past or even to a single eternal object. It has the utter disengagement from time that an atemporal form has, while enjoying subjectivity and consciousness. Since the actual is formally identical with its atemporal possibility, God's nontemporal synthesis *does* include the total universe. (Here Whitehead is relying on his formal analysis of actualities in terms of infinite abstractive hierarchies. Later on, to be sure, he was to hold: "An actual entity cannot be described, even inadequately, by universals" (PR 48), but that was not yet his position.)

"The aspect of the realm of forms as qualified by the world" seems to refer to the realm of eternal objects insofar as it is organized into actualizable ideals for the world, while "the aspect of the world as qualified by the forms" might refer to actualities considered as complex structures with perhaps their near alternatives. Note that both aspects are aspects of the *same* eternal realm. It is just different features of that realm, differently arranged. The interpretation of this sentence must remain somewhat tentative, but the surrounding context suggests that here at least Whitehead conceives of God as exclusively nontemporal.

2. The world is at once a passing shadow and a final fact. The shadow is passing into the fact, so as to be constitutive of it; and yet the fact is prior to the shadow. There is a kingdom of heaven prior to the actual passage of actual things, and there is the same kingdom finding its completion through the accomplishment of this passage (RM 85).

If we identify without qualification the kingdom of heaven with God (as RM 148 appears to do) then God completes himself by means of (his experience of) temporal actualization in the world. I would suggest, however, that by "kingdom of heaven" Whitehead might mean here the objectification of God for the world, which would be the total realm of eternal objects. This he takes to be both prior to the world, and something which is completed by the world. Later, he will modify the first claim: "Viewed as primordial, . . . he is not *before* all creation, but *with* all creation. . . . He is not the beginning in the sense of being in the past of all members" (PR 343, 345).

3. Religion is the direct apprehension that, beyond such happiness and such pleasure, there remains the function of what is actual and passing, that it contributes its quality as an immortal fact to the order which informs the world (RM 77f).

Here the ambiguity of Whitehead's language poses the problem. The passage does propose the consequent nature, *if* we take the entire phrase "the function of what is actual and passing" to refer to God, and if we take "passing" to mean the consequent nature. But I submit that by God Whitehead intends only the phrase "the function." "What is actual and passing" refers to the world, particularly in its transitory existence, needing the assurance of permanence that God and religion can provide. Religion, he argues, is founded "on our apprehension of those permanent elements by reason of which there is a stable order in the world" (RM vii).

The remaining excerpts are all taken from the final section of *Religion in the Making* (4.4), which contains the most exalted writing by Whitehead prior to Part V of *Process and Reality* and the final chapter on "Peace" in *Adventures of Ideas*. In this final section he seeks to integrate "dogma," i.e., general (metaphysical) insights broadly based on the extraordinary, religious experience of mankind, with the metaphysics of ordinary experience he had outlined in the previous chapter. Here he is most sensitive to the yearnings of the faithful, giving them maximum scope consistent with the ordinary metaphysics already established. Here he is pushing his speculative vision to the uttermost, stretching to touch the fringes of his thinking.

It is conceivable that Whitehead in 1926 intuited some of the functions of God which in 1928 could only be assigned to the consequent nature. But it is doubtful whether he ever discerned the conceptual means necessary to sustain these insights, such as a consequent nature based on divine physical feelings.

Here are the passages taken from the final section:

4. The kingdom of heaven is not the isolation of good from evil. It is the overcoming of evil by good. This transmutation of evil into good enters into the actual world by reason of the inclusion of the nature of God, which includes the ideal vision of each actual evil so met with a novel consequent as to issue in the restoration of goodness.

God has in his nature the knowledge of evil, of pain, and of degradation, but it is there as overcome with what is good. Every fact is what it is, a fact of pleasure, of joy, of pain, or of suffering. In its union with God that fact is not a total loss, but on its finer side is an element to be woven immortally into the rhythm of mortal things (RM 148f).

This passage certainly resonates with Whitehead's claim in *Process and Reality* that God "prehends every actuality for what it can be in such a perfected system—its sufferings, its sorrows, its failures, its triumphs, its immediacies of joy—woven by rightness of feeling into the harmony of the universal feeling" (PR 346). It surely seems to require the consequent nature of God. Moreover, "this transmutation of evil into good enters into the actual world" by the way in which God's consequent nature seems to be prehended in the provision of specific initial aims. Since the only evidence for creaturely prehension of the consequent nature is to be found in that highly enigmatic fourth phase (PR 351), Cobb recognizes that "the evidence for it is less clearly found in *Process and Reality* than in *Religion in the Making*," evidently with this passage in mind.[11]

The interpretive crux in this passage concerns how God acquires his knowledge of evil. If he acquires that knowledge by physical prehension of the world, then the foregoing analysis is valid, including the actual occasions' prehension of God's consequent nature, a favorite process doctrine not clearly affirmed in Whitehead's later writings. But if God acquires that knowledge in another way, the passage has a quite different meaning. In God's synthesis of omniscience he knows all formal possibilities—and actualities inasmuch as these are objectified as complex eternal objects. Since he knows everything, he knows evil, pain, degradation, but as these are overcome with good. That is, to every evil, God correlates that possibility which can restore the good.

"The kingdom of heaven is not the isolation of good from evil," for God does not merely know the good and not the evil. He knows all formal possibilities, and therefore also all evils, but these as correlated with good. These correlations provide the novel consequents for the world. "Every event on its finer side introduces God into the world. Through it his ideal vision is given a base in actual fact to which He provides the ideal consequent, as a factor saving the world from the self-destruction of evil" (RM 149). Since every occasion is a fusion of all actuality, it includes God within its experience as well. So the entire realm of eternal objects is prehended by every actuality. Somehow the occasion particularly prehends that formal possibility within that realm which corresponds to itself, thereby being lured by the novel consequent which God has correlated with it, but how this is done is never made very clear. Perhaps

Whitehead proposed it to himself as part of his future program, but was never able to resolve it satisfactorily.

   5. His purpose is always embodied in the particular ideals relevant to the actual state of the world. Thus all attainment is immortal in that it fashions the actual ideals which are God in the world as it is now. Every act leaves the world with a deeper or a fainter impress of God. He then passes into his next relation to the world with enlarged, or diminished, presentation of ideal values (RM 152).

If the passage said that the world leaves a deep or fainter impress upon God, or that God receives an enlarged, or diminished, experience of the world, this would be strong evidence for the presence of the consequent nature here. But it does not. Even the way attainment is immortal is that its exact formal character is known by God forever. Just a few pages before Whitehead emphasized the non-temporality of God's knowledge: "He is complete in the sense that his vision determines every possibility of value. Such a complete vision coordinates and adjusts every detail. Thus his knowledge of the relationships of particular modes of value is not added to, or disturbed, by the realization in the actual world of what is already conceptually realized in his ideal world" (RM 147f). This leaves no room for any divine temporal experience of the world.

   6. He is the ideal companion who transmutes what has been lost into a living fact within his own nature (RM 148).

In Whitehead's later doctrine, the transient events of this world are cherished forever in God's experience and thereby achieve "everlastingness." That certainly appears to be his teaching here, but is it? We may perhaps read too much into "transmutes," as if God actively appropriates and integrates "what has been lost" with other values within his own experience, all of this being understood as a temporal transaction. But think of it as a nontemporal activity, whereby *all* possible alternatives, including those which are lost (perhaps because of their disvalue) are correlated with novel consequents, all within God's own nature. This transformed loss is "a living fact" because of the goodness by which it is overcome and because it is actively entertained by God forever.

   7. Each actual occasion gives to the creativity which flows from it a definite character . . . In another way, as transmuted in the nature of God, the ideal consequent as it stands in his vision is also added (RM 151).

If the occasion is "transmuted in the nature of God" by being prehended, then this is definitely evidence for the presence of the consequent nature here. But I believe "transmuted" here may mean little more than that the same formal character exemplified in temporal existence is also present nontemporally in God's synthesis of omniscience. Since that character is directly correlated with its ideal consequent, and since the supervening occasions prehend that ideal consequent, it also is present in the world, adding its character to the creative advance.

Our purpose here has been quite narrow: we have sought to give an interpretation of these passages consonant with what seem to be Whitehead's working principles of the time, in terms of which he would seek to justify his claims. Yet this language is highly proleptic, foreshadowing things to come. His way of expressing himself often stimulates further discovery, and this might well be such an instance where earlier statements take on added meaning from a changed perspective. As we shall see when we consider the original version of *Process and Reality*, Part V in the chapter on the Giffords draft, Whitehead was capable of assigning functions to the primordial actuality which in the completed theory could only be assigned to the consequent nature. Introducing the primordial/consequent distinction had a way of narrowing down the role of the primordial. For *Religion in the Making*, then, we may conclude that God was conceived as a primordial, nontemporal actuality of conceptual feeling alone, endowed however with many of the functions Whitehead was later to assign to the consequent nature.

5. Note: Wieman's Development of Whitehead's Idea of God

For an indication of one of the ways in which Whitehead's seminal concept of God could be further developed, we might consult Henry Nelson Wieman's genial response to *Religion in the Making*, published the next year.[12] Excluding reviews, this was the first substantive response Whitehead's novel conception of God elicited. Wieman was in a good position to appreciate Whitehead's argument, as both were seeking for God in a world of creative advance. For both, at least then, there was considerable creative activity or "concretion" going on without God, whose task is to enhance the achievement of this "concretion."

"Concretion" and "prehension" are used almost interchangeably to describe the way in which all things enter into every particular thing.[13] Wieman, excited by Whitehead's ideas, was willing at this time to include even "abstract forms" (eternal objects) among all those things to be unified.[14] "Now the principle of concretion is this structure of the universe by virtue of which all being does thus come to a focus in each thing. The principle of concretion is this system of organization which makes all abstract forms and all events have some share in the constitution of any flower or grain of sand." [15] These sentences are somewhat ambiguous, for they can be taken to mean that the principle of concretion is quite individualized for each situation, as just that factor needed to bring about that particular concretion. Or it can mean that which is the source of all these particular creative factors. Wieman apparently means the latter: "That order pervading the universe that makes it concrete is God. God is not himself concrete, says Whitehead, but he is the principle which constitutes the concreteness of things." [16]

There is one false note that Wieman introduces into this account of *Religion in the Making*, and that is the notion of degrees of concretion. For Whitehead it is not a matter of degree: a thing is either fully concrete, or it is not yet actual. For Wieman things are more or less concrete, as they are more or less good. "God tends to make the universe ever more concrete. The principle of evil tends to break down its concreteness." [17] In later years this principle of concretion is ever more immanently understood as creativity, or as "growth" suitably universalized. For Wieman, it is always the source of good. For Whitehead, creativity is quite neutral with respect to value, creating both good and evil indifferently, while the source of value is vested in God, who is carefully distinguished from creativity.

On other points Wieman's exposition, and further explanation, is quite accurate and illuminating, particularly with respect to that famous dictum, "religion is what the individual does with his own solitariness" (RM 16).[18]

His most provocative modification of Whitehead's concept is made with respect to the particular providence of God: "It is God who constantly reorganizes this realm of abstract forms in order to preserve and often enhance the concreteness of each thing and of the universe. God does not do this as an external agent, for he is simply that persistent order of all being by virtue of which this reorganization constantly occurs. Because of the principle of concretion all the infinity of abstract forms assumes a different relevance whenever any new thing comes into existence." [19] Clearly this is a major step in the direction of a God who could provide particular "abstract forms," particular aims for particular occasions in the later philosophy. Is it a way in which Whitehead could have gone?

In Whitehead's terms, this would have involved the temporalization of the primordial nature. Wieman's proposal ignores the nontemporal way in which God contemplates the eternal objects. His is a purely immanental approach. He is willing to use personalistic language about God, provided it can be translated literally in terms of some underlying principle about the working of the world, and he understands Whitehead in *Religion in the Making* to be doing just that. Since the world is temporally involved in process, any God immersed in this activity would be temporally involved as a matter of course.

God, as the principle of limitation, was quite impersonal, but not for that reason immanent in the world. As later developed in the primordial envisagement, the decision limiting the world to those eternal objects which are genuinely actualizable possibilities could be achieved nontemporally, and was achieved nontemporally as a way of marking the (partial) transcendence of God over the temporal world. On this issue of nontemporal transcendence Whitehead was, at least at this time, thoroughly traditional in his concept of God.

When Whitehead did come to embrace a temporal nature for God, he did not transform the primordial nature along the lines proposed by Wieman, but treated them as complementary to one another. This had the effect of explicitly individualizing God in such a way that he could no longer be understood as purely immanent in the world, as Wieman would wish it. Although Whitehead had already conceived God as conscious and personal in the last two chapters of *Religion in the Making*, this view of God first became inescapable in the final pages of *Process and Reality*.

From near-identity of views in 1927, Wieman drifted further away in later years. His final views, both methodologically and substantively, resemble those of John Dewey in *A Common Faith*, when expressed with greater religious sensitivity.

NOTES

1. Victor Lowe, "Whitehead's Gifford Lectures," *The Southern Journal of Philosophy* 7/4 (Winter 1969–70), 331a.

2. Charles Hartshorne, *Whitehead's Philosophy* (Lincoln: University of Nebraska Press, 1972), p. 2. See also *Two Process Philosophers*, ed. Lewis S. Ford (American Academy of Religion: Studies in Religion 5, 1973), pp. 55f, 74f.

3. *Whitehead's Philosophical Development* (Berkeley: University of California Press, 1956), p. 285.

4. For a careful analysis of "Religion and Solitariness," see Donald A. Crosby's essay in the *Journal of the American Academy of Religion* 40/1 (March, 1972), 21–35, republished in *Explorations in Whitehead's*

Philosophy, ed. Lewis S. Ford and George L. Kline (New York: Fordham University Press, 1983), pp. 149–69.

5. This is my own position in *The Lure of God* (Philadelphia: Fortress Press, 1978), Chapter Two.

6. A vestige of this same strategy may be found in *Adventures of Ideas.* The divine Eros (i.e. the primordial, nontemporal nature of God) is mentioned throughout the book, but the Adventure of the Universe as One—Whitehead's term for the consequent or temporal nature of God—is only introduced on the last two pages. Specific themes dependent upon religious experience are reserved for the final chapter on "Peace."

7. Lewis S. Ford, "Some Proposals Concerning the Composition of *Process and Reality,*" *Process Studies* 8/3 (Fall, 1978), 154, with respect to Jorge Nobo.

8. John B. Cobb, Jr., *A Christian Natural Theology* (Philadelphia: Westminster Press, 1965), pp. 164, 149.

9. On theories of consciousness, see Chapter 8, Section 2(3) and Chapter 9, Section H.

10. See Chapter 9, Section I.

11. Cobb, *A Christian Natural Theology,* p. 167.

12. *The Wrestle of Religion with Truth* (New York: Macmillan, 1927), chapters 11–13.

13. *Ibid.,* pp. 182f.

14. *Ibid.,* pp. 183f.

15. *Ibid.,* p. 185.

16. *Ibid.* (cf. SMW 178).

17. *Ibid.,* p. 189.

18. *Ibid.,* 206–09.

19. *Ibid.,* pp. 194f.

SEVEN

The Metaphysics of 1926–27

IN this chapter we shall analyze Whitehead's further metaphysical development up to the summer of 1927, when he started to draft the Gifford Lectures. In that way we can come to understand the philosophical position which guided Whitehead in the initial composition of his major work. To be sure, given his practice of constantly revising his concepts, the position Whitehead may have begun *Process and Reality* with need not be the position he finally adopts. We may be able to discover this initial position from the texts themselves, but we will be guided by clues about that initial position derived from whatever external evidence we have about his position leading up to the summer of 1927.

After *Religion in the Making* (Spring 1926), however, the first broadly metaphysical work Whitehead published was *Process and Reality* itself. A slender volume, *Symbolism, Its Meaning and Effect*, to be sure, did appear in the Spring of 1927, but it is primarily devoted to Whitehead's newly developed theory of perception. Thus, if we seek to chart the vicissitudes of Whitehead's metaphysical reflection during this period, we need to resort to essays and other materials. Fortunately there are three documents which we may turn to:

1. The brief but very compact address on "Time," presented at the Sixth International Congress of Philosophy held September 13–17, 1926, at Cambridge, Massachusetts (IS 240–47, republished here as Appendix 2).

2. We possess a very good set of student notes for Whitehead's Harvard Lectures, 1926–27. These were compiled by George Bosworth Burch, then a graduate student, later for many years Fletcher Professor of Philosophy at Tufts University.[1] Burch's notes are republished as

Appendix 3 of this study, and will be cited according to paragraph numbers, which have been introduced into the text for convenience.

There are also other students' notes for this academic year, most notably those by Everett J. Nelson and Lester S. King, which I may cite from time to time. Burch's notes, by comparison, are very selective. Sometimes whole days pass without being noted. But when the issue is important, particularly for Whitehead's own philosophy, Burch's account is very detailed and accurate. Burch's notes do not specify the date, as do the other two, but it is comparatively easy from their notes to determine when Whitehead said something in class. On the whole, though, these other notes do not add enough to our understanding of Whitehead's lectures at Harvard to warrant separate publication. (Photocopies of these notes should be available at the Center for Process Studies, 1325 N. College Avenue, Claremont, California 91711.)

3. On March 4, 1927, during the second session of his "Seminary in Logic 20" at Harvard, Whitehead presented a very compact summary of his philosophical outlook in some 22 propositions, which we have reproduced as Appendix 4.

From the sheer temporal proximity we may anticipate that the metaphysical position emerging out of these documents from 1926–27 would have considerable continuity with what Whitehead wrote that summer. Such is in fact the case. Thus the study of these materials should prepare us for the developmental study of *Process and Reality*.

The study of his 1926–27 metaphysics may best be accomplished by three sub-studies: (A) a combined study of "Time" and the fall 1926 lectures, as there appears to be no significant shift in these two documents; (B) a detailed comparison of the 6 metaphysical principles of 1926 with the 8 principles of 1927 (Appendix 5); and (C) a brief commentary on the 22 propositions of March 1927.

1. THE METAPHYSICS OF FALL, 1926

In the course of his philosophical reflection, Whitehead uses two concepts to articulate process: "transition" and "concrescence." "Transition" usually signifies the shift *between* occasions, "concrescence" the growing together of feelings *within* a single occasion.[2] Although the term was not yet introduced, the earlier writings understand process solely in terms of "transition." "Supersession" is Whitehead's term for this notion of transition, in a more extended sense, in this essay on "Time;" it is used prominently only in this essay. It emphasizes not only the shift between occasions, but also the way in which the new replaces the old. "If time be taken seriously, no concrete entity can change. It can only be superseded" (IS 240), It "perishes," in Locke's sense, for "the phrase 'perpetually perishing' is used in the same sense as 'supersession' here" (IS 240).

As in the "Relativity" addition to *Science and the Modern World*, time is epochal. "Supersession is not a continuous process of becoming" (IS 246). Instead of the complex argument Whitehead used for this thesis in the "Relativity" addition, he introduces a streamlined one, couched in supersessionist terms: ". . .if B supersedes A, then the continuity of B requires that some earlier portion of B has superseded A antecedently to the later portion of B. This argument can be repeated on that earlier portion of B, however you choose that portion" (IS 246). This infinite regress can be avoided only by rejecting continuity in favor of the atomicity of occasions. The same argument, differently expressed and further elaborated, is used in *Process and Reality* (PR 68f), but with a more far-reaching conclusion. In the first two contexts in which Whitehead employed arguments for atomicity, time was the subject of discussion; in *Process and Reality*, it is the act of becoming. The act of becoming is "not extensive in the sense that it is divisible into earlier and later acts of becoming" (PR 69).

This may seem like a fairly minor difference, but it has considerable effect upon the doctrine of internal supersession, which Whitehead espoused in the "Time" essay: "Supersession is a three-way process. Each occasion supersedes other occasions, it is superseded by other occasions, and it is internally a process of supersession, in part potential and in part actual" (IS 241). If one suboccasion supersedes another, such that a secondary, mental unification supersedes an initial, physical unification, then there are earlier and later acts of becoming within the same occasion, i.e., within the same act of becoming. Internal supersession is excluded by the application of the argument for atomicity to all forms of becoming, but Whitehead clearly did not hold to this view in the fall of 1926. Why not?

First, it appears that the idea of internal supersession had a conceptual development quite independent of the epochal theory of time. As we have seen, Whitehead apparently held broadly pansubjectivist views on such issues as the interiority of events and perhaps the nature of prehension since the Lowell Lectures, but he seems to have explained mind differently, in terms of ego-objects. If Whitehead was then a pansubjectivist but not a panpsychist (understanding "psyche" rather narrowly as mentality), then it may have been his originally *non*-panpsychist leanings that led him to distinguish between the physical occasion and the mental occasion. This was a way of securing the thesis that many, if not most, actualities might be utterly devoid of mentality, as well as the thesis that all mentality is embodied in, and partially dependent on, non-mental actuality. Whitehead complicated this model somewhat in *Religion in the Making* by also introducing the contrast between ground and consequent, for he sought to account for novelty even with respect to purely physical occasions. Otherwise no evolutionary advance would be possible, for there could not be any emergence of mentality in associated mental occasions without the possibility of novelty in physical occasions. The essay on "Time" simplified this model by assimilating the role of novelty to the mental occasion and thereby eliminating any separate distinction between ground and consequent, but this has the implication of rendering his system panpsychist in the sense that every actual occasion has some degree of mentality: "we must hold that each occasion is dipolar" (IS 240).[3]

The essay also specified the supersessive relation between the physical occasion and its associated mental occasion: "the mental occasion supersedes the physical occasion" (IS 241). As Whitehead reasoned, this was the only possible relationship. The mental occasion was dependent upon the physical occasion, not vice versa. Nor could the two suboccasions be out of the supersessive relationship entirely, like simultaneous occasions, for then they would lack any essential connection. Thus the mental occasion must supersede the physical. This is the prime example of internal supersession, creating the category.

In order to reconcile such internal supersession with the epochal theory, Whitehead made two evasive moves: (1) The scope of the argument was implicitly restricted to time, while (2) the mental occasion was held to be outside time; ". . . the linkage between the physical and the mental pole of an occasion illustrates the truth that the category of supersession transcends time, since this linkage is both extratemporal and yet is an instance of supersession" (IS 241). This second doctrine persists into the later philosophy, as we are told: "Every actual entity is 'in time' so far as its physical pole is concerned, and is 'out of time' so far as its mental pole is concerned" (PR 248). Eventually it is extended to cover all genetic activity within concrescence: "This genetic passage from phase to phase is not in physical time" (PR 283), although previously he had been content to speak of *earlier* and *later* phases of concrescence. The first doctrine, however, is abandoned. Whitehead comes to regard each act of supersession as an act of becoming, and to view each act of becoming as indivisible. This excludes internal supersession.

Thus the theory of the mental occasion superseding the physical occasion did not persist into the composition of *Process and Reality*. As we shall see, it is not explicitly articulated in the 22 propositions of March, 1927. While it lasted, however, Whitehead had developed the theory to a considerable degree, understanding the physical occasion as a synthesis of the past, with mental occasions as their analysis. The "Time" essay speaks of "the mental occasions which achieve knowledge by their conceptual analysis of their associate physical occasions" (IS 242).

This is a very strange teaching, if we think of mentality as primarily assisting in the achievement of unification. That is its role in his final position, but not originally. Here unification is vested in the physical occasion. As initially conceived, *all* actualities possessed physical occasions, while some in addition had associated mental occasions. That meant that each physical occasion had to be a complete prehensive unification or synthesis of its world. There was no need for the superseding mental occasion to duplicate that synthesis, so Whitehead hit upon the opposite activity: conceptual analysis. Concepts differentiate; they bring to articulate awareness what is massively felt. Here Kant's dictum about intuitions without concepts being blind could be a guide to his thinking, particularly as prehensive unifications are called in *Religion in the Making* "acts of blind perceptivity."

Though not explicitly discussed as such, this model of synthesis/ analysis persists in Whitehead's philosophizing further than is often realized. The Giffords draft, to be discussed in the next chapter, dropped the language and conceptuality of internal supersession, but retained (implicitly) the synthesis/analysis model. There was only one concrescent act for the occasion, but that would start with a single unified *datum*, the synthesis of the entire past world. "The datum, which is the primary phase in the process constituting an actual entity, is nothing else than the actual world itself in its character of a possibility for the process of being felt" (PR 65). Feelings start from this original datum, and are analytic of it in the sense that each appropriates part of it. The concrescence of feeling has no need to go outside the occasion to receive anything from past occasions, for all of its content is derived from that original datum. The original datum *looks like* the synthesis achieved by an antecedent physical occasion, but Whitehead is careful not to make this claim, for a physical occasion followed by an act of concrescence would entail successive acts of becoming within a single occasion. But he is largely silent as to how that original datum was derived. Later, to be sure, he speaks of an initial phase of many simple physical feelings prehending the many *data* of the past, but that raises questions about the unity of incomplete phases he was not ready to handle earlier.

As long as Whitehead endorsed internal supersession, as in his Harvard lectures for the fall of 1926, however, he was free to speculate on its implications, which were not exhausted by its prime example, the mental occasion superseding the physical occasion. It can be used to distinguish "duration," the property of each single occasion, and "endurance": "The epochal occasion which we apprehend as the present is one occasion, but it might have been twenty epochal occasions. Endurance is an instance of unrealized potentiality" (par. 29). This may explain what Whitehead means by potential internal supersession (cf. IS 241).

This comment of November 23, 1926, is expanded in Nelson's notes: "We have an epochal occasion realized as a totality, but its endurance consists in the unrealized potentiality of [its] sub-divisions. It *might* have been twenty epochal occasions, but *was* just one. Every epochal entity contains within itself the potentiality of a breaking up into many entities. *Endurance is the potentiality of many and the actuality of one.* The potentiality of many is indeterminate. The character of having potentiality is confused with various feelings, e.g. tedium. Endurance is an instance of unrealized potentiality."

Later Whitehead analyzes potentiality in terms of the divisibility of the achieved satisfaction, but here he seems to analyze the one act of becoming into possible smaller acts of internal supersession. But there may also be actual internal supersession besides the phys-ical/mental: "The actual entity is a succession of acts of experience" (Burch, par. 32). Does Whitehead intend this as a way of accounting for the apparent continuity of subjective experience?

Besides supersession, there is another feature of the essay on "Time" about which Whitehead later is largely silent: the doctrine of "incompleteness" (yet PR 214f). "Time requires incompleteness. A mere system of mutually prehensive occasions is compatible with the concept of a static timeless world. Each occasion is temporal because it is incomplete. Nor is there any system of occasions which is complete; there is no one well-defined entity which is the actual world" (IS 242). This last assertion, to be sure, becomes a permanent feature of his thinking, necessitating (as he here saw) that the term "actual world" is as token-reflexive as "yesterday." Actual occasions, on the other hand, though explicitly incomplete in this "Time" essay, are later regarded as complete (PR 25f, cat. expl. 25). What could have caused Whitehead to alter his mode of expression here?

The temporal incompleteness of occasions is a dramatic and insistent way of articulating the flow of creativity, something basic to Whitehead's whole way of thinking, of which he was becoming increasingly aware. "The creativity *for* the creature has become the creativity *with* the creature; and the creature is thereby superseded" (IS 243). If the creature is *essentially* related to the superseding creativity, then by itself it is incomplete.

Yet this theme of incompleteness appears to be absent from the fall lectures at Harvard. It may be that Whitehead then regarded it as derivable from the principle of solidarity, which states: "Every actual entity requires all other entities, actual or ideal, in order to exist" (Burch, par. 20).

Internal supersession and incompleteness are mutually supportive. A suboccasion, if superseded by another, is incomplete in exactly the same sense that a total occasion is incomplete. It belongs to the essence of each that it will be superseded. Once supersession is abandoned, the incompleteness of a phase of concrescence is radically different. The process of unification does not terminate until the phases are complete. Since a single occasion is complete in this sense, it would be too confusing to insist that it is also incomplete in the old sense of the "Time" essay. In the transformation from internal supersession to concrescence, "completion" finds a new meaning.

The essay on "Time" teaches that each occasion is internally related to its future: "The incompleteness of an actual occasion A means that A prehends in its concretion objectification of occasions X, Y, Z . . . which must supersede A but, as in A, have not the actuality of determinate concretions" (IS 243; cf. 243f). This continues the line of thought expressed in the Lowell Lectures which lasts to the 12th chapter of *Adventures of Ideas*, although very little is said in *Process and Reality*. In the Lowell Lectures Whitehead had said: "An event has a future. This means that an event mirrors within itself such aspects as the future throws back on to the present, or, in other words, as the present has determined concerning the future. Thus an event has anticipation" (SMW 72f). The way an occasion relates itself to the past and the future is there called "memory" and "anticipation," qualified in the "Time" essay as "physical memory" and "physical anticipation." Since "every occasion holds in itself its own future," "anticipation is primarily a blind physical fact, and is only a mental fact by reason of the partial analysis effected by conceptual mentality" (IS 243). This teaching about internal relatedness to the future was never fully abandoned by Whitehead, and in a qualified sense is maintained in *Adventures of Ideas.*

For many schooled on the asymmetry of relations, whereby the present is internally related to the past, but the past is only externally related to the present, it seems that the future must be externally related to the present. But this asymmetry of prehension is not explicitly endorsed by Whitehead at any point in his career. To be sure, Whitehead makes the crucial distinction, that the relation need not be either symmetrically internal or external. Thus in a given instance "the relationship between A and a is external as regards A, and is internal as regards a" (SMW 160), but he applies this only to the relation between an eternal object (A) and an actual occasion (a). If he applies this to prehensions between occasions, he does not make it very explicit.

If relations to the past and the future are handled in terms of physical memory and physical anticipation, relations to the present are expressed in terms of physical imagination operating in the mode of presentational immediacy. "This presentational immediacy of the world simultaneous with A embodies the originative character of A. . . . To explain it, you must analyze A, and not the simultaneous world [which is causally independent]; since it constitutes A's peculiar originality. Thus presentational immediacy has the character of physical imagination, in a generalized sense of that word. This physical imagination has normally to conform to the physical memories of the immediate past; it is then called sense-perception, and is nondelusive" (IS 245).

This passage summarizes much of Whitehead's final teaching on presentational immediacy, which appears here for the first time, and whose origins we need to rehearse. Very early, already in the philosophy of nature, he had identified what he came to call the "presented locus" (PR 126), that simultaneous cross-section through all contemporaries which is the locus of what we immediately perceive. This "duration," as he simply called it then, was regarded as temporally thick, retaining in itself the passage of nature (CN 53–56). Later, in the Lowell Lectures, he generalized the perception of this present duration, thereby linking all events past, present, and future by means of the perceptual analogy. To be sure, prehension of the past was described in terms of memory, but that tended to be understood as some sort of perception of the past (SMW 72).

Here in the "Time" essay a crucial step is taken: "physical memory *is* causation" (IS 244). Prehension, whose origin lies exclusively with perception, is here, in one of its forms, identified with causation.

This is an enormously fruitful relationship, for in this way the great explanatory power of causal theory is retained without requiring any concomitant causal determinism. In one stroke Whitehead has joined the phenomenology based on perception of his philosophy of nature with scientific explanations based on causation. Both are instances of prehension.

But if prehension is understood causally as well as perceptually, then present occasions are connected to past ones, although not to any contemporaries. By definition in relativity theory, contemporaries are causally independent. Yet we perceive that which is simultaneous with ourselves. This datum, which had been with Whitehead throughout his reflection on the problem, cried out for an explanation, which he sought to give in his theory of physical imagination. Our immediately conscious perception is basically imaginative. That imagination is not capricious, however, since it usually conforms to the physical memories of the immediate past. Thus we are first causally connected to past events, then imagine present relationships.

Here Whitehead is very close to developing his mature theory of perception in terms of three modes. Only one key element is not here: perception in the mode of causal efficacy.

We may be tempted to ask, why not? If he already has specified one mode of perception with respect to presentational immediacy, would not Whitehead be anticipating other modes as well? But Whitehead does not talk of (conscious) perception, but of *prehension* in this mode, contrasting it with other temporal modes, not other perceptual modes. The contrast is between physical imagination (present), memory (past), and anticipation (future). Perception belongs to physical imagination, and hence to the mode of present simultaneity. Later of course, this temporal mode of immediacy becomes a "perceptive mode" when contrasted with other "perceptive modes" and is so specified (PR 172). In time he contemplated these other modes as well, but right now he may not have felt any need for alternatives.

Whitehead describes presentational immediacy in one place with these words: "It is the self-creative self-enjoyment of A in its character of a concretion" (IS 245). This is closely related to the theory of "self-presentation" in the Harvard lectures: an actual occasion is "an individuation or concretion of the entire universe into the one real actual unity which is self-presentation, i.e., a presentation of itelf to itself in its character of being that representation of the universe" (par. 11).

This doctrine is contrary to his later thesis that "no actual entity can be conscious of its own satisfaction" (PR 85), expressed as early as the 9th proposition of March 1927. If there is a single act of becoming, and all experience is within that act, it has no presentational or superjective unity until the very end when subjective immediacy has perished. But in the fall of 1926 Whitehead was working with a succession of acts of becoming. The physical occasion could unify the past world and present itself as a single unified datum to the mental occasion. Thus he speaks of "the physical occasion, the primary self-presentation arising out of the representation in itself of the entire universe. It is pure perceptivity, whereby an actual object emerges from the limitations imposed on it by the universe" (par. 16). The rejection of internal supersession brought an end to this theory, but beforehand "self-presentation" played an integral role in his metaphysics.

One final shift that the "Time" essay introduces is the use of the term "concrescence": "The occasion B which acquires concretion so as to supersede A embodies a definite quantum of time which I call the 'epochal character' of the concrescence" (IS 246). Here "concrescence" may be contrasted with "concretion" as its more dynamic counterpart, but it is difficult to determine the difference. "Concretion" is otherwise used throughout the essay at least seven times in the sense of concrescence, being initially introduced in these terms: "An occasion is a concretion—that is, a growing together—of diverse elements" (IS 241). "Concrescence" is used just once, at the very end. It seems Whitehead is experimenting with a new variant.

If the "Time" essay uses "concretion" primarily, the Harvard lectures use "concrescence" regularly. To be sure, Burch records "concretion" the first time (par. 11), "concrescence" thereafter (e.g., pars. 14, 22, 28). Our other two reports have "concrescence" from the start. It may be that Burch, expecting "concretion" from Whitehead's usage in *Religion in the Making*, misheard Whitehead's introduction of the word "concrescence" the first time. In any case, this is merely a terminological shift, not a conceptual one.

Two further features of the 1926 lectures, not present in the "Time" essay, should be noted. The first concerns philosophical criteria, and should be compared with the four given at the outset of *Process and Reality*: coherent, logical, adequate, and applicable (PR 3f). "Philosophy is a criticism of belief—preserving, deepening, and modifying it. Standards of criticism are: (1) intensity of belief, (2) concurrence in belief, (3) clear expression of belief, (4) analysis of belief, (5) logical coherence of belief, (6) exemplification of belief, and (7) adequacy of belief" (par. 4). These seven criteria are not further elaborated, so we cannot be certain what is intended precisely in each instance. The criteria of *Process and Reality*, with the exception of "coherence," are given in the last three criteria, "exemplification" in (6) being another way of expressing "applicability." Now it may seem that (5) combines both the later criteria of "logicalness" and "coherence," but it is more probable that "logical coherence" in the 1926 lectures means little more than logical consistency, and the peculiarly Whiteheadian sense of "coherence" imperceptibly developed later.

The tasks of criticizing beliefs and framing speculative philosophies of absolutely general ideas would seem to be different tasks, so that Whitehead is more rigorous in limiting his criteria in the latter instance. Thus the first four standards of criticism drop away, except that Whitehead informally seeks concurrence (2) for his doctrines with some of the major philosophers: Plato, Aristotle, Descartes, Locke, Hume, Kant (cf. PR 39). That massive pool of philosophic wisdom ought not to be ignored.

The other feature to be noted in these 1926 lectures is its classification of entities: "There are three types of entities: eternal objects, actual entities, objective occasions; the third is derivable from the other two (par. 19). (As these notes were taken from oral delivery, "objective occasions" might possibly have been "objectifications.") This notion of a threefold division, whereby the actual entity in concrescence is considered a distinct entity from its objectification (=concretum), is remarkably similar to George L. Kline's proposal in "Form, Concrescence, and Concretum." [4] Clearly there is a basic distinction between the concrescent activity and concrete outcome of an actual entity which remains a basic feature of Whitehead's philosophy, but is it best expressed by holding these to be distinct *entities?*

Before the year was out, Whitehead laid stress on there being just "two primordial genera of entities," actual entities and eternal objects, all others being derivative.[5] These other entities were not specified, but when they were, as in the catagories of existence, they did not include "objective occasions." The other categories of existence specified parts or groups of actual entities, whereas the "objective occasion" indicated the *same* actual occasion, except now as past. It is important that "concrescence" and "concretum" be understood as being the same actuality, differing only in temporal aspect. This feature would be obscured by regarding them as distinct entities. For this would be contrary to Whitehead's concern spelled out so clearly in *Religion in the Making:* "There are not two actual entities, the creativity and the creature. There is only one entity which is the self-creating creature" (RM 99). I doubt that he ever abandoned this insight, although it was in temporary tension with the notion of three distinct types of entities.

2. THE METAPHYSICAL PRINCIPLES COMPARED

In the Harvard lectures during the fall of 1926 Whitehead also presented six metaphysical principles (par. 20). These seem to have little connection with the categoreal scheme of *Process and Reality*, unless first compared with the eight principles proposed to his Harvard class in October 1927. Those principles, here published as Appendix 5, represent Whitehead's further revision and expansion of his principles made in the light of his draft of the Gifford Lectures, composed during the intervening summer. We shall refer to the six 1926 principles by B1-B6 (for George Burch, the compiler of these notes) and to the eight 1927 principles by M1-M8 (for Edwin L. Marvin, their compiler). One of these principles (M3) is explicitly referred to as the "third metaphysical principle" in the Giffords draft (PR 212), but these principles are ultimately incorporated in the greatly expanded list of the categories of explanation (CEs). Unlike the original list, the eight 1927 principles are couched in the language of the categoreal scheme, so we can indicate the categories they correspond to.

The arrangement of these first two lists is quite similar, with some variation at the end. The 1926 principles are reordered the next year in this fashion: 1, 2, 3, 6, 5, 4. Then two principles are sub-divided into two new principles each, making a total of eight: B6 becomes M4 and M5, B5 becomes M6 and M7. The 1926 principles are all named; only one of these names—the ontological principle—carries over to the 1927 principles (B4=M8). The 1927 principles are all stated as dependent clauses prefixed with "That," but neither here nor in the categoreal scheme are we told the nature of the main clause. Presumably it would be something like "It is stipulated . . . ."

Let us compare these principles seriatim, reserving B1 for the end.

B2. "The principle of creative individuality. Every actual entity is a process which is its own result, depending on its own limitations."
M2. "That in the becoming of an actual entity, the *potential* unity of many entities acquires the actual unity of the one entity—the whole process is the many becoming one, and the one is what becomes."

Both B2 and M2 stress that the process is its own result, but the concern of B2 with "creative individuality" is replaced by a more definite understanding of the process as "the many becoming one." Since "creative individuality" is not clearly part of the B2 principle, we may wonder whether it was not just a convenient title. The later concern with "the many become one" does not fit with the earlier internal supersession, whereby an initial unification (the physical occasion) is followed by a secondary unification (the mental occasion). Once this two-fold unification was eliminated, Whitehead could then speculate about a single unification such as articulated in M2. In M2 we find perhaps the concerns of the category of the ultimate expressed for the first time.

With some further revision, M2 becomes the second category of explanation (abbreviated, CE 2).

B3. "The principle of efficient causation. Every actual entity by the fact of its own individuality contributes to the character of processes which are actual entities superseding itself." M3. "That the potentiality for acquiring real unity with other entities is the one general metaphysical character attaching to *all* entities, *actual* or nonactual—i.e., it belongs to the nature of a 'Being' that it is a potential for a 'Becoming'." This in turn becomes CE 4, the principle of relativity.

M3 here generalizes B3, which is limited to actual entities, so that it may apply to all entities. At the same time it gives qualified assent to the truth of the principle of solidarity (B1). According to B1, "Every actual entity requires all other entities, actual or ideal, in order to exist." M3 has the connection to all other entities, but here the connection is only potential, not explicitly actual.

In *Science and the Modern World* each actual occasion prehended every eternal object. Unless there were an ordering of these ideal entities by God as the principle of limitation, there would be "indiscriminate modal pluralism" (SMW 177) as all sorts of impossibilities would be prehended along with the possibilities. *Religion in the Making* continues the principle of all-inclusion, but qualifies the mode of inclusion: "Each such instance [=actual occasion] embraces the whole, omitting nothing, whether it be ideal form or actual fact. But it brings them into its own unity of feeling under gradations of relevance and of irrelevance, and thereby by this limitation issues into that definite experience which it is" (RM 108). All this is in accordance with the principle of solidarity of 1926.

Much later this principle of solidarity is qualified by the restriction that while all actual occasions are felt, only a selection of eternal objects are (PR 41). M3, like CE 4, is compatible with this new stance, and may reflect this shift. On the other hand, M3 is also compatible with the earlier position. It expresses the metaphysical stance of the Giffords draft, which appears to contain no explicit specification that only a selection of the eternal objects are felt. All the explicit passages seem to be intimately connected with negative prehension, which is a later doctrine.

B4. "The ontological principle. The character of creativity is derived from its own creatures and expressed by its own creatures." M8. "That every condition to which the process of becoming conforms in any particular instance has its *reason* in the character of some actual entity whose objectification is one of the components entering into the particular instance in question (the ontological principle— the principle of extrinsic reference). Actual entities are the only *reasons*; to search for a reason is to search for an actual entity."

Here Whitehead's explicit designation of both as the ontological principle directs our correlation, for the two formulations are quite different. B4 is more properly called an ontological principle, since it specifies the relation between the ultimate ontological foundation and its expressions. Later Whitehead expresses its truth: "In all philosophic theory there is an ultimate which is actual in virtue of its accidents. It is only capable of characterization through its accidental embodiments, and apart from these accidents is devoid of actuality. In the philosophy of organism, this ultimate is termed 'creativity'; and God is its primordial, non-temporal accident" (PR 7).

If we focus on a single instance of creativity, however, it is derived from other creatures of creativity in such a way that these function as [the extrinsic] reasons for each condition of that instance. In some such way M8 can be derived from B4. This principle is more properly called the "principle of extrinsic reference." It is only the ontological principle by courtesy as its lineal descendant. In neither of these formulations does Whitehead allude to the general Aristotelian principle, that only actual entities primarily exist, while all other entities derive their existence from actual entities.

Note that M8 is restricted to extrinsic reasons, while CE 18 makes the existential move that subjective decisions can also function as (intrinsic) reasons by adding the proviso that reasons can be found in past actualities "*or* in the character of the subject which is in process of concrescence."

B5. "The principle of esthetic individuality. Every actual entity is an end in itself for itself, involving its measure of self-satisfaction individual to itself and constituting the result of itself-as-process." That each occasion enjoys an inner worth becomes a basic tenet of

Whitehead's philosophy, which if anything deepened in his later thinking. But this principle of esthetic individuality loses its status as a metaphysical principle. Perhaps he wished to show how it could be derived from the others. By removing its teleological factor, two principles could be derived from it:

M6. "That two descriptions are required for an actual entity: (a) one of them analytic of its potentiality for its 'objectification' in the becoming of other actual entities and (b) the other analytic of the process that constitutes its own becoming." With very minor variation, this is CE 8.

(M6 could with equal reason be derived from B2, except for the correlation we discern between B2 and M2.)

M7. "That *how* the actual entity *becomes* constitutes *what* the actual entity is, so that the two descriptions of an actual entity are not independent. All *explanation* of an actual entity exhibits its process as the reason for its potentiality, and all description exhibits the realized objectifications of that actual entity as a partial analysis of its own process." This second sentence is dropped in the final formulation of this principle in CE 9, which is then called the "principle of process."

While the second sentence of M7 is dropped from Whitehead's final categoreal formulation, it remains a basic feature of his philosophy. "Description" here refers to the activity of science in analyzing that being which appears in the world, while "explanation" signifies that ultimate accounting of that being in terms of becoming. As formulated in 1927, there need be no redundancy between M7 and the ontological principle (M8). When Whitehead reformulates this principle in CE 18 by vesting some of the reasons in the process of becoming itself, and these reasons become the dominant reasons, then it becomes difficult to distinguish between "explanation" and the giving of reasons according to the ontological principle. This partial redundancy may have led Whitehead to abandon the second sentence of M7.

B6. "The principle of ideal comparison. Every creature involves in its own constitution an ideal reference to ideal creatures: (1) in ideal relationship to each other, and (2) in comparison with its own self-satisfaction." This continues the teaching of *Religion in the Making* that in God's timeless ordering there is a complete conceptual realization of all ideal possibilities which becomes available to the creatures as they come into being (RM 146–49). But we are not told how this could be accomplished. Who selects the ideal possibilities, God or the creature? If the creature, how can it select the possibility before coming into being, at least partially, while it needs that ideal possibility in order to come into being? If God, however, how can God make the particular temporal decision if purely nontemporal (as God was conceived at this time)?

Eventually B6 reasserts itself in the doctrine of God's provision of initial aims, but this is considerably after the Giffords draft and the formulation of the 1927 principles. In the meantime, Whitehead appears to have backed off from the strong claims of B6, awaiting further justification. What replaces the principle of ideal comparison are two rather innocuous claims about eternal objects:

M4. "That there are two primordial genera of entities: (a) eternal objects and (b) actual entities, and that all other entities are derivative complexes involving entities from both of these genera." (This becomes CE 19.) M5. "That an eternal object can only be described in terms of its potentiality for 'ingression' into the becoming of actual entities and that its analysis only discloses other eternal objects." (Becomes CE 7.)

B1. "The principle of solidarity. Every actual entity requires all other entities, actual or ideal, in order to exist." This is a favorite early principle of Whitehead's, going back to his monistic days, formulated in sharp opposition to the easy assumption that the causes of things are readily specifiable. In part it is retained throughout, particularly in the insistence that a concrescing occasion in some way or other prehends every past actuality whatsoever. But he more and more explicitly excludes future and contemporaries occasions, and all but a selection of the eternal objects.

Before these developments, however, the principle of solidarity was undercut by the development of the principle of efficient causation (B3) into M3. M3 states that all entities, actual or ideal, are potentials for becoming. This is the reciprocal of B1, except that B1 requires that every entity *must* be ingredient in becoming. M3 says only that they *may* be. Thus when Whitehead recognizes that only a selection of the eternal objects must be felt, this necessitates no revision of M3, whereas it would have of B1.

Either B1 combines with B3 to form M3, allowing for M1 as a new principle, or B1 is replaced by M1, there being no other principle to which it could correspond. "That the actual world is a process and that this process is the becoming of actual entities." This becomes the first half of CE 1.

After enunciating the six 1926 principles, Whitehead adds: "These principles are essential to actuality, and so apply equally well to God (pure act). It follows that God is a creature; the supreme actuality is the supreme creature. The only alternatives are to say that God is not actual or that God lies beyond anything of which we can have any conception" (par. 21). Then follows a brief discussion as to how some of these principles apply to God.

This is the first expression of two of Whitehead's most characteristic claims about God, that he is a creature of creativity and that he is the chief exemplification of all metaphysical categories (PR 343). The second denies such claims as Paul Tillich's which would put God beyond all being and thus beyond all the categories of being. The insistence that God, if there be one, exemplify the categories places a constraint of precision upon our philosophical understanding of God, as well as upon our formulation of the categories, which must now be pertinent to the existence and nature of God.

Yet, while it is relatively easy to see how God exemplifies "the" metaphysical principles of 1926, when there were only 6, it is more difficult to see how he exemplifies the 27 categories of explanation and the 9 categoreal obligations of the final formulation. Here we may be able to exclude the categoreal obligations from applying to God, on the basis of a later insertion (analyzed in chapter 9, section J).

During much of the composition of *Process and Reality*, "actual entities" and "actual occasions" were interchangeable terms. The fact that God was solely a mental being did not make him uniquely so, because there *might* be other purely mental beings, such as spirits or disembodied souls. With the discovery of the consequent nature, and the contrast between the physical and mental poles, God could be conceived as systematically unique. While all actual occasions initiated from physical feeling, God was the sole actual entity to initiate from his conceptual feelings. Armed with that distinction, Whitehead inserted the stipulation that most of his discussion of "actual entities" did not apply to God: "In the subsequent discussion, 'actual entity' will be taken to mean a conditioned actual entity of the temporal world [in other words, an actual occasion], unless God is expressly included in the discussion" (PR 88). The most systematic part of that discussion, as well as the part most recently formulated, would be Part III with its categoreal obligations.

The reason God's relation to the expanded list of the categories of explanation is unclear is that Whitehead finally used it for principles which apply to entities other than to actual entities. Naturally such would not apply to God. The original list of 1926 all pertains to actual entities, and hence to God as chief. Thus the rule we should follow is to limit ourselves to those categories of explanation that concern actual entities. These are the metaphysical principles that God is said to exemplify.

To exemplify the metaphysical principles does not mean to exemplify some of the most basic pervasive features of actual occasions. Whitehead did not apply the notion of internal supersession, whereby the mental occasion superseded the physical occasion, to God, who is described as "pure act." Although all other actual entities were temporal, God remains completely nontemporal in Whitehead's conception at this time. It was other considerations, quite apart from divine exemplification of principles, which led him eventually to espouse a temporal side to God.

3. THE MARCH 1927 PROPOSITIONS

The 22 propositions published in Appendix 4, which Whitehead presented to his logic seminar in the spring of 1927, are not merely about logic. They resemble Leibniz's "Monadology" in being a compact summary of Whitehead's philosophy at that time. In the first four propositions he engages in various logical maneuvers to obtain the "basic" or (roughly) "atomic" proposition, but in prop. 5 he already moves into metaphysics with this justification: "The source of all types of complex units [including propositions, by prop. 1] is to be sought in their derivation from the individual unification of the universe in each actual entity." This proposition also expresses, in its next sentence, the principles both of solidarity and of individual creativity, the first two of the 1926 principles: "An actual entity is an individual unification of the universe with its own particular individuality." Many other continuities with characteristic earlier doctrines are apparent. For example, prop. 18 expresses the "incompleteness" theme of the "Time" essay.

We can most conveniently examine this metaphysical sketch in terms of three topics: consciousness, the act of experience, and propositions.

(1) *Consciousness*. Props. 13–15 present the first developed theory of consciousness, and thus deserve particular scrutiny. In the philosophy of nature he concentrated on the perceived, the contents of consciousness, bracketing the question as to the nature of the consciousness itself. In the Lowell Lectures he closes a brief, preliminary discussion with the remark: "This question of consciousness must be reserved for treatment on another occasion" (SMW 152). Whitehead recognized that a theory of consciousness ought to be on his

agenda, but perhaps was not yet ready to offer one. A year later he offered this rudimentary sketch: "Such consciousness is a mental occasion. It has the character of being an analysis of physical experience by synthesis with the concepts involved in the mentality" (RM 114). Thus right from the start consciousness is seen to involve a contrast between the mental and the physical, and not just a factor of mental experience alone. Also the contention of William James (in his celebrated essay, "Does Consciousness Exist? ") that consciousness is a function, not an entity, is accepted at the outset.

Props. 13–15 do not explicitly affirm that consciousness is a function of propositional feeling, but on occasion they come very close. They describe consciousness as "the synthesis of various objective unit entities [presumably objectified actual entities] with predicates [=eternal objects: prop. 11] which might not be theirs or may be theirs" (prop. 13). The reason for this is that Whitehead is already interested in the affirmation/negation contrast, which require the contrastive elements of a proposition. There are two basic forms of consciousness: the yes form and the no form. The yes form affirms what is physically experienced; since there is no contrast between the conceptual and the physical here, "you vaguely know that you are perceiving" (prop. 14). In the no form, the conceptual content is quite different from what is physically felt, so there is the contrastive basis for clear and precise consciousness.

Since perception in the mode of presentational immediacy is both imaginative (i.e., contrasting with physical experience) and clear, it can provide an apt instance of consciousness in its no form. Since Whitehead now had a contrasting yes form for consciousness in general, he may have inquired as to whether there were a corresponding mode of perception. He knew several of its characteristics to look for: it would be most intimately bound up with the physical prehension of past actualities, and it would be vague. Some such reflections may have led to the discovery of perception in the mode of causal efficacy, and to the construction of the theory of perception found in *Symbolism*.

The relationship between the March 1927 propositions and the Babour-Page Lectures on *Symbolism* (delivered April 18–20 that same year) is difficult to disentangle because of their close temporal proximity, but it seems the propositions are first. There appears to be no influence, explicit or implicit, of the *Symbolism* lectures on the propositions, and this is best explained by assuming that at that time the diverse modes of perception had not yet been clearly anticipated. On the other hand, prop. 14 with its yes/no forms of consciousness, and notion of vague perception, could easily have suggested perception in the mode of causal efficacy. If there is any influence, it would be one way.

The dates are close but not impossible. On December 10, 1926, when Whitehead agreed to give the University of Virginia lectures, he proposed "Symbolic Expression, Its Function for the Individual and for Society." [6] This suggests the topic of the third lecture, but one would hardly expect to find a new and original theory of perception under this title. One reason for this, I propose, is that Whitehead did not then have such a theory, and so did not anticipate lecturing about it at Virginia. The 22 propositions were presented at the second session of the logic seminar on March 4, 1927, as we have seen, but they may have been formulated earlier in preparation for that course. As a result of the stimulus from these ideas of consciousness, Whitehead may have been so intensely working out this new theory of perception that he stole time set aside for the Barbour-Page Lectures. When symbolism proved to be an appropriate bridge between the two primary modes of perception, Whitehead could justify presenting his newly discovered theory in the first two of his three lectures.

(2) *The Act of Experience.* In charting the changes in Whitehead's thinking during the spring of 1927, prop. 9 is particularly significant. As we have seen, the essay on "Time" postulates, first, a physical occasion which is then superseded by a mental occasion. Here process is primarily understood as transition, the way one entity gives way to another. By the time of the later stages of the Giffords draft the emphasis is all on concrescence, the way the many feelings within an occasion grow together toward unity. Which way does an intermediary statement such as prop. 9 lean? It is extremely difficult to say. The language of supersession is absent, but so is the language of concrescence. No word at all is given for the over-all activity, whether it be "process" or "becoming" or "concrescence."

This evasion appears deliberate for it is very difficult to phrase these issues without commiting oneself one way or the other. Thus if the divisions are each acts, then the occasion is a series of distinct processes, as in internal supersession; but if the divisions are simply phases of one single process, then we have concrescence. The issue may well be evaded if Whitehead were then uncertain whether to reaffirm the internal supersession of the "Time" essay or to develop new categories of concrescence.

We shall quote proposition 9 in its entirety, with a running commentary:

"9. An act of experience or actual entity, or actual occasion in the temporal world, is only:

" (1) A synthesis of perceptivity of other acts of experience, together forming the actual universe. Its perception of how the other acts of experience, the rest of the actual universe, is synthesized into the one entity which is the act of experience in question."

This is the former physical occasion in its own self-constitutive activity, or perhaps simply as datum for further activity (cf. PR 149f).

" (2) The emotional or esthetic intensity which is the primordial individual fact constituting the meaning or outcome of this unity. It is an esthetic intensity which is an enjoyment of being that synthesis."

Whitehead does not present these steps in genetic order, and has leaped forward to the satisfaction, which includes the element of subjective appropriation which is synthesized along with the original objective content.

" (3) The conceptual functioning whereby what might be enters into a synthesis with what is, and is thereby analytical of it by reason of the yes and no types of analytical unity. Concept meets percept. If of the yes type, there is a certain unity and identity of relationship to the percept. If of the no type, there is a certain diversity."

This corresponds to the previous mental occasion, except for some advanced features which are reserved for the fourth step. It is analytic of the physical synthesis. What is new is the division of concepts into the yes type and the no type. These seem identical with the yes and no forms of prop. 14.

" (4) There is the additional self-creative activity of the self-judgment of the act of experience upon the complex stages of the nontemporal constitution of the actual entity. The entity is analyzable into layers, each of which presupposes one another logically. [Hence genetic succession is nontemporal, yet logically ordered. This order is subsequently seen to be earlier/later.] The new element is the self-judgment on what is logically antecedent in the entity, so that the esthetic emphasis of the earlier stages is controlled and adjusted. What is made important depends on that. [This readjustment is necessary if there is to be any freedom, since the act of physical unification is blind; whatever individual determination there is must come from this adjustment of emphasis in the earlier synthesis.] In this way there is control and adjustment of what is put forward or led back. The occasion begins as an emotional intensity which is then reconstituted by an act of self-judgment."

This step may be conceived as the more complex phase of the mental occasion, but it represents an additional line of thought beyond the analysis in the "Time" essay. This step of self-judgment of the act of experience, "so that the esthetic emphasis of earlier stages is controlled and adjusted," is seen to be required. Otherwise the theory is in danger of becoming epiphenomenalistic. In the old theory, only the physical occasion affected the future beyond itself, and there did not seem to be any mental input into the physical occasion. There was an analysis of the physical synthesis in the mental occasion, including free decision and sometimes consciousness, but this apparently had no impact on the physical occasion. Now, with the notion of self-judgment, that initial physical occasion could be modified.

The possibility of self-judgment, in turn, suggests a movement toward concrescence. For the physical occasion is now conceived as something modifiable within concrescence, not something already completely determinate as it presents itself to supersession.

Conceivably reflection about consciousness could have led to the postulation of a more complex mental phase. But Whitehead makes no firm assignment here of consciousness to any of the phases. If "Consciousness emerges with the emergence of unverified propositions" (prop. 14), then this would be with the concepts of the no type in step (3). Again, reflection about propositions could conceivably have led to the fourth phase, but there is no indication the question as to the location of propositions within concrescence had even been raised yet.

" (5) There is the emergence of the final actual occasion providing a new creative character for the universe whereby creative passage is conditioned beyond the act in question. This doesn't sit in judgment on itself or know itself."

Later, Whitehead distinguishes between the "satisfaction" and the "decision" of an occasion, i.e., the way in which it will influence supervening occasions (PR 150). This stage properly belongs to the "decision."

As noted before, this appears to be the beginning of Whitehead's teaching that no occasion is conscious of its own satisfaction: it "doesn't sit in judgment on itself or know itself." For once complete, made enough (satis + facere), the occasion is no longer subjectively capable of reflecting upon itself, but purely objective.

Because of our inveterate habit of thinking of satisfaction in terms of the gratification of desire, it is easy to interpret it subjectively. But if satisfaction, in its root meaning, entails the completion of something, then in this case it means the completion of concrescence, to which no additions can be made.

Jorge Nobo distinguishes between "subjective satisfaction" and "superjective satisfaction": "The subjective satisfaction is the final *creative* phase of the actual occasion." [7] After that, the subjective immediacy perishes and the satisfaction moves over into its superjective nature. He bases this distinction largely on the following passage, which appears to be the only one explicitly mentioning "subjective satisfaction." Whitehead speaks of the datum "absorbed into the subjective satisfaction" as " 'clothed' with the various elements of its 'subjective form'." The subjective form as a factor of a positive prehension is further described as "the feeling whereby this datum is absorbed into the subjective satisfaction" (PR 52). I take "subjective" here primarily to refer to "subjective form," and interpret "subjective satisfaction" to be that side of the final objective unity which concerns the unity of all the subjective forms together. It appears to be a very late development in Whitehead's position. His understanding of satisfaction as objective was so total that he seems not to have been alert to the possible ambiguity of "subjective satisfaction."

(3) *Propositions.* After an extended metaphysical interlude (props. 5–18), Whitehead returns to the theme of propositions at the very end, treating propositions 19–22 in considerable detail. Since this is his first considered statement on propositions, we can use it to determine which features are part of the theory initially and which features were added later.

Previously, in his chapter on "Abstraction," Whitehead referred to propositions with these remarks: ". . . every actual occasion is set within a realm of alternative interconnected entities. This realm is disclosed by all the untrue propositions which can be predicated significantly of that occasion. It is the realm of alternative suggestions, whose foothold in actuality transcends each actual occasion. The real relevance of untrue propositions for each actual occasion is disclosed by art, romance, and by criticism in reference to ideals. It is the foundation of the metaphysical position which I am maintaining that the understanding of actuality requires a reference to ideality" (SMW 158).

This passage is rich with ideas of alternative values, but for our immediate purposes we shall only note that a "proposition" may not yet be conceived as anything more than a certain kind of complex eternal object. It belongs to that "ideality" ordinarily reserved for the eternal. Nor should this surprise us. As one of the authors of *Prncipia Mathematica*, Whitehead may be expected to follow its theory of what a proposition is. Its whole theory of "empty classes" is a device to transform substantial logical subjects into placeholders specifying eternal objects, thus transforming propositions into complex eternal objects.

Although presented to a logic seminar, metaphysical rather than logical considerations prevailed with respect to the determination of propositions. Whitehead here sought a hybrid entity between the strict universality of an eternal object and the insistent particularity of actual entity. Thus "a proposition is an intermediate universal" (prop. 19). It is the specification of a given eternal object (the predicate) to a range of actual entities (the logical subjects). Otherwise the eternal object would simply apply to *any* actual entities whatsoever. (Because actual entities in the specified range of a proposition are ordinarily meant, he usually refers to the logical subjects in the plural, lapsing once or twice by conforming to customary usage here, but later very infrequently (cf. PR 186).

Yet while, for the exigencies of finding a genuine cross between actuality and ideality, Whitehead turns from *Principia Mathematica* to Aristotle to affirm real actualities as subjects of his propositions, he does not share Aristotle's logical concern as to the primary function of propositions. For traditional logic propositions are basically affirmations and denials. Whitehead sees interest in propositions beyond simple truth or falsity: "in practice, we may know that a proposition expresses an important truth, but that it is subject to limitations and qualifications which at present remain undiscovered" (SMW 183). There are also all those untrue propositions important to art and criticism. He may not yet have summed up these observations with the generalization that the primary function of propositions is to serve as lures for feeling (so PR 184), but it is clear in any case that they are not primarily affirmations and denials.

Whitehead distinguishes between the "logical subjects" and the "percipient subject" of a proposition. The logical subjects provide the (Aristotelian) subject-matter; they constitute that which the proposition is about, and to which it refers. It is for the percipient (Cartesian) subject who experiences the proposition. (This latter subject is called in *Process and Reality* the "judging subject" [PR 189–193].)

With the distinction between the "logical subjects" and the "percipient subject," we can perhaps unravel this basic but difficult sentence: "A proposition about the actual world is itself the universal which expresses the hypothetical objectification of any set of acts [i.e. the logical subjects] from any one act of another set [that one act being the percipient subject]" (prop. 19 (3)). Here the shift in the meaning of "subject" is important.

These features, the nature of the proposition as a hybrid entity between an actual entity and an eternal object, and the distinction between the logical subjects and the percipient subject, become basic to Whitehead's account of the proposition in chapter 8 of *Process and Reality*, part II. Other adventitious features survive, such as the example, "Caesar crossed the Rubicon." The "rustic on the bank looking at Caesar" (prop. 22) may have been metamorphosed into "one of Caesar's old soldiers [who] may in later years have sat on the bank of the river and meditated on the assassination of Caesar" (PR 196). There is, however, as yet no theory of indication, whereby logical subjects are distinguished from actual entities *simpliciter*. Nor are propositions important as interesting, functioning as lures for feeling. There is no mention of propositional feeling, nor of the location of propositions within the phases of concrescence. The nature of "metaphysical propositions" (not so named) is specified: "Some propositions, like those of arithmetic, are for all subjects because they are about any act of experience, and exist for all acts of experience" (prop. 22). But the topic of "metaphysical propositions" is not developed as in sect. 4 of chapter 8, nor is the contrasting topic of inductive propositions (sects. 5–8) developed at all.

Thus a small but sufficient basis for the theory of propositions has been established in this March, 1927, statement, allowing the full theory to develop without any major revisions.

NOTES

1. As edited by Dwight C. Stewart, these were published in *Process Studies* 4/3 (Fall, 1974), 199–206.

2. These are the meanings which become standardized in *Process and Reality*. Here "transition" is not yet used as a technical term, while "concrescence" is not yet conceived as a species of process.

3. This brief summary of some reflections found in chapter 6, section 1, is quite one-sided, insisting on a limited domain for complete occasions (RM 114). If *every* occasion found in nature is a complete occasion, as it is quite possible to understand the text, then Whitehead came to his panpsychist views as early as *Religion in the Making*, possibly even in the final paragraph of the essay on "Abstraction" in *Science and the Modern World*.

4. *The Southern Journal of Philosophy* 7/4 (Winter, 1969–70), 351–360, since republished in a revised and considerably expanded version in *Explorations in Whitehead's Philosophy*, ed. Lewis S. Ford and George L. Kline (New York: Fordham University Press, 1983), pp. 104–46.

5. See next section on "Metaphysical Principles," M4.

6. Victor Lowe, "Whitehead's Gifford Lectures," *The Southern Journal of Philosophy* 7/4 (1969–70), 332.

7. Jorge Nobo, "Transition in Whitehead: A Creative Process Distinct from Concrescence," *International Philosophical Quarterly* 19/3 (September, 1979), 270.

EIGHT

The Giffords Draft

SINCE we have only very limited evidence concerning Whitehead's metaphysical position during the academic year 1926–27, we must content ourselves with relatively meagre results from the analysis of that evidence. I have sought to be thorough, since this evidence can be precisely dated, and indicates his position just on the verge of composing *Process and Reality*. It shows, moreover, the beginnings of a major revolution in Whitehead's position. In reviewing his philosophy after February, 1925, we may discern three major shifts, together with a number of other changes:

1) from temporal continuity to temporal atomism (within SMW)
2) from monism to pluralism (within RM)
3) from supersession to internal process (early 1927)

This last shift may be discerned in the application of the epochal theory to becoming generally, not just to temporal becoming (PR 68). (See our discussion of the 1926 essay on "Time" in the last chapter.)

Nevertheless a large gap remains between the metaphysics of 1926–27 and Whitehead's characteristic metaphysics in *Process and Reality*, such that it is difficult to discern any continuity between these two positions. Intermediary theories are needed. Fortunately some seem to be discernible in *Process and Reality* because of the idiosyncratic way that book was put together. Just as in *Science and the Modern World*, the major position of the book has been transformed by later additions from another point of view, while the whole has been largely interpreted from this later perspective.

The method of composition was the same, but the degree to which Whitehead modified his text in *Process and Reality* is considerably greater. Chapters are rearranged. The chapter on "Organisms and Environment" (now II.4) is twice referred to as "Part II, Ch. VIII" in uncorrected references (PR 286, 291), suggesting that once this part was so arranged that this chapter was in eighth place. Later on we shall see reasons why chapters 4 and 8 originally belonged together, as did chapters 3 and 9. Later insertions abound, coming not just in sequences of entire paragraphs as in *Science and the Modern World*, but in units ranging from entire sections (e.g., II.9.8) to sentence fragments. A favorite device of his seems to be to write a prefatory passage transforming the meaning of a given section without, however, carefully editing and revising the section itself to remove infelicities resulting from the former perspective. Sometimes two disparate topics are jammed together in the same paragraph.

This method of composition makes for a less orderly systematic presentation of Whitehead's ideas in *Process and Reality* than might be desired, but it grants us a rare glimpse into the creative process by which a philosophical genius in our century forged his ideas. Whitehead reached such heights, it appears, because he was constantly willing, ready, and able to revise his previous ideas in the light of his own criticisms.

If we can devise a method suited to the idiosyncrasies of this book, we may be able to discern the stages both of its growth and the growth of Whitehead's ideas. Our method involves three steps: (a) Passages are isolated by means of anomalies, terminological shifts, and faulty references (here the original, uncorrected edition is most useful). They may also be isolated by means of the continuity the text displays if the suspected passage were absent. (b) We then determine whether there is any interpretive dissonance between each passage, interpreted most primitively, and its surrounding context. By the most primitive interpretation of a passage I mean that interpretation which relies only upon those concepts outside the passage itself for which we have reason to suppose that they have already been introduced in earlier passages. Genetic interpretation here is often at odds with systematic interpretation. Genetic interpretation seeks for the smallest unit of interpretation, while systematic interpretation, often in a harmonizing fashion, seeks the widest possible unit of interpretation. (c) These passages are arranged as later than each other by their dependence on one another or by their continuation of characteristic terms, while some are discerned as early by their similarity to the philosophical position of 1926–27.

Process and Reality is a rich and formidable text, and this method of compositional analysis is very exacting in its execution. While I have engaged in its compositional analysis extensively, the results are by no means complete. Moreover, it is a task which would be best completed by a team of scholars working cooperatively to test each other's findings. In the absence of any definitive analysis, we cannot give a detailed examination of Whitehead's development within *Process and Reality*. On the other hand, our study would be radically incomplete if I did not say something about this work. The metaphysics of 1926–27 is too unfamiliar, and looks impossibly primitive in itself, to be clearly related to Whitehead's mature philosophy. Hence we shall complete this study with two chapters provisionally sketching the course of Whitehead's development to his final philosophy, so that these connections may be seen.

External evidence concerning the composition of *Process and Reality* is fragmentary. In August, 1924, Whitehead had expressed his "hope in the immediate future to embody the standpoint of [his philosophy of nature] in a more complete metaphysical study" (PNK ix). Much of this was then sketched out in the sections on constructive philosophy included with *Science and the Modern World*. Later, according to a letter dated May 16, 1926, he wanted "to follow it [SMW] up with something purely addressed to philosophers—*short* and *clear*, if I can make it so!" [1] Seven months later Whitehead received added impetus to write his book on metaphysics, in the form of an invitation to give the Gifford Lectures in Natural Theology at the University of Edinburgh in June, 1928. The original invitation was tendered January 19, 1927. Whitehead cabled his acceptance February 26, and wrote Prof. Norman Kemp Smith, who was primarily responsible for Whitehead's nomination, on April 6, proposing "to deliver ten or twelve lectures [subsequently restricted to ten], and then expand them for publication." [2]

The summer of 1927, which the Whiteheads spent in a cottage on the shore of Caspian Lake in Greensboro, Vermont, was devoted to the Gifford Lectures, as these were originally conceived. On August 22 he wrote his son North: "It seems years and years since I wrote to you. But I have written nearly half a book on Metaphysics this summer, and have not wanted to break my thoughts in any way. Anyhow I have now got nearly 9½ out of a projected plan of 20 or 25 chapters [PR has 25 chapters]. I am rather pleased with the result, so far. Since August 15th I have been taking a complete holiday. . . ." [3] Whitehead refers to his "book on Metaphysics," but there is ample reason to think that he meant the ten intended Gifford

Lectures, which were to form part of that book. Evelyn Whitehead, his wife, acting as his business agent, had reported to the publishers on August 9, 1927, that "9 of the 10 Gifford Lectures are written." [4] (These intended lectures, as we shall see, were not identical with the Giffords as actually delivered the following June. See Appendix 6.)

It may be difficult, but not impossible, to identify these 9½ chapters, which coincide largely, though not exclusively, with part II. I find this the single most helpful external clue as to the composition of *Process and Reality*, for by its means we can isolate what was written before the end of the summer of 1927. As it happens, the most important shift in the book occurs in those texts written after this time. The Giffords draft, as I shall call the writings of that summer, is comparable to the Lowell Lectures for *Science and the Modern World*. Both are extensive formulations of one point of view which have been incorporated into a larger work expressing another point of view.

1. THE EARLY CONTENTS OF PROCESS AND REALITY

Before considering these 9½ chapters of the Giffords draft we need to inquire whether any parts of the book were basically finished prior to that summer. Two parts are likely candidates:

A. The Basic Theory of Extension
(IV.2–3, 5 in part)

These chapters probably stem from the summer of 1926. In Whitehead's earlier philosophy of nature the method of extensive abstraction was expressed in terms of inclusion. As early as 1921 Theodore de Laguna proposed that this method could be improved by the substitution of "containing" as the basic primitive, but Whitehead did not immediately pick up on the idea. Later on he enthusiastically adopted this suggestion, as the testimony of de Laguna's wife indicates. Victor Lowe reports the following from notes of an interview with Mrs. Grace de Laguna, November 11, 1966: "The de Lagunas first got to know the Whiteheads in Greensboro, Vermont, probably in the summer of 1926. . . . In the summer of 1927 they saw the Whiteheads again. Mrs. de Laguna remembers her husband explaining his criticism of extensive abstraction to Whitehead, and proposing "extensive connection" (as Whitehead termed this relationship) as the primitive relation. Whitehead thought for a minute, then said, 'Yes! You're right!' or something to that effect." [5]

As against Mrs. de Laguna's memory, some 29 years after the event, we have students' notes of Whitehead's lecturing on the method of extensive abstraction, which show that he first introduced 'extensive connection' as his basic primitive in the spring of 1927. That strongly suggests that de Laguna's emendation, always gratefully acknowledged, was appreciated the previous summer of 1926. The chapters on extensive connection and flat loci (IV.2–3) could easily have been developed out of that insight, while the material on measurement (IV.5.4–6) forms an important application, as Whitehead wanted to base measurement on straightness, and not, as is customary, the other way around.

B. The Original Treatise on Perception
(II.4.5–8 and II.8)

This Original Treatise on Perception, as I have called it, was probably composed together with the first two lectures on *Symbolism*, lectures delivered in early April 1927. They treat of the same three modes cf perception: causal efficacy, presentational immediacy, and symbolic reference, with the same basic theory holding them together. Since it appears to be highly uncharacteristic for Whitehead to write up two accounts of the same thing, we may wonder why he did so in this case. The most plausible hypothesis is that Whitehead wrote the Original Treatise first, as a part of his projected book on Metaphysics, working out this novel theory of perception. Then, once he had resolved to present this theory as part of his lectures on *Symbolism*, he found the Original Treatise unsuited for this task, and so rewrote the *Symbolism* lectures from scratch. This second presentation is the more congenial, certainly for independent reading.

Although during the summer of 1927 Whitehead had intended only the Giffords draft for his Gifford Lectures, by the spring of 1928 the many shifts in his thinking prompted him to give a precis of the entire project, insofar as it was completed. The prospectus shows that many topics were included, which might have been deemed unsuitable for a general audience: categories of existence and explanation, intellectual feelings, external connection, flat loci, etc. This suggests that if a topic is missing, it was probably not then to be included in the book on Metaphysics. Such is the case with the Original Treatise, whose topics are absent from the prospectus for the Gifford Lectures (Appendix 6).

Another topic missing is "Strains." If, after Whitehead presented the Giffords in June, 1928, he worked out the problem which "Strains" confronted him with, and decided to include this solution in his book on Metaphysics, then it would be convenient to have in the same book a preliminary account of the theory of perception this problem grows out of. Then the Original Treatise would have been resurrected to play this role, while "Strains" would be placed in part IV as the first application of straightness, measurement then becoming its second application.

As it stands now, "Symbolic Reference" (II.8) does not make a very self-contained chapter. Its initial discussion of the pure mode of presentational immediacy makes no contact with the previous chapter on the (reformed) subjectivist principle (II.7), and it introduces the "presented locus" without any adequate preparation (PR 168). On the other hand, an adequate preparation can be found in sections of "Organisms and Environment" (II.4.5–8). The earlier sections of II.4 consider a variety of topics, but focus on perception with section 5, which opens with these words: "The current accounts of perception are the stronghold of modern metaphysical difficulties" (PR 117). This may well be the initial words of an independent treatise. Both of the first two modes of perception are then introduced, together with the complexities of the "presented locus." We believe that "Symbolic Reference" (II.8) originally followed these three sections if we eliminate the last two sentences of II.4.8. These sentences are designed to lead into the later discussion of "Strains" appended in the next section (PR 126).

C. The Giffords Draft

With these preliminary considerations out of the way, we are prepared to consider what constitute the 9½ chapters of the Giffords draft completed the summer of 1927:

1. *"Speculative Philosophy" (I.1)*. Although there is some evidence Whitehead may have written this chapter later on in the summer, he seems always to have intended this general reflection on "speculative metaphysics" to be first. There is some evidence that it was one of the very last chapters he wrote before delivering the Giffords, since this chapter mentions "the consequent nature of God" (PR 12f). For reasons that will emerge later, we take the distinction between the primordial and the consequent natures to be one of the last additions made before the Giffords were presented. If that dis-

tinction forms an integral part, then this chapter must also be very late. But there is good evidence that this single paragraph (spanning PR 12f) concerning the ontological status of truth is a speculative reflection later inserted into this chapter. The passage runs smoothly without this interruption. Also, in the one other mention of God in this chapter this distinction is not evident (PR 7). For it is *only* with respect to the primordial nature, not the consequent nature, that God is the nontemporal exercise of creativity. As Whitehead simply says here that "God is its primordial, non-temporal accident," the consequent nature seems not yet to be thought of.

2. *"Fact and Form" (II.1)*. This discussion of "Fact and Form" in terms of the age-old issue of universals and particulars, explored in terms of Plato and Locke, contains very early material. There are several later insertions, however, two of which deserve notice. Section 4 introduces the ninth categoreal obligation (PR 46), while the rest of the Giffords draft does not discuss the categoreal obligations in detail. Even the later revisions of the Giffords draft only envisage eight categoreal obligations (PR 222, 248). The eighth categoreal obligation was originally described as "this final category" (PR 278). The ninth one was freshly envisaged later, and was inserted here as one of the last acts in preparing the book for publication. The insertion is not just section 4, but the last three paragraphs of the preceding section as preparation.

Later, sections 6 and 7 repetitiously introduce a discussion of Locke on power. One of these would be quite enough, if expounded in sequential order, suggesting some later insertion. The last two paragraphs of 1.6 may be a later insertion using late terminology, such as "intellectual feelings."

3. *"The Extensive Continuum" (II.2)*. This chapter contains the discussion of epochal becoming which seems to have led Whitehead to give up the internal supersession of the essay on "Time" of 1926. It may be earlier than the summer of 1927, but its origins are obscure. Its abrupt beginning suggests that it orginally belonged to a longer discussion of the various perceptive modes, while its use of "presentational objectification" (PR 61, 64) suggests a tie-in with 1.7, which is the only other section to use this peculiar formulation (PR 58).

4-5. *"Locke and Hume"* and *"From Descartes to Kant" (II.5-6)*. These discussions of his philosophy in the light of Descartes, Locke, Hume, and Kant may draw upon Whitehead's practice of making extracts from the philosophers he was reading, with brief comments thereon. It is possible that chapter 6 now contains two additions: (a) 6.3b: The passage beginning, "The four stages constitutive of an actual entity can be named datum, process, satisfaction, decision" (PR 149f), to the end of 6.3. (b) 6.5a: From the beginning of 6.5 to PR 155.14.[6] The discussion of Kant proper, the original subject of that section, begins with "In comparing Kant's procedure with that of the philosophy of organism . . ." (PR 155.17). The intervening three sentences are transitional.

These additional passages of a more systematic sort interrupt the flow of the historical commentary. It is difficult to determine when they were inserted, but their doctrine belongs squarely with that of the rest of the Giffords draft.

Originally chapter 6 may well have included an additional section: 7.1. Chapter 7 does not form a cohesive whole: 7.3–4 with 7.2 form a unit over against 7.1 and 7.5. It is difficult to conceive of these being drafted in consecutive order from the start, and much more plausible to think of them being assembled from other sources. The final section on the reformed subjectivist principle (7.5) was added in order to signal Whitehead's change of views on this important topic. It would have saved much confusion if Whitehead had thoroughly revised 7.1 instead of contenting himself with this addendum.[7] That 7.5 was added at the end of the chapter indicates that the chapter 7.1–4 had already taken shape as a unit.

6. "The Order of Nature" (in part) with "Organisms and Environment" (in part) (II.3.1–4 + 4.1–4). The rest of chapter 3 (5–11) is a sustained discourse utilizing such very advanced notions as "structured society," "living person," and "hybrid physical prehension." "Physical prehension" is not mentioned otherwise in the Giffords draft by our reckoning, and the notion of "hybrid physical prehension" is much later. Since 3.5 announces that its discussion is going to replace I.3.2, that section may have originally stood here in its place. At that time chapter 3 would appear to have only five sections. Was it the half-chapter Whitehead spoke of in saying that he had finished 9½ chapters?

It is unlikely that Whitehead could have foreseen that particular completion of chapter 3, since it depended so crucially on unanticipated concepts. On the other hand, without the Original Treatise on Perception, II.4.1–4 had no home in a single chapter. The two could be combined into one: 3.1–4 + I.3.2 + 4.1–4. Much of this corresponds to the Giffords prospectus for the fifth lecture (Appendix 6).

Several additions to the first section of chapter 3 will be considered later.

7. *"Propositions" (II.9)*. The opening sentences of chapter 3 tell us: "In this, and in the next chapter, . . . we are . . . concerned with . . . the allied problems of 'order in the universe,' of 'induction,' and of 'general truths.' The present chapter is wholly concerned with the topic of 'order' " (PR 83). The other two topics of induction and general (or metaphysical) truths are not taken up until II.9.4–8. This suggests that these two chapters originally stood adjacent to each other.

Whitehead's use of the date, "July 1, 1927," for "now" is strong evidence that chapter 9 was written during July, 1927, as we would suppose it to have been (PR 199).[8] The brief original reference, "in this and the next section" (PR 201), indicates that once 9.6 closed the chapter, to which are appended two additional justifications of induction. The last, which is based on the late notion of the primordial nature of God, was added even after the end-note of the chapter had been put in place.

8. *The Original Theory of Feelings (III.2.2, augmented)*. In some of the earlier essays, such as the additions to II.6, Whitehead devoted partial sections to the description of the phases of concrescence. Now he appears to devote a chapter to the topic, utilizing III.2 and possibly 7.3–4, with part of 7.2.

Reading "The Primary Feelings" (III.2) from the standpoint of the later doctrine that all conceptual feeling is derived from physical feeling, we assume its second section is primarily about conceptual feeling. But this is not the case. It is about the two main species of primary feelings, conceptual feelings and simple causal feelings. They are not derived from past actual entities nor from each other. Section 2 originally initiated the chapter, for III.2.1 is very likely a later insertion, reflecting the altered theory Whitehead espoused after the Giffords draft (see the next chapter). Section 3 is even later, applying categoreal obligations 1 and 7. When Whitehead came later to block out a whole part (PR III) devoted to concrescence, he made use of III.2 from the Giffords draft, relegating the rest to II.7.

9. *"The Final Interpretation" (PR V)*, as originally drafted. Part V, in its original form, probably constituted a single chapter. Its most

distinctive feature, the contrast between the primordial and the consequent natures of God, is probably quite late. When God is designated in the Giffords draft, it is usually as "the primordial actual entity" (PR 65). Just as the formative elements in *Religion in the Making* contain an "actual but non-temporal entity" (RM 88), actual occasions and eternal objects "are mediated by a thing which combines the actuality of what is temporal with the timelessness of what is potential. This final entity is the divine element in the world, by which the barren inefficient disjunction of abstract potentialities obtains primordially the efficient conjunction of ideal realization. This ideal realization of potentialities in a primordial actual entity constitutes the metaphysical stability whereby the actual process exemplifies the general principles of metaphysics" (PR 40). This is the chief role of God as primordial actual entity: to insure the basic metaphysical stability and general order by functioning as the underlying principle of limitation.

A "primordial actual entity" need not have two distinct natures, and we should not generally expect the distinction in the absence of one or the other of these two contrastive terms, "primordial nature" or "consequent nature." When they do appear in the chapters assigned to the Giffords draft other than in Part V, it is invariably in the form of later insertions, made when Whitehead was revising his lecture notes for publication, as we will see in the next chapter (section J).

If the development of this distinction between the two divine natures is late, we might expect Part V to be late as well. On the other hand, the Giffords draft constituted what in the main Whitehead intended to lecture about the following June in Edinburgh, and it would be most unusual for these lectures in natural theology not to conclude with a chapter on God, or God and the world, particularly as Whitehead had something original to say on these topics.

There is also more specific evidence that Whitehead wrote at least part of this material before he drafted II.10. The truncated character of V.1.2, now consisting of only two paragraphs, should indicate that something is missing. The first section of "Process" (II.10), from its beginning until one sentence beyond the verse quoted "Abide with me; Fast falls the eventide" (PR 209.7) fits seamlessly with V.1.2, if we omit the first two sentences (PR 338.11). That excerpt from II.10.1 seems to have originally belonged in V.1.2. It was as if Whitehead, wanting a good characterization of the contrast between flux and permanence for his discussion of the two kinds of fluency in II.10.1, excerpted this passage from what he had previously written, replacing it somewhat lamely with the two sentences which initiate V.1.2 in its present form.

If so, at least part of V.1–2 was written during the summer of 1927. It was probably intended to constitute one chapter. A scrutiny of part V indicates that there is sufficient material consonant with the general viewpoint of the Giffords draft for such a chapter. It could well have closed with the last three paragraphs of V.2.6, which end with these dramatic words: "The concept of 'God' is the way in which we understand this incredible fact—that what cannot be, yet is" (PR 350). At one point in the composition of the book, Whitehead probably intended that this sentence should complete it.

The first paragraph of that section (V.2.6) suggests this discussion concerns the role of the consequent nature, as does the opening sentence of the next section: "Thus, the consequent nature of God is composed of a multiplicity of elements with individual self-realization" (PR 350). There can be no doubt that the later Whitehead saw this role of experiencing the world as belonging solely to the consequent nature. But no such distinctions are made in these three paragraphs here. We learn only of God's unification of the eternal objects, which is described as God's "conceptual realization." "But God's conceptual realization is nonsense if thought of under the guise of a barren, eternal hypothesis" (PR 349). Then follows an eloquent, highly visionary passage in which the transiency of the world is described as being reclaimed in God, that is, in his *conceptual realization.*

Long before Whitehead had discovered the necessary concepts for his endeavor, even before he had officially adopted theism, he was grasped by an idea which later comes to be expressed by the doctrine of the consequent nature. In *Concept of Nature,* he wrote: "We can imagine a being whose awareness, conceived as his private possession, suffers no transition, although the terminus of his awareness is our own transient nature" (CN 67). It is the *timeless* awareness of the temporal that enables Whitehead to speak of it as a "conceptual realization." He may have initially thought of this timeless awareness as a *totum simul,* embracing all time and passage (cf. CN 69), but he finally comes down on the side of a gradual, continuing passage of the world. Thus, in these three final paragraphs of the Giffords draft, we are told: "This final phase of passage in God's nature is ever enlarging itself" (PR 349). How this is to be reconciled with God's timelessness is by no means clear, but it does anticipate later developments.

10. *"Process" (II.10).* This summary overview of Whitehead's basic notion "process", as developed thus far, has a fitting place in the Giffords draft. Its central thesis, that there are two species of process— "conscrescence" and "transition"—is fundamental to this earlier position. Also, this chapter is our best candidate for the half-chapter required for "9½ chapters." Guided by the discussion of "flux" and "permanence" in section 1, I had suggested that this treatment of "flux" was meant to be complemented by an emphasis on "permanence", i.e., God, in the remainder.[9] But if Whitehead borrowed his discussion of "flux" and "permanence" from material concerning God he had already written, that could not be the plan. A closer scrutiny of "Process" (II.10) reveals that Whitehead announced the two species of process in the opening and closing sections (10.1 and 10.5), and then discussed only one of these species, "concrescence," in the intervening three sections. A comparable treatment of "transition" is absent, and we submit that this was to be the topic of the missing half-chapter. As we shall see, that absence is not adventitious. It may be questioned whether he could have developed the notion any futher given the conceptuality he was working with. Subsequent developments rendered the issue superfluous, and he never returned to complete the chapter.

These 9½ chapters isolate about two hundred pages of text which, if due allowance is made for later insertions, lack such well-known technical concepts as simple physical feelings, negative prehensions, the derivation of conceptual from physical feelings, conceptual reversion, transmutation, intellectual feelings, hybrid physical feelings, subjective aim, and the distinction between the primordial and consequent natures in God. All these terms, and their accompanying conceptualities, were introduced by Whitehead in the final revisions, after this draft was composed. The most singular doctrine of the Giffords draft is the theory that concrescence *starts from* a single unified datum, "the datum of the concrescence," rather than starting from a vast multiplicity of initial data, which are reduced to unity in the final satisfaction. The initial phase here is not a multiplicity of simple physical feelings of past actualities, but a single datum: "The datum, which is the primary phase in the process constituting an actual entity, is nothing else than the actual world itself in its character of a possibility for the process of being felt" (PR 65). "No actual entity can rise beyond what the actual world as a datum from its standpoint—*its* actual world—allows it to be" (PR 83).

Before we analyze the theory of the Giffords draft any further, we should inquire whether any other chapters in *Process and Reality* might have been part of it. To be sure, our proposal is a fallible conjecture, which may well have to be modified in detail should new evidence come to light. Yet there may be large scale alternatives which propose quite a different set of chapters for our consideration. One such alternative suggests that Whitehead was concerned to get his theory straight first off, and therefore wrote the theoretical chapters first, before the chapters on applications. Now Whitehead could have done this the summer of 1927, writing first such chapters as II.2, II.3a/4a, II.9, II.10, III.2, before II.1, II.5–6. (It is far less plausible that he should have written III.3 or IV.1, as these contain ideas which may well have been *unanticipated* during the summer of 1927.) Once we bracket III.–IV.1 from consideration, then the amount of pure theory which part II contains can be seen to be considerable.

Suppose, however, the core of the alternative proposal is that these 9½ chapters contain at least these chapters: II.10, III.1–3, IV.1. Against this proposal we observe that IV.1 should be considered late because it is not mentioned on the prospectus for the Gifford Lectures and uses such late terms as "coordinate division" (for "morphological analysis"), "subjective aim," "eternal objects of the subjective and objective species" (IV.1.6). If III.1–3 were to be included, we might as well include III.4–5, for they take very little unanticipated theory to complete once the rudiments have already been established. But then we might have too many chapters for our 9½. If III.3 were part, it would stand in strong tension with III.2.2. (III.3 holds that all conceptual feelings are derived from physical feelings, while III.2.2 knows nothing of the sort.) While III.2.2 and 2.4 are part of the Giffords draft according to our reckoning, III.2.1, the linchpin of this chapter, stands in the sharpest tension to the Giffords draft. III.2.1 speaks of simple physical feelings of past actual occasions, while for the earlier theory, the concrescence of feelings always takes place within the occasion, arising out of the single original datum for that occasion. If the 9½ chapters should include any of the chapters I have proposed, such as II.10, then III.2.1 would stand in tension with it. If it were a part of a chapter within the 9½, then it would be inaugurating a new line of inquiry (III.3,5), rather than completing an earlier one. These considerations also apply, although to a lesser degree, to III.1.

2. Some Distinctive Characteristics of the Giffords Draft

(1) *The Original Datum.* For the time being, then, we shall assume that the 9½ chapters specified constitute what was completed during

the summer of 1927 as Whitehead's draft for the Gifford Lectures he would deliver the following June. As already indicated, their most characteristic teaching, at least with respect to what is to be rejected in the final revisions, is the doctrine that concrescence begins from a single unified datum. We find this teaching already as early as the Original Treatise on Perception, which speaks of a particular datum, "the visual datum for the percipient" in which "general geometrical relationships" are illustrated by "colour-sensa." The complexity of this datum is appreciated, for "the responsive phase [which follows upon this initial phase] absorbs these data as material for a subjective unity of feeling" (PR 172). If the issue of the unity of the primary datum were not so important to Whitehead, he could have written "data" throughout.

Later, we are told that "the first stage of the process of feeling is the reception into the responsive conformity of feeling whereby the datum, which is mere potentiality, becomes the individualized basis for a complex unity of realization" (PR 113). In one of the last chapters of the Giffords draft, II.10, Whitehead writes: "The objectified particular occasions together have the unity of a datum for the creative concrescence" (PR 210). This doctrine, that concrescence starts from a unified datum, and not from a multiplicity of initial data, so permeates the Giffords draft that it even appears in quite tangential contexts. Thus, "triviality and vagueness are characteristics in the satisfaction which have their origins respectively in opposed characteristics in the datum" (PR 111).

This particular teaching in intelligible only if we see it as an intermediate step between the metaphysics of 1926–27 and the final theory of concrescence. In the early metaphysics, every occasion possessed two suboccasions, a physical occasion superseded by a mental occasion. If such internal supersession is later prohibited by Whitehead's teaching on epochal becoming in II.2 (PR 69), then the theory of sub-occasions will have to be drastically remade. The activity of process could only be vested in one of the two, not in both. In the Lowell Lectures, he had vested all process in events, which were later to become "physical occasions". That early theory was forced to deal with mind in strange ways, in terms of "percipient objects" and "ego-objects". What we normally think of as subjects here became objects in contrast to events, since mind was excluded from events.

Hence Whitehead now adopts the opposite strategy for the Giffords draft by vesting all process in the mental occasion. The concrescence which springs from the original datum needs no physical feelings; it is a succession of phases of conceptual and supplemental feeling achieving its subjective appropriation. The datum is simply the former physical occasion objectified, conceived as devoid of process. The role of the physical occasion in amassing, ordering, and unifying all the content derived from the actual world is explained in terms of a theory of "objectification," itself apparently abstracted from process.

Imperceptibly, by means of this philosophical reflection, process has become almost exclusively identified with mentality, and vice versa. This is so characteristic of the later Whitehead that we tend to interpret the actual occasions of *Science and the Modern World* as mental. If anything, it would be more accurate to read "actual occasion" and "prehension" there as purely physical. But now in the Giffords draft, Whitehead has moved fully on the side of mentality, and can talk about the way the self comes into being by its appropriation of the original datum. This is a theory of "self-creativity," such as *Religion in the Making* called for, since the datum lacks all subjectivity as it lacks all process, and the occasion acquires it only in the process of concrescence.

On the other hand, this kind of self-creativity is less radical than the later theory in which the occasion itself (and not just some part labeled the "self") comes into being by the activity of concrescence. The Giffords draft theory remains more traditional: first the occasion comes into being as a datum, and then acts by means of concrescence. It does not "act" before it comes into being. As such, this is not a theory of "self-creativity" in the sense that that which is created is itself brought into being by that process. Here by "self" we do not mean (only) subject so much as the entity itself conceived reflexively. In the final revisions, Whitehead adopts just such a theory, which requires the creative unification of a multiplicity of initial data which only become one being at the end of concrescence. Radical creation can only be creative unification, for the unified being must emerge from the process. A being can either be created by itself or by another, but not by both. In the Giffords draft, a being is created in the emergence of the primary datum. It is created by its past. A self may also be created in the Giffords draft, but only as part of the total being of the occasion, not as the occasion itself.

The theory of the original datum from which concrescence begins is perhaps the most distinctive feature of the Giffords draft, but there are also several other differences from Whitehead's final theory that should be noted.

(2) *All Eternal Objects are Felt*. The Giffords draft adopts the principle that "every item of the universe, including all other actual

entities, are constituents in the constitution of any one actual entity" (PR 148). This principle, in turn, justified such claims as: "every so-called 'particular' is universal in the sense of entering into the constitutions of other actual entities" (PR 48). The principle White-head appeals to is the principle of solidarity, most clearly stated in the fall of 1926 as: "Every actual entity requires all other entities, actual or ideal, in order to exist." [10]

This principle as such does not carry over to the summer of 1927, but the third metaphysical principle (which becomes the fourth category of explanation) can be interpreted to entail the principle of solidarity if we assume that every potentiality will be actualized. The third metaphysical principle holds: "That the potentiality for acquiring real unity with other entities is the one general metaphysical character attaching to *all* entities, *actual* or non-actual—i.e., it belongs to the nature of a 'Being' that it is a potential for a 'Becoming.' " [11]

Later, however, not all eternal objects ingress in every actual entity. With the introduction of a principle of elimination by negative pre-hension, "only a selection of eternal objects are 'felt' by a given subject, although all actual entities are felt." (PR 41).[12] The excess ontological ballast is reduced considerably. Now, however, the prob-lem of novelty comes to the fore. That had not been a problem before. Since the primary datum included all the eternal objects whatsoever, each nascent occasion could select whatever creative possibility it needed for its own actualization. Now, however, White-head needs both a theory of the derivation of conceptual feelings from physical feelings, and a principle of conceptual reversion in order to explain the emergence of novelty in the world. The categoreal obligations were first formulated in the final revisions, but even the ideas they embody were absent from the Giffords draft. They were not needed then.

(3) *The Theory of Consciousness.* The theory of consciousness is less developed in the Giffords draft than in later revisions. Whitehead as much as says so in the opening paragraph to III.4: "The nature of consciousness has not yet been adequately analyzed. The initial basic feelings, physical and conceptual, have been mentioned, and so has the final synthesis into the affirmation-negation contrast," but not the intermediate use of propositional feeling, let alone the use of intellectual feeling, which depends upon the propositional feeling (PR 256).

This particular quotation presupposes a revised III.2, at least to the extent that the first section on simple physical feeling has been added. The Giffords draft lacks the concept of a physical feeling, since its function was then exercised by the primary datum. In the absence of physical feelings, it is difficult to conceive of the synthesis of physical and conceptual feelings in propositional feeling.[13] "Propositions" (II.9) developed the concept of a proposition with its logical subjects, which were in turn identified with actual entities, but it did not attempt to locate propositions within concrescence, or propose any "propositional feeling," let alone determine its derivation.

A fundamental conviction Whitehead held throughout his philosophizing is the principle "that consciousness presupposes experience, and not experience conscious" (PR 53). Only certain kinds of experiences are conscious: "the negative perception is the triumph of consciousness" (PR 161). It is a contrast between what is and its relevant alternatives, that which it is not; a contrast between the actual and the possible. "Consciousness requires more than the mere entertainment of theory. It is the feeling of the contrast of theory, as *mere* theory, with fact, as *mere* fact. This contrast holds whether or no the theory be correct" (PR 188).

Later on, it is appreciated that consciousness is not a factor in the datum of a feeling, in what is felt, but a factor in how it is felt. Then Whitehead applies the concept of the subjective form to consciousness: "Consciousness is the subjective form involved in feeling the contrast between the 'theory' which *may* be erroneous and the fact which is 'given' " (PR 161). As yet, this section (II.7.2) makes no mention of 'propositional feeling', the notion which later becomes the backbone of Whitehead's final theory of consciousness.

Thus, the basic ideas as to what consciousness is (the felt contrast between what is and what might be) is present already in the Giffords draft, but the conceptuality for expressing this (propositional feeling, intellectual feeling, subjective form) comes later.

(4) *The Theory of Subjectivity.* The Giffords draft has a theory of subjectivity cast in terms of final causation. As we saw above under the first distinctive feature, the original datum includes all the eternal objects, from which the occasion derives its 'ideal of itself.' "Process is the growth and attainment of a final end. The progressive definition of the final end is the efficacious condition for its attainment" (PR 150).

Certain features of the concept of 'subjective aim' are already present here. There is an individualized final causation operative throughout concrescence, whose nature is partially determined by the occasion itself. Its derivation, however, is more closely associated with the past than with God. Most importantly, the 'ideal of itself' does not play nearly as a central role in concrescence as the 'subjective aim' comes to play simply because it is not required in a process initiated by the original datum. Given the multiplicity of intial data, 'subjective aim' is needed in order to coordinate the activity of creative unification. The term 'subjective aim' and its special enlarged role only comes much later in the final revisions.

We shall attend to the nature of the 'ideal of itself' later in this chapter when considering possible transitions within the Giffords draft (Section 3[3]).

(5) *The Nature of 'Perishing.'* While the sense of "objective immortality" remains the same, the sense of "perishing" is quite different in the final revisions. There he writes: ". . . actual entities 'perpetually perish' subjectively, but are immortal objectively. Actuality in perishing acquires objectivity, while it loses subjective immediacy" (PR 29).[14] In this passage, subjectivity refers to the process of becoming by creative unification, which *necessarily* ceases once final determinate unity is achieved. But while unification must perish, the being of the occasion does not also perish. For it was the attainment of just that being (unity) which was the final end of the unification. The unification ceases in the unity, but the unity is then objectively immortal.

The force of this argument depends on the strict identification of subjectivity with creative unification, which was not possible within the Giffords draft, for it assumed an underlying subject arising out of the original datum, a being which then acts in achieving its own determinate concrescence. As a being this subject does not perish with the attainment of full determinate being, for it becomes merged with that determinate being. "Subjective immediacy" can be lost, because the occasion is no longer concrescing, but subjectivity per se cannot be lost, if it is at all a being, except by the loss of the being itself, which Whitehead does not argue for. That would contradict the principle of relativity by which, among other things, all past actualities are prehensible by all supervening ones. How could actualities be prehended if they were no longer in existence?

Even though the subject may not perish as in the later revisions, much does perish in the loss of subjective immediacy as envisaged in the Giffords draft: all dynamism, all flux, all creativity. The process of concrescent unification, which is the basis of the occasion's individual privacy, ceases with the final attainment of the satisfaction: "The 'perpetual perishing' (cf. Locke, II, XIV, 1) of individual absoluteness is thus foredoomed. But the 'perishing' of absoluteness is the attainment of 'objective immortality' " (PR 60). Or consider this text, which is either an anticipation or an alternative rendition of subjective perishing: "Locke's notion of time hits the mark better: time is 'perpetually perishing'. In the organic philosophy, an actual entity has 'perished' when it is complete. The pragmatic use of the actual entity, constituting its static life, lies in the future. The creature perishes *and* is immortal" (PR 81f).[15]

Another passage citing Locke belongs to the final revisions, having its own way of expressing subjective perishing: "The ancient doctrine that 'no one crosses the same river twice' is extended. No thinker thinks twice; and, to put the matter more generally, no subject experiences twice. This is what Locke *ought to have meant* by his doctrine of time as a 'perpetual perishing' " (PR 29, italics added). But Locke, lacking an understanding of subjectivity even as advanced as the view of the Giffords draft, did not mean that. This is what Whitehead ought to have meant by 'perishing' throughout *Process and Reality*. But in most contexts his thought is still very proleptic, finding completion only in the final theory of subjectivity as creative unification.

Much later, after Whitehead develops physical feeling for God in terms of the consequent nature, he may have first become fully aware of the "ultimate evil" in the temporal world which his new temporal theism can remedy: "the past fades, . . . time is a 'perpetual perishing.' Objectification involves elimination. [This is perspectival elimination, not the elimination of the whole. Otherwise there could be no objectification.] The present fact has not the past fact with it in any full immediacy" (PR 340). This sense of 'perishing,' which we may term 'superjective perishing,' in contrast to the 'subjective perishing' so prominent in the final revisions, is finally overcome in God.

This reception of the (otherwise) fading superject into the divine nature is *not* what Whitehead means by 'objective immortality'. That term was first introduced in the essay on "Time" (1926): "Each occasion A is immortal throughout its future. B enshrines the memory of A in its own concretion, and its essence has to conform to its memories. Thus, physical memory *is* causation, and causation *is* immortality" (IS 244). 'Physical memory' later becomes physical feeling, such that a past occasion is immortal by the way in which it is objectified in the present occasion. No appeal to God here is necessary. Nor does Whitehead mention any contrasting term to 'objective immortality,' a term which in any case is rarely used in the Giffords draft.

At least one mention does occur (II.10): each occasion "really experiences a future which must be actual, although the complete actualities of that future are undetermined. In this sense, each actual entity experiences its own objective immortality" (PR 215). This use of 'objective immortality' is consonant with its use in "Time."

It is only in the final revisions that 'objective immortality' secures its proper contrast, which is with subjective 'perishing'. For it is the 'being' which survives the 'becoming', and it is only the 'being', not the subjective 'becoming', that can be objectified. Subjective perishing is the precondition for objective immortality, while superjective perishing is at odds with objective immortality. As Whitehead notes later, the occasion "passes from a subjective aim in concrescence into a superject with objective immortality" (PR 245).[16] The superject never perishes completely, for by the principle of relativity, it must be prehended by every supervening actual entity. On the other hand, it is precisely the superject which perishes in the sense of ever fainter objectification by these supervening occasions, a loss which can only be overcome by God. Thus, we can say that the superject, as objectively immortal, nevertheless perishes. The theory is consistent, but the rhetoric jarring. Whitehead would have a much better rhetorical stance if he restricted himself to subjective perishing and superjective immortality.

Just as in the Giffords draft he avoided 'objective immortality', so in the final revisions he avoids using 'perishing' to mean superjective perishing (for this would interfere with the newly discovered subjective perishing). Nevertheless, he needs that which superjective perishing was designed to handle: the loss engendered by temporal supersession. With the invention of the consequent nature Whitehead has even greater reason to stress such loss, since now he has the conceptual instrumentality needed to express its divine overcoming clearly. Part of the problem is solved by finding an appropriate contrasting term for superjective perishing: 'everlastingness'. For he recognizes that ordinary objective immortality involves ever-diminishing objectification. "But objective immortality within the temporal world does not solve the problem set by the penetration of the finer religious intuition. 'Everlastingness' has been lost" (PR 347).

Thus 'objective immortality' is distinguished from 'everlastingness'. While occasions without God have 'objective immortality', they fade, for they lack 'everlastingness'. This 'everlastingness' is achieved by their prehension into God, for " 'everlastingness' is the content of that vision upon which the finer religions are built—the 'many' absorbed everlastingly in the final unity" (PR 347).

(6) *The Primordial Actuality.* As we have already seen, God in the Giffords draft is simply conceived as a primordial, or nontemporal actuality, having only conceptual feelings. This may seem anomalous, since Whitehead assigns to this 'conceptual realization' many of the functions which later could only apply to the consequent nature, e.g., the absorption of the world into the divine nature (see V.2.6). If God is an actual entity, but lacks physical feelings, while all other actual entities have both, it seems but a short step to experiment with assigning physical feelings to God as well, particularly as this would clarify functions already assigned to God.

When Whitehead did come to experiment with the idea of physical feelings for God, his conceptuality was sufficiently advanced to encourage and support such a venture. Given the underlying assumptions of the Giffords draft, however, it would be extremely difficult if not impossible for Whitehead to have seriously entertained such a possibility.

Whitehead came to the conviction that God exemplifies the categories quite early, at least by the fall of 1926, for he appends these remarks to the six principles of that year: "These principles are essential to actuality, and so apply equally well to God (pure act). It follows that God is a creature; the supreme actuality is the supreme creature." [17]

Since the eight metaphysical principles listed in Marvin's notes (Appendix 5) apply to the Giffords draft, these would be the principles God exemplifies in that conception. None of them requires any specific form of concrescence, nor that all actualities have both physical and conceptual feelings. A purely conceptual actuality, such as God was conceived to be, exemplifies these principles fully.

Also, how could we ascribe physical feelings to God when, as we have seen for the Giffords draft, *no* actuality whatsoever had any physical feelings? Physical feelings replace the concept of a primary or original datum, which is basic to this earlier conception. It is hardly likely that this doctrine of an original datum could be thought to apply to God. At least not in terms of a prior physical actuality. If God's concrescence were eternal, how could it be derived from some original datum? What could that datum possibly consist in? Here it makes little difference whether we construe 'eternity' as 'everlastingness' or as timelessness.

This technical problem is symptomatic of a deeper difficulty. In transitional unification, as conceived in the Giffords draft, the past collectively brings the occasion (qua original datum) into being. The past is active, the present occasion merely passive. (Since the occasion does not yet exist in any sense, it is perhaps better to say that it is not even passive.) Applied to God these considerations would seem to require that if God exemplifies the principles governing actual occasions, God's existence would be derivate from the world, and/ or whatever influence is received from the world would be received passively. Traditionally, such passivity was clearly regarded as a mark of imperfection.

In the final revisions after the Giffords draft, Whitehead won his way to the position that while becoming was not yet being it was not therefore simply nothing. In becoming it was possible for a concrescing occasion to prehend and to actively unify what it prehended. Thus God, in becoming, could also actively prehend and unify. If God was dependent upon the world for the data he prehended, God was not dependent upon it for the activity of prehending, as the Giffords draft might have suggested. Furthermore, this prehending was not a passive undertaking, but an active reception of actual data. Receptivity is here transformed from passivity into activity, and should no longer be considered as a divine imperfection.[18]

Once Whitehead perfects his understanding of physical feeling in "The Theory of Feelings" (III.1; also 2.1: D-E), it would be possible to ascribe physical feeling to God. This was not felt necessary, however, until the development of intellectual feelings (III.5: H) showed that God without physical feeling would be unconscious.

3. POSSIBLE TRANSITIONS WITHIN THE GIFFORDS DRAFT

For the most part the Giffords draft shows considerable consistency of doctrine, as might be expected from a series of lectures all drafted in one summer. It is possible, however, that there are some slight shifts, such as in Whitehead's understanding of concrescence, or in his understanding of the self.

Some of these texts, particularly those which reflect his growing awareness of the complexity of the original datum, or lead to the formulation of the concept of 'subjective form,' may not have been written during the summer of 1927. They could well be later reflections which were then inserted into his draft. Nevertheless, they have been classified with the Giffords draft because they continue to retain (although sometimes with evident strain) its most distinctive trait: the claim that concrescence originates from a single unified datum. Yet they may equally well be seen as preconditions for the shift which leads into the final revisions analyzed in the next chapter.

As we shall then see, this shift is largely based on the identification of the feelings within concrescence with (positive) prehensions. The identification requires the distinction between positive and negative prehensions, which in turn may well depend on the notion of subjective form. It is conceivable that the discovery of subjective form brought about the conceptual breakthrough we associate with the final revisions.

(1) *From "Process" to "Conscrescence", and from "Objectification" to "Transition"*. Whitehead's initial name for the inner activity of an occasion in the Giffords draft is "process." Thus the four stages constitutive of an actual entity are named "datum, process, satisfaction, decision" (PR 149f). While Whitehead used the term 'concrescence' in the 1926 lectures and in the essay on "Time," it does not appear among the earliest strata of *Process and Reality*.[19]

Towards the end of the Giffords draft, Whitehead apparently introduces "concrescence" as an alternative term for "process." They seem to be used interchangeably in II.6.5a, while II.7.4b speaks of "concrescence" as flowing from an "original datum," remarking upon "the complexity of the datum" (PR 165).

Now concrescence is used here in a double sense: (1) to signify the process of rendering something concrete; (2) in its etymological sense of "growing together." "Concrescence" is the unification of the many into one (especially so in II.10.2). A most striking example of this usage is given in this passage: "No actual entity can rise beyond what the actual world as a datum from its standpoint—*its* actual world—allows it to be. Each such entity arises from a primary phase of the concrescence of objectifications which are in some respects settled" (PR 83). The objectifications are unified into the occasion's original datum. What is here called "concrescence," to indicate the unification involved in forming the original datum, is later called transition to contrast it with concrescence as a process within the occasion. In the latter sense of "conscrescence," this growing together of objectifications is not a concrescence, but it is a concrescence in the former sense of unification.

Initially, Whitehead seems to have introduced the theory of "objectification" in order to explain how past actualities could be ingredient in concrescing occasions in some way not requiring "process." In that way all process could be assigned to the inner activity of occasions. This is also the position of the final theory, without the intervention of an intermediate step of a datum achieved by objectification which is then first felt in the process of concrescence. In the Giffords draft, objectification is the precondition of feeling, while in the final revisions the steps are joined: "an actual entity as felt is said to be 'objectified' for that subject" (PR 41). The initial data of past actualities, as felt, are brought together in concrescence.

As Whitehead states explicitly much later, objectification is conceived as the converse of prehension,[20] as prehension was understood in *Science and the Modern World*. Just as there is direct prehension of the remote past, so there is direct objectification of the remote past in the immediate subject, even though it may be practically negligible (PR 63). Just as there is perception in the modes of causal efficacy and presentational immediacy, so their converses appear in terms of causal and presentational objectification (PR 64; see also 62f). Perception and causality are here inseparably linked since "objectification" is the way of being " 'present in another entity' " (PR 50). Thus Locke adumbrates "the principle that the 'power' of one actual entity on the other is simply how the former is objectified in the constitution of the other. Thus the problem of perception, and the problem of power are one and the same . . ." (PR 58).

The theory of an original datum requires that the objectifications of the past actual world so constitute themselves as to form one consistent, complete, and unified entity for the concrescence. In "The Extensive Continuum" (II.2), extension is sufficient to accomplish this end: "Extension, apart from its spatialization and temporalization, is that general scheme of relationships providing the capacity that many objects can be welded into the real unity of one experience" (PR 67). In "Process" (II.10), however, objectification is seen to require elimination as well, and this requires process: "The objectified particular occasions together have the unity of a datum for the creative concrescence. But in acquiring this measure of connection, their inherent presuppositions of each other eliminate certain elements in their constitutions, and elicit into relevance other elements. Thus objectification is an operation of mutually adjusted abstraction, or elimination, whereby the many occasions of the actual world become one complex datum" (PR 210).

Objectification here is conceived as a process, "whereby the many occasions of the actual world become one complex datum." This is another process of unification, akin to concrescence. So Whitehead experiments with the notion that there are two processes of unification, a macroscopic process of "transition," and a microscopic process of "concrescence" (II.10).

Creativity as unification becomes the guiding thread shaping Whitehead's final philosophy, but at this point it poses some major problems: If concrescence is to be a real unification, there must be a real many to unify. But the internal process Whitehead has so far described starts from one single original datum, though there is another (external) process by which that later datum is obtained. "The creativity by which any relative complete actual world is, by the nature of things, the datum for a new concrescence, is termed 'transition' " (PR 211). In the next section we shall see that original datum described in terms of data, for that is what is needed for true concrescence. But the tension is still there, as long as Whitehead wishes to retain the initial unity (being) which the theory of the original datum was designed to protect.

For transition, there seems to be a very straight-forward process of unification: from the many actual occasions of the past to the one original datum. This would entail a concrescence of prehensions, as prehensions had been described in *Science and the Modern World* in terms of extensive internal relations, producing what was then described as the "physical occasion." But the more we try to work out the implications of this process of transition, the more it seems to involve a supersession whereby a transition (= physical occasion) is superseded by concrescence (= mental occasion). This is precisely the internal supersession which was rejected at the outset of the Giffords draft by the argument concerning epochal becoming.[21] I believe this was the reason why the chapter on "Process" (II.10) was left a half-chapter at the end of the summer of 1927. The sections on transition resisted any clear presentation. Later Whitehead was embarked on an entirely new way of conceiving the relation between transition and concrescence; which rendered any completion of II.10 obsolete. On his new view, "transition" would be conceived, not supersessionally, but coordinately (III.1.2).

(2) *From "Datum" to "Data."* First we should consider a particular form of the datum: the "objective datum." The "objective datum" does not first arise from the contrast between the initial and the objective datum, for this contrast is absent from the Giffords draft. There is one apparent exception, but what is here called "the initial datum" turns out on closer inspection to be what is to be called "the objective datum" from which concrescence starts: ". . . the way in which the antecedent universe enters into the constitution of the

entity in question so as to constitute the basis of its nascent individuality . . . is the initial datum in the process of its concrescence. When it is desired to emphasize this interpretation of the datum, the phrase 'objective content' will be used synonymously with the term 'datum' " (PR 152). From there it is only a short step to combine these synonyms, "datum" and "objective content," into "objective datum."

"Objective datum" is used at least twice in the Giffords draft (PR 164, 212), and possibly in one other text: in contrast to Kant (cf. II.6.5), Whitehead seeks "to describe how objective data pass into subjective satisfaction" (PR 88).

Until Whitehead composed his initial discussion of propositional feelings (III.4.1–2), he appears to have reserved "datum" (and "objective datum") for the entire concrescence, not for all individual feelings. In simple causal and simple conceptual feelings the subject felt actual entities and eternal objects respectively, both derived from the (original) datum (III.2.2), but these feelings are not yet said to have their own individual data. Propositional feelings, however, have propositions as their data. Here Whitehead also uses "objective datum" for that which is felt (PR 257, 259).

The doctrine of a single objective datum from which concrescence begins may be quite alien to our ordinary notion of Whitehead's philosophy, but it is quite appropriate to the Giffords draft. It represents the least necessary revision of the bipolar model of an actual occasion as both physical and mental occasion once internal supersession has been refuted (as in II.2.2). Yet, if concrescence is increasingly appreciated as a process of unification, the original datum would be seen more and more as a multiplicity. Once Whitehead speaks of "the complexity of the datum" (PR 165), another time of the "multifold datum" (PR 185). From then on he seems willing to speak simply of the original datum as "data" (PR 164, 213). In one place Whitehead speaks of the "objective datum" as the "reception of the actual world as a multiplicity of private centres of feeling" (PR 212).

Perhaps the best example of the use of 'data' for the original datum within the Giffords draft may be found in the chapter on "Propositions" (II.9.6). As if to ward off the suggestion that Whitehead adopts in his later theory, we are told that "these data are not extrinsic to the entity [as past actual entities would be]; they constitute that display of the universe which is inherent in the entity" (PR 203). This display can only be the original datum from which the occasion begins. But "datum" is avoided here in favor of "data."

Originally we were inclined to regard the shift from "datum" to "data" as the key to the shift from the Giffords draft to later revisions, but texts such as these suggest otherwise.

(3) *The Self and the "Ideal of Itself."* Now we should turn our attention to the other pole of the concrescence, the subject, to see how Whitehead conceived of it.

The datum, as originally conceived, was determinate with respect to exactly *what* shall be felt from the past actual world, but indeterminate with respect to *how* that shall be felt. Thus "the datum is indeterminate as regards the final satisfaction. . . . The determinate unity of an actual entity is bound together by the final causation towards an ideal progressively defined. . . . The ideal, itself felt, defines what 'self' shall arise from the datum; and the ideal is also an element in the self which thus arises" (PR 150).

This theory, that the self arises from the datum, makes use of "an ideal progressively defined." This clearly anticipates the term "subjective aim." But the "ideal of itself" is not used for the subjective aim's most distinctive function, which is to provide subjective unity for the incomplete phases of concrescence. Here it is enough for the self gradually to appear at the end. This ideal is variously called 'the full ideal,' 'the ideal peculiar to each actual entity,' 'the private ideal, gradually shaped in the process itself,' but Whitehead seems to have settled upon 'ideal of itself' as his technical designation.

Thus in "The Order of Nature" (II.3.1) Whitehead speaks of "the attainment of the full ideal. . . . In each case there is an ideal peculiar to each particular actual entity, and arising from the dominant components in its phase of 'givenness' " (PR 83f). "In its self-creation the actual entity is guided by its ideal of itself as individual satisfaction and as transcendent creator" (PR 85).

In describing concrescence in "Process" (II.10.3), Whitehead says: "The second stage is governed by the private ideal, gradually shaped in the process itself; whereby the many feelings (of the one original datum), derivatively felt as alien, are transformed into a unity of aesthetic appreciation immediately felt as private" (PR 212).

In a passage which is probably a very early insertion within "Propositions" (II.9.1), Whitehead formulated the notion of an "objective lure" as that from which the "ideal of itself" can be derived.[22] We think this passage is an addition because the topic of the "objective lure" is not directly germane to the issue at hand, which is the specification and description of propositions, and because of the intrusive way in which these passages are introduced. It was as if

Whitehead worked out the notion of "objective lure," and then hunted around for a likely context in which to insert his thoughts.

The initial paragraph of this insertion deserves to be quoted in full: "The 'lure for feeling' is the final cause guiding the concrescence of feelings. By this concrescence the multifold datum of the primary phase is gathered into the unity of the final satisfaction of feeling. The 'objective lure' is that discrimination among eternal objects introduced into the universe by the real internal constitutions of the actual occasions forming the datum of the concrescence under review. This discrimination also involves eternal objects excluded from value in the temporal occasions of that datum, in addition to involving the eternal objects included for such occasions" (PR 185).

"Objective lure" functions here as a technical term for the "lure" or element of final causation ingredient in the original datum. With a concern for novelty which ultimately leads to the category of reversion, Whitehead notes that the "objective lure" also involves relevant eternal objects unrealized in that datum. The relation between an eternal object and its relevant actual occasions takes the form of a proposition: "A proposition is an element in the objective lure *proposed for feeling*, and when admitted into feeling it constitutes *what is felt*" (PR 187). Since the objective lure is derived by objectification, and is thus not amenable to any subjective determination, it functions primarily as a reservoir of possibility for the occasion, from which selection is made. It is the source for the "lures for feeling", including the "ideal of itself." In any case, the ideal is ultimately derived from the past, and not, as will later be the case, from God. "In each case there is an ideal peculiar to each particular actual entity, and arising from the dominant components in its phase of 'givenness' " (PR 84).

A second "objective lure" passage, now using "data" instead of the "multifold datum," may be found in the chapter on "The Order of Nature", section 1 (II.3.1), beginning with the fifth paragraph (PR 84).[23]

This addition contains a number of later insertions within it, the first of which is designed to identify the later term "subjective aim" with the "ideal of itself." Without this two-sentence insertion the text would read: "In its self-creation the actual entity is guided by its ideal of itself as individual satisfaction and as transcendent creator. This lure for feeling is the germ of mind" (PR 85). Its ideal of itself is the one of the lures for feeling stimulating the process of concrescence.

While the original single datum now dissolves into many initial data, Whitehead retains the notion of a single objective lure constituted by the relevance of various eternal objects to the actual occasions initially felt. Thus "the *relevance* of an eternal object in its role of lure is a fact inherent in the data. In this sense the eternal object is a constituent of the 'objective lure' " (PR 86). "The gradation of eternal objects in respect to this germaneness (to the basic data) is the 'objective lure' for feeling" (PR 87). Again, the objective lure is not what is finally felt. Subjective decision can exercise its power in the selection made: "the concrescent process admits a selection from this 'objective lure' into subjective efficiency. This is the subjective 'ideal of itself' which guides the process" (PR 87). Although insisting upon the purely objective character of the objective lure, Whitehead notes: "But admission into, or rejection from, reality of conceptual feeling is the originative decision of the actual occasion. In this sense an actual occasion is *causa sui*" (PR 86).

This pair of concepts, the "objective lure" and the "ideal of itself," serve as the conceptual material from which Whitehead later fashions "subjective aim."

(4) *The Emergence of "Subjective Form."* As we have just seen, several key terms and concepts appear towards the end of the composition of the Giffords draft, such as "concrescence," "transition," "data" (when applied to the original datum), "ideal of itself," and "objective lure." There is also one more term, which appears very late, and which will play an important role in the final revisions: "subjective form." While the term "subjective form" appears many times in the chapters we have assigned to the Giffords draft, invariably these turn out to be later insertions Whitehead introduced when he edited his manuscript for final publication.[24] Only two passages using "subjective form" can be closely associated with the Giffords draft, indicating that while the term was late in coming, it should be classified with that draft. Those two sections are from the chapters on "The Subjectivist Principle" (II.7.4) and "From Decartes to Kant" (II.6.5).

(a) Let us first consider the second half (7.4b) of this section (starting with PR 164.39). Both halves assume there is a single datum from which concrescence flows, 7.4a speaking of "the objective datum from the past" which is the "transcendent decision" (PR 164), while 7.4b mentions the "complexity" of "the original datum" (PR 165). Yet while 7.4b is on the verge of introducing subjective forms, it never does so, while 7.4a mentions them several times.[25]

Now 7.4b clearly anticipates the idea of "subjective form." Whitehead speaks here of "the adjustment of subjective importance by functioning of subjective origin. The graduated emotional intensity of the subject is constituting itself by reference to the physical data, datively there and conformally felt. . . . Supplementary feeling is emotional and purposeful, because it is what is felt by mere reason of the subjective appropriation of the objective data. . . . The conformal stage merely transforms the objective content into subjective feelings. But the supplementary stage adds, or excludes, the realization of the contrasts by which the original datum passes into its emotional unity" (PR 164f).

Whitehead is aware of the complexity of the original datum, recognizing that each conformal feeling appropriates only part of the datum. Here the function of supplementary feeling has a very close bearing upon subjective form, for both are concerned with the emotional, subjective response to what is given. In Whitehead's more developed conceptuality, every feeling has a subject, a datum, and a subjective form. The datum is *what* is felt, while the subjective form expresses *how* that datum is felt. That distinction is missing here, for here the supplementary feelings are themselves full-fledged feelings in their own right, whereas subjective forms are conceived as *aspects* of feelings, which also have data of their own distinct from those subjective forms. It is difficult to conceive how Whitehead could have composed 7.4b the way he does if "subjective form" were already part of his conceptuality. On the other hand, 7.4b would certainly contribute to the ferment leading to the emergence of this concept.

This section (7.4), moreover, distinguishes between the dative phase and conformal physical feeling. In the dative phase the datum is simply given to the concrescence. It is pure objectification. That datum is then appropriated for the nascent occasion by its many conformal physical feelings which the concrescence can then integrate. Note that these conformal feelings, like all other feelings, are entirely *within* the occasion, unlike prehensions, which mediate *between* occasions. At this point feelings and prehensions do not seem to be identified, as they soon will be.

After Whitehead adopted the concept of subjective form, he apparently made the addition found in 7.4a. Since it dealt with many of the themes of 7.4b, particularly with the ferment that half-section caused, it was natural, given Whitehead's characteristic methods of revision, that he supplement 7.4b with a preface detailing his newly won position.[26]

In 7.4a the meaning of "subjective form" is still quite fluid. The immanent decision describes "the process of acquisition of subjective form and the integration of feelings" (PR 164). Here we cannot determine whether subjective form applies to each feeling individually or to the whole concrescence. Or perhaps we should understand it as the form of the subject to be realized by the process.

(b) The text from "From Descartes to Kant" (6.5a) seems to be a later insertion into the Giffords draft, which Whitehead used to preface his historical discussion of Kant (beginning at PR 155.17). Given Whitehead's earlier commitment to a unified primary datum, he could then set up a neat contrast with classical philosophy: "The philosophies of substance presuppose a subject which then encounters a datum, and then reacts to the datum. The philosophy of organism presupposes a datum which is met with feelings, and progressively attains the unity of a subject" (PR 155). This general comparison could then be applied to Kant.[27]

Two passages here might support an earlier understanding of subjective form as applying to the whole: "The problem which the concrescence solves is, how the many components of the objective content are to be unified in one felt content with its complex subjective form" (PR 154). And: "But 'process' is the rush of feelings whereby second-handedness attains subjective immediacy; in this way, subjective form overwhelms repetition, and transforms it into immediately felt satisfaction; objectivity is absorbed into subjectivity" (PR 155).[28] Neither of these passages, however, is decisive, and the other three mentions of "subjective form" clearly apply to individual feelings.

The introduction of "subjective form" at this point in Whitehead's philosophy was most salutary, for without "subjective form," it might not have been conceptually possible for Whitehead to have identified "prehension" and "feeling." In the next chapter we shall see how much this identification lies at the very heart of the metaphysical revolution which prompted the final revisions.

NOTES

1. Victor Lowe, "Whitehead's Gifford Lectures," *The Southern Journal of Philosophy* 7/4 (Winter, 1969–70), 331f.
2. *Ibid.*, 329f.
3. *Ibid.*, 333.

4. I am indebted to my student Michael Hertzig for this information, which he found among the Macmillan correspondence with authors housed in the Archives of the New York Public Library.

5. Letter to author, July 17, 1978. Because of the exigencies of analyzing PR, terms simply mentioned will be often enclosed in single quotation marks in chapters 8 and 9.

6. Decimal places indicate the line number when this is desirable in page citations. These are easily determinable with a calibrated rule set alongside the margin of the page.

7. As well as the insertion 189.30–191.21 to II.9.2.

8. See also the footnotes to PR 200.

9. "Some Proposals Concerning the Composition of *Process and Reality,*" *Process* Studies 8/3 (Fall, 1978), 150.

10. B1. See Appendix 3.

11. M3. Whitehead's emphasis. Appendix 5.

12. This sentence is found in a negative prehension addition which includes the entire last paragraph of II.1.1 with the exception of the very first sentence (PR 41f). See also PR 239.

13. For this reason, and because the term "physical feeling" is used several times, III.4.1–2 should be assigned to the final revisions, even though otherwise nothing here is incompatible with the primary datum theory.

14. Whitehead evidently has not yet made the distinction between actual occasions and actual entities (which include God), else he would have written that only actual occasions perish.

15. This passage shows explicitly that the function of objective immortality is identified with the superject, but also the continuity of the "subject-superject." Whitehead introduced this term in the final revisions, in III.1, either in 1.3 or 1.10: "The subject-superject is the purpose of the process originating the feelings" (PR 222). "An actual entity is at once the subject of self-realization, and the superject which is self-realized" (PR 222). The hyphenated term was designed to stress the identity of the two, since the subject is not an external agency bringing about the superject. That would not be self-creation. On the other hand, the doctrine of the "subject-superject" could emphasize the continuity of the occasion, a continuity which could easily be lost by a one-sided emphasis on subjective perishing. Even though the "subject" perishes in becoming the "superject," these cannot be conceived as two distinct entities. There is only the one entity, which can only be called the "subject-superject." The subject-superject is also mentioned at PR 28, 29, 47, 83, and 233.

16. This text comes from the last two paragraphs of II.2, which is probably an addition. It has nothing to do with perception and "symbolic transference," the theme of the immediately preceding chapter, but it does discuss change, which Whitehead could easily have taken as one of the main themes of the chapter, and simply appended this note, probably to call attention to *Timaeus* 28A as germane to the problem of perishing. While these two paragraphs have been inserted later, we cannot tell clearly whether they belong to the Giffords draft or to the final revisions.

Locke's "perpetual perishing" is cited four times, while Plato is only cited once on this theme. Whitehead was a great admirer of Plato; why was he not cited more often than Locke, whose discussion of time on the whole is rather pedestrian? I suspect that when Whitehead was reading Locke he read his own idea of time as "perpetual perishing" into Locke, and was tremendously excited by the idea, and proceeded to cite him on this idea during the summer of 1927. Later he found this citation from Plato to use. If this passage quoting the *Timaeus* is part of the Giffords draft, then only one more citation of Locke is forthcoming. Otherwise this could be the final citation of Locke, showing the roots of this reflection in Plato.

17. Appendix 2, paragraph 21.

18. Here see my essay, "Whitehead's Transformation of Pure Act," *The Thomist* 41/3 (July, 1977), 381–99.

19. The adjectival counterpart, "concrescent", appears once in II.1.7, twice in II.2.1, and four times in II.4.8, all very early texts probably composed before the summer of 1927, perhaps before Whitehead had fixed his terminology.

20. See category of explanation 14.

21. See chapter 7, first section, with respect to PR 68f.

22. This first "objective lure" addition seems to have consisted of paragraphs 5, 6, part of 7, and 17 of II.9.1 (PR 185.14–186.16 + 187.17–24). The 17th paragraph speaks of "these hybrid entities," a reference making no sense in context but fitting well with the distantly prior paragraph 7, describing a proposition as "a hybrid between pure potentialities and actualities." On the other hand, the rest of paragraph 7 specifying a "singular proposition" is necessary for the original context.

23. That is, PR 84.21–89.2, including other insertions. See the original continuity which existed before these insertions. The earlier paragraphs of II.3.1 are summarized in this way at the beginning of this insertion: "Thus the notion of 'order' is bound up with the notion of an actual entity as involving an attainment which is a

specific satisfaction." Just this theme is resumed in 3.2: "the notion of 'order' is primarily applicable to the objectified data for individual actual entities" (PR 89). No mention is made of the intervening discussions of objective lure, subjective aim, and God.

24. I have proposed a provisional list of these insertions in "The Concept of 'Process': From 'Transition' to 'Concrescence'," an essay appearing in *Whitehead and the Idea of Process*, ed. H. Holz and E. Wolf-Gazo (Freiburg: Verlag Karl Alber, 1984), fn. 12.

25. I take 7.4b to have originally begun more formally: "There are four modes of functioning . . ." The first part of that paragraph, and some comments in the preceding paragraph, appear to be transitional material linking the later 7.4a with 7.4b.

26. The text of 7.4a includes one later insertion: 164.3–12. Previous to 7.4a Whitehead spoke of "decision" simply in terms of the decision that the past world lays upon the concrescing occasion (PR 150). Here in 7.4a this decision as "transcendent" is contrasted with the "immanent decision." In the insertion Whitehead wants to associate this "transcendent decision" with God's decision, which was nowhere contemplated in the original discussion.

The insertion's use of "subjective form" is subtly different from that in the original 7.4a.

27. The transitional material patching these two sections together would be 155.14–17.

28. This is the final sentence of 6.5a proper.

NINE

The Final Revisions

In this chapter we come at last to that philosophical outlook which most regard as characteristically Whitehead's. Here concrescence is conceived as a process of unification of simple physical feelings of a multiplicity of past actual occasions, a process presided over by a subjective aim whose initial phase is provided by God. Yet there is no single self-contained final treatise setting forth these conclusions. Whitehead had already written his treatise in the form of the Giffords draft; here he contented himself by making revisions in the form of appended chapters and sections to what he had already written.

The basic conceptual revolution is effected in the opening chapter of Part III (III.1.2), which we shall examine shortly. On its basis Whitehead appears to have devised the first three categoreal conditions and to have examined the natures of "contrasts," "nexūs," and "subjective forms": these comprise the topics of the first chapter. That chapter forms the beginning of a short treatise, to be sure, when combined with a plan to determine the theory of concrescence as now reconceived on its new basis. For this purpose the discussion of primary causal and conceptual feelings (III.2.2) was supplemented by the introduction of simple physical feelings (in 2.1) and of consciousness as an integrated feeling (2.4). When Whitehead came to realize that an integrated feeling based upon his theory of propositions would speak to the problem of consciousness, he developed the propositional feelings of "Propositions and Feelings" (III.4.1–2).

These sections (III.2.1–2.4 + 4.1–2) may originally have belonged to the same chapter, but when Whitehead decided to adopt Hume's principle of deriving all conceptual feelings from physical feelings, the elaboration of categoreal conditions 4–8 in the chapter on "The Transmission of Feelings" (III.3) was interposed. In working out the final categoreal conditions, he seems to have devised the full concept of 'subjective aim' for the first time, and to have realized that it could only come from God (3.1).

The necessity of distinguishing between "physical purpose," which all occasions must have, and "propositional feelings," which only the higher occasions would have, led to the invention of the "intellectual feeling." The complexity of the "intellectual feeling" gives Whitehead the required flexibility to distinguish conscious perceptions, intuitive judgments, direct and indirect authentic feelings, etc., which constitute the core of "The Higher Phases of Experience" (III.5). Its developed theory of consciousness, that physical feelings be a required part of integrated intellectual feelings, which alone are conscious in their subjective forms, demands that God either have physical feelings or be unconscious. This naturally leads to the experiment of endowing God with a physical nature, resulting in the extended revision of Part V on "God and the World."

At this point we have recounted all the changes and additions that would have occurred between the end of the summer of 1927 and June, 1928, when Whitehead gave the Gifford Lectures in Edinburgh. He still had to prepare the manuscript for publication, and set about editing it, trying to render the earlier sections consistent with his final views. His primary method seems to be the insertion of paragraphs or sentences designed to encourage the reader to interpret the passage in question in terms of his final view. In that respect we must judge him largely successful, for most interpreters have supposed that *Process and Reality* propounds one consistent viewpoint.

Besides these additions, three more chapters were yet to come. The problem of identifying a percipient occasion's presented locus with one of its contemporary durations suggests the notion of "strain-feelings," leading to II.4.9 and IV.4 (probably also part of IV.5). The concept of the "hybrid physical prehension" enabled Whitehead to explain more precisely how the initial aim was derived from God (III.3.2), and to abolish the category of conceptual reversion (3.3, final paragraph). It also permitted a more satisfactory explanation of the living person (II.3.11).

Finally, as a way of integrating the theory of concrescence in part III with the theory of extension in part IV, the chapter on Coordinate Division (IV.1) was introduced.

This summarizes Whitehead's progress in completing the theory of *Process and Reality*. We shall now attend to the individual steps, showing why we believe this to be the proper order, insofar as it can be ascertained at present.

D. "The Theory of Feelings"
(III.1, especially 1.2)

The concept of an original datum from which concrescence flowed, which had been the staple of Giffords draft theory, became increasingly problematic as concrescence was conceived more and more as a process of unification requiring an initial many to unify, and transition was treated as process unifying the many "objectifications." Such a view of transition could make sense of the original datum, but at the cost of transforming the process into two successive unifications, the sort of internal supersession excluded by the doctrine of epochal becoming (II.2.2). Instead of this double process Whitehead needed a single process moving from the many past actualities to the final unity of the satisfaction.

Whitehead found the means for achieving this end in an identification of feelings and prehensions, and in a "miniaturization" of the Giffords draft theory to apply to each individual feeling.

The distribution of the term "prehension" is not yet adequately understood, but it seems to be used rarely, if at all, in the Giffords draft. If used at all, it would be in the older sense of *Science and the Modern World* as pertaining to spatio-temporal relations between actual occasions. These relations were largely reconceived in terms of objectification. At any rate, such prehensions would pertain only to the objective content of occasions. Feelings, in the Giffords draft, applied to subjective activities within concrescence.

The introduction of subjective form, however, greatly facilitated the identification of prehension and feeling, for now prehensions could be endowed with the subjectivity of response expressed by the subjective form.

Yet, we prehend far more than we feel. By the theory of prehension we are related to all other actualities in the universe, though this is much more than can be finally felt in satisfaction. So Whitehead introduces the distinction between positive and negative prehensions, allowing only "positive prehensions" to be strictly identified with "feeling." But what is the status of that which is prehended but not felt? If what is negatively prehended were to have no impact whatsoever, then why would it not be non-existent for that occasion? How can we say that the occasion negatively prehended anything? Without the recently acquired concept of subjective form Whitehead would be hard pressed to give any answer, but now he can simply say: in negative prehension, the datum is inoperative, but the subjective form of exclusion is felt as contributory to the final subjective form.

If we were to construe "feeling" to mean the entire concrescence of an actual occasion, such that the "initial data" constitutes the entire past actual world, and recognize that "transition" has taken on a new meaning, then one core assertion can be interpreted in terms of the original datum theory of the Giffords draft: "A feeling— i.e., a positive prehension—is essentially a transition effecting a concrescence. Its complex constitution is analysable into five factors which express what that transition consists of, and effects. The factors are: (i) the 'subject' which feels, (ii) the 'initial data' which are to be felt [in this case, all past actual occasions], (iii) the 'elimination' in virtue of negative prehensions, (iv) the 'objective datum' which is felt, (v) the 'subjective form' which is *how* that subject feels that objective datum" (PR 221). On this interpretation, the objective datum would be the original datum from which the concrescence flows, and the subjective appropriation would be made in terms of the subjective form.

But this core assertion is prefaced by an account of the many feelings of concrescence, and this assertion applies to *any* of these feelings. The conceptual moves required to revise the original-datum theory are very few. Basically Whitehead has individualized the earlier theory to apply to each feeling, which is now also endowed with the properties of being a positive prehension. By a prehension a subject prehends more than can be felt. In addition to the concept of "negative prehension," Whitehead invents the concept of "initial data," and the distinction between the "data which are to be felt" and the "datum which is felt." In those cases in which a feeling employs all five factors, the one objective datum is derived from many initial data, but these are not fully felt.

The idea that data, as a sheer multiplicity, cannot be felt is finally articulated in terms of the reformed subjectivist principle: there can be no "togetherness" except "togetherness in experience" (PR 189f). The many finally cannot form a many, unless somehow "together," which is possible only in experience. Only that which has the minimal unity of a single datum can be the object of a feeling. For this reason a multiplicity is not a "proper entity"; in fact, it is difficult to see how it is any entity at all. It has only the spatiotemporal internal relatedness of its many members expressed by their mutual prehension of one another.[1] If the multiplicity can only be felt *as* a unity, then the multiplicity specifies only what "is to be felt," not what is finally felt. Each feeling then is a reduction of multiplicity to one. It is "essentially a transition effecting a concrescence," since each contributes to the overall unificatory process.

For example, if we consider a propositional feeling, some proposition is its objective datum, but the components of that same proposition, the logical subjects and the predicative pattern, constitute its initial data. They are not felt by the propositional feeling, but by prior physical and conceptual feelings. Should these integrate to form a propositional feeling, the initial data are integrated into one complex objective datum, the proposition. Not all feelings are so complex, and for them the first three factors can be telescoped. For example, "in a conceptual feeling there is no necessary progress from the 'initial data' to the 'objective datum'" (PR 240).

"Transition" and "concrescence" are now conceived coordinately as applying to each individual feeling. They are no longer successive processes, but aspects of the same process. "There is a transition from the initial data to the objective datum effected by the elimination" (PR 221). This would be fully intelligible in terms of the Gifford draft theory, but Whitehead now applies it to any feeling. Thus it applies to propositional feelings, although the accent would naturally fall upon simple physical feelings. But notice also the carefully constructed parallel statement: "There is a concrescence of the initial data into the objective datum, made possible by the elimination, and effected by the subjective form." Transition as a unification is a concrescence, while concrescence is a transition from data to datum. In concrescence it is effected by the subjective form, but only because these feelings are compatible for integration, according to the first categoreal obligation, brought about by perspectival elimination.

By means of this revised conceptuality, process is a single act of unification, starting from many actual entities of the world. Now Whitehead is fully embarked on his particular task in metaphysics: to explain subjectivity in a radically non-substantive fashion, in a way which cannot presuppose any being, especially any unified datum, at the outset.

A section found in "The Theory of Feelings" (III.1.5) appears to be Whitehead's first attempt to comprehend the conditions of concrescence under these transformed circumstances. With the use of three basic categoreal conditions, particularly the first, the category of subjective unity, Whitehead sought to preserve some of the advantages of the former datum theory he has now abandoned. Its chief advantage is the compatibility for integration it insures for the objective content of any feeling. According to the earlier theory, all possible incompatibilities among the many actual data of the past world would have been adjusted to one another by the activity of transition producing the unified datum. Then Whitehead could write: "the settled world provides the 'real potentiality' that its many actualities be felt compatibly; and the new concrescence starts from this datum" (PR 150). The unity of this datum, moreover, assured that the subjective appropriations of it by means of conformal physical feelings, as well as any integrations thereof in supplementary feelings, would all be mutually compatible. All this seemed to be in jeopardy once the theory of an initial single datum was abandoned. What could guarantee that a sheer multiplicity of feeling would spontaneously possess this degree of inner harmony?

Here Whitehead's solution seems somewhat forced, for it is difficult to see the justification for every feature of the first category. It seems to be promulgated by simple fiat: "The many feelings which belong to an incomplete phase in the process of an actual entity, though unintegrated by reason of the incompleteness of the phase, are compatible for synthesis by reason of the unity of their subject" (PR 223).

One striking feature of this formulation is the final justification: ". . . by reason of the unity of their subject." But the subject has not yet fully come into being. We might have expected something like: "by reason of the unity of the subjective aim." But the original text of this section does not appear to contain any trace of 'subjective aim'.[2]

Whitehead offers a justification for this absence. In systematic interpretations the passage we shall now consider is often put to other uses because of its close verbal affinities with "subjective aim," but that particular phrase, particularly in its technical meaning, was in all probability not yet even anticipated: "It is better to say that the feelings *aim at* their subject, than to say that they *are aimed at* their subject [by, among others, the 'ideal of itself']. For the latter mode of expression removes the subject from the scope of the feeling and assigns it [the feeling] to an external agency. Thus the feeling would be wrongly abstracted from its own final cause. This final cause is an inherent element in the feeling, constituting the unity of that feeling" (PR 222). Here the final cause does not yet function as a separate feeling within the concrescence, but rather simply as an element inherent in every feeling. It does not guide the individual feelings by aiming them at their ultimate subject.

An important role for subjective aim later on will be to provide some sort of subjective unity now that any initial objective unity has been discarded. Whitehead initially accounts for that subjective unity in quite another way, in terms of the mutual sensitivity of subjective forms. This follows from the commonplace in aesthetic experience that all components interpenetrate in one final feeling. Whitehead at first broadens the scope of that principle's application in two ways within the occasion: (1) Contemporary feelings, as long as they are within the occasion, can mutually influence one another. (Strictly speaking, the macroscopic aesthetic experience only relates past components to present perception. Contemporaries are causally independent.) (2) Earlier and later feelings within the same occasion influence each other. Such *unrestricted* mutual sensitivity of feeling allows for the latter, and this is sufficient to insure subjective unity throughout the occasion, as that final subject can influence the whole process.

Later, mutual sensitivity becomes restricted, but here are some examples of this early unrestricted use: In discussing the first category Whitehead tells us that "the one subject is the final end which conditions each component feeling. Thus the superject is already present as a condition, determining how each feeling conducts its own process. Although in any incomplete phase there are many unsynthesized feelings, yet each of these feelings is conditioned by the other feelings" (PR 223). "There is a mutual sensitivity of feelings in one subject, governed by categoreal conditions. This mutual sensitivity expresses the notion of final causation in the guise of a pre-established harmony" (PR 221).

E. The Second Theory of Concrescence
(III.2.1–2.4 + 4.1–2)

After devising the first three categoreal conditions and specifying some key terms, Whitehead appears to have set about revising his theory of concrescence in the light of his newly-won identification of feeling with positive prehension. He was able to utilize the second section of "The Primary Feelings" (III.2.2) pretty much as previously written by means of two stratagems. In order to make it (2.2) his basic discussion of conceptual feeling, he prefaced it with another section (2.1), which introduces "simple physical feelings." Originally the second section was intended to introduce both types of primary feelings, simple causal feelings and conceptual feelings. These causal feelings, moreover, as originally conceived, differ from simple physical feelings in that they do not "reach out beyond" the occasion to other actualities; they are wholly within the occasion, as derived from the original datum. This can be seen by reading the accounts of simple causal feeling strictly by themselves, without regard to the first section. Now, however, Whitehead modifies that original meaning merely by stipulating that causal feelings are to be identified with simple physical feelings (PR 236).

The analysis of the simple physical feeling in section one follows the same pattern of analysis that Whitehead had laid down for any feeling (III.1.2). Rhetorically (although not conceptually) there is one difference, since a simple physical feeling has a single initial *datum*, whereas a feeling as analyzed previously (in III.1.2) has many initial *data*. But a datum actual occasion can be thought of as constituting many data by coordinate division. Thus, if we chose, we could say that the many initial data, which are to be felt, are the many feelings comprising the satisfaction of the past actual occasion, while the objective datum is that past occasion's one feeling by which it is finally felt. All of the five factors, initial data, elimination, objective datum, subjective form, and subject, are thus present in the simple physical feeling, although the initial data collectively are here named the initial datum for the convenience of analysis.

After physical and conceptual feelings were introduced in the first two sections of chapter two (III.2), Whitehead could use their integration as a way of articulating the contrast in consciousness between what is and what might be in the final section (2.4). He already had the contrast in the Giffords draft (II.10.3, the middle paragraph), but then he lacked the conceptual means of specifying the element of fact in terms of concrescence. Physical feeling, first introduced in the first section of this chapter (2.1), supplied that means.

This final section (2.4) presupposes another conceptual innovation: the understanding of consciousness in terms of "subjective form." As we have seen in the final section of the last chapter, "subjective form" seems to be a very recent emergent, coming in the final transitional stages of the Giffords draft.

None of these transitional passages (including 2.4), in their original forms, mentions "propositional feeling". Whitehead had worked out the notion of "proposition" fairly thoroughly, both in his Harvard classes and in II.9, yet without considering its status within the phases of concrescence. The means for doing so, at least in any direct fashion, were missing during the summer of 1927. Before a propositional feeling could be conceived, there had to be physical feelings which could be integrated with conceptual feelings, and individual feelings had to have their own (objective) data, such that a propositional feeling could entertain a proposition as its datum. Physical feelings and individualized data did not become features of Whitehead's system until the final revisions, when feelings and prehensions could be identified. That was not possible until the concept of 'negative prehensions' could be invented. This, in turn, would have to wait upon the notion of "subjective form."

This final section (2.4) appears not to anticipate propositional feelings, but later Whitehead evidently came to appreciate that his theory of propositions could provide the requisite features for a theory of consciousness. If we recast propositions as propositional feelings, they provide the integration of physical and conceptual feeling needed for consciousness. All the ingredients for propositional feelings were on hand: propositions, the contrast between physical and conceptual feelings, and an individualized notion of objective data; hence III.4.1–2.[3]

Not every propositional feeling is now conceived as involving consciousness. "It may, or may not, involve consciousness. . . . The subjective form will only involve consciousness when the 'affirmation-negation' contrast has entered into it. In other words, consciousness enters into the subjective forms of feelings, when those feelings are components in an integral feeling whose datum is the *contrast* between a nexus which *is*, and a proposition which in its own nature *negates* the decision of its truth or falsehood" (PR 261, Whitehead's italics). This clearly anticipates the "intellectual feeling," though that term is absent from this chapter. The "integral feeling" has almost the nature of an "intellectual feeling," yet without its specificity.

At this point Whitehead makes one important concession: "all forms of consciousness arise from ways of integration of propositional feelings with other feelings, either physical feelings *or conceptual feelings*" (PR 256, emphasis added). By this qualification God, as yet conceived as the nontemporal unification of conceptual feeling only, could still be assumed to be conscious, since his conscious feelings required no recourse to physical feelings.[4]

F. The Remaining Categoreal Conditions
(III.3.3–5, 5.8)

Quite possibly III.2.1–2, 2.4, 4.1–2 were intended, at one time, to form a single chapter, but this plan was disrupted by the adoption of five additional categoreal conditions.[5] These categoreal conditions are the result of working out what is entailed by the adoption of

Hume's principle that everything within the mind is derived from sensations.

In terms of the original theory of the Giffords draft, the primary datum for a given concrescence was conceived to be constituted by the objectifications of all other actual entities and by all relevant eternal objects. Thus, all actuality and possibility were at the disposal of the concrescence, and there could be no problem of novelty, since *any* possibility the occasion could actualize was already contained within its objective lure as part of the primary datum.

With the dissolution of the primary datum into the many simple physical feelings of the initial phase, it became questionable whether *all* the eternal objects were being prehended as before. If physical prehension were to restrict us solely to realized eternal objects, there would be no room for novelty. Initially Whitehead appears to have resisted Hume's principle, regarding the origination of physical and conceptual feelings as quite separate (III.2.2).

Perhaps in the spirit of resisting Hume's principle, Whitehead points out that "Hume's assertion is too unguarded according to Hume's own showing" (PR 242). In fact, "he makes two concessions which ruin his general principle. For he allows the independent origination of intermediate 'shades' in a scale of shades, and also of new 'manners' of pattern" (PR 260f). This claim is documented, at least with respect to the first part, by a long extract from Hume concerning whether a possible missing shade of blue could be imagined by someone who had never seen it for himself (II.3.1).

Initially Whitehead seems to have referred to the missing shade in order to justify his own non-adoption of Hume's principle, but later he decided to generalize it as the principle of conceptual reversion. Just as the missing shade is cognate to those shades already perceived, sharing both partial identity and partial diversity with them, so reverted eternal objects are relevant to those from which they are derived. Since conceptual reversion now provides those unrealized eternal objects necessary for any creative advance, Whitehead could now adopt the fourth categoreal condition as his restatement of Hume's principle, together with the category of reversion and the other categoreal conditions, thus forming the bulk of the chapter on "The Transmission of Feelings" (III.3.3–6: PR 247–55, 277ff).[6]

These two categories of derivation and reversion form the necessary basis for the category of transmutation, the sixth categoreal condition. Reverted feelings are often necessary to "smooth out" our variegated prehensions, and to provide the particular kind of simplification that transmutation affords. Transmuted feelings form a special class of propositional feelings, as Whitehead acknowledges: "It will be found that transmuted feelings are very analogous to propositional feelings" (PR 253). Other kinds of propositional feelings emphasize their conceptual element and are primarily mental, while the predicative pattern in a transmuted feeling only serves to unify the physical feelings. For this reason, "a transmuted feeling comes under the definition of a physical feeling" (PR 253).

Since the last two categoreal conditions are intimately bound up with the emergence of "subjective aim," we shall defer their consideration until the next section.

The first two sections of this chapter (3.1, 3.2, and most of the first paragraph of 3.3) are later additions we shall consider in due course. This later material concerns the provision of initial subjective aims by God. The first paragraph of section 3 discusses God's impact upon the nascent occasion "as an inescapable condition characterizing creative action" (PR 247). So far, however, initial aims have not yet been envisioned, and God's impact is conceived in extremely general terms: "This ideal realization of potentialities in a primordial actual entity constitutes the metaphysical stability whereby the actual process exemplifies general principles of metaphysics, and attains the ends proper to specific types of emergent order" (PR 40).

G. The Emergence of 'Subjective Aim'

In his final theory Whitehead assigns at least two functions to "subjective aim" (or at least to the divine provision of eternal objects for the nascent occasion):

(a) Telic direction: It directs the concrescence towards that particular goal it strives to achieve.

(b) Subjective unity: Although the occasion only achieves full determination as superject, the concrescence must be sufficiently unified to function as a process of unification. Subjective aim provides that partial measure of unity.

The first function of telic direction is already present in the Giffords draft, in terms of the twin concepts, the "ideal of itself", and the "objective lure". The "ideal of itself" is the final conceptual pattern of the satisfaction, progressively defined in concrescence. "The progressive definition of the final end is the efficacious condition for its attainment" (PR 150). The "objective lure" is the array of relevant eternal objects which we take to be part of the primary datum.

With the demise of the theory of the original datum, the concept of the "objective lure" gradually disappears. It had been postulated as a way of deriving the "ideal of itself," which Whitehead now tries to derive in another way, using the fourth category of conceptual valuation. This category not only provides for the derivation of a conceptual feeling from every physical feeling, but for its valuation in terms of the subjective form of this conceptual feeling. "Conceptual valuation introduces creative purpose. The mental pole introduces the subject as a determinant of its own concrescence. The mental pole is the subject determining its own ideal of itself by reference to eternal principles of valuation autonomously modified in their application to its own physical objective datum" (PR 248). This reference to "eternal principles of valuation" indicates the necessary role of God in the cosmic background, but all the specific particularities of the "ideal of itself" are derived from the conceptual valuations, themselves derived from physical feelings of the past actual world.

Telic direction was a part of Whitehead's program from the Giffords draft, and its derivation was apparently satisfactorily accounted for under changed circumstances. The "ideal of itself" persists in its subordinate role. But the questions of subjective unity becomes quite acute. While the primary datum theory arose as a result of the theory of objectification, it provided an easy solution to this issue. Since the primary datum had the unity of a being, the occasion could be conceived as already a being before undergoing its concrescence. Since feelings must have a subject, this subject could be conceived as a being determining itself, rendering itself more determinate in the process.

Once the primary datum dissolves into a multiplicity of initial data, this type of unity is no longer available to the concrescing occasion, and Whitehead must fashion another. One such attempt may be found in "The Theory of Feelings" (III.1.3). Here the occasion as a whole is taken as the subject of its feelings. More precisely, Whitehead proposes, we should think of this subject as superject. All the feelings of the occasion are conceived to aim at the superject as their final cause (PR 222).

Although this passage introduces the term "subject-superject" for the first time, Whitehead seems merely to identify the two. Either "subject" or "superject" means that at which all the feelings aim. Later on, however, while retaining that meaning of "superject," he intends some overall agency within concrescence as the subject which directs the individual aiming of the various feelings, thus distinguishing "subject" and "superject". Thus the seventh categoreal condition of subjective harmony was originally formulated: "The valuations of conceptual feelings are mutually determined by their adaptation to be joint elements in a satisfaction aimed at by the subject" (PR 254f).[7]

The term "subjective aim" first emerges in the discussion of the eighth categoreal condition (III.5.8). Yet the original formulation of this category is radically defective, not even grammatical. "The subject aim . . . is intensity of feeling . . ." (PR 277, 1929 text). Reconstructing this text in context, without immediately assimilating it to the later formulation of the categoreal scheme, we find that the category may have originally read: "The subject aims at balance and intensity of feeling (α) in the immediate subject, and (β) in the relevant future."

At first, it is the subject which aims. Yet this notion of the subject resists any further explication, for in the early incomplete phases there are merely many individual feelings having no unity such as a subject could be supposed to provide. Instead of the notion of "the subject aiming," Whitehead needs the notion of one feeling which is basically telic and peculiarly appropriate to the emerging subject.

In an addition composed together with, or after the final categoreal conditions, he introduces the notion of one particular "conceptual feeling of subjective aim," present from the primary phase to the end, suffering various modifications en route, each determining the "subjective end" evolved for that phase (PR 224). Here a conceptual means was found for the self-determination of the final ideal, as well as a way of abandoning the difficult notion whereby in mutual sensitivity later phases might be thought to influence earlier ones. Now mutual sensitivity of subjective forms could be implicitly restricted to feelings within the same phase.

The notion of "subjective aim" can combine both the notions of "telic direction" and "subjective unity," because that one conceptual feeling of subjective aim, by the notion of a "subjective end," can influence all the many feelings of an incomplete phase. "The many feelings, in an incomplete phase, are necessarily compatible with each other by reason of their individual conformity to the subjective end evolved for that phase" (PR 224).

Unlike the "ideal of itself," the subjective aim is not primarily situated at the end of concrescence. It is present throughout concrescence to insure the aesthetic compatibility of all the many feelings, and to guide them toward final unification. Unlike the "ideal of itself," then, it cannot be derived from conceptual feelings themselves derived from the many physical feelings of the past actual world. It must be derived from a conceptual source that can provide for the ideal unity of past multiplicity. This can only be God. "Each temporal entity . . . derives from God its basic conceptual aim. . . . This subjective aim, in its successive modifications, remains the unifying factor governing the successive phases of interplay between physical and conceptual feelings. These decisions are impossible for the nascent creature antecedently to the novelties in the phases of its concrescence" (PR 224).[8]

The derivation of initial subjective aims from God is classically presented in the opening section of "The Transmission of Feelings" (III.3.1) as a preface to the formulation of the final categoreal conditions. Initial aims are customarily said to be derived from the "primordial nature of God" by means of "hybrid physical feelings," but neither of those concepts is yet present. (The technical derivation of these aims by hybrid physical feelings is the topic of 3.2, a later addition.)

H. Intellectual Feelings (III.5)

Had it not been for one difficulty, this elaboration of the phases of concrescence, the categoreal conditions, and the nature of "subjective aim" could have sufficed for part III. But the difficulty would not go away. It concerned the structural similarity in the derivation of "physical purposes" and "propositional feelings," apparently first noticed after both concepts had been devised.

"Physical purpose" apparently makes its first appearance in the discussion of the fourth categoreal condition of conceptual valuation. The conceptual feeling derived from its physical feeling is valued up or down in terms of its subjective form, and this subjective form is reenacted by that physical feeling. "This is the phase of physical purpose" (PR 249). The name was apparently chosen to contrast with "conscious purpose" to indicate a purposive valuation of physical feeling lying below the level of consciousness.[9]

So formulated, the phase of "physical purpose" seems to leave the phase of conceptual valuation behind. For if the subjective form of the conceptual valuation is to influence the final physical feeling, there must be some synthesis of physical and conceptual feeling. If there is such an integration, then a "physical purpose" would have the same general structure as a "propositional feeling." Whitehead had devised propositional feelings primarily to explain consciousness, and physical purposes were emphatically not conscious.

Also, as Whitehead comes to realize, "the cosmological scheme which is here being developed requires us to hold that all actual entities include physical purposes" (PR 276). Since concrescence is the unification of many physical data, with the various conceptual phases assisting in this unification, there must be a final unity of physical data in the satisfaction as guided by the conceptual feeling. All occasions, in their satisfactions, would have some physical purposes if they had *any* conceptual feeling, and all have some. Otherwise, among other things, there would be no hope of any advance into novelty. But if *all* actual entities have physical purposes, and hence the structure of propositional feelings, what would prevent all actualities from being conscious, even though in lesser degrees?

In some ways this problem recalls the issues which led Whitehead to propose the double distinction between "ground" and "consequent" and between "physical occasion" and "mental occasion" in *Religion in the Making*. The distinction between "ground" and "consequent" corresponds to that between physical feeling and conceptual feeling which here finds its synthesis in "physical purpose." All actualities were "physical occasions," while only those which were subjective, particularly those which were conscious, were "mental occasions." In terms of the later theory "mental occasions" alone would have propositional feeling. In the later theory, all occasions are intended to have physical purposes, while only the more advanced would have propositional feelings, but the structural similarity between these two types of feelings threatens to blur the distinction.

Chapter four on "Propositions and Feelings" makes no contrasts whatever with "physical purpose," [10] suggesting that Whitehead was not yet aware of this difficulty. Yet the chapter has the main ingredients for a solution. The theory of indication it uses for the logical subjects of propositions had already been worked out in the Giffords draft (II.9.3). In indication an actuality is singled out merely in terms of its individuality, not in terms of any quality or characteristic it might possess, since all such features would belong to the predicate and not to the indicated logical subject. "Each logical subject becomes a bare '*it*' among actualities, with *its* assigned hypothetical relevance to the predicate" (PR 258).

By this theory of indication a proposition can be reconceived not so much as a synthesis of actual entities and eternal objects, but as a specification of an eternal object's scope, restricting it to certain indicated logical subjects. It is like the difference between a pure unrestricted possibility and a real possibility restricted to specific conditions for actualization. Then the synthesis between this conceptually understood propositional feeling and the contrasting physical feelings of the requisite indicated actualities forms a complex comparative feeling we can designate as an "intellectual feeling." If only intellectual feelings have consciousness in their subjective forms, and are effective contrasts between "what is" and "what might be," then we have a credible theory of consciousness which can be restricted to only the higher actualities. For while all actualities may have physical purposes, not all can have intellectual feelings. Structurally physical purposes and propositional feelings may shade off into one another, but this is no problem as long as all of them are considered to be unconscious.

In the absence of any theory of intellectual feelings, we could read chapter four (especially 4.4 and 4.5) in terms of consciousness. The direct (no intervening transmutations) authentic (no reversions) perceptive feeling (4.4) seems to describe our veridical perception, while imaginative feeling, where the physical basis for the predicative pattern is not identical with the logical subjects, purports to describe our ordinary, waking imagination (4.5). Yet these are only particular species of propositional feelings, which according to the theory of intellectual feeling can only be unconscious. Hence in chapter five a set of counterparts is devised in terms of intellectual feelings which alone are conscious. "Conscious perception" signifies that intellectual feeling which has a "perceptive feeling" as its component propositional feeling, while "intuitive judgment" signifies one having an "imaginative feeling" as its component.

When Whitehead planned six chapters to Part III (PR 193n., 1929 text), he may well have intended to include a section correlating this new theory of "conscious perception" with his earlier theory of perception in the modes of causal efficacy, presentational immediacy, and symbolic reference, perhaps in accordance with an earlier reference (PR 121n.4). Systematically and topically this would have made excellent sense, but we have seen that Whitehead approaches issues somewhat differently, largely in terms of challenges prompted by difficulties in his emerging theory. The analysis of the three modes of perception came very early in the development of *Process and Reality* (Spring 1927) when Whitehead faced the question: How can we perceive contemporary space when all causal conditioning factors must already be past to influence us? The theory of "conscious perception" arose (Winter-Spring 1928?) as a derivation from intellectual feelings, devised to explain consciousness, and to distinguish it structurally from physical purpose.

We might suppose the theoretical challenge of correlating these two theories would suffice to prompt Whitehead to work out their interconnection, but apparently it was not enough. The most straight-forward solution, according to which each perception in the three modes would be treated as a "conscious perception" perhaps struck Whitehead as over-elaborate and too complex. An alternative solution would be to identify perception in the mode of causal efficacy with physical feeling, perception in the mode of presentational immediacy with that propositional feeling having the percepta as its predicate, and perception in the mode of symbolic reference as the 'conscious perception' synthesizing these two subordinate feelings. In this so-lution only perceptions in the mode of symbolic reference would be conscious, and we could not be directly conscious of any perceptions in the two pure modes. This contravenes Whitehead's earlier argument in *Symbolism*, which may be the reason why he rejected this alter-native. But all that phenomenological description in *Symbolism* could be saved under this alternative hypothesis by treating examples of perception in the mode of causal efficacy as experiences of symbolic reference where the component elements are overwhelmingly phys-ical, or examples in the mode of presentational immediacy as ex-periences in which the component elements are overwhelmingly conceptual. The experiences could be nearly pure, but not so pure that all consciousness would be lost.

I. The Consequent Nature of God

With the development of intellectual feelings, Whitehead could well have discovered that his conception of God as a synthesis of purely conceptual feeling was deficient: ". . . conceptual feelings, apart from complex integration with physical feelings, are devoid of consciousness in their subjective forms" (PR 343). Without intellectual feelings, God could not be conscious, and these required a basis in physical feeling.

Whitehead could have preserved the nontemporality of God in line with traditional theism by any one of a number of strategems: (1) The concept of consciousness could be revised so as not to involve physical feeling. (2) God could be conceived to be "superconscious," conscious in some way transcending any application of the concept of intellectual feeling. (3) God could be conceived not to be conscious at all, thus reserving consciousness to temporal beings which excluded God.

Whitehead opted for none of these alternatives. The perfected concept of consciousness was achieved at some conceptual cost, and should be revised only for good reason. The way of analogy or indirect predication suggested by the second alternative runs counter to Whitehead's practice of univocal specification. In the early days of *Science and the Modern World* he did embrace the conception of God as an unconscious principle of limitation, but now it would run counter to his dictum that God is the chief exemplification of the metaphysical principles (PR 343). If all actual entities enjoy subjectivity, and the higher organisms among them enjoy consciousness, should not consciousness pertain to the highest subjectivity of all?

The experiment of ascribing physical feelings to the primordial actuality was very easy to execute since all other actual entities were already conceived as syntheses of both physical and conceptual feelings. God's temporality followed ineluctably from this decision to conceive God as prehending all actual occasions. Since occasions were prehensible only in terms of their determinate satisfactions as they came into being, God's physical feelings could only be conceived as forming an everlasting concrescence, absorbing all objectifications in turn, not as something nontemporal.

Because Whitehead had conceived of God solely as the primordial actuality throughout most of the composition of *Process and Reality*, and because the idea of God's physical feelings was so new to him, he opted for the (formal) distinction between two natures: the primordial and the consequent nature. Some of the difficulties of his approach might have been avoided had the two sides of God been better integrated. Ultimately, the only reason for treating these two natures separately lies in the historical accident of the book's composition.

Now, with physical feelings ascribed to God, Whitehead had the conceptual means to articulate the vision he already attributed to God (cf. V.2.6), which leads to the expansion of the Giffords draft chapter on "God and the World" into the present Part V. Also placing physical feelings within God enabled him to conceive of *all* actual entities as having both physical and mental poles. If so, God could be uniquely distinguished from all other actual entities by a reversal of the poles, since every finite actual occasion was dependent upon an initial phase of physical feeling. This could not apply to that being which is primarily nontemporal. This reversal of the poles permits him to claim that God is the *only* actual entity that is not an actual occasion. Previously this distinction could not be made, so that "actual entity" had been used interchangeably with "actual occasion" (e.g. PR 18, 22, 31). While God had been possibly the only being who possessed only conceptual feelings, there *might* have been others: disembodied spirits, immortal souls, pure angelic intelligences, and the like.

Whitehead promises to take care of "the objective immortality of the consequent nature" in part V (PR 32), but the only text pertaining to this would be the final two paragraphs of the book. Without modifying the claim of his previous section, that the final phase corresponds to God's consequent experience of the world, this last section (V.2.7) adds another phase: "The action of the fourth phase is the love of God for the world. It is the particular providence for particular occasions. What is done in the world is transformed into a reality in heaven, and the reality in heaven passes back into the world" (PR 351; contrast PR 349).

We are not told, however, how God as an everlasting concrescence can ever be objectified for the world in a system where concrescences must be completed in determinate unity before they can be prehended. This is an example of Whitehead's proleptic writing, where his intuitions outrun his concepts. In *Religion in the Making* and in the Giffords draft (V.2.6) he had envisioned God (then conceived as a purely conceptual reality) as embracing the progress of the world, but by introducing the consequent nature he achieved the means to justify this vision. He had already seen that God would be the source of initial subjective aims (III.3.1), but he lacked the means for rendering this claim precise until he devised hybrid physical prehensions, which are then introduced in the following section (3.2). In this particular case (V.2.7) his intuitions seem to have outrun any means he was later able to devise, so the problem has been bequeathed to his followers.

J. The Gifford Lectures and Subsequent Additions

Up to this point we have recounted the growth of Whitehead's manuscript in preparation for delivering the Gifford Lectures at Edinburgh in June 1928. This appears to be the totality of the material Whitehead drew upon in presenting his lectures.

Judging from the prospectus (Appendix 6), what Whitehead actually presented was a very condensed summary of *Process and Reality* in just ten lectures. This seems a far cry from what he had intended to deliver just the summer before, the Giffords draft, and not nearly so accessible to an audience for whom this would all be new and highly unfamiliar. We may particularly miss the historical chapters discussing Descartes, Locke and Hume, which could have helped his audience regain their bearings (II.5–6). These chapters were sacrificed, presumably, in order to gain room for more systematic presentations of his philosophical outlook.

The prospectus is sufficiently detailed that we can determine which topics were omitted (such as II.5–6). It also omits those sections in Part II about perception in the three modes which are largely duplicated by *Symbolism*, the advanced discussion of living persons (II.3.5–11), the material on Strains, the chapters on "The Subjectivist Principle" (II.7), and on "Coordinate Division" (IV.1). From the topics announced for Lecture V we may surmise that the first parts of "The Order of Nature" (3.1–4) and "Organisms and Environment" (4.1–4) originally formed one chapter. The material concerning the three modes of perception was probably left out because its theory was already available in *Symbolism*, but the other topics are not present, we submit, because they were not yet part of Whitehead's manuscript, but belong to later developments.

Despite the great differences between what Whitehead presumably intended in August 1927 to present at Edinburgh, and what he actually presented ten months later, there is an important continuity which should not be overlooked. In both cases there is an attempt to encompass his total philosophy. To be sure, lecture IX on "Prehensions and the Extensive Continuum" summarizes topics from Part IV (2, 3 and 5) which are primarily mathematical. Yet Whitehead evidently felt the need to relate his theories of concrescence and extension. In the absence of a chapter devoted to this topic, such as the later "Coordinate Division" (IV.1), he drew upon already existing material. Another topic that could be forbidding was Lecture II, "The Scheme of Interpretation," but quite possibly the categoreal scheme had not yet been as elaborately worked out as we now possess it, allowing Whitehead more opportunity to introduce some of his key ideas early.

Since the great bulk of *Process and Reality* seems to have been written in advance of the Gifford Lectures, we may suppose that the next half-year devoted to getting it ready for publication would have been relatively easy. This is not how Whitehead reported the process to his son North on December 23, 1928: "This last term has been the greatest tax on my imagination that I have ever had—*not* the most tiring physically. But I have been making the final draft of my

Giffords—and having to keep the whole scheme of thoughts in my head, so as to get all the points written up in order." [11]

The writing of particular sections, especially under the stimulation of recent insight, relishing in the unanticipated and the adventuresome, was not Whitehead's problem. Revision and organization was, particularly as his philosophy had grown so complex in such a short time. Because of this growth, there were bound to be inconsistencies and incongruities between parts composed from different perspectives. Nevertheless Whitehead was apparently resolved neither to eliminate nor to revise extensively those passages belonging to earlier viewpoints. Once he had satisfied himself that he had expressed himself satisfactorily for publication, he rarely went back to revise it. If this is a defect, it is the defect of his genius, which lay in perpetually seeking for new insights, reaching beyond present insights to grasp the unattainable. If he were constantly revising what he had already written in the light of new insights, he would never get done. The author of a well-organized book must be willing to be bored by his own ideas, and this Whitehead appears never willing to be.

The strategem he adopted for getting his manuscript in shape appears to be the use of insertion. In *Science and the Modern World*, these insertions were limited to two chapters and three other additions, each measurable in units of paragraphs. *Religion in the Making* and *Symbolism* do not show any signs of interpolation, but then there may have been no need for it. *Process and Reality* was a much more complex undertaking, particularly in the light of unexpected breakthroughs after the summer of 1927. This called for massive interpolation, to reorient the reader from the start to his newest vision, and to introduce key concepts early.

A very straightforward example of such an insertion may be found in a section of "Fact and Form" (II.1.4), which introduces the ninth categoreal obligation of freedom and determination. As we have seen, the elaboration of the categoreal conditions develops only eight such conditions (III.3) while the earlier Giffords draft, within which this insertion is embedded, otherwise mention no categoreal conditions. This is the first categoreal condition to be named a "categoreal obligation" on its introduction, indicating the shift to Whitehead's final terminology. [12]

Many of these insertions can be recognized by their use of special technical terms such as 'subjective form,' 'subjective aim,' 'negative prehension,' 'primordial nature of God,' later terms appearing in what may otherwise be regarded as earlier passages. Thus, the use of 'subjective forms' in the penultimate paragraph, second section, of

"Process" (II.10.2) suggests an insertion, which appears to be that paragraph together with the first sentence of the last paragraph. Notice the continuity which would exist in the absence of those sentences by considering the sentences preceding and following them: "We thus say that an actual occasion is a concrescence effected by a process of feelings. . . . This process of the integration of feeling proceeds until the concrete unity of feeling is obtained" (PR 211). Only such an arrangement provides a proper referent for the "this."

Frequently when editing his text, Whitehead brings to it other concerns than he had when writing the text initially, and embodies some ideas in insertions which are fairly intrusive with respect to the original sense of the passage. Thus in one passage (II.7.3) he describes the nature of higher types of experience: "The clash of uncoordinated emotions in the lower categories is avoided: the aspect of inhibition and of transitory satisfaction is diminished. . . . [But] it involves enhanced subjective emphasis. The occasion has become less of a detail and more of a totality, so far as its subjective experience is concerned" (PR 163). Two sentences situating experience in the consequent nature of God have apparently been interpolated here, and the fit is not exact.[13]

Or consider the opening third and fifth paragraphs of "Propositions and Feelings" (III.4.1), which build up to a description of the "propositional feeling" by indicating the differences between eternal objects and propositions. Third: "Now an eternal object, in itself, abstracts from all determinate actual entities, including even God" (PR 256). Fifth: "But a proposition, while preserving the indeterminateness of an eternal object, makes an incomplete abstraction from determinate actual entities" (PR 257). In editing this passage, Whitehead evidently became concerned about any possible ontological independence for the eternal objects the first statement suggested, so in the intervening fourth paragraph he worked out their relationship to the primordial nature of God.

Another instance of insertion may be found in the section introducing 'nexus' (III.1.9), comprising the third paragraphs from the end (together with the very last sentence of the preceding paragraph). Without this interpolation the passage would be a straightforward account of the nature of a "nexus." Now, however, Whitehead can resolve one problem about the ontological status of the independent nexus he could not resolve at the time of composition: "According to the ontological principle, the impartial nexus is an objective datum in the consequent nature of God; since it is *somewhere* and yet not by any necessity of its own nature implicated in the feelings of any determined actual entity of the actual world" (PR 231). By designating this the first use of "nexus" and interpolating it where he did, Whitehead got himself in the awkward position of stipulating the second use before the first.

Many of these insertions concern the primordial and consequent natures of God, as Whitehead apparently seeks to interweave this newly-found notion into the fabric of his presentation. A particularly important insertion on this theme may be found in "The Order of Nature" (II.3.1: PR 87.40–88.30).[14] Here Whitehead is challenged by his own threefold description of an actual entity in terms of its 'given' character, its subjective character, and its superjective character, to see if he can apply that description to God. The 'primordial nature', with heavy qualification, corresponds to the first, and the 'consequent nature' to the second. For the third Whitehead appropriates the precise language of the "superjective character" substituting only "the 'superjective' nature of God." Context and punctuation indicate that Whitehead had no definite, third 'superjective nature' for God in mind.[15] This is the only place in the book where the 'superjective' nature of God is mentioned. This may be another of the promissory passages, for as we have seen, Whitehead had difficulty finding the appropriate conceptuality by which to back up his claims concerning the impact of the consequent nature upon later occasions.

Additions are often difficult to determine if there has been no difference in position between the two passages. For example, Whitehead may have originally terminated the analysis of epochal becoming with this sentence and its successor: "In respect to time, this atomization takes the special form of the 'epochal theory of time' " (PR 68), contenting himself with the reference to *Science and the Modern World*, chapter 7 as the warrant for this claim. Later he could have added a longer systematic justification in terms of Zeno's paradoxes (PR 68f). But this surmise cannot be established, not to the degree that we can establish the last three paragraphs as a later insertion, for these last paragraphs use terms not otherwise introduced into the Giffords draft, such as 'subjective aim' and 'conceptual prehension.'

K. Strains (II.4.9, IV.4, 5.1)

Sometime during the composition of *Process and Reality* Whitehead came to appreciate the non-identity, although close approximation, of the "presented locus" (the locus we directly perceive) and some duration in unison of becoming with the percipient occasion. These are meant to be the same, but are defined in very different ways. The theory of "strain-feelings" is designed to reconcile them, and to this end Whitehead has included the chapter on "Strains" and related passages (II.4.9, IV.4, and IV.5 [in part]).[16]

The material about "strain-feelings" is difficult to place, but there is good reason to place it before the introduction of 'hybrid physical prehension' (to be made in L). The fact that the present section (K) describes "a high-grade percipient" as an occasion in "the historic route of an enduring object" (PR 318) rather than in a "living person" suggests this, or at least that it is prior to the "living person" addition (see next section). The mention of such terms as "the category of conceptual reproduction," "the category of transmutation," and "physical purpose" suggests that it comes after the introduction of "intellectual feelings," already discussed in the fifth section of this chapter. It *could* be this early, as it makes no mention of the primordial/consequent nature distinction in God, nor of the "subjective aim." But it is more probable that the material on "strain-feelings" comes after the Gifford lectures were delivered, as the prospectus makes no mention of them.

Only three sections are fully devoted to the issue that "strain-feelings" were introduced to resolve (4.1, 4.4, and 5.1). Four other sections have only relatively small insertions (4.2, 4.5, 5.2, and 5.5). In one case, for example, the insertion consists only of the initial paragraph and the words "and of the strain-locus" in the very next sentence. Without those words that sentence would read: "It is to be noted that this doctrine of presentational immediacy . . . entirely depends upon a definition of straight lines in terms of mere extensiveness" (PR 323). Without these brief "strain-feeling" additions, several (4.2, 4.3, 4.5, 5.2 [and 5.3?]) probably constituted a single chapter[17] addressing the question of "Projection and Presentational Immediacy," a topic of the ninth Gifford Lecture according to the prospectus. Since that doctrine depends upon a definition of straightness in terms of mere extensiveness (and not simply as "the shortest distance between two points," which makes straightness dependent upon measurement, rather than vice versa), Whitehead felt it necessary to include in his metaphysical treatise the two mathematical chapters (IV.2–3) designed to give a proper definition of straightness.

That this material is prior to the introduction of "hybrid physical prehension," the topic we turn to next, may also be inferred from this passage. Each occasion prehends every actuality in its universe, including God. "Then, by the category of conceptual reproduction, the vector prehensions of God's appetition, and of other occasions, issue in the mental pole of conceptual prehensions . . ." (PR 316). There is no mention of "hybrid prehensions," when this would have been most relevant. The same applies to "subjective aim," here conspicuous by its absence.

L. Hybrid Prehension, Abolition of Reversion, and the Living Person (III.3.2, II.3.5–11)

The principal text introducing hybrid prehension may be found in "The Transmission of Feelings" (III.3.2), a text offering a precise technical amplification of the way God provides initial aims, which had just been announced in the previous section. Here the distinction between "pure" and "hybrid" physical prehensions is formally made, and it is observed that there are two sub-species of hybrid feelings, those pertaining to other actual occasions, and those feeling the conceptual feelings of God. "Those of God's feelings which are positively prehended are those with some compatibility of contrast, or of identity, with physical feelings transmitted from the temporal world. But when we take God into account, then we can assert without any qualification Hume's principle, that all conceptual feelings are derived from physical feelings. . . . Apart from the intervention of God, there could be nothing new in the world, and no order in the world" (PR 247). With hybrid prehensions the category of reversion becomes superfluous, since all relevant novelty can be directly derived from God. The category is not yet abolished, however, for in this text Whitehead simply restricts its scope to apply to transmission within the world, leaving God out of account.

Possibly an earlier passage concerning hybrid prehension may be found among the additions to the first categereal condition, which comprise all the material beyond the first two paragraphs. The first addition or additions introduce the phases of subjective aim and its derivation from God, including this sentence: "Each temporal entity, in one sense, originates from its mental pole, analogously to God himself," because it derives from God "its basic conceptual aim" (PR 224). At this point there is no anticipation that that aim could be physically derived. Characteristically Whitehead does not modify that assertion in his final recension, but adds an explanatory note, the passage we are interested in, which begins with these statements to introduce hybrid prehensions: "But this statement in its turn requires amplification. With this amplification the doctrine, that the primary phase of a temporal actual entity is physical, is recovered" (PR 224f). From a strict systematic perspective, if it is true that every temporal actual entity starts from its physical pole, it is always true, and the statement that it originates from its mental pole is incorrect, and should be omitted. Whitehead's way of adding amplifying notes obscures this systematic intent, but it does give us further insight into the philosopher's own reflections, an insight we would not otherwise have.

This passage, which extends to the presentation of category II, is more rudimentary than the text concerning the provision of initial aims (3.2). The contrasting term "pure physical prehension" does not appear, nor are the two sub-species mentioned, nor is there any discussion of its relation to conceptual reversion. This addition may well be the first introduction of hybrid prehension, which is then more fully developed later (in 3.2), but its mention of "Categoreal Obligation" suggests otherwise. The other passage (3.2) still uses the earlier language of "categoreal condition." There seems no other explanation for this than that it (3.2) is the earlier text, while this passage has been later appended (to 1.5) in order to correct the claim that: ". . . each temporal entity . . . originates from its mental pole."

Hybrid prehensions are also mentioned in the section presenting the category of transmutation (III.3.4). Before the category is formally introduced there is some trace of hybrid prehensions, if only by the insertion of the phrases "pure or hybrid," "some pure and some hybrid," and "pure, and hybrid" in the first two paragraphs (PR 250). Later on there seem to be two insertions (PR 251.44–252.13 and 252.18–252.25).[18] In the original text Whitehead had been primarily concerned how reverted feelings play their part in "smoothing out" experiences of transmutation, where the variety of physical feelings is reduced to one feeling in terms of one common eternal object. In these insertions he recognizes that hybrid feelings can perform that same function. These insertions are important in showing how reverted and hybrid feelings continued side by side, even though reversion had now been rendered superfluous.

The next passage to consider, however, calls for the abolition of reversion. It is the final paragraph of the discussion of the categories of conceptual valuation and reversion (III.3.3). Heretofore, reversion has been simply superfluous; here he argues it is also deficient because it cannot ground the reason for the specific relationship between any reverted eternal object and the characteristic eternal object of the prehending occasion in any actual entity, as required by the ontological principle. "A more fundamental account must ascribe the reverted conceptual feeling in a temporal subject to its conceptual feeling derived . . . from the hybrid physical feeling of the relevancies conceptually ordered in God's experience" (PR 250). Since the reason for the relationship among unrealized eternal objects can only be found in God's primordial envisagement, a reason which is lacking for purely mundane reversion, and since hybrid prehension can supply all the novelty that reversion could, reversion is simply replaced by hybrid prehension. "The category of reversion is then abolished" (PR 250).

Many interpreters find it difficult to take these words at face value. If reversion is really abolished, they reason, why is reversion used as a valid principle later on in the book, even in the very next section (III.3.4) ? If the book had been rigorously revised for publication in the normal fashion, then the categoreal obligations should have been completely recast to omit all reference to reversion. Whitehead's method, however, at least in this instance, seems to be autobiographically dialectical, whether intentionally or not. He first shows the reader the train of reasoning leading him to espouse reversion, and then abolishes it. An author who could stipulate part way through that henceforth 'actual entity' shall ordinarily mean 'actual occasion' could also stipulate the abolition of reversion. In the end, reversion was not a fundamental category for Whitehead.

None of these 'hybrid prehension' passages explicitly refers to God as 'primordial' or 'consequent,' and the second one uses a phrase which might be more apt of the former conception of God as the primordial actuality: "God is [not: forms] the eternal primordial character" of creativity (PR 225, emphasis mine). Thus it is possible that the introduction of hybrid physical prehension antedates the distinction between the two natures of God. This would be less true, however, of the application of hybrid prehension to the concept of the "living person," which we find in the expansion of "The Order of Nature" (II.3.5–11). Since that expansion is not among the topics listed in the prospectus for the Gifford Lectures, it seems most appropriate to assign its place after the lectures were given, particularly as it uses such a late term as 'categoreal obligation.' [19]

The expansion begins with these words: "It is obvious that the simple classification (Cf. Part I, Ch. III, Sect. II) of societies . . . requires amplification" (PR 99). It means to replace that earlier section, and probably displaces it from an original location in Part II. Whitehead recognizes that the earlier section (I.3.2) has been superseded and needs to be replaced, but he is apparently loath to abandon the section entirely, and so includes it among the introductory materials of Part I.

The expansion in its original form, introduces such concepts as the "structured society" and nexus of "entirely living occasions" but rather surprisingly not the "living person," the one concept dependent on hybrid prehension. Some of the essay stands in tension with the notion of a "living person." Thus to the question, "whether the living occasions, in abstraction from the inorganic occasions of the animal body, form a corpuscular sub-society, so that each living occasion is a member of an enduring entity with its personal order," the answer is "no" (PR 104). This could be interpreted to mean there are no disembodied minds, but Whitehead is fixed on the conceptual problem of an *enduring* mind, even if embodied. "Life is a bid for freedom: an enduring entity binds any one of its occasions to the line of its ancestry. The doctrine of the enduring soul with its permanent characteristics is exactly the irrelevant answer to the problem which life presents" (PR 104). The unresolved problem for Whitehead here is how to order novel occasions within a personal society.

This problem is resolved by the adoption of the "living person" whereby the living occasions are personally ordered in a linear series by the use of the hybrid prehensions. The passage discussing the "living person" constitutes only the first three paragraphs of the final section (3.11), and this could easily be an insertion. Note that the remaining material of this section forms an independent unit addressing the traditional mind-body problem. It also reverts to Whitehead's more customary way of thinking about minds as enduring objects. The more advanced conceptuality of "living person" and "hybrid prehension" is not used beyond these three paragraphs.

Lastly, a passage mentioning hybrid prehension as a way of explaining mental telepathy deserves brief mention. Like the others, this is an insertion in a previoiusly completed text. It comprises all but the first major paragraph of IV.3.4. I suspect that paragraph had originally been the final paragraph of the previous section and that Whitehead used the device of posing two questions about the nature of "external connection." The first, purely geometrical question goes back to the very first layer of *Process and Reality*, written perhaps as early as the summer of 1926, while the second question introduces the very late notions of "conceptual prehension," "coordinate divisibility," and "hybrid prehensions."

M. Coordinate Division (IV.1)

Probably the last chapter to be included in *Process and Reality* concerns "Coordinate Division" (IV.1). Its subject-matter is not to be found among the topics in the prospectus for the Ninth Gifford Lecture on "Prehensions and the Extensive Continuum," where it would naturally belong. Since the inclusion of this chapter in the Gifford lectures would have suited Whitehead's purposes better than most of the topics of the ninth lecture, it would be most surprising if he had omitted an already existing chapter. The probability is strongly against the existence of IV.1 until after the Giffords were given.

There does not seem to be any way of ascertaining the relative order of composition between the expansion of chapter 3 (II.3.5–11) and this chapter (IV.1). There is some slight evidence that this chapter is later than the essay on "Strains," for it refers back to the theory of perception as including the introductory section on Strains (II.4.9).[20] If this reference is original with the text, then it would be later than the analysis of strains. That it is original with the text is probable because the text *twice* refers to "II.4" as "II.8" in the 1929 text (PR 286 and 291), suggesting that at one time Whitehead had intended to make "Organisms and Environment" the eighth chapter of part II.

Part III presents the general theory of concrescence; part IV the theory of extension. The theory of extension was either written very early, focusing on the mathematical problem of deriving straightness from the properties of extensiveness alone (IV.2–3, 5) or much later to address a very specific and rather technical problem in the theory of perception (IV.4). Some bridge connecting these disparate theories was needed to coordinate the whole. In working out this chapter, Whitehead may have utilized earlier material. The mention of "physical occasion" (PR 287f), though presently quite qualified, indicates some very early material.

There may well be another reason for this chapter. Whitehead appears only gradually to become aware of the commensurability of genetic and coordinate divisibility. The term 'divisibility' is first used of genetic growth in the prospectus for the seventh Gifford lecture: "General Theory of Prehensions—Divisibility of Actual Entities into Prehensions: Genetic and Co-ordinate Divisions." In *Process and Reality* it is first used in this chapter (IV.1). Since both were now seen as species of divisibility, some sort of systematic correlation of genetic and coordinate divisibility was called for.

Previously Whitehead had referred to genetic *analysis* and extensive *division* (PR 227, 235). When in the "subjective aim addition" to "The Extensive Continuum" (the last three paragraphs of II.2.2), we are told that "the subjective aim does not share in this divisibility"

(PR 69), we are not explicitly told whether this is 'genetic' or 'co-ordinate.' But at the time this was written the question of any possible ambiguity could not have arisen, given his particular usage: The subjective aim is not divisible, i.e., extensively divisible, although it is (genetically) analyzable.[21]

One of the very last passages that Whitehead may have included concerns the description of the category of the ultimate (PR 21f).[22] On October 8, 10, and 13, 1928, Whitehead dictated to his class at Harvard a categoreal scheme, that is, the categories of existence and explanation, and the categoreal obligations, excepting the category of the ultimate. Since all these other categories are presented, in the same order as, and with no significant variation in phraseology from, the published version, while neither the category of the ultimate nor the rhythm of the one and the many are mentioned, we infer that this material was formulated and included later.[23]

In place of the category of the ultimate, these lectures have the following reflection on October 8:

"It is useless to explain [the] emergence of more concrete things by abstract things. Concrete fact cannot be replaced in terms of abstractions. [The] proper philos[ophical] question is to ask how concrete things exhibit abstract [properties]. [The] original meaning [of] concrete = grown together. This meaning [is] lost in modern usage. [We] should return to [the] original meaning. This is concrescence. This is creativity [which] can't be defined further. It is most general. It is the ultimate behind all forms, inexplicable by its forms and conditioned by its creatures." [24]

———

In the Giffords draft there were two species of process: first, the transition which brought about the objective datum, secondly, the concrescence which unified the feeling into a self. After the transformation, transition disappears as a separate supersessive activity. Concrescence no longer depends upon an initial objective datum from which it begins. Through simple physical feeling it now reaches out into the past actual world itself. Concrescence is now one continuous act of unification, and it therefore starts with the multiplicity that the past world is.

This concrescence is a genuine coming into being, something it could never be if it first proceeded from some objective datum. To be sure, the self could come to be from the datum, but this subjective response would not be a being in its own right if dependent upon a prior objective being. A being can only be brought into being once. If by transition, then not by concrescence, and vice versa. The Giffords draft sought to straddle the fence, ultimately to no avail.

Transition may still be retained as a concept describing one aspect of creativity, particularly with respect to macroscopic behaviour, but there is no longer the supersession of transitional unification by concrescence. If there is still a separate species of creativity named "transition," its role has become quite transformed from the Giffords draft.

It is a basic mistake to interpret Whitehead's final theory as a philosophy of flux; it is not even a philosophy of transition, understood as succession. Endurance and change (flux) are the two species of succession, the one stressing sameness between occasions, the other difference (PR 73, 80). Concrescence is neither, but the deeper source of both. Ultimately, the concept of *process* is inadequate to what concrescence is all about.

I prefer to call it *creation*, for concrescence is the way an actual occasion comes into being from its past and its initial subjective aim, by means of its own decision. To be sure, Whitehead does not give us a theory of divine creation as this is traditionally understood, which was more an article of faith than a carefully worked out, rationally defensible theory. But there is no reason why the classical theory of divine creation should preempt all use of "creation," particularly when Whitehead's theory of creation is the more fully developed.

The theory of self-creation is fundamentally based on unification. All the constituents had their being as constituents, and the becoming is the bringing of these elements together. It is this particular whole which never existed before, and which does yet not exist until the final completion. Just as being and unity are convertible, we might think of becoming and unification as convertible. Whitehead may not describe it this way, but unification is also the key to subjectivity and to activity. The self exists insofar as it becomes the one superject.[25] A self-creative concrescence actively brings its actuality into being while at the same time functioning as its subjective core.

This theory was hardly evident when Whitehead embarked on his metaphysical adventure, but it is the achievement of that endeavor.

NOTES

1. Here 'prehension' must be understood in terms of its former meaning, as universal internal relatedness among events, such as is found in *Science and the Modern World*, and not in terms of any of the specific kinds of prehension, such as the simple physical prehension.

2. That is, III.1.2–11. 1.1 is probably much later, added with IV.1 in mind. 1.12 was added after the term "subjective aim" was introduced. Two sentences were added to the first paragraph of 1.4 when Whitehead decided to enlarge his list of categoreal conditions from 3 to 8. Even so, the ninth Categoreal Obligation (II.1.4) is not even mentioned—presumably because it was not yet anticipated. Finally, the last four paragraphs in 1.5 discussing the first category show signs of being two distinct additions, the last dependent upon the very late notion of a hybrid physical feeling of God. If we omit this material, the three discussions in 1.5 are evenly proportioned: the statement of the category itself followed by one fairly brief paragraph of explanation.

3. The elaboration of propositional feelings into perceptive feelings (4.4) and imaginative feelings (4.5), above all the derivation of propositional feeling (4.3) come later, for they are all dependent upon the remaining categoreal conditions of III.3, whereas 4.1–2 makes no mention of these conditions.

4. At this time propositional feelings could be apparently regarded as mental (as in PR 191, 241f). We regard this paragraph as a later interpolation within III.2.4, perhaps made at the same time with III.4.1–2 introducing propositional feelings. (See also PR 191.)

5. Whitehead notes that "five additional categoreal conditions must be added to the three" which have been already explained (PR 248). Thus the last two sentences of the opening paragraph of III.1.4 are best regarded as interpolations. Even so, only eight categoreal conditions are anticipated. (See PR 278 in the original text: twice the eighth categoreal condition is called the "final category.")

When the ninth category was eventually introduced, it was the first to be called by its final designation, "obligation" (II.1.4). Presumably Whitehead wanted to stress that his categories were not constitutive of objectivity, like Kant's, but of subjectivity. A subject is obliged to do that which is required of it, even though these obligations are metaphysical rather than moral.

6. We take the original presentation of the eighth categoreal condition, now found in III.5.8, to have once been III.3.6.

7. In 1.3 feelings are not aimed at by anything. Whitehead wanted to exclude any external agencies from doing the aiming, and had not considered the subject-half of the subject-superject as possibly performing this role. This categoreal condition is reformulated in the categoreal scheme. The last five words now become: "congruent with the subjective aim" (PR 27).

8. This may well be a continuation of the same insertion. We take the rest of this paragraph, however, to be a later insertion based on the "hybrid physical prehension of God." Note the later usage of "categoreal obligation" for "categoreal condition."

9. This same understanding of "physical purpose" is also present at PR 184, 244, and 253f, the first named being a later addition to II.9.1.

10. Except in the note to PR 256, which could easily have been added later.

11. Victor Lowe, "Whitehead's Gifford Lectures," *The Southern Journal of Philosophy* 7/4 (Winter, 1969), 329–38.

12. By the reference to the ontological principle at the outset of 1.4, and the mention of God's primordial nature in the last three paragraphs of 1.3, we deem these to belong to the same insertion as 1.4. Without this insertion there is greater continuity between the rest of 1.3 and 1.5.

13. The two sentences read: "Experience realizes itself as an element in what is everlasting (cf. Part V, Ch. II), and as embodying in itself the everlasting component of the universe. This gain does not necessarily involve consciousness."

14. The insertion could begin two paragraphs before, or that could be a separate insertion occasioned by reflections about "subjective aim." In any case the final paragraph of the section continues the line of thought about "objective lure" of the passage just before these two paragraphs.

15. Here see my note "Is There a Distinct Superjective Nature? " *Process Studies* 3/3 (Fall, 1973), 228f. The difference between these various natures, as indicated by the punctuation, is not maintained in the corrected edition of PR.

16. Also, the last two sentences of II.4.8 were added to introduce 4.9.

17. I take " (but cf. Section VI) " in 4.5 to refer to 5.1 when it was reckoned as 4.6, and the two references in 5.2 to the "previous chapter" (PR 324f) to be to the chapter on "Flat Loci," which was then the previous chapter for all these sections.

18. There is clear continuity if these two insertions are omitted. The second insertion starts out being more mindful of the interruption it causes than of the immediate passage it succeeds.

19. It is not so late that it recognizes the category of reversion to be abolished.

20. Whitehead's reference to "Sects. IV to IX" (PR 286), however, may refer to the remainder of the chapter (II.4.4–8, 10) *before* the section on 'Strains' (4.9) was added.

21. *Contra* Edward Pols, *Whitehead's Metaphysics: A Critical Examination of* PROCESS AND REALITY. (Carbondale: Southern Illinois University Press, 1967), whose critique depends critically upon the genetic indivisibility of subjective aim. See esp., p. 105. See also my critical study, "Can Whitehead Provide for Real Subjective Agency? A Reply to Edward Pols' Critique," *The Modern Schoolman* 47/2 (January, 1970), 209–225.

(There is one context, however, in which " 'genetic' analysis" is contrasted with " 'coordinate' analysis" [PR 220].)

22. The category of the ultimate may be a generalization of Whitehead's discussion of 'concrescence' in the chapter on "Process" (II.10.2), once transition has been given a derivative status (cf. PR 211f).

23. William A. Christian regarded creativity and the category of the ultimate to be "pre-systematic" notions. ("The Concept of God as a Derivative Notion," *Process and Divinity*, ed. William L. Reese and Eugene Freeman [Lasalle, Illinois: Open Court, 1964], p. 183.) They may not be "systematic" terms, as Christian means them, but our genetic analysis suggests they might be "post-systematic" terms. For a non-genetic critique of Christian's position, see William J. Garland, "The Ultimacy of Creativity," *Southern Journal of Philosophy* 7/4 (Winter, 1969–70), 361–76, reprinted in a revised version in *Explorations in Whitehead's Philosophy*, ed. Lewis S. Ford and George L. Kline (New York: Fordham University Press, 1983), pp. 212–38.

24. From the notes of Whitehead's Harvard Lectures for the Fall of 1928 as recorded by Sinclair Kerby-Miller. A photocopy of these notes should be available at the Center for Process Studies, 1325 North College Avenue, Claremont, California 91711.

25. Whitehead continues, however, to depict the subjective aim as a sort of embryonic self growing throughout concrescence. Thus in the addition to II.2.2 he writes: "This subjective aim is this subject itself determining its own self-creation as one creature" (PR 69). It would be more consistent with his own deepest insights, I submit, if subjectivity were *exclusively* identified with unification, so that all unity would be objective.

TEN

Recapitulation

In four short years, from the sketch contained in the Lowell Lectures of February, 1925, until January, 1929, when he submitted the final manuscript of *Process and Reality* to the publishers, Whitehead worked out a stunning metaphysical synthesis. If the original sketch is rather meagre, this merely shows how far Whitehead travelled the next few years. In this summary we shall simply list the major conclusions we have reached, omitting all argument and qualification. The chapter should also facilitate the use of this book as a ready reference, as these conclusions are difficult to keep straight. It can provide a preliminary orientation for readers interested in specific chapters as well. (The numbered sections summarize particular chapters of the book.)

I. Before the Composition of *Process and Reality*

1. *Science and the Modern World* is usually interpreted in the light of Whitehead's later metaphysical writings, but if the original Lowell Lectures are isolated from the total text, they reflect a metaphysics having much greater kinship with the earlier philosophy of nature. We may specify three basic characteristics of the later philosophy that are largely absent from the earlier thought: temporal atomicity, pansubjectivity, and theism. In the earlier philosophy of nature, events are infinitely subdivisible, while the later actual occasions, being temporally atomic, cannot be. There is no temporal atomicity nor explicit theism in the Lowell Lectures, and pansubjectivity only in a very qualified sense. All events have interiority, but not necessarily mentality.

The Lowell Lectures, "with some slight expansion" (SMW viii), comprise chapters 1, 3, 4, 5, 6, 7, 8, 9, and 13 of the book. According to my investigations, this slight expansion consists in three additions:

(a) The "Triple Envisagement" addition of three paragraphs (overlapping SMW 105)
(b) The "Relativity" addition: the last ten paragraphs of chapter 7 (SMW 122f–127)
(c) "The Quantum Theory" addition: the last four or five paragraphs of chapter 8 (SMW 135–137)

Since the basic text in *Science and the Modern World* for temporal atomicity is this "Relativity" addition, and since temporal atomicity is presupposed by the later layers of the text, but contrary to the nature of an event, as conceived in the earlier layers, Whitehead seems to have adopted it during the composition of this book. The entire book is usually interpreted in the light of this doctrine, but we can make better sense of the text if we isolate the earlier portions to interpret them according to their own presuppositions. This is the task of chapter 2.

By a detailed examination of the first paragraph of the "Triple Envisagement" addition we can show the contrast in meaning with respect to the related notions of "endurance" and "vibration" occasioned by the shift introduced by temporal atomicity (ch. 1, sec. 3).

2. The original Lowell Lectures of 1925 are based on the notion of divisible and overlapping events, in accordance with the earlier philosophy of nature (PNK and CN). There are two differences. The many different types of objects (sense-objects, perceptual objects, percipient objects, etc.) are now grouped in terms of eternal objects (mostly, sense-objects) and enduring objects (the rest). Prehension now replaces extension as the primary relation between events (cf. PNK 202). Prehension is not yet allied with feeling, nor does it have a subject or a subjective form. It is perhaps best understood as symmetrical internal relatedness conceived from the standpoint of one of its relata. "Prehensive unification" is perhaps best understood as a precursor of the concept "concrescence".

Whitehead understands his "philosophy of organism" in terms of "organic mechanism," in which the plan of the whole influences the plan of the part, and vice versa. Mind/body interaction is seen in terms of how the enduring pattern of the whole organism affects the part. Mentality and consciousness, occasionally termed 'ego-objects', constitute objective characteristics of "bodily events."

3. Since the "Relativity" addition (the last ten paragraphs of that chapter) introduces the pivotal notion of temporal atomicity, we have devoted a chapter to its intensive examination. This difficult and intricate argument is not completely conclusive, and is replaced in later contexts by a Zeno-like argument which is both simpler and more potent. Yet the argument of this addition is more intimately bound up with the set of problems Whitehead was then wrestling with, and gives us more clues as to how he personally first came to espouse temporal atomicity.

The structure of Whitehead's argument appears to be: (a) An event is what it is by virtue of its internal relatedness to all other events. (b) If so, an event can be analyzed into an underlying substantial activity of individualization, and into a complex of apects so unified by this activity. (c) An event is internally related to the entire duration of simultaneity in which it lies. (d) [implicit] To be perceivable, a temporal slice of nature cannot be instantaneous; it must be a temporally "thick" duration. (e) These last two steps suggest that the percipient event, as cogredient in its duration, is not only temporally "thick" but is also temporally atomic.

4. The two "metaphysical chapters" on "Abstraction" and "God" appear to have been appended to *Science and the Modern World* after these additions with their espousal of temporal atomicity. We tend to interpret "Abstraction" as the first systematic elaboration of Whitehead's final metaphysics, as it pertains to the eternal objects. In the context of Whitehead's development, however, these two chapters offer a fairly complete metaphysical analysis of the cosmological doctrine he had presented in the Lowell Lectures, as seen in the light of the transformation temporal atomicity introduced. This doctrine is analyzed in terms of its basic elements, those concerning form and abstraction in the first chapter, those concerning actualization and concretion (God and the substantial activity) in the second.

The term "eternal object" carries the same meaning as in the Lowell Lectures, but its scope is considerably enlarged. In the earlier philosophy it referred mainly to the extrinsic characteristic of an event, where the distinction between actual and possible events was not sharply made. Now it could also designate the intrinsic property of a (not yet realized) possibility. The chapter on "Abstraction" explores the nature of a possibility, the mode of its ingredience, the individual and relational essences of eternal objects, the contrast with actuality, and the extent to which actuality can be described by purely formal characteristics (infinite abstractive hierarchies). My analysis of 'eternal objects' is prefaced by consideration of anticipations of this teaching in the Harvard Lectures of April and May, 1925 (see section 2).

5. After the abstractness of pure form has been examined, its concretion or actualization in matter of fact is taken up by considering the conditions of actualization. The transcendent role eternal objects now assume generates an infinity of possibilities which Whitehead conceives as influential upon all occasions, not just those which are sentient. Since the actualization of these possibilities indiscriminately, without regard to any general principles of order, would lead to chaos, Whitehead introduces a principle of limitation. Since this principle of limitation orders the cosmos, it fulfills a traditional role for God, as foreseen in the teleological argument. It can properly be called "God," yet it lacks the trait of traditional concepts of God which Whitehead held objectionable, that of being the transcendent creator. (In an event ontology, that which brings any event into being would also determine that event's nature. Such determination would preclude the possibility of human freedom.)

As the principle of limitation, God is conceived neither as a particular actuality among others nor as a super-actuality inclusive of all others. In the original Lowell Lectures an event could not be the unit of things actual, since an event could be of any size whatsoever. Whitehead concluded that nothing short of the whole could be regarded as finally actual, and endowed that total event with an underlying substantial activity in order to account for the world's dynamism. This basic monism carried over into the additions and supplementary chapters. That underlying substantial activity was conceived to have two attributes, "eternal possibility and modal differentiation" into actual occasions (SMW 177). The principle of limitation became the third attribute.

Chapter 5 also considers some details about Whitehead's changing attitudes towards religion, especially as found in the address "Religion and Science" and tries to specify the relation between the three forms of limitation (logic, causality, and particularity) and the principle of limitation.

6. In *Religion in the Making* (1926), a second but shorter series of Lowell Lectures, Whitehead proposes to exhibit the concept of God as enhanced by "dogmas," his special term for those particular principles discernible by religious experience. His strategy is to explore the nature and general history of religion and dogma in the first two chapters, sketch a theistic metaphysics based on ordinary ex-

perience in the third chapter, and show how this metaphysics is enhanced by dogma in the fourth.

A comparison of this metaphysics with his previous writings shows that he has shifted from a previous monism based on the underlying substantial activity to a pluralism of occasions. This underlying substantial activity assigned previously to the whole is here assigned to each occasion, thereby making it self-creative, although the exact sense in which it is self-creative is yet to be spelled out. In order to explain the creative advance into novelty, Whitehead introduces the contrast between ground and consequent, which is complexly related to the contrast between the physical occasion and the mental occasion.

While the shift to pluralism obviously took place sometime between 1925 and 1926, there is some slight evidence to date it more precisely. It may have happened after Whitehead had drafted the first two lectures, while he was examining the foundations for his metaphysical sketch in the third chapter.

Several passages in *Religion in the Making* strongly suggest to many readers that Whitehead already had by then the concept of the consequent nature of God in mind. To be sure, God is here conceived as personal, conscious, dynamic, and possibly even receptive to the temporal world, features which in Whitehead's final vision can only be ascribed to the consequent nature. It poses severe difficulties, however, to our understanding of *Process and Reality* to suppose that God could be ascribed physical feeling as early as *Religion in the Making*. While many very strong intuitions of God's temporality may well now be present, the conceptual device termed the "consequent nature" seems to have been invented late in the composition of *Process and Reality*. Here God appears to be conceived solely as a synthesis of ideal entities or as a nontemporal concrescence of pure conceptual feeling.

7. During the academic year 1926–27 Whitehead published no books save for the lectures on *Symbolism, Its Meaning and Effect* (April 1927), which primarily restrict themselves to a new theory of perception. They are best considered together with those chapters of *Process and Reality* analyzing the three modes of perception (see chapter 8). For clues concerning his metaphysics during this transitional year we have three sources to examine: (1) The address on "Time" delivered at the international philosophical congress in September, 1926 (Appendix 2). (2) Notes of his lectures at Harvard, Fall 1926, compiled by George B. Burch (Appendix 3). (3) A compact summary of his metaphysical position in 22 propositions which

Whitehead presented to his students in seminar during March, 1927 (Appendix 4).

The "Time" essay collapses the double distinction between physical and mental occasion, and ground and consequent, by applying the former distinction to all occasions, thereby making his doctrine explicitly panpsychist. It also champions internal supersession, whereby an initial process of physical unification is superseded by a derivative act of mental unification. It is just such internal supersession which I take to be prohibited by the later epochal theory of becoming (PR 68), but in September 1927 the epochal theory was limited to time, and so did not apply to the mental occasion which was conceived to be extra-temporal.

Another theme in the "Time" essay largely reversed in later thought is its insistence that time requires incompleteness. "Each occasion is temporal because it is incomplete." Contrast this with the category of explanation 25, that the satisfaction is determinate in every respect. Though "concretion" is primarily used, "concrescence" is here introduced for the first time, and used throughout the Harvard lectures.

In the essay on "Time," Whitehead discusses presentational immediacy, but not yet the contrasting mode of causal efficacy. Yet perhaps the crucial step towards his distinctive theory of perception was taken in the idea that "physical memory *is* causation." (IS 244). For if prehension were conceived as primarily causative, then the causal independence of contemporaries would throw into question the easy assumption of the earlier writings that prehension of contemporaries is possible.

The Harvard lectures contain six metaphysical principles which are quite unlike any contained in the final categoreal scheme, even though one of them is titled "the ontological principle." But by comparing them with the eight principles presented the next fall, in October 1927 (Appendix 5), after Whitehead had drafted most of the intended Gifford lectures, we can gain considerable insight into the evolution of the categoreal scheme. For the 1927 principles resemble their counterparts among the categories of explanation.

The March 1927 metaphysical sketch presents his first theory of consciousness as involving a contrast between the mental and the physical. Following William James, consciousness is a function, not an entity. The role of propositional feeling in consciousness is yet to come, but there are some vague anticipations. Whitehead does sketch out of theory of propositions as intermediate universals: eternal objects which have been restricted in their application to specific actual entities, their logical subjects. Logical subjects are distinguished from the "percipient subject" (later, the "judging subject"). Even some of the later illustrations involving Caesar are present here. This small basis is sufficient for the development of his theory (as contained in the intended Gifford lectures) without any major revisions. But there is yet no mention of propositional feelings, nor of the location of propositions within the phases of concrescence.

II. THE COMPOSITION OF *PROCESS AND REALITY*

8. As in *Science and the Modern World*, there is a basic shift in the midst of *Process and Reality*, taking place between the Giffords draft, our name for those chapters completed during the summer of 1927 (the subject-matter of chapter 8), and the subsequent revisions (the topic for chapter 9). The Giffords draft assumes that concrescence begins from a single unified original datum (itself perhaps the product of transitional unification), while the final revisions reconceive concrescence as a single process of unification beginning from a multiplicity of initial data.

Compositional analysis suggests two sections of *Process and Reality* were written prior to the summer of 1927, and were not originally intended for the Gifford Lectures:

A. The Basic Theory of Extension (IV.2–3, 5 in part). Theodore de Laguna seems to have convinced Whitehead of the importance of "extensive connection" in the summer of 1926, and Whitehead may have directly begun the work of axiomatizing his theory and drawing out its consequences for measurement on this new basis.

B. The Original Treatise on Perception (II.4.5–8 and II.8). Though somewhat scattered, these sections form one continuous whole, and may well have formed a preliminary study for the April, 1927, lectures later published as *Symbolism, Its Meaning and Effect*. Later, when Whitehead developed his theory of "Strains" (IV.4), these chapters were included in the book as necessary background.

From correspondence we learn that Whitehead wrote 9½ of the ten Gifford Lectures he intended to deliver the following June during the summer of 1927. (These are not the Lectures he finally presented, as Appendix 6 will indicate.) It is possible to risk a tentative identification of these 9½ chapters:

C. The Giffords Draft

1. "Speculative Philosophy" (I.1),
except for one paragraph (spanning PR 12f), a later insertion.

2. "Fact and Form" (II.1).
This chapter has many later insertions, most obviously the fourth
section introducing the ninth categoreal obligation.

3. "The Extensive Continuum" (II.2).

4. "Locke and Hume" (II.5).

5. "From Descartes to Kant" (II.6).
This last chapter may contain two important early additions summarizing Whitehead's early theory of concrescence: the last part of
section 3 discussing "datum, process, satisfaction, decision" and the
first part of section 5, before the discussion of Kant proper. The
chapter may also have included another section (now 7.1). Chapter
7 does not seem to have been originally drafted as a single chapter.
The middle three sections display a unity in tension with the first,
while the final section on the reformed subjectivist principle (added
much later) signaled Whitehead's change of views on this principle.

6. "The Order of Nature" with "Organisms and Environment"
(II.3.1–4 + 4.1–4).
The rest of chapter 3 (3.5–11) is a sustained discourse using such
advanced notions as "structured society," "living person" and "hybrid
physical prehension" which come much later, after the delivery of
the Gifford Lectures. Without these later sections, chapter 3 is truncated, but it is unlikely that Whitehead then thought of these sections
as forming a half-chapter. For without the Original Treatise on
Perception, the first part of "Organisms and Environment" lacked a
place in an independent chapter. These two parts may have originally
been combined in a single chapter. Much of this corresponds to the
Giffords prospectus for the fifth lecture (Appendix 6).

7. "Propositions" (II.9).
The opening sentences of chapter 3 suggest that chapters 3 and 9
originally belonged together. The last two sections of chapter 9 show
signs of being added later.

8. The Original Theory of Concrescence (III.2.2, as augmented).
This chapter, perhaps drawing upon materials from "The Subjectivist
Principle," (7.2–4), is based upon the second section of "The Primary
Feelings." The first section of this chapter appears to be a later

insertion based upon the final revisions. It has dominated the interpretation of this second section. Considered independently, the second section concerns two main species of primary feelings, conceptual feelings and simple causal feelings, which are neither derived (directly) from past actual entities nor from each other.

9. "The Final Interpretation" (Part V), as originally drafted.
In its original form, without the sections contrasting the primordial and the consequent natures of God, part V probably constituted one chapter. The whole of part V did not originate with this distinction, for there is good evidence at least part was written prior to the chapter on "Process" (II.10). The initial section of "Process," down to one sentence beyond "Abide with me; Fast falls the eventide" (PR 209.7) fits seamlessly with V.1.2, if we omit the first two sentences (PR 338.11). Whitehead seems to have written this description of "flux and permanence" originally for "The Final Interpretation," then lifted it for use in the chapter on "Process".

10. "Process" (II.10), as a half-chapter.
In this brief systematic summary, Whitehead proposes that there are two species of process, concrescence and transition, particularly in the first and final sections. The middle three sections discuss concrescence, but there is no corresponding analysis of transition. This, I submit, was to be the burden of the projected half-chapter. Whitehead may have found it impossible to work out a theory of transition, for any detailed account comes close to postulating two successive acts of unification (a transitional act establishing the original datum, and an act of concrescent appropriation) for a single occasion, in violation of his theory of epochal becoming. After the shift signaled by the final revisions, an independent theory of transition was no longer necessary.

These 9½ chapters isolate about two hundred pages of *Process and Reality*. If due allowance is made for later insertions, they lack such familiar concepts as simple physical feelings, negative prehensions, the derivation of conceptual from physical feelings, conceptual reversion, transmutation, intellectual feelings, hybrid physical feelings, subjective aim, and the distinction between the primordial and consequent natures in God. All these terms were introduced by Whitehead in the final revisions, after this draft had been composed.

The most distinctive doctrine of the Giffords draft, from the standpoint of later revisions, is that concrescence starts from a single unified datum, rather than from a multiplicity of initial data. Thus "the datum, which is the primary phase in the process constituting an actual entity, is nothing else than the actual world itself in its character of a possibility for the process of being felt" (PR 65). This theory is the direct descendant of the teaching in *Religion in the Making* and the 1926 essay on "Time" that a complete occasion consists in a sequence of two sub-occasions, a physical occasion and a mental one. The physical occasion is here reduced to its outcome as a datum unifying the causal influences of the universe as they impinge upon this event. The mental occasion now becomes the concrescence by which this datum is analyzed and subjectively appropriated. This is one theory of self-creativity, for the subjectivity of the occasion only emerges in concrescence, but it is not the radical theory of self-creativity that Whitehead was later to achieve. For in conformity with tradition the occasion first acquires being (as a unified datum), then acts (through concrescence). It does not yet come into being through its acting, by unifying the initial multiplicity it inherits.

While the theory of the Giffords draft is generally constant throughout, there are some hints of an impending change towards the end. Thus there are a few instances in which he recognizes "the complexity of the datum" (PR 165), speaking of the "multifold datum" (PR 185) or even of "data" (PR 164, 213) even while not yet denying its basic unity (see 8.3 [2]). While "subjective aim" has not yet been introduced, some of its functions are present in the pair of concepts, "ideal of itself" and "objective lure" (see 8.3 [3]). The term "subjective form" emerges in the final stages of the Giffords draft, particularly in respect to the fourth section of "The Subjectivist Principle" (II.7.4). The second half of this section, which anticipates the emergence of "subjective form," shows signs of being written before the first half, which uses the term explicitly (see 8.3 [3]).

The Giffords draft evolves a theory of consciousness culminating in this definition: "Consciousness is the subjective form involved in feeling the contrast between the 'theory' which *may* be erroneous and the fact which is 'given' " (PR 161). As yet neither propositional feeling nor intellectual feeling, necessary features of the final theory, have been introduced (see 8.2 [3]).

Ch. 9. The Giffords draft seems to be the only full-scale metaphysical treatise that Whitehead attempted for *Process and Reality*. While his revisions of the theory propounded in the Giffords draft are considerable, constituting his metaphysical theory as commonly understood, they did not lead to a separate treatise conceived on the same scale as the Giffords draft. Whitehead rather contented himself with making numerous piecemeal supplementations to what he had already written, the most systematic of which concerning the phases of concrescence being grouped in part III. We may perhaps discern some ten stages governing his theory in these supplements:

D. "The Theory of Feelings" (III.1, especially 1.2).
If we were selecting one text which expresses the fundamental theoretical shift from the Giffords draft to the later revisions, it would be the second section of this chapter. The earlier theory of transition followed by concrescence, a theory which originally applied to the entire activity of an occasion, is here transformed by being applied to a single feeling in a careful sentence outlining the five factors of a feeling (PR 221). Feelings, which heretofore had only operated within concrescence, in terms of an occasion's subjective appropriation, now reach out beyond concrescence to the past actual entities themselves by the simple expedient of identifying feelings and prehensions. But we prehend more than we feel, so it was necessary for Whitehead to introduce negative prehensions. If a prehension only distinguished between subject and datum, it could be very difficult to make sense of a prehension whose datum is inoperative, but by this time Whitehead also had the concept of "subjective form" as a third distinguishing factor at his disposal.

Given this new conception of a feeling-prehension, Whitehead could now conceive of concrescence as a single process of unification starting from a multiplicity of simple feelings of the world, and no longer as a two-step process whereby first the original datum was unified by the activity of transition, to be followed by a second process of appropriation (concrescence). It could be a single process whereby the many became one. On the basis of this transformation Whitehead set about developing a theory of feelings, including the first three categoreal conditions, as well as the concepts of "contrasts," "nexūs," and "subjective forms."

E. The Second Theory of Concrescence (III.2.1–2,4 + 4.1–2).
The new theory obviously meant that the original theory of concrescence in the Giffords draft (see 8.1:C.8) would have to be completely overhauled. The section on the two primary species of feelings, simple causal and conceptual (III.2.2), could be retained by just stipulating that by simple causal feelings simple physical feelings were meant. (Other sections of the original theory were dispersed [e.g. to II.7] or possibly eliminated.) The prefatory section on simple physical feelings (III.2.1) was drafted anew on the basis of the revised theory.

Higher feelings were conceived as based on synthesis of these two primary species of feeling. Once physical feeling was introduced it became possible to analyze the origin of a proposition in terms of physical and conceptual feelings, thus giving rise to propositional feelings. More importantly, Whitehead found in propositional feeling, at least for the time being, the sort of feeling which could be the vehicle for consciousness. Consciousness was the subjective form of a certain contrast, the Giffords draft had concluded; now Whitehead could specify the feeling of that contrast in terms of propositional feeling. At this point the revised theory of concrescence probably consisted of five sections combining materials later found in chapters 2 and 4.

F. The Remaining Categoreal Obligations (III.3.3–5, 5.8).
If a single chapter on the second theory of concrescence was planned, it was disrupted by Whitehead's decision to adopt Hume's principle that everything in the mind (conceptual feelings) was derived from sensations (physical feelings). Apparently the flexibility and multiplicity of simple physical feelings, replacing the old theory of the original datum, gave Whitehead the confidence to identify with this understanding of sensations. Heretofore he had resisted Hume's principle on the grounds that it could not provide for novelty, but now he generalizes Hume's exception concerning the missing shade of blue (PR 86f) into a theory of conceptual reversion. Just as the missing shade is partly identical with, partly different from, extant shades already perceived, so reverted eternal objects are relevant to those derived by conceptual valuation.

These two principles of valuation and reversion lead Whitehead to expand the list of categoreal conditions provisionally to eight, which were then articulated to form the basis of "The Transmission of Feelings" (III.3.3–6). (The eighth categoreal condition, now housed in the very last section of this part [III.5.8], probably belonged to this chapter originally.) Transmutation depends upon early phases of valuation and reversion to provide a single or simpler characteristic for our fused sensations. The last two categories of Subjective Harmony and Intensity seem to have been originally intended to direct the concrescence towards a final unity.

G. The Emergence of "Subjective Aim."
The role of purposive direction, which Whitehead assigns to subjective aim, may be traced back to the "ideal of itself" and to even earlier concepts in the Giffords draft. The concept of the "ideal of

itself" persists as far as the discussion of the category of conceptual valuation (PR 248). But the distinctive function of subjective aim, that of accounting for the unity of an occasion during concrescence, does not seem to be assigned to the "ideal of itself."

This question of unity became acute once the original datum was dissolved into a multiplicity of initial data. The unity could no longer be taken for granted as the outcome of transitional activity. Since now no objective unity was possible short of objectification, some understanding of subjective unity needed to be forged, assuming that concrescence, as a something, is best understood in terms of unity. Whitehead seems initially to have thought this unity could be provided for in terms of the universal categoreal conditions. The unity could be conceived in terms of the integrity of a subject aiming at the satisfaction it will attain. In its original version, the eighth categoreal condition may have read: "The subject aims at balance and intensity of feeling (a) in the immediate subject, and (b) in the relevant future" (see PR 277, 1929 text).

This generic way of accounting for concrescent unity ultimately proved unsatisfactory, perhaps because it did not connect that unity with the particular individuality the occasion would become. In any case Whitehead reassigned this role of providing for subjective unity to the element in concrescence which bore the particularity of the outcome: the telic, purposive factor heretofore known as "the ideal of itself." Instead of the subject as a whole, as constituted by the categories, aiming, we now have its role taken over by the "subjective aim," conceived as a particular feeling running through concrescence, subject to continual modification.

Unlike the "ideal of itself," the subjective aim does not primarily emerge at the end of concrescence. It is needed throughout concrescence, even in the initial phase of simple physical feeling, if it is to provide a measure of subjective unity. Otherwise, especially in that initial phase, the occasion would fall apart into complete multiplicity. If this is the case, the subjective aim cannot be derived from the concrescence itself, or from any particular phase. Whitehead proposes that it be derived from an external conceptual source, God, who primordially envisages all aims as possibilities. So the first section of "The Transmission of Feelings" was prefaced to the discussion of the later categories (III.3.1). The derivation of the initial subjective aim by means of hybrid physical feelings (3.2) comes later (**L**).

H. Intellectual Feelings (III.5).

The final chapter of part III most likely owes its existence to a technical difficulty which Whitehead now realized was emerging from his system. The derivations of "physical purposes" and "propositional feelings" are structurally all too similar. For all actual entities whatsoever have "physical purposes," which are the integration of their conceptual component with the final physical feeling. Since only very few actual entities enjoy consciousness, "propositional feeling" forms a poor vehicle for consciousness if it is so similar to "physical purpose." By using the theory of indication already worked out in the Giffords draft (II.9.3), Whitehead nearly empties "propositional feeling" of all physical content (substituting bare *it's*), while proposing a higher synthesis of propositional feeling with reinfused physical feeling. This higher synthesis, termed "intellectual feeling," is alone regarded as conscious with respect to its subjective form.

The rest of chapter five is largely a reworking of parts of chapter four (4.4–5) in order to account for the consciousness of perception, illusion, and imagination in terms of intellectual feelings.

I. The Consequent Nature of God.

If only intellectual feelings can be conscious, as Whitehead now held, and these are necessarily derived (in part) from physical feelings, then any pure synthesis of conceptual feeling alone would have to be unconscious. Yet after *Religion in the Making* Whitehead conceived God as wholly constituted by conceptual feeling, and he seems never to have thought that a personal God could be unconscious. The conflict between his newly developed theory of consciousness and his theory of God stimulated a major revision of his theism, resulting in the characteristic process theism by which Whitehead's thought is known.

Now that consciousness required physical feeling, Whitehead experimented with the alternative of ascribing physical feelings to God as well. Since the metaphysical implications of physical feeling and their subsequent integrations were already worked out, he needed only to apply this theory, which provided the appropriate vehicle for articulating his religious vision. To accommodate this new theory to the text thus far written, he renamed "the primordial actuality" (i.e., God as hitherto conceived) "the primordial nature" to contrast it with "the consequent nature," the supplementary physical feelings he now introduced. The primordial nature may not be conscious (PR 345), but the final synthesis is. God had been conceived as purely eternal, in line with traditional thinking; now God is conceived as both eternal and temporal.

Since God was now endowed with both mental and physical poles, God's uniqueness could be specified in terms of a reversal in origination in contrast to ordinary actual occasions. This enables God to be uniquely designated as the one actual entity which is not an actual occasion (PR 88).

J. The Gifford Lectures and Subsequent Additions.

Judging from the prospectus (Appendix 6), what Whitehead actually presented in his ten Gifford Lectures of June, 1928, was rather different from the Giffords draft he had drawn up the previous summer (see **C** above). His theory had grown considerably since then (**D-I**), so he resolved to give a precis of the whole, omitting some historical chapters (II.5-6) and the discussion covered in *Symbolism* (II.4.5-8, II.8). There is also no mention of Strains (II.4.9, IV.4), nor the advanced theory of living persons (II.3.5-11), nor the chapter on "Coordinate Division" (IV.1), but these probably had not yet been developed. From the topics announced for Lecture V we infer that "The Order of Nature" (II.3.1-4) and "Organisms and Environment" (4.1-4) were originally intended to form one chapter.

After the Giffords Whitehead set about preparing his lectures for publication. The materials were largely written, except for the chapter on Coordinate Division (IV.1) to pull parts III on concrescence and IV on extension together. (The other new materials were the result of new difficulties and ideas, and could not be anticipated beforehand.) Whitehead's method of revision seems calculated to preserve as much of what he had written as possible, even if from another and conflicting point of view, by inserting additional material which would reinterpret what had already been said along the lines of his current thinking. This material could be a paragraph or two, or several pages, or a part paragraph (a paragraph concerning two very different topics is a frequent device of his), or even a sentence or phrase. These insertions have largely fulfilled their purpose in redirecting our attention to the final theory and away from the process whereby Whitehead achieved that theory. Several examples of these insertions are given.

K. Strains (II.4.9, IV.4, IV.5.1).

One technical difficulty Whitehead came to appreciate in his theory of perception is the non-identity, even though very close approximation, between the "presented locus" (the locus of that which we directly perceive) and the "duration" or contemporary event within which the percipient occasion is situated. The theory of "strain-feelings" is designed to reconcile them, and to that end Whitehead produced this material. Since only three sections (4.1, 4.4, and 5.1) are fully devoted to the topic, with many of the other sections having relatively small discussions of "strains," which could easily be insertions, it appears that several sections initially constituted a single chapter (4.2–3, 4.5, 5.2 and possibly 5.3), discussed in the ninth Gifford Lecture on "Projection and Presentational Immediacy".

L. Hybrid Prehension, Abolition of Reversion and the Living Person (III.3.2, II.3.5–11).

The section inserted into "The Transmission of Feelings" (III.3.2) precisely explaining the way God can provide initial subjective aims by way of hybrid physical feeling may introduce this latter notion into Whitehead's theory, or it may have been anticipated in an addition discussing the first categoreal condition (PR 224f). Secure in a definite theory of divine provision of aims, appreciating the scope of unrealized possibility these aims can provide, Whitehead now calls for the abolition of reversion as superfluous in a final paragraph attached to the section that had introduced it (PR 249f).

The notion of hybrid physical prehension also enables Whitehead to combine continuity and novelty in the concept of a "living person." Since the actual discussion of the "living person" takes place only in the first three paragraphs of the final section of Whitehead's expansion of "The Order of Nature" (II.3.5–11), the rest may well have been written first. From the opening remarks of this expansion (PR 99), it appears to have been meant as a substitute for an earlier section, now relegated to "Some Derivative Notions" (I.3.2).

M. Coordinate Division (IV.1).

This may have been the final chapter written, although the sequencing of these last three sections (**K, L,** and **M**) relative to one another is difficult to ascertain. It provides a more systematic relation between parts III and IV than otherwise would have been possible. Another reason for the chapter may lie in Whitehead's increasing willingness to accept the commensurability of genetic and coordinate divisibility. Heretofore he had referred to genetic *analysis* and extensive *division* (PR 227, 235). Now he recognizes two species of divisibility, which need to be correlated.

From the notes of Whitehead's lectures to his students at Harvard, October 8–13, 1928, we can infer that the introduction of the Category of the Ultimate (PR 21f) was probably one of the very last acts in the composition of *Process and Reality*.

In the course of Whitehead's metaphysical adventure the meaning of his basic term "process" undergoes a subtle transformation. In the Lowell Lectures of 1925 it signifies a philosophy of change or of flux, marking a philosophy of events replacing traditional notions of substance. By the time of the Giffords draft endurance and change are both secondary considerations, pertaining to the similarity or difference between successive occasions. "Process" now meant the two-fold activity of "transition" and "concrescence." With the final shift after the Giffords draft (**D**), this "process" was simplified into a single act of self-unification requiring ultimately a past multiplicity and a divinely provided subjective aim. "Process" is now the coming into being of an actual occasion; it is "becoming," in contrast to the "being" achieved, which is the other half of the title, *Process and Reality*. Instead of calling this process *flux*, which is now no longer appropriate, I think we should call it "creation," although of a radically different form from traditional divine creation. Whitehead has managed to conceive a new species of "creation," opening up the discussion in new and fruitful ways.

Appendix 1

THE HARVARD LECTURES, FOR 1924–25

edited by Jennifer Hamlin von der Luft

THESE notes of Whitehead's first course at Harvard were taken by one of his colleagues, William Ernest Hocking, and are here reproduced (in part) with the permission of his literary executor, Richard Hocking. The manuscript is deposited with the Houghton Library, Harvard University, Cambridge, Massachusetts 02138, and a facsimile should be available at the Center for Process Studies, 1325 North College Avenue, Claremont, California 91711. The lectures beginning with October 21, 1924, and ending with March 28, 1925, have been briefly summarized. The lectures beginning with March 31, 1925, and ending with May 26, 1925, because of their relevance to this study, have been put into publishable form without any major changes. A few changes in grammar and spelling were necessary, but nothing has been altered that would affect the meaning of what was written. Hence these notes retain the character of lecture notes. Often sentences are very short, sometimes not sentences at all. Sometimes it has been possible to render these more intelligible by supplemental bracketed material.

Two topics have major significance in the lecture notes, time and eternal objects. Whitehead did lecture part of the time on logic but these particular lectures (February 17 to March 3, 1925) show that Whitehead was trying to discover a method for comparing time in different time systems. He put his arguments into symbolic notation, but he was not studying principles of logic, methods of logic, or even different systems of logic.

Whitehead ended these lectures by putting forth his new and important discovery of temporal atomicity of occasions. Although Whitehead skirted the issue all through these lectures, he did not present his discovery until April 7, 1925. A reading of the notes will show that Whitehead was lecturing on things that were new to him as well as new to his students. He lectured as he discovered, so there is no reason to assume that Whitehead made his discovery of the atomicity of time appreciably earlier than he announced it in class.

All through the notes there is the tension between the eternal and the temporal process of this world. There is also the tension between the past and present and the future and the present. Whitehead has very little trouble dealing with the subject of space but time puts him in a muddle. It is not until the atomicity of time is discovered that these tensions begin to straighten themselves out. It is this discovery that solves many of his problems, as can be seen by reading the notes.

These notes are fragmentary, even when completely transcribed, but it is possible to see Whitehead experimenting with some of the ideas that characterize the later stages of *Science and the Modern World*. Yet he does not incorporate them into the philosophy he was willing to publish until after the discovery of temporal atomicity. We also see him experimenting with new terminology, terminology which must have been very strange to his auditors, including technical terms since dropped such as "subsequence" (November 21). "Subsequence" apparently signifies the effect an actuality has on *subsequent* actualities.

SUMMARY, OCTOBER 21, 1924, THROUGH MARCH 28, 1925

October 21–25, 1924
Beginning with the first lecture, Whitehead argues against Aristotelian thought, especially on the topic of change.
Law of excluded middle gets us into trouble.
P is already present as a possibility before it appears. Not-P does not exclude the possibility of P (but rather indicates it).
We can perceive the term and its relation without perceiving [the] relatum. This makes induction possible.

Nov. 1
Actuality is being an occasion of Realization—like an event.
The eternal is contrasted with the enduring.
The Ground exhibited in every occasion is: 1) "that which is true respecting every occasion because it is an occasion," 2) "the processional character in itself," 3) "the substance of which the occasion is a limited affection," 4) "the substance which requires all occasions," 5) "the substance determining the processional occasions," 6) "the ground of generality," 7) "fact as self-contained with, or exhibiting, its own reason."

Nov. 4 (taken from [Dr. Ralph] Eaton's notes)

Process of the world is not linear but expansional. Realization is limitation.

Whitehead protests against both realist and transcendentalist (Kantian) ways of looking a things. Whitehead says that subject and object can only be explained by making them a part of a larger togetherness.

What is immediately realized is a relation to ourselves—the impress. Whitehead escapes solipsism by saying that the mind is in the idea not the idea in the mind. The mind is in the impress.

Nov. 8

"The inmost character of realization is after all this atomic individuality achieved by structural definition." It is this individuality which allows the impress to get itself into something. The eternal is enriched by its particularization into particular occasions.

The eternal "emerges into an individuality of value which is in a sense eternal." It is this eternality which allows for memory. No assurance of the truth of the past is possible "unless there is something eternal in things."

"The realm of ideas in its pale apartness is neither true nor false. Truth has to do with the act of realization."

Endurance differs from spatial extension. If space is cut in half two bits are left; if time is cut in half a whole space is left. To abolish distinction between space and time is to abolish the distinction between sense and nonsense.

"The mind is nothing but the flow of its perceptions with something to pull it together as one mind."

Nov. 11

Whitehead "arrested by a doubt." It seems to concern the definition of speculative philosophy. Whitehead mentions Broad, who wants to disallow religious and ethical experience from speculative philosophy. Whitehead on the other hand states, "We cannot go a step beyond experience, but we must go all the steps that experience imposes on us."

Nov. 13

Objects [eternal objects] have relational essences. It is what it is in itself and in relation to others.

Eternal objects are limits to process. In this limitation value emerges.. This emergent value has endurance.

Nov. 15

Whitehead discusses the processional nature of the World. Everything is in relation to something else. "Reality is becoming. . . . Can't catch a moment by the scruff of the neck—it's gone you know." "A togetherness of things" is realized in this process. The structure of this togetherness is limitation. Togetherness is not merely formal; what and who the elements are makes a difference.

"Becoming is not managed from without." What we're talking about must be all inclusive. "I *emerge* from my details as an entity. I do not lie behind them."

Nov. 18

Mind does not create objects. Objects same for all entities as they are eternal, they stand up against the mind in their own right.

Two kinds of Objects, Primary and Emergent. Greenness would be a primary object. There are two kinds of Primary Objects—Pure and Social Objects. A Pure Object "is purely an object, not a concept of an occasion." A Social Object is also "the concept of an occasion—structural relation, a concept of a togetherness."

Emergent Objects—"Has to do with the definite limitation of eternal principle by fact of actuality." Basic object of zero grade whose ingredients are pure objects. Process continues. Example: molecules fuse into an organism. An emergent object becomes more and more complex.

But what is realization? The first accent of reality is the fact that it has limitation of selection. The second accent is that there is transition in selection with an aspect of the selection, and an aspect of display.

Nov. 20

1) Description must be founded on observation.
2) In perception
   a) Relation of here to there
   b) The physical feels another active—*there*
   c) Immediate recollection of past
   d) Anticipation—present is known as having its aspect in the future. Relation of objects to occasion is complex.
3) Four essentials of an object—Categories: Actuality, Selection-or Finiteness, Pattern or System, Unification.
4) *Actuality*—Limited exhibition of the Eternal. "Time depends on actuality."

5) Systematic *Selection*—Selection is omission. Unification is structural. "Ingression of a pure object into a basic object is in a particular part and in another sense in other parts." Ingression of pure objects differs depending on the standpoint of the object.

6) What is Unification?

   a) Category of quantitative cumulation—Intensive quality and vividness

   b) Category of qualitative cumulation—Refers to diversity

   c) Category of qualitative contrast—But also relation arising from diversity

Nov. 21

1. Evolution is production of superior types out of inferior types. Nature of things based on two aspects; 1) monistic totality of realization, 2) pluralistic aspect based in world of potentiality. No emergent entity is fundamentally independent. Entrance of pure object into space-time is of a complex character. "The invention of 'ingression' suggests the various types of relations."

2. A basic object B in process of realization is very complex. For any region P there is an aspect of B called the P aspect of B. B is in a sense there. "This is the 'subsequence' of B, [that which is] pervaded by B. . . . All sorts of *thereness* in the subsequence [:] perception, memory, field, causality."

3. Anticipation— When a passes into b, a is not b simpliciter but a anticipates b by allowing for the possibility of b.

4. Emphasis upon the togetherness of concrete fact as expressed in poetry, e.g. Shelley's "Mont Blanc".

5. For a basic object B at P there is a fusion of pure objects into a pattern at P. "But the fusion does not abolish separateness."

Nov. 24

The environment is conceived as having a pattern embedded in it by the emergence of B. This "I call the subsequence of B."

1) Intrinsic and Extrinsic Reality of B.

2) "What do I mean by concreteness? There is no unconditioned actuality." Something is only real by its position in an environment. A concrete entity has three aspects:

   a) *display*—Individual internal achievement

   b) *formulation*—Individual determination of achievement

   c) *universal*—Embodying Eternal Principle which underlies all achievement.

Nature of realization finds itself in these three characteristics. "Apart from its environment the object is in abstraction and loses its concreteness."

"Logic is nothing but the science of formulation considered in itself. The emergent entity is how formulation looks in realm of realization."

Nov. 29 [An analysis of fusion]

1) Pure objects have no location in space-time. Objects in space-time are only in a relation of governing region P to some subsequent region Q. Objects are in the subsequent region Q as derivative from the governing region P.

2) Grades of realization—full concreteness in individuals

3) Ideal existents—plurality of isolated entities

4) Realization achieves unity of all being (monism)

5) The aggregate of modal presences in Q is dependent on what exists at P. The contents of P antecedent to the contents of Q and the contents of Q are subsequent to contents of P.

6) Q has an "Actual Potentiality" different from "Ideal Potentiality."

7) Internal relations—"There is something in P which is Q." "P is beyond Q."

8) Q, which is present, is "a meeting point of past and future." Past and future cannot be nothing since you cannot have relations to nothing.

9) The principle of realization is "the integration of ideal diversity into unity." "An event . . . implies some grade of emergent unity." Only where there is some realization of structural pattern is there complete realization.

10) The very essence of reality is the achieving of something by selection, for its own sake. What is realized is value.

11) Three categories apply: 1) the ideal of unification; 2) the ideal of display; 3) the ideal of selection.

Dec. 2

1) Metaphysics is a purely descriptive science; also it is most general. All special sciences must be able to stand within one's metaphysics. One gets one's metaphysical concepts "by starting with some special science and pushing its concepts back and back."

2) Epistemology is "the first critic and first source of metaphysics," but it is not the foundation of metaphysics.

3) Whitehead's thought differs from absolute idealism in that for him the absolute is not a super-reality. Whitehead's ground of reality

is no more real than the given. "Reality is always emergence into a finite modal entity. Realization is always unification, whose conditions are always a discrete plurality of existents."

4) The process of becoming one is the emergence of a limited entity and it also refers to process beyond itself.

5) The fundamental description of an emergent entity is not in terms of Subject-Predicate but requires reference by the entity to something beyond itself. Q, a present entity, is both something for its own sake and contains the impress of P, a past entity. "Realization is a realization of everything there is for realization."

6) An entity P does not modify its next-door neighbor; there is no next door neighbor. "The present is arising out of a past and passing into a future, and is relevant to both."

7) Freedom lies in the fact that present emergent events are more that a sum of past and future. Each entity "chooses what it is going to be."

Dec. 4

1) Emergent Entity—

"Run away from the unity. Then the entity q is made up of its parts. What are the parts made of? Other parts. Infinite regress. Got to stop it. Only two ways." 1) parts which are not events, "something different with mysterious external relations." But this is a "metaphysical fairytale." 2) An emergent entity's actuality is inherent in its unity. A room is not a bare piece of space-time. Space-time characteristic of mere roominess is an abstraction.

2) "It has emerged as an end in itself and is therefore of the nature of value."

3) The "Actual Potentiality" is what is accepted from the past. The "Actual Effectiveness" is how what is beyond the emergent entity receives actual potentiality from it.

4) Retention is illustrated by time. Present occasions retain past occasions.

5) "We've got to dig out the enduring object from the event. . . . Something has been passed which is identical and equally present in any segment." This is the historical route. "The object pervades its route. . . In all realization we have the self-affirmation of a pattern for its own sake." This is how continuation of identity is achieved.

Dec. 11

We must "stop [our] effort to frame a general metaphysical outlook and come back to the *order of nature.*"

1) "The idea of an enduring entity: an identity of pattern throughout an historic route."

2) "Each organism helps to create its own environment." Organisms which passively change to suite environment, die when environment changes, but organisms which help to form their environment survive.

3) "Can't stop evolution at some 'final' point." Nor can we start from some point of time before time. It is not a linear process; it is an expansion of progression, an expansion which "stands behind it."

Dec. 16 (taken from Eaton's notes)

Definiteness, the fact that every matter of fact is definite, is the only eternal matter of fact.

The order of nature is an abstraction that gives a particular order which is a particular space-time.

The order of nature is an emergent mode. The order of nature ought essentially to exhibit itself as a (part) of a wider community.

"Process is deeper than space-time. Space-time is a particular mode of process; it is a process under the form of spatialized retention and temporal passage."

Dec. 18

"An enduring object is a pattern in space-time."

Assume that there is a timeless space and a time. Then an electron "is nothing but the modification which it introduces into the electro-magnetic field."

"The electron is the functioning of the pattern."

"The concrete entity cannot be abstracted from its environment."

Dec. 19

1) The key to nature lies in organism, not matter.

2) The concept of matter is proving inadequate to the depth of the new situation.

3) In every case the parts have to be interpreted in terms of the whole.

4) The actual pattern cannot be divorced from the environment. "You cannot consider the nature of an electron without considering the whole, nor the whole without considering the electron."

"The organic principle must not be brought in on top of [the] mechanistic principle."

5) What is realized at a particular standpoint is a definite value or effectiveness. "Cognition is our immediate perception of what there is about us." The "value of things is permeated through and through with effectiveness." The simplest thing is not a billiard ball atom, but a basic object, an emergence, an enduring object, an organism.

6) "A group is isolated when it is not being *much* affected by other things in respect to the perspectives that interest you."

7) A favorable environment is "one in which each subordinate organism has a function." The totality "is an essential condition for the continuance of its ingredient parts. This is an organism."

Jan. 6, 1925
"Arrived at [the] idea of organism—"

1) The problem of vitalism is wrongly stated, for it assumes mechanism prevails throughout the inorganic and the vitalism first appears with the organism.

2) Mechanism argues from parts to whole. Vitalism argues from whole to parts.

3) The mechanist is a materialist, starting with the part as concrete and sufficient to itself. "Organism insists you must bring the whole into your argument."

4) "If you let mechanism in [to explain cells, bodies, gyroscopic action] you have hard work to push it out."

5) We know we have an interest in our bodies as a whole. "Mechanism leaves out my obvious interest in lunch."

6) Mechanism has its strongest point in that it is built up on the Baconian basis. Vitalism cannot disturb the whole procedure of modern science.

7) Mechanism presupposes matter, simple location, substance and extensiveness.

8) Must decide whether to proceed on an objectivist or a subjectivist basis.

9) Whitehead going to proceed on an objectivist basis. What we observe is what we observe. "Awareness must be confined to awareness in relation to body."

Jan. 8
Whitehead calls eternal existences "eternal objects."

Connection between *two events* always marked by the eternal object and vice versa. "I take prehension as holding together without reference to cognition, which I am not sure is involved."

Your organism is the event which is the prehension into unity of the aspects or pattern thereof.

The endurance of objects—Pattern is the only thing which endures. There is no matter in the background. "But we have prehensive activity. Displayed spatially and enduring temporally."

"There must be some element of pattern, [an] aspect which is found equally in all segments. Endurance means persistence of this part; [the] pattern [endures] throughout the event. . . . The unity of pattern is derived from inheritance within the event."

Jan. 10

We must get at the binding element in the transition between occasions.

Two points of view on this: 1) the analysis of transition in terms of something outside of transition; 2) the self-determination of the flux which is the relation of occasion to occasion.

Occasions are the realization of some form of togetherness of pure objects. Does this leave any relation between occasions besides comparison?

The examination of bodily events is helpful here. We perceive a bodily event as a whole. There is no such thing as simple location in case of eternal objects. Simple location leads to bifurcation of nature.

The substitute for simple location is the functioning of eternal objects in the connection of events.

Eternal objects such as shape or color are not in an event as an aggregate of aspects but as a pattern of aspects.

An event therefore is an organism.

"The underlying activity realizes itself in the event and therefore it is in the event that you get a *mode* of substance. It is only real in the unity of modes."

Jan. 13

The object is the prehension into unity of the pattern. It has two roots inherited from the past and from the environment. A physical object inherits aspects and continues these as its predecessors did. If a physical object gets into "a strikingly different environment," is it still the same? Yes, the identity continues if there is enough in common between earlier and later physical objects.

Jan. 15

The event responds to its environment. The quantitative aspect of effectiveness is called intrinsic energy. "The response to the environment is the capture of intrinsic energy."

"The organism tends to organize itself so as to preserve its pattern. . . . Nature is built on shock." An electron will change its pattern in response to a stressed environment.

Jan. 17

Time differs from space in that one can divide the event so that the pattern reappears as a whole in the individual segements. Pattern consists in spatially connected segments. "Pattern is founded on the unity of the event."

The space-time continuum is for enduring objects. Events do not require objects but objects require events.

Is there only one public time? Whitehead discusses Einstein's relative time. What is needed is "some way of expressing motion which is independent of which body you take as to rest."

Jan. 20

"The instructive assumption of an order of nature had got implanted in the European mind by fifteen centuries of Christianity and the mediaeval rationalism, believing in the immediate interference of God. [Many are] haunted by this point of view. Modern science is not so haunted."

[February 1925]

"Laws of thought can be stated only because they might be otherwise and are yet *that*. You can't talk of anything that might not be otherwise."

"Extending over. Mustn't use the idea of points to explain 'extending over' if you are going to use 'extending over' to explain points."

"Reasoning, to be powerful, must be perfectly general."

Feb. 17

To express inclusion:

i) The idea of inclusion excludes the case of including itself.

ii) given any entity *a*, it includes event *x* and is included by event *y*.

iii) *a* can include *b*.

iv) transitive law of inclusion

v) some event can always come between two other events

vi) one event x can extend over two other events a and b
Intersection: if common part x of a and b
Separation: no common part
Touching: one point in common
Dissection: one part completely inside another

Feb. 19

If x and y share more than one point they make a new event. One point or less shared makes two separate events.

"Creative activity itself not in the idea of [a number] but in the idea of classes."

Feb. 21

The doctrine of internal relations taken seriously leads to the relations modifying the essences. You cannot explain what the entity is without considering its relations. "An entity is the prehension of all other entities under a limitation of aspects."

". . . it is not possible [for man] to deal with [the idea of the] universe without abstraction. With God it may be possible."

Our senses are always inexact, but it is nonsense to say they are inexact unless we know what exactness is.

Feb. 24

Lecture concerns abstractive classes and the definition of "covering."

Feb. 26

Congruence can be made a primary idea, but Whitehead feels that it can be analysed further.

Structure is "endurance of a pattern."

"Congruent things have homologous relations to gemoetrical structures."

"When two abstractive classes are to be equal the point instant is to be the whole species of classes with the same convergence."

Feb. 28

Concerns primes, antiprimes, and routes of approximation.

March 3

How to deal with time:

Only a duration can enclose a duration. If two durations intersect they do so in a duration of the same kind. An intersection is the having of events in common.

"If we leave go the systematic character of space-time we leave go the sheet anchor of how knowledge is possible. . . . in the organic character of the universe everything is in its nature modified by everything else."

A moment is a class of co-equal antiprime durations.

"In practice our apprehension of a moment is a duration within which transition is negligible."

March 5

We are now using hypothesis; we are going beyond clear experience.

The use of hypothesis:

Everything comes down to direct experience; here Whitehead is a pragmatist. An hypothesis must have some bearing on direct experience. Perhaps it will enable you to apprehend something you would not otherwise. A good hypothesis leads to observation. It is a creation of the intellect; it prepares the mind for perception. Its chief use is to increase the direct apprehension of truth. It binds together vague apprehensions by making precise a vaguely felt unity.

March 7

An hypothesis may induce docility.

An hypothesis must satisfy a vague apprehension of what is the case and must take us beyond what we know. The assumption of science in the mid 1880's was that everything had been cleared up. Science must never assume that it has a system all worked out; it must always question.

A nobler hypothesis brings in a wider harmony.

March 10

A moment is a class of antiprimes with the same convergence.

What is meant by a point comes to the same as what is meant by a moment.

For Euclid, a point is that which is indivisible.

Aristotle makes no distinction between a point and where it is. No accumulation of points can make a continuity.

Plato did not recognize points as a class of being at all; he regarded them as geometrical fictions.

March 12

There may be alternative time systems. Different endurances may use different rules of succession. "What we are aware of is the time system of our own endurance." A timeless space would be neutral in regards to all moments.

March 14

Space alone is not a sufficient structural principle. Space and time must be taken together. Only an indefinite number of temporal successions will allow us to explain the structural ideas that arise in geometry. Alternative time systems present themselves by means of geometrical structure.

March 17

An instantaneous three-dimensional space is merely a concept of structure. Change is nonsense in that kind of world.

"The timeless enduring point. The Greeks muddled it up with the instantaneous point event."

March 19

There is a need for a method whereby the measurement of time in two different time systems can be compared. "I maintain that the only method of comparison is by seeing a geometrical structure and [by] observing that the elements compared have an analogous position in that structure."

March 21

Whitehead does not believe that in measuring, the observer forces his concept on the material because the relations are already there in the material. Three types of space: a) Euclidian, b) hyperbolic, c) elliptic.

March 24–28

Whitehead discusses whether the times in two different time systems can be compared, whether their velocities can be compared, and whether there can be any congruency between different time systems.

TRANSCRIPT, MARCH 31, 1925, THROUGH MAY 26, 1925

March 31

1. "The relativity hypothesis presents us with the notion of alternative progressions in time—not obvious to myself, only by a miracle that I have made it obvious to you."

Get rid of the linear idea of becomingness.

Plato in *Timaeus*—

2. In what does the distinction consist between different views of time[?]

"Bergson has the merit of philosophic originality even greater than clearness—seeing the real philosophic problem, even if he can't get it clear."

Bergson says *Durée* is indivisible—difficult. A time system is a definite scheme of divisibility.

3. Paradoxes in the idea of alternative time system.

A. A man on Mt. Wilson observing a star, S, whose light has taken some hundreds of years to come.

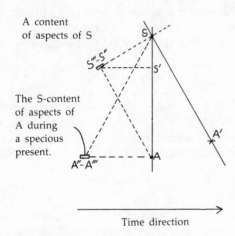

A content of aspects of S

The S-content of aspects of A during a specious present.

Time direction

But what at this moment is going on in the star[?] The question has some sense.

Observer at S is also wondering what is going on at our sun, which he locates at A^1 which is in the future (?). You have inconsistent views of simultaneity. A^1 is future, but you can't draw lines into non-entity. Can't put off as mere thought, as I can think Jack Giant Killer.

4. [These] difficulties were not wantonly raised in modern doctrine of relativity. Were there before in another form. Take the old idea of the flux of time.

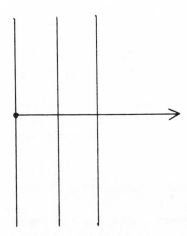

Kant's Analytics, Müller, 143, 149.

Axioms of intuition. All phenomena are extensive quantities "drawing on intuition." So time—a successive synthesis of part w[ith] part, and these parts are antecedent to the whole!

"Points and moments mere places of limitation." Can't compose time or space of *them* but only of times and spaces. W[hitehead] is in perfect agreement w[ith] Kant, who is not here expressing his own particular ideas. You've got to have some theory of the parts and the wholes.

Zeno made an unfortunate choice in dealing with motion and space—muddling up time and space together.

Egyptian law. If you have been acquitted three times for brigandage you must be expelled from the country—(lest you kill the judge and the jury).

So Zeno refuted often enough—suspect something permanently true there.

Zeno: How are you going to move forward into the future? How is process possible? If you conceive it under the guise of a temporal transition into the non-existent, you can't get going. There is nothing you can point to into which there is a transition, or is then and there created.

April 2

Doesn't extensive quantity contain in itself an inherent contradiction[?] It's the basis of the alleged unreality of time and space in Bradley—something wrong about it. All extensive quantity tracks back to space and time.

Take Kant's statement that the parts are antecedent to the whole— therefore every part itself is a whole w[ith] antecedent parts. Vicious regress.

"Previously" means the rel[ation] of part to whole enters into [the] essence of the whole, an internal relation so far as [the] whole is concerned. I believe I am nearly alone in holding that the relations in space-time are internal: they are usually taken as the very example of external relations.

Both must be put on same footing—the whole is of the essence of the part, just as the part is of the essence of the whole (cf. doctrine of aspects). Kant's idea of antecedence "was bursting with Newton's fluxions when he wrote that."

Whitehead's delight in Kant, one of the reasons he turned to philosophy. Caird didn't seem to know this—treated Kant as a product of Oxford Greats school.

You have got to make what lies beyond any part or event as of the essence of the part. The beyond is necessary to organize your ideas of space and time.

How does the unlimited become limited? Pythagoras—Spinoza. The infinite is only exemplified in limitations. How do the modes get into the substance is the Pythagorean difficulty.

Zeno asks[:] how is generation possible?

Aristotle's idea[:] We ought to start with points and moments and avoid all these difficulties. Points and moments with external relations.

But if your relation is external it is not of the nature of the term. Then the point has lost its space, or a moment its time. But a moment has an essential reference to other moments and you are wrong in regarding the relation as external.

Then there is something wrong in the notion of such a point as occupied. Makes a perfectly absolute theory of Space-Time necessary. If you don't hold this theory, a point must be a way of talking of a relation between things.

| Moment | | What is that moment? I say it is that particular concrete relatedness of that past to that future. We do not deal with the past passive[ly?] but with past events. In their rel[ation] to future events. |

Before (Past) | After (Future)

We only get hold of the unbounded via system. We discern system. Apart from system you can't know anything until you know everything. My answer to that puzzle is, you discern system. As in the example of simultaneity.

How are we going to express this relation of the unbounded past to [the] unbounded future?

April 4

1. Realization is a generative process.

Qua generation—Selective actuality of realization

Qua eternal—space-time as the scene of potentiality

Divisibility is the actuality—we have got to preserve that.

These are the elements of thought we have got to play with. Also in science, continuity and atomicity [are] always haunting [us] and under the influence of the quantum theory the atomic aspect has become more urgent than before.

Trying to conciliate these points of view [is] the business of philosophy.

2. Qua eternal you lose distinction between time and space in the time-space continuum, because it is all there. Time has to do only with generation. Space-time as the locus of all possibility. But as the home of *all* possibility [it has] no value. Here Plato went astray—regarded the eternal as the home of all value.

"But there is a halfway house which it is the business of theology to explore;—not my business."

3. Ideal conditions exemplified in every flux, but [are] not [them-

selves] in flux. Mathematicians emphasize it. Biologists try to keep
it in the background. The mathematician is trained to deal with what
is left when you have abstracted from every particular thing. So
Pythagoras worried about the infinite, how does the unbounded
become bounded. The discoverer of mathematics discovers this problem. Generation is limitation.

Plato also had the venturing of the idea in generation.

Aristotle, biologist, son of a doctor, wants to put the ideal into
the flux, whereas Plato wanted to put the flux into the ideal.

Fails to explain generation without an appeal to potentiality. But
potentiality is a positive fact. If it is nothing, it *is* nothing, it doesn't
help you.

---

4. Potentiality is so called in contrast with actuality. But a contrast
implies a positive element.

Spinoza does justice to this positive side of potentiality. Space and
time as attributes of the eternal were possible.

Descartes "the father of all bifurcation." Mind the receptacle of
ideas. Matter the basis of generation. Very good as a guide to the
science of his time. As Galileo and the Inqu[istion were] both wrong,
but Galileo's idea [was] the guide to the science of his time.

Berkeley and Hume: Mind of God. Hume [has] vague reference
of impressions.[?] Ends in skepticism.

Kant—lands in an impasse—but extraordinarily useful. But he has
stable conditions of organization of experience. Excessive subjectivism
lands him in perfectly hopeless difficulties. We must keep an eye
on Kant. Try to do the same sort of thing he does and get rid of
the subjectivist basis.

Hegel tried to do this. The idea as generation. The unbounded
becomes bounded. Trying to sum up what was inherent in all
philosophy. He got in very much too much necessity. The idea too
much and the generation too little. But Hegel and Pythagoras shake
hands.

Where I think Hegel missed it. The contribution of philosophy to
thought, an adjustment of Eternal to actuality, has to bring into
accord the hypothetical adjustments of each particular region of
experience—as in logic, science, etc. Philosophy must have its hypothetical element, taking account of the hypothetical stages of each
department of thought.

Bradley represents a revolt against generation; Bergson a revolt against the eternal side.

Speculative element must have some element of fairy tale in it. If any philosophy seems not to have it, it is because we are used to its terminology.

5. The naturalness of the atomic view.

I have been insisting that the moment is a high abstraction.

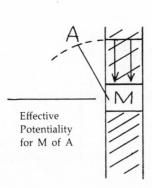

Effective
Potentiality
for M of A

M. = Man (What is your name. N or M [NN?]). The aspect of a pattern grasping together of a totality as all "now". "A reproduction in the bounded of a character of the un-bounded."

The given, spatio-temporal. The whole of the given is "for that"—a subjective aspect. It is how all *that* is related to *that*—internally.

Transmission from A to M. M cannot be itself without adjusting itself to what it has received from A.

April 7

[Whitehead] professes a state of muddle, due to the state of the subject.

1. Science at present is asking for an atomic theory of time. Shall metaphysics say to science it can't have it? This is not the function of metaphysics. Can we find any ground for it[?]

2. Consider events as extending over one another. You can only get it by making temporality something beyond inclusion, extending-over. This distinction between temporality and extensiveness has already been suggested. The question of the direction of time is fundamental. Can't slip it in in a nicely constructed sentence. The idea of extension doesn't include time-direction.

3. Mere extension soon demands that you should go beyond it. Hegel's dialectic has some application. A set of abstractions demands, in order that you shall [not] land in no-meaning that you go beyond them.

4. The temporalization of extension, via realization of the potential. The individualization of each event [is brought] into a peculiar to-getherness. The future, qua relevant to reality, is merely for something

which is real. An event as present is real for itself. It is this becoming real which is temporalization.

5. But here we bump up against the atomic view of things, also the subjective view. The subjective view has got to be expressed within the objective view. It is there—the psychological field. You have got to express the subject as one element in the universe [as there is] nothing apart from that universe.

Indefinite antecedent
past out of which
the present has
emerged

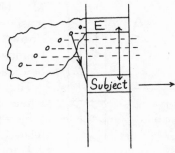

The subject has to realize
itself qua the influence of
the past on it.
Limitation

A subject is a parallelogram in our myth, having divisiblity and transitions within itself.

Its reality is the realization of something as entering into its own being. "The pulling together of a duration from its own viewpoint, i.e. as entering into its own essence."

The event, E, is within, enters into the essence of the subject not as being merely the subject but as [the] being itself. The subject is what that grasping-together is. "I am the apprehension of that"— you people, the Presidents' house, all these things, of a whole simultaneity. The whole duration as realized for the subject.

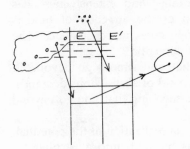

Atomicity

Realization may require a minimum duration.

There is nothing in a moment.

The becoming real is not the production via the parts of the duration—contradicting Kant.

"The transition is in the nature of what has become real, but it hasn't become real because of the transition."

The second extract from Kant was inconsistent with the first (on extensive quantity): if you throw over the first, you get your idea of atomic quantity.

The time transition must be a *transition within what is already there*. The simple thing to say is that the future is simple non-entity. [But] there is no relation between something and nothing. You see the transition within the given, the trolley car going before you.

The atomic view of succession: E, E', [etc.] Eddington's view takes the psychological projection out of physical nature. Einstein said he was not talking about the psychological field. The physical universe simply becomes the scheme of thought. But it is a scheme of thought about your psychological field [since there is] nothing else to be thought about—lands you straight into solipsism.

April 9

1. *Is the monadic view contradictory to continuity?*

Berkeley and Leibniz introduce a *deus ex machina* to overcome the difficulty of atomism and continuity. Subjectivism and objectivism reach the same impasse.

Starting with events, and bringing the future and past into it, didn't give enough differentiation. Had to introduce 'reality' as 'real togetherness', bringing in the time-idea. If you take time as merely generating the event, Zeno gets at you. There is no such thing as a moment. What must be real is the togetherness of the content of the event.

---

2. Cognition is self-cognition. What is an event for itself? The subject of Descartes' *Meditation[s]*. If you differ from a philosopher you differ from him before he has begun, in his presuppositions.

Descartes' cogitation involves '*inspectio*' of what is other than himself, raising the epistemological question in its most acute form. *Cogitata*—things cogitated. The first thing he finds in asking what he is is that the ideas of substance and quality don't apply. *Cogitata* cannot be represented as qualities of the mind.

Self-consciousness is simply self-knowledge. The true way of putting it starts from [the] idea of internal relations. The relation of subjectivity to objectivity modifies its own essence. In asking what it is in itself you can't avoid taking account of what the other real things are. Any real subject is one among other things, constituting a community of internal relationship. Better than substance-quality idea vs. Aristotle.

3. How represent these internal relationships? The mind is not something standing behind events but something realized in events. It is of the essence of what is being realized.

Object event as lending its aspects to Eternal Objects and vice versa. "That is colored," or "Color is there."

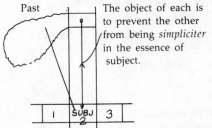

Past

The object of each is to prevent the other from being *simpliciter* in the essence of subject.

Taking the subject as real is to take it atomically as having in itself the flux of time, spatio-temporal. Realization is limitation, [and] embodies the whole in limitation. How does the subject achieve this?

1. The whole is as NOW, a duration.

2. The beyond-the-now. (PAST) The past is for the subject qua realized.

What the subject is for itself includes the present as issuing from the past. Internal relations with the past.

[Consider a] schoolboy catching [a] cricket ball. [The] perceptual object [is constituted by] data appearing as issuing from a strain of control. Not so far from what Kemp Smith has been saying in his recent book. Which everybody has been saying is so inadequate. Would have done better if he had drawn a diagram.

Continuity of the subject.

Inheriting a pattern. (2) inherits from (1) the totality of the subject as being past. The subject inherits its own unity, its own grasping-together, as the same process only with the aspect of being behind. "Every *enduring subject* inherits (or anticipates) itself under *the aspect of other circumstances*" (written on board). What is it that I am the same person as lectured to you last time—seems portentous to me.

Physics is the account of how *this* (past) modifies the essence of this subject. How the passage is accomplished. How this subject can find itself under different circumstance[s]. How the reality of the past affects the conditions so that the subject passes from event 1 to event 2.

What Spinoza left out is that the underlying substance is always in its limitations. [It] is always itself in a limitation. What is odd is that there is one universe instead of an infinite number of universes. Imagine a solipsist deity enjoying every world at once, [then] he is realizing nothing, [for these worlds] can't be discriminated. There [must be] a definite achievement. Here freedom comes in. The underlying activity has to be definite and exclusive.

April 11

1. Internal relations—

Means that the essence of the individual is what it is by virtue of the relatedness.

This brings you to monism. *MONISM.* "You never get away from the totality." "There you are with Spinoza." But you take a step which I think Spinoza ought to have taken: that the one attribute of your monistic substance is that it is realized in a pluralistic actuality that is in each individual realization because it is a limitation of the substance qua aspects.

2. Wherever you get the aspect of continuity in space-time relation, you are dealing with possibilities. Whenever you talk of space-time you always get the termination "-able."

We have the process of becoming—the realization of a pattern. See *Concept of Nature,* Ch[apter] on time. On why time seems more fundamental than space.

The ego of any entity is out of space. [It is] the monistic total[ity] as exhibiting itself in that individual activity of realization.

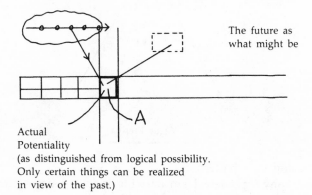

The future as
what might be

Actual
Potentiality
(as distinguished from logical possibility.
Only certain things can be realized
in view of the past.)

Individual as in time. Its life history.

This again, in order to be real[,] individualizes itself. (drawing cross line)

Must express its relations to every other part of the whole.

A is what it is in its immediate realization.

Expresses the totality in two ways. The Present as in its immediate self. And also as its own past.

The burden of the Platonic and Pythagorean message is that possibility cannot be non-entity.

You don't recollect what happened to somebody else, you see.

April 14

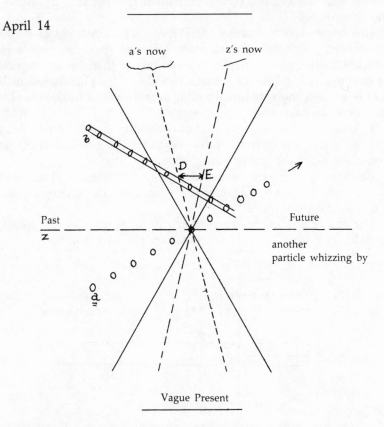

Vague Present

Reiteration of a pattern.

[The] metaphysical view I am drawing is in a sense a monism [for the one substantial activity] not one [activity] among others. But it is the essence of the activity that it individualizes itself in a plurality of real things.

The body is to be looked on as a method of keeping out [causal influences rather than as a method for] letting [them] in. It selects what aspects shall be considered.

A at A_0. Perceptive experience is knowledge of 3-termed rel[ations] between A_0, B and D.

Z at Z_0 Perceptive experience is kn[owledge] of a 3-termed relation Z_0, B and E.

The small boy catching a ball is not catching roundness but the determinateness of the universe in respect to the ball being there. [He is] not [catching] sense-data. [There is] a strain of control issuing into the future. [I] very much disagree with the idea of private worlds. If there is no apprehension of what the event in itself is "here," you can't get on at all. The essence of A_0 is being modified by the aspects of B, etc.

[Otherwise we are] then in danger of bifurcation [into] psychological space-time and the actual space-time.

April 16

The world as real, selected from abstract possibility.

The mind as subject and the object as predicate.

Modern psychology with physiology as its guide shows that the S[ubject]-Obje[ct] view won't do. The nerves are something, not just predicates of the mind. Subj[ect]-Obj[ect] view is a compromise [though] more complete than Subj[ect]-Pred[icate] view, or Subject-Attribute [view] of Descartes.

The object is obviously the ghost of a predicate—not the fact of experience. I walk into the room. I enter the room. The room doesn't enter me in any sense at all. Our experience is always one of entering into the world, not into the world as supported by oneself in any sense at all.

Subject—lying under—wrong.

We are always entering into things.

I-amid-objects is the truth of things. Myself within this room. Subjectivism gets rid of and abstracts from that.

My relations to the other entities enter into my constitution now.

2. Modality of limitation has a 3 fold character—

a. As of present

b. As of recollection

c. As of thought

We perceive the past as issuing into the present as in the cricket ball.

"Definite knowledge that there is something definite to be known always involved in hypothesis." Hence [my] disagreement with James and [F.S.C.] Schiller [the British pragmatist (1864–1937)].

Any sound metaphysics must preserve hypothesis, else there would be no error. It would be cosy to get a neat theory without error. "James' service to metaphysics [lies] in bringing out error and patting it on the back. Always on the side of the underdog—one side of it."

3. Recollection. Me-then as modifying Me-now. Permanent Me as an individualized activity of realization.

4. Eddington tends to take up extreme subjectivism.

Halfway house: Kant.

Objectivism. Whitehead. Elements perceived by senses are the elements of a common world. Things are to be distinguished from our kn[owledge] of them. We have enjoyment of [the] senses distinct from cognition—Bacon. Things enter with subject on equal terms—hence subject [?] to.

[5.] Objections to Subjectivism

1. Direct Perception. I am *within* space. Seen to be elements of [the] world. Instead of making this world depend on us, [he] holds with naive experience.

2. Particular content of experience. Historical kn[owledge]. Ages in the past. Star systems beyond our ken. Distances [between] interior of earth and far side of moon.

3. Action. Instant for self. Transcendent activity passes beyond self. Kant should have put his 3 critiques together. But activity goes to determinate ends [as the] known word transcends self.

Everybody wants to struggle back to an objectivist position.

Russell and Mrs. Ladd Franklin. [Christine Ladd-Franklin (1847–1930) was lecturer in logic and psychology at Johns Hopkins, later at Columbia. Her theory of color vision was widely accepted, displacing the theories then current.]

I do not see how a common world of thought can be established apart from a common world of sense. Can't remedy it by saying "anyhow we have a common world of thought." Any community must presuppose the immediate objective position of the world of immediate experience.

Realist and Idealist division does not coincide with this. Objective

Idealist finds the common world, but finds it involves mentality in every detail. Here realism departs. [We] should start with provisional realism.

Next: thought and abstraction.

April 18

[The] Subject-Object [theory] has in its background the Subject-Predicate Conception. The essence of the mind [is] the holding-before-it of objects. One objects to this as the prime expression of the metaphysical situation. The relation is one of parity.

Immediate apprehension of oneself in a world [is] the axiom. If you once drop this, you can never recover it, and it is an immediate question what point *of view you can hold.*

The internal relation is the fundamental metaphysical idea. As soon as you are dealing with what is real. The ego-object [is] in a world of objects. The world of objects modifies the essence of each object in that world.

The ego object knows itself as amid other objects. The predicate-subject p[oin]t of view. The idea of the essence is an abstraction from the other relata.

Relation of ideas to what is actual.

Difference of emphasis: Plato, Aristotle. Plato, mathematician; Aristotle, doctor. Plato considers abstraction: actual presupposes ideal. Aristotle first saw the stuffed bird and then found the idea.

Potential underlies the actual—any mathematician agrees to this.

But these ideas are held before the realizing process as potential *for it.* Can't tear the two apart. "I speak here with immense ignorance of what I am talking about. So please understand that."

If you insist that all your universals are in the particular realized entities, you get into a muddle. Can't see how the world then is to get onto anything new.

But they are always in a general relation to what is real.

Thought is a manifestation of the selectiveness.

As for the eternal objects. The relations they enter into are external. Hence [they are] logically antecedent to realization. This gives content to relation of identity (see beginning lecture of this session).

It's nonsense if you have not got two instances of the same thing.

Activity-process. Underlying activity.

Our perception of the enduring object is how our essence is modified by its aspect.

[I] can't make out how Hume says of impressions that we perceive nothing that connects impressions of past with future.

Its first importance[?] must be entirely arbitrary.

[It is] obvious, however, that in saying that anything—this chalk—is an object, you are perceiving something on the same level as yourself and as issuing into the future and thereby determining what the future is to be to you too. In perceiving an object you perceive that the future is to issue from that object, tho[ugh] you don't know what the future is to be. Your apprehension of the object is thus, as Descartes said, to be discriminated from the sense datum. [He] called it *inspectio*. On this ground we object to the whole materialism of science, [which conceives of] passive matter in space and time and in external relationships. Then [you] have to endow it with a field of force, as Newton did. Once [you] admit that the perceptual object is merely where it is and what it is, Hume has you, for you have exhausted all you have seen. Faraday (1849) said an electric charge is nothing but its tubes of force.

April 28
Cognitive Experience

A subject hitherto kept in the background. [We are] amplifying Bacon—as Bacon would be surprised to follow [*sic:* know?].

What are we driv[ing] at by the point of view of [this] course?

Cog[nitive] exp[erience] [concerns] how the essence of an immediate occasion is modified by, or partly constituted by its relations with other entities.

[Whitehead] believes he [is] in complete agreement w[ith] James in his essay, "Does C[onsciousness] Exist? " [James is] objecting with the idea of a stuff of mind, and in complete disagreement with Descartes.

Subjective side of C[ognitive] Exp[erience]. It is essentially self-knowledge (requiring a discussion of 'self'). Everybody knows the difficulty of getting away from [the] solipsist [objection:] "Your reason ought to spring out of your philosophy, and not out of the fact that you don't believe your philosophy."

"Consciousness is a relation between an emergent entity and the composite potentiality fr[om] wh[ich] it emerges."

A paradox: Cognizance presupposes the entity as less than itself.

An occasion may permit cognizance without requiring it or including it. The *standpoint* occasion and the *cognizant* occasion.

The translucence of cognizance. It does not alter the facts. An occasion *inclusive* of c[ognizance] presupposes the same facts *exclusive* of cognizance. The essential belief of realism.

You may look on cognition as *distorting* the cognita in some way, or as apprehending *representatives* of reality (Spencer), or as *finding* the cognita (realism). Here absolute idealism comes close to realism. If you have been brought up in Oxford, you call yourself an idealist. [If in] Cambridge, a realist. [It is] a matter of *emotional reaction*. Russell and Bosanquet agreed on value of symbolic logic for Bosanquet's kind of philosophy.

As long as one admits that c[ognizance?] does not alter the facts, the absolutists are harping on the importance of c[ognizance] in the universe. [This is] indubitable. The realist harps on the translucence of consciousness.

A parallel distinction [can be made] in re[gard to] the enduring entity. The self [is] the reiterated emergence of the same achieved value for its own sake.

The self of cognizant occasions must be discriminated from the self of standpoint occasions. Cognizant self and experient self [need to be contrasted. The experient self(?) is] industrious [and] active.

Cognizant self [is] fitful and variable in its analysis of the essence of any occasion. In relation to endurance, the important self is the experient self. There are many cognizant selves—sleeping, waking. "The cognizant occasion is the immediate *image* which constitutes the immediate knowledge of the cog[nizant] self." When we talk generally of the self we mean the experient self. It is within the images [rather than] the images within the self. *Mind is imaginal [rather than] images [being] mental.* Images as modification[s] of the universal mind distorts the cosmic situation [in] terms of substance and attribute or predicate. That which is permanent is not cognitive qua mental—associated rather w[ith] image. Descartes tacitly identifies the self which endures with the immediate cognitive occasion. The self which has endured since birth is not cognitive. "The man's judgment is warped by envy." Much . . . has not entered into this cognitive self at all.

April 30
[Raphael] Demos [raised these questions:]

1. How can c[ognizance] be translucent in view of the doctrine of internal relations? Should not c[ognizance] modify its object?

2. Is it correct to throw c[ognizance] into the flux—seems to be neither transient nor enduring—as when I say the sun is shining.

---

1. *In re* internal relations we must admit an essential difference between past, present, and future. [Otherwise?] the total content of the time-process is given. Unless you do that [admit the difference, it] relates time-process to c[ognizance], and [it becomes just as determined as the] turning over leaves of a book. We must have a universe in which there is room for freedom.

Anything which is not now [but] in the future can modify the present only "systematically"—via the essence of the actual, as containing in itself the condition of how it can affect the future. It stands within the essence of the actual occasion [as to] how it is modifying the future.

Now we come to the Demos' question, "how the present is modified by the present."

Standpoint a, which is now. [Let us] suppose [that] in this the universe is synthesized doubly (or trebly).

1. Under the modal limitation of being included in the immediate present.

2. [It is] further limited as being the present from *standpoint a*.

A takes the past as issuing [from] C', C'', into the present [and] perceives sensa (eternal objects we called them before).

A's experience or essence is *of* A as modified by other essences; this is

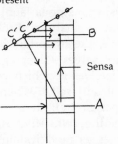

Trolley issuing into the present

Sensa

true without consciousness. But now we have to provide for sense-data.

There is an immediate inspection of B, but not of (whether) the endurances which are illustrated in B. [Nor?] of *what the present is in itself.*

The atomic independence of [all occasions] is necessary if you are to have a breath of *freedom* or of *error*. Radical pluralism. I am here and that chair is there.

Translucence of c[ognizance] is only an illustration of the atomic independence of all occasions in the present time.

---

2. How do I get A into the flux? By inspection it doesn't seem to be there. But the awareness does take place in time. Read "Time" in the *Concept of Nature*.

May 2
"The creature emerges by virtue of the niche that is there for it in the universe."

Cognitive experience is always a selection from the whole experience. Only requires the whole in its systematic aspects. Abstraction without distortion is possible because relations to the whole may omit details.

Correspondence theory of truth.

Intrinsic realities of the present are veiled from us. We have only the intrinsic sun of eight minutes ago.

May 5
Back to content of experience.
1. An ontology that finds no room for knowledge stands self-condemned. But it is not true that the first step in philosophy is an inquiry how knowledge is possible.
2. All cognitive experience has form[. The] immediate occasion is modified by its relations with other entities. Modified by = partly constituted by.
3. We apprehend not images in our mind, but entities [out] there. Our expression [is] only a restatement in general form of simple experience.

4. The experient self embodies [a] creative activity whose law is self-perpetuation. A creature emerges because of the niche there is for it in the universe.

Individual embodiment is the active principle involved in the formation of the chain of particular instances.

"Definiteness of achievement is such an odd fact. Such an odd fact that Bradley couldn't believe in it, as over against an Absoluteness which is everything at once. The supreme wonder [is] that a particular individual should be sitting here."

5. Antecedent sources of Definiteness

    a. Systematic relations in a general scheme whereby a niche is provided.

    b. In respect to this niche there is a *potentiality* arising from

    c. A definite character of the individual embodiment of creative energy. This question of creative character is somewhat arbitrary.

May 7

Idea of the Self last Time.

Today: Relation to Abstraction.

[I] don't want to run into solipsism. [Therefore I] have to describe kn[owledge] so it can be wrong.

1. Does error begin with conscious experience[?]

Do you think wrongly because you are an erroneous individual[?]

Bergson rather exalts intuition, and tends to assume that error begins with thought. When man begins to think, he thinks wrongly.

With self-c[onsciousness] error grows in *importance*. Children are sacrificed to Moloch.

But the real question is whether instinct is inerrant. The actions of animals are most ill-judged. And in the long run, c[onsciousness] is a mode of enabling you to avoid error.

[Wolfgang] Köhler was judging the presence of thought by the ability of apes to overcome an obstacle.

N. [W?] believes [the reason that] we think wrongly is because we are already erroneous, [but] then the error is magnified in importance.

2. We must therefore analyze the whole of experience without reference to thought.

First you must have experience as of external relations, otherwise everything depends on everything else.

Where does the external rel[atio]n come in?

Over[?] that principle that the present is only known to us through its systematic relationships.

Any event in itself is a mere triviality unless there is embodied in it an enduring pattern, self-inherited.

$$A, \bar{a}, \bar{\propto}, \left\{ A_3, A_2, A_1, A \right\} \quad \bar{\propto} = \bar{a}$$

A = present experience in itself

$\bar{a}$ = enduring entity

$\bar{\propto}$ = universal pattern the unity running through A's in series

How are we to analyze up the essence of A? [It is] eight different things.

more or less adept [?]

Essence of A. (Various Sources of modification thereof)

1. A as conditionally realized in the sequence $A_3A_2A_1$, etc.

+A as conditionally realized [in] $X_3X_2X_1$ any other enduring object

+A as conditionally realized [in] U,V,W, antecedent events

+A as standpoint for [the] ingression of eternal objects, β in sequence of occasions $(B_1B_2)_\beta$ in present and of $(C_1C_2$———$)_i$ in present, etc. "Appearance"—Red is there for me here, etc.

+ (and here is where error comes in) Moon could have vanished in the 1⅓ seconds [it takes] for light to come over. I do say I see the moon, not merely the patch of color. [I see] an enduring entity. The idea of self, *qua* idea, is [an] enduring object as much as any.

I am bound as serving this point of view of bringing in the ingression of selfhood.

+A as standpoint for ingression of selfhood in occasion $(B_1B_2)_\beta$ in present

+A as conditionally realizing the future via system

+A as conditionally realized from the past via system

+A as with preferential abstract envisagement of eternal objects

+A as intrinsically emotional and purposive—(Character of the underlying creative activity)

May 12

Thought and Private Worlds.

Essential to Realism that there be no private world. Everything there is is entering into the character of everything.

Natural to look on thought as in the nature of the case private. Yet they say God knows all our thoughts. How can he, if they are in the nature of the case private? [I] object to God being brought in to do impossibilities.

What if the mind shapes in synthesizing? "If you run [*sic:* allow?] any privacy, you will find it an infection difficult to get rid of."

To explain what you mean by error is another way of explaining what you mean by truth. But it is more important to attend to the [truth than to] explaining error. Only one way to do that—*Grades of experience.* And your old friend primary and secondary [qualities] must turn up in such way.

[Whitehead] holds that our experience of ourselves in the past is the same in principle as of anything else in the past. [There is a] *general publicity* of the past in every present occasion of concrete experience. If you don't have that publicity, you will sooner or later find yourself in great difficulty.

Secondly, you have got to have facts that can in some way be isolated from internal relations.

Necessary to get a cross-classification of experience to bring out the meaning of experience.

A = Standpoint Occasion

(Primary)

No room for error
above this line.

{
Memory Exp[erience] (Past as in A)
Anticipatory Exp[erience] (Future as in A)
Ingression Exp[erience] (Present as in A)
Abstract Exp[erience] (*Eternal Objects* as in A)
Emotional Exp[erience] (A as in itself,
    its own value)
}

We are bound to come → Secondary Exp[erience] (Ingression: more
down to some form of   abstract; more definite)
"Not private! "

[Secondary Experience is] an outcome of all the above as a reen-visagement, an ingression of eternal objects into events, which is a relation of eternal objects to the primary exp[erien]ce.

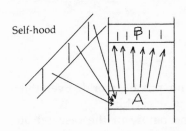

Self-hood

Hume. You have your impression. Then you have faint copies of your impressions. Copy = secondary. [Whitehead] differs from Hume and Descartes in putting Abstract[ions] into the Primary Experiences. [So PR 239f.]

Thursday, May 14
Emergence of Thought
Having arrived at a maximum of incredibility, we turn to reconsider the general principles. Details always reach the incredible.

Very much the same general line as Lloyd Morgan and Alexander. (Whitehead was prior) in Emergent Evolution.

Dissatisfaction with Alexander

1. [Alexander is] in a muddle in his early chapters on Space-Time. [I] never found anybody who did [make sense of them].

2. In handling the idea of emergence, [he did] not [put] sufficient emphasis on the provisions of the *niche* for emergence. He says that where you have a sufficiently complicated state of affairs there *is* cognitive experience. He ought to have a principle such as shows you in analysis that there is provided a niche for the *emergence* of something else. The niche is the relationship between elements which is the *possibility* of a synthesis. Get red and green together, you have left a niche for the particular togetherness, as "swearing" at each other, or harmonizing, eluding all empirical description. Can describe everything except what it *is*.

[This] procedure [is] endless because whatever emerges has new relationships. You can never exhaust the analysis of concrete fact by means of universals.

The most W[hitehead] has done has been to demonstrate [that there is] a niche. "To say this is cognizance is to go beyond anything I have demonstrated." What one described led to seeing that there was that relationship for realization. Cognizance is precisely what emerges as the realization of *that* possibility. Can't foretell the specific character of c[ognizance] anymore than of the sweariness of red and green.

3. The creative side of the synthesis. "The universe is such that given this occasion [it is the case] that the emergent entities are exactly what they are." What emerges is always what your analysis has left out. You have provided the type and the words, but the *story* has been left out. You can never get away from a creative activity with a creative character.

In respect to what situations do you recognize a niche? Can't tell it without bungling it. "Any metaphysics is a good meta[physics] which takes you a good long way without its metaphors breaking down."

Hegel [has] a certain arrogance. "When Hegel finds himself bound in a contradiction, that must be the character of things in themselves, and not of Hegel's thought." [He] doesn't go back to revise his own metaphors, or change his errors of misplaced concreteness and oversimplified relations. [The] attribution of redness to the cloud carried you a long way, or the [attribution of a] sixpence size to a star.

Two ways of metaphysics.

1. Try to reproduce in yourself Plato's state of mind, [or] Aristotle's [state of mind] etc., [and then] try to see how things were for them.

2. Describe things as well as you can, and revise [your description]. See that your description is a generalization of what people have said before. Keep philosophy in connection with the concrete state of mind of your own epoch.

You can never get back to the absolutely general. There is always something matter of fact about it. Why 3 dimensions, or 4? Always get something which is so and might be otherwise, even in logic.

Standards of music and ethics are there. [They are] matters of fact. [There is] something beyond it. Metaphysics always has to begin with that. Religion concerned here.

May 19

[I was] Absent in N.Y. Saturday, May 16, reading a paper on Hist[ory of] Mathematics [which is] to be published [SMW ch.2].

Pythagoreanism.

Classifying on Aristotelian ground tended in [the] Mid[dle] Ages to displace measuring. How much we might have learned had this not been so [cf. SMW 28].

Modern mathematics shows the emergence of new formulae by further generalization. Relation of relations, etc., being equivalent to new niches.

In becoming abstract, trigonometry became useful [SMW 31]. [Mathematics (?)] broadened out into diversity of possible explications. The utmost abstractions are the true weapons for controlling concrete fact.

Christianity was not the product of a happy epoch [Cf. SMW 33f]. It is only in a happy epoch that the age can undertake the revision of fundamental concepts. Then mathematics becomes relevant to philosophy, and you are then very near a Platonic view of philosophy.

May 22
Pythagoras' problem. How is abstraction possible? [This problem is] more fundamental than Kant['s].

How are actual events implicated in relationships?
    emergent objects
    eternal objects.
Relations progressively drop their character of internality in this series. It is the essence of an eternal object that it does run about on its own.

Are they merely external? Not quite. Any eternal object A has determinate relations to other eternal objects, and indeterminate relations to actuality. It doesn't lie in the nature of red whether a given bull somewhere in Mass[achusetts] will see red tomorrow. Red may or may not have that relation and yet be the same thing.

Prin[ciples]
    I. An entity cannot stand in external rel[atio]ns until it is indeterminate in its rel[atio]ns to [the] others which it is patience to.
    II. An ent[ity] wh[ich] stands in *internal* rel[atio]ns has no being as an entity *not* in these relations.

Individual essence, Relational essences, Patiences.
Analyze an eternal object A:
    1. Its A-ness
    2. Its determinate relations to every other eternal object
    3. A as patient of relationships which may be realized
A simpliciter is (1) and (2)

Bergson and Aristotle said it: What happens is an exclusion of what doesn't happen.
Every occasion is a synthesis of being and not being.

Every eternal object which is synthesized qua-being is also synthesized as not-being. (*not* Hegel)

I am not in that chain [i.e. series of actual occasions] but in this one. I should not have said "I"—I am not an eternal object.

R(A,B,C,)   is another more complex eternal object.

A B C D$_1$ D$_2$ . . . D$_n$ These exist.

What is actual is an abstract[ion] from the world of possibility.

Every actual occasion synthesizes every eternal object, including the complex eternal objects, either as existing or as not existing. This is the reason why every actual occasion is a limitation.

May 26
Whitehead—last lect[ure].

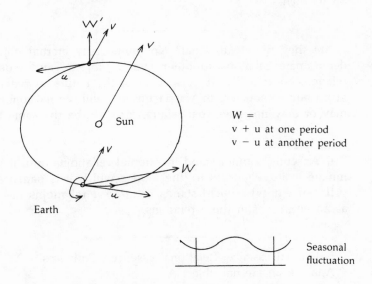

W =
v + u at one period
v − u at another period

Seasonal
fluctuation

Miller's positive result. You don't quite know what to expect because you don't know the resultant motion.

If the earth drags the ether along with it—then the result at the top of M[oun]t Wilson might be more that on the ground.

$$m \frac{d^2(X_\alpha Y_\alpha Z_\alpha)}{dt^2} = (F_1 F_2 F_3)$$

Newton's laws.

$$\frac{d^2 X_\alpha}{dt^2} = \frac{d^2 X_\beta}{dt^2}$$

---

1. Naturalism

18th and large part of 19th C[enturies]: You have explained a thing when you have brought it under these equations.

Clerk Maxwell produced another set of equations and died thinking he had made a step to bringing electricity under his equations.

Hertz pointed out that "Maxwell's Theory is Maxwell's Equations."

Since that time the electrical theory of matter has turned up.

Now the dynamic equations are derivatives from the Maxwell equations. Rel[atio]n inverted.

Maxwell's equations however are not invariant—for different axes. According to him the important thing is whether you are at rest w[ith] ref[erence] to the ether. Would be very muddled if you have your ether dragged about. So you are "up against a very well documented theory."

Larmon and Lovery found out the new equations which would be invariant.

Larmon's equations

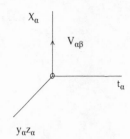

X_α

$V_{\alpha\beta}$

t_α

$y_\alpha z_\alpha$

P. $(x_\alpha y_\alpha z_\alpha t_\alpha)$
$(x_\beta y_\beta z_\beta t_\beta[)]$

Now refer this to a system of axes moving along x axis with velocity $V_{\alpha\beta}$.

$$\Omega_{\alpha\beta} = \frac{1}{\sqrt{1 - \dfrac{V^2_{\alpha\beta}}{C^2}}}$$

$$X_\beta = \Omega_{\alpha\beta} (x_\alpha - V_{\alpha\beta} t_\alpha)$$
$$y_\beta z_\beta = y_\alpha z_\alpha$$
$$t_\beta = \Omega_{\alpha\beta} \left(t_\alpha - \frac{V_{\alpha\beta} x_\alpha}{C^2} \right)$$
$$X_\beta - x_\beta = \Omega_{\alpha\beta} \left[(X_\alpha - x_\alpha) - V_{\alpha\beta} (T_\alpha - t_\alpha) \right]$$
$$T_\beta - t_\beta = \Omega_{\alpha\beta} \left[(T_\alpha - t_\alpha) - \frac{V_{\alpha\beta} (X_\alpha - x_\alpha)}{C^2} \right]$$

The ordinary Newtonian system.

$$x_\beta = x_\alpha - V_{\alpha\beta} t_\alpha$$
$$t_\beta = t_\alpha$$
$$X_\beta - x_\beta = (X_\alpha - x_\alpha) - V_{\alpha\beta}(T_\alpha - t_\alpha)$$
$$T_\beta - t_\beta = T_\alpha - t_\alpha$$

Whitehead regards it as a question of fact whether any given body is using any special space-time system. Neither view excludes the possibility that there shall be one unique determination of time. See Nat[ural] Kn[owledge] p. 163. If you assume relativity you get a nicer doctrine. Connect your metaphysical doctrine with your physical entities. Get a nice explanation of the different connections of a point and of the 3 dimensions of space.

Appendix 2

"TIME" (SEPTEMBER 1926)

(FROM *Proceedings of the Sixth International Congress of Philosophy*, 1927, reprinted in *The Interpretation of Science* (IS), ed. A. H. Johnson (Indianapolis: Bobbs-Merrill, 1961), pp. 240–247. Pagination of IS is shown between brackets, e.g. [240], and the paragraphs have been numbered for ready reference.)

SECTIONS: *I, Supersession; II, Prehension; III, Incompleteness; IV, Objective Immortality; V, Simultaneity; VI, Time as Epochal.*

I.1. *Supersession.*—In his book, *Space, Time, and Deity,* Alexander enforces the precept that we should take time seriously. No philosopher takes time seriously who *either* conceives of a complete totality of all existence, *or* conceives of a multiplicity of actual entities such that each of them is a complete fact, "requiring nothing but itself in order to exist, God only excepted." If time be taken seriously, no concrete entity can change. It can only be superseded. Also it must be superseded because supersession is part of its real essence, in Locke's sense of the term "real essence."

2. Thus in the place of Descartes's substance with "endurance" as one of its principal attributes, we must put the notion of an "occasion" with "supersession" as part of its real essence. By Locke, the phrase "perpetually perishing" is used in the same sense as "supersession" here.

3. Also, in the place of Descartes's doctrine of the two species of substances, bodies and minds, we must hold that each occasion is dipolar, and that one pole is the physical occasion and the other pole is the mental occasion. The physical occasion, as conceived with the abstraction of the mental occasion, and the mental occasion, as conceived with the abstraction of the physical occasion, are each of them devoid of the full concreteness of the dipolar occasion. In order to avoid misunderstanding, I interject the statement, otherwise irrelevant to this paper, that there is a contrast of importance as between [241] the two poles, and that in this contrast the relative importance of either may be negligible.

4. Supersession is a three-way process. Each occasion supersedes other occasions, it is superseded by other occasions, and it is internally

a process of supersession, in part potential and in part actual. One example of the actual internal supersession in an occasion is that the mental occasion supersedes the physical occasion. Thus the physical pole must be explained before the mental pole, since the mental pole can only be explained as a particular instance of supersession disclosed in the analysis of the fully concrete occasion.

5. Time is concerned primarily with the physical poles of occasions, and only derivatively with the mental poles. But the linkage between the physical and the mental pole of an occasion illustrates the truth that the category of supersession transcends time, since this linkage is both extratemporal and yet is an instance of supersession.

II.6. *Prehension.*—The concept of time is complex, and arises from the interplay of three fundamental categories, namely, *Supersession, Prehension,* and *Incompleteness.* The category of Prehension expresses how the world is a system of organisms. An occasion is a concretion— that is, a growing together—of diverse elements; that is why each occasion is an organism. The elements thus organized fall into two classes; (i) the other occasions, and (ii) the universals—or, as I prefer to call them, the eternal objects; these eternal objects are the *media* of actuality, whereby the *how* of each actual occasion is determinate. Because the other occasions are each in a definite way required for the organization of any one occasion A, the world is called a system. The definite way in which A includes other occasions in its concretion is here called "Prehension." By this term, blind physical perceptivity is meant. We recall Kant's doctrine that "Intuitions without concepts are blind." The physical world exhibits itself as a system of organisms arising out of concretions of blind intuitions.

7. The physical world includes the eternal objects as its defining elements; but not conceptually, only intuitively. The [242] conceptual introduction of eternal objects is effected by the mental occasions which achieve knowledge by their conceptual analysis of their associate physical occasions. But pure perception is the fundamental relationship of physical occasions in the physical world. It has wrongly been assigned to mentality, which is merely analytic; though this analysis, being partial and also having regard to the exclusions as well as the inclusions, can exhibit a contingent originality, in the forms of "attention" and "imagination."

8. There are comparative depths of actuality, and each occasion only achieves its depth by reason of its limitations, that is, by reason of its exclusions. Occasion A does not prehend occasion B *simpliciter,* but B under a limitation which is its objectification. This objectification is provided by the eternal objects whereby B is prehended into A

as an example of those objects. Thus B is objectified for A, and the eternal objects are the relational elements which effect the objectification.

9. The eternal objects are said to have modes of *ingression* into the actual occasions. These modes define the objectivity of the prehended occasions in any one physical occasion, and they define the concepts whereby the associate mental occasion analyzes the physical occasion, thereby effecting a new synthesis which is the unity of consciousness. Thus eternal objects define—both for physical and for mental poles—the functional processes of concretion, and are thus always relational in their operation.

III.10. *Incompleteness.*—Time requires incompleteness. A mere system of mutually prehensive occasions is compatible with the concept of a static timeless world. Each occasion is temporal because it is incomplete. Nor is there any system of occasions which is complete; there is no one well-defined entity which is the actual world. This phrase, "the actual world," means the past, present, and future occasions as defined from the standpoint of some present occasion. It is a demonstrative pronoun, analogous to "he," "she," "it," "tomorrow," and "yesterday." Its meaning is defined by its context.

[243] 11. The incompleteness of an actual occasion A means that A prehends in its concretion objectification of occasions X,Y,Z, . . . which must supersede A but, as in A, have not the actuality of determinate concretions. Thus the objectification of its own supersession belongs to the real essence of A. A calendar of next year, and a railway timetable, render this truth about our physical occasions intellectually explicit in our mental occasions.

12. Thus the category of incompleteness means that every occasion holds in itself its own future; so that anticipation is primarily a blind physical fact, and is only a mental fact by reason of the partial analysis effected by conceptual mentality.

13. Physical anticipation illustrates the truth that the creativity, whereby there is supersession, cannot be disjoined from the creature which is superseded. The character of the creativity is found in the analysis of the creature. The creativity *for* the creature has become the creativity *with* the creature; and the creature is thereby superseded. This doctrine, that the objectified future is prehended in each actual occasion, is only a version of the old doctrine that the process of becoming is a union of being with not-being.

IV.14. *Objective Immortality.*—Physical memory is another exemplification of the category of incompleteness. In occasion B there is a physical memory of each antecedent occasion, such as A. Since A is antecedent, B prehends A into itself as contributing a measure of determinate completion. This prehension of A into B is a relational functioning with an individual character expressible in terms of eternal objects. These eternal objects, thus functioning, determine the objectification of A whereby it becomes a constitutive element in the concrescence of B. This transaction exhibits A as relatively determinate, except for its indetermination arising from the indetermination of B in the converse anticipatory objectification of B in A. Thus the full transaction between A and B, consisting of the pair of objectifications, constitutes A and B as poles in a linkage. A, in its function of a constituent member of this linkage, [244] A and B, is more complete than A in abstraction from the linkage. For the indetermination of B in A, which clings to A in abstraction, is removed by the actual concretion of B in the full linkage. Thus, in the community A and B, the incompleteness of A by reason of B is rectified by the completion of B so far as its transaction with A is concerned: A has thereby an added meaning. Hence each occasion A is immortal throughout its future. For B enshrines the memory of A in its own concretion, and its essence has to conform to its memories. Thus physical memory *is* causation, and causation *is* objective immortality. Also conscious memory is that partial analysis of causation which is effected by the associate mental occasion.

15. Thus Hume, when he asks for direct consciousness of causation, should be directed to memory.

16. The ordinary mechanistic account of memory is obviously inadequate. For a cerebration in the present analogous to a cerebration in the past can, on this theory, only produce an image in the present analogous to the image in the past. But the image in the present is not the *memory* of the image in the past. It is merely an image in the present. This criticism also applies to Locke's doctrine of memory.

17. According to the doctrine which is now being developed, the image in the present is the outcome of the gathering up of the true memory into the creativity of the present. Hume's "faint copy" is the image in the present, but its equally present character of being a copy arises from its comparison with the objectification of the past which is the true memory.

18. The irreversibility of time follows from this doctrine of objective immortality. For the later occasion is the completion of the earlier occasion, and therefore different from it.

V.19. *Simultaneity.*—Past and future have thus been explained as referring to causal relationships in which an occasion A is involved. But there are occasions which are not prehended in A in any causal sense, except as conforming to the general systematic character of the universe. These occasions are the occasions *simultaneous with* A. Thus, if there be any contingency in the universe, the contingency inherent in the concretion [245] of A is independent of the contingencies inherent in the occasions simultaneous with A.

20. But A does prehend these occasions in the mode of *presentational immediacy*. The eternal objects functioning in this prehensive mode are termed the "sense-data."

21. This presentational immediacy of the world simultaneous with A embodies the originative character of A. It is the self-creative self-enjoyment of A in its character of a concretion. To explain it, you must analyze A, and not the simultaneous world; since it constitutes A's peculiar originality. Thus presentational immediacy has the character of physical imagination, in a generalized sense of that word. This physical imagination has normally to conform to the physical memories of the immediate past; it is then called sense-perception, and is nondelusive. It may conform to the physical memories of the more remote past: it is then called the image associated with memory. It may conform to some special intrusive element in the immediate past such as, in the case of human beings, drugs, emotions, or conceptual relationships in antecedent mental occasions: it is then variously called delusion, or ecstatic vision, or imagination. Partial consciousness of this physical imagination is effected by the conceptual functioning of the mental pole.

22. Here an ambiguity arises, which has been disclosed by the modern physical theory of relativity. There are two available senses for "simultaneity." It may mean those occasions which are not causally related to occasion A, either as causing or caused. But it may mean those occasions which are prehended in A with presentational immediacy. If we identify these two meanings we are reduced to the classical view of time as strictly serial. If we hold that the presentationally immediate occasions are only some among the occasions which are not causally related, we can include the modern relativity theory in this doctrine of time. But apart from the paradox of nonseriality, the whole paper is directed to explain the relativistic conclusion that individual perceptivity is the ultimate physical fact.

[246] VI.23. *Time as Epochal.*—Supersession is not a continuous process of becoming. If we try to combine the notions of supersession and continuity we are at once entangled in a vicious infinite regress.

24. For if B supersedes A, then the continuity of B requires that some earlier portion of B has superseded A antecedently to the later

portion of B. This argument can be repeated on that earlier portion of B, however you choose that portion. Thus we are involved in an infinite regress. Also the supersession of A has to commence at what should be the infinite end of the regress. But there is no infinite end. Hence supersession cannot be regarded as the continuous unfolding of a continuum. I express this conclusion by the statement that time is "epochal." The occasion B which acquires concretion so as to supersede A embodies a definite quantum of time which I call the "epochal character" of the concrescence. The epochal theory of time is the foundation of the theory of atomic organisms, and of the modern physical quantum-theory.

25. I do not say that all the time-quanta involved in supersession are equal. But some time-quantum is always involved. But we could not even discuss the relative sizes of time-quanta unless these quanta were also divisible, and were also comparable in respect to their parts, thus elicited. For if time-quantum T_1 be greater than time-quantum T_2, it must mean that T_2 is comparable to some part of T_1 in respect to equality. Thus there is also a continuity in time, arising from indefinite divisibility. This continuity is an instance of the potentiality which is an essential element in the actual world. The epochs in the past are what they have been. But if we abstract from the realized self-enjoyment which is the individual residuum of each epochal occasion, that occasion, considered with the abstractions of physics, might have been subdivided into epochal occasions which together complete that one occasion. This is the potential supersession internal to each actual occasion. Thus there is no continuity of becoming, but there is a becoming of continuity.

[247] 26. The question of the extensive relation whereby time acquires its extensive character, termed "duration," and the question of the connection between temporal and spatial relations, and the question of the measurement of space-time, cannot be considered without extending this communication beyond its assigned limits.

Appendix 3

THE HARVARD LECTURES FOR THE FALL OF 1926

(Compiled by George Bosworth Burch, edited by Dwight C. Stewart; reprinted from *Process Studies* 4/3 [Fall, 1974], 201–206, with numbered paragraphs.)

1. There is no philosophy of science; we are concerned with those parts of philosophy which are suggested by science. In three epochs science has suggested philosophical ideas: the Greek period, the seventeenth century, and the twentieth century.

2. Descartes, Leibniz, Locke, and Kant assume that the underlying reality of the world is a permanent substance which has adventures.

3. Our scientific habits are set by ignoring the inexplicable. In every intellectual epoch the adequacy of the evidence for the prevailing beliefs seems overwhelming. We must not ignore the inexplicable; we should imitate our ancestors who beat gongs when the moon was eclipsed. But mere notice of unusual phenomena is not sufficient; we must give them rational attention. Science and philosophy are united in a common goal, explanation. (Dewey says the goal is action.) Action and use are a test of explanation, and explanation is the basis of action, but explanation is an end in itself and is the chief end of science and philosophy. Scientists who are clear in their concepts are at least thirty years behind their times.

4. Progress in philosophy involves the explicit statement of assumptions implicit in previous philosophers. Rationalism never deserts standards of criticism. We philosophize because we believe; we do not believe because we philosophize. Philosophy is a criticism of belief—preserving, deepening, and modifying it. Standards of criticism are: (1) intensity of belief, (2) concurrence in belief, (3) clear expression of belief, (4) analysis of belief, (5) logical coherence of belief, (6) exemplification of belief, and (7) adequacy of belief.

5. The old notion of self-evidence obviously refers to an ideal, not a fact. The old rationalism was founded on the ideal of the clear intellect—but there is no such intellect. Some facts are luminously obvious, but the rest of our experience is obscured in a deep, penumbral shadow with reference to which our intellectual faculty varies from that of a savage to that of a jellyfish. A most colossal

example of exploded self-evidence is the long-held belief that Euclidean geometry applies to real space.

6. Descartes emphasizes the permanent and enduring, as opposed to the flux. He sees the world as definite substances. He is a mathematical intellect and always states definitely and clearly what he means.

7. Descartes was a mathematician; his philosophy was a philosophy calculated to include mathematical physics, and it is pervaded by the mathematical intellect. We must compare Descartes with Plato, also a mathematician. Aristotle revolted against the rationalism of Plato; Dewey against that of Descartes. Whitehead's type of rationalism takes a middle course which corrects the false method of Descartes and which is easily reconciled with the pragmatic point of view.

8. The Greeks thought that their logic and mathematics exhausted the possibilities of rationalism, and they also thought that the Greek language was adequate for philosophical discussion.

9. Rationalism is an ultimate faith. Descartes' metaphysical method is the method of Euclid. This is a false method. Pure thinking cannot produce knowledge about the real world.

10. Cartesian rationalism proceeds by discarding complexity in order to arrive at simple notions immediately obvious. Modern rationalism uses the Cartesian method of discard as a preliminary guide to imaginative construction; but its essential point is that it starts with an imaginative system of ideas, the logical connections of which have been thoroughly explored. The logical exploration shows that there is no one set of premises from which the remainder of the system is a deduction. Nor is there any one set of simple notions from which the remainder are simple constructions. Modern rationalism must have recourse to the obviousness of experience.

11. The ultimate real actual entity is to be considered an *actual occasion*—something that happens, and its time-fulness is of the essence of it—which is an individuation or concretion of the entire universe into the one real actual unity which is self-presentation, i.e., a presentation of itself to itself in its character of being that representation of the universe. This self-presentation is also to be looked on as a self-valuation, and in being an end for itself it thereby constitutes the character of the concrescence which succeeds it.

12. *Eternal objects* (universals) have ingression into actual occasions. These modes of ingression of the eternal objects constitute the relations among the actual occasions.

13. The most concrete occasion is dipolar. The two poles, mental and physical, cannot be separated, but the two may not be of the same strength or importance. One pole is the primary and synthetic side of the actual occasion; we call that the physical occasion. It is to be described in synthetical terms. The other pole is the secondary and analytic side of the actual occasion; this we call the mental occasion. It is the self-knowledge which supersedes on the synthesizing of the actual occasion. It is an endowing of the physical occasion and a putting together of it afresh.

14. Knowledge is the concrescence of two modes of functioning (ingression) of the eternal object. Both have a common past and a common future, but they are mutually independent in respect of their originality. The first mode of ingression is perceptual (physical); the second is conceptual (mental). Conceptual functioning is a mode of analysis of the physical occasion.

15. Whitehead does not believe that there are different kinds of actual things. The same principle explains everything. Different things fall into different categories, but the fact of being actual is a common fact explainable in a single way. "Being actual" cannot be equivocal.

16. Meanings of *immediate experience:* (1) the physical occasion, the primary self-presentation arising out of the representation in itself of the entire universe. It is pure perceptivity, whereby an actual object emerges from the limitations imposed on it by the universe; (2) the mental occasion, originating from the imagination; (3) the ultimate concrete occasion, both physical and mental, the ultimate concrete fact. The actual fact is the immediate experience, but by this we sometimes mean some abstraction from it.

17. Predication has not an unequivocal meaning. The confusions of metaphysics are due to failure to distinguish the various meanings of predication. The assumption that there is a definite metaphysical fact underlying the *is,* is false. Every proposition must be considered with reference to the whole universe. (This is Bradley's doctrine.) Reality is the final subject of every proposition. An offshoot of the subject-predicate theory of knowledge is the subject-object theory of knowledge; after the subject modified by *its* object comes the subject qualified by *its* ideas. The subject with its private complex of predicates is a trap into which the philosophers fall; there is no such privacy, because of the relevancy of the whole universe. The subject-predicate theory holds that the vulgar form of language enshrines metaphysical reality; this is the easiest metaphysics to grasp, but not true. We must start with some more general notion than that of predication. This general notion we shall call *relevance.* There are

stages of relevance and intensity of relevance; irrelevance is the lowest stage of relevance. Descartes' philosophy corrects some of the major excesses resulting from the subject-predicate complex which dominated medieval philosophy. Locke corrected it further. But neither grasped the fact that the notion of substance is a result of the subject predicate logic and has no metaphysical status. Whenever they are not thinking of what they are criticizing, they fall into the trap.

18. Inadequacies of Cartesianism: (1) Descartes' view of substantial independence is the subtle psychological origin of many of the shortcomings of our modern civilization. Moreover, it is a view fatal to the essential doctrine of the solidarity of the universe. The view of substantial independence has haunted all modern philosophy, including the anti-Cartesian; it is responsible for Hegel's absolute, Spencer's unknowable, Bradley's absolute. It is also destructive of ethics; social ethics is the conciliation of two doctrines: thou shalt not steal (individualistic, substantial independence), and property is robbery (socialistic solidarity). Law and social ethics are concerned with conciliating these two attitudes, individualism and solidarity. This is also, more generally, the business of metaphysics; how can there be individuals with separate ends and yet combined in a solid community? (2) Cartesianism makes any reference to a general end irrelevant to existence.

19. Criticism of Descartes: (1) Whitehead agrees with Descartes in identifying substance with the actual entity. (2) Whitehead disagrees with Descartes in rejecting the subject-predicate form of expression as representing any metaphysical truth. (3) Whitehead disagrees with Descartes in maintaining the notion of the universal relevance of all entities, actual and nonactual. There are three types of entities: eternal objects, actual entities, objective occasions; the third is derivable from the other two. All are universally mutually relevant. (4) In Descartes, God is the only self-creative substance, the process of creation being also the creator. In Whitehead, this is the general characteristic of all actual entities.

20. Six principles of metaphysics:[1]

1. The principle of solidarity. Every actual entity requires all other entities, actual or ideal, in order to exist.

2. The principle of creative individuality. Every actual entity is a process which is its own result, depending on its own limitations.

3. The principle of efficient causation. Every actual entity by the fact of its own individuality contributes to the character of processes which are actual entities superseding itself.

4. The ontological principle. The character of creativity is derived from its own creatures and expressed by its own creatures.

5. The principle of esthetic individuality. Every actual entity is an end in itself for itself, involving its measure of self-satisfaction individual to itself and constituting the result of itself-as-process.

6. The principle of ideal comparison. Every creature involves in its own constitution an ideal reference to ideal creatures: (1) in ideal relationship to each other, and (2) in comparison with its own self-satisfaction [cf. RM 148].

21. These principles are essential to actuality, and so apply equally well to God (pure act). It follows that God is a creature; the supreme actuality is the supreme creature. The only alternatives are to say that God is not actual or that God lies beyond anything of which we can have any conception.

22. The doctrine of concrescence is derived from the first two principles. The actual entity is not an individual apart from its solidarity with the whole universe; it is an individual by means of that solidarity. The specific value of the individual occasion arises from the end obtained individually, but it includes in its concrescence the relevance of ends beyond itself. This is the doctrine of social solidarity.

23. By the ontological principle there is a creature by virtue of which creativity bears its character; there is a creature by virtue of which there is a science of metaphysics. Thus, there is a creature with a general relation to all creatures including itself. This creature requires all other creatures in order to exist and, yet, is in a sense ontologically prior to them since its character determines the metaphysical laws and is determined by them. This creature is a process which is its own result, like all other creatures; it is in a sense self-creative. It depends for its actuality upon its own limitations. God is limited by his goodness. This creature contributes to the character of all the creatures superseding it. This creature is an end in itself. It involves in its own constitution an ideal reference to ideal creatures in ideal relationships to each other.

24. There are only two metaphysical principles in virtue of which the existence of an actual entity can be inferred; to wit, the principle of efficient causation, and the ontological principle, in virtue of which

any generality of character shared among entities presupposes a character of generality. The ontological principle denies that whatever is to be known is derivative from actual fact. Knowledge is the synthesis of the two poles of the actual occasion (mental and physical) described from the point of view of what the mental activity contributes. There is an actual entity which is more than its objectification.

25. Demonstration is how the relativity of objectification is transcended.

26. Given an actual entity, B, consider how an eternal object A may have ingression into B. (1) A *may* have ingression into B as constituting a physical relationship between B and some other actual entity, B'. (2) A does enter into B as constituting a conceptual relationship between B and each particular occasion X, whereby the patience of X for its physical relationship to B is objectified for B. This mode of ingression involves the yes-form and the no-form of comparison. (3) A does enter into B as constituting a conceptual relationship between B and the universe as systematically patient of A. (4) A does enter into B as constituting a conceptual relationship between B and the *environmental* universe as systematically patient or impatient of A by reason of its environmental character.

27. There is an actual universe which is a multiplicity of actual entities. An actual entity is an act of percipience. Every actual entity has its peculiar mode of percipience. The universals are the specific character of specific perceptions. There are no dead (nondynamic) entities. Every entity expresses some way in which the creativity is objectified. Creativity is the most general form. It acquires its specific character in each individual actual entity. A historic creature is a succession of actual entities peculiarly congruent to each other. One's view of his own past is the same in principle as his view of the past of another person or thing, but so tremendously different quantitatively in intensity as to amount practically to a qualitative difference.

28. The potentiality of a creature is the range of alternative characters for that creature which are compatible with the efficient causation whereby the concrescence of that creature is derived from other creatures. Potentiality is definite with respect to the generic sort but ambiguous with respect to the specific mode. The creature realizes not only the specific mode that it is but also the genus of modes which it might have been. The notion of probability is derived from that of potentiality.

29. Curiously mixed with the notion of potentiality is the notion of endurance. Descartes distinguishes between endurance and mea-

sured time. The fact of self-existence has duration. The epochal occasion which we apprehend as the present is one occasion, but it might have been twenty epochal occasions. Endurance is an instance of unrealized potentiality.

30. We can define what we mean by things going on without reference to the idea of stuff, but we do require the notion of an actuality which emerges from a potentiality. We can define an ether of events as opposed to an ether of stuff. The condition of the immediate can only be formed in terms of a continuum, but the group of actual entities which arise are definite quanta determined by the conditions of the past and by what (if anything) is added by the act of self-creation. The process of self-formation is not in time, but is determined by the way the organism feels in the nontemporal process of being itself.

31. *Ether*, the one genus of physical fact. Whitehead agrees with the principle upheld by nineteenth-century materialists, that there is only one genus of physical facts. This is where Descartes started: all physical facts are facts about corporeal substance. The substance emerges from the activity which synthesizes the attributes. It is wrong to think of the attributes as emerging from the substance.

32. The seventeenth-century metaphysical foundation of science was good for 300 years—proof of its great merit. They attempted to start from something which is in our immediate knowledge. But now we look on a physical object, not as a continuous corporeal reality only relatively at rest, but as a violent activity of infinitesimal organisms. The fundamental idea we have in experience is that of an actual entity. We experience ourselves as actual entities in a community of actual entities. In seeking to know what we mean by an actual entity, we should have recourse to ourselves. This is what Descartes did, but he only found a mind, at least at first. What we know of ourselves is not, as usually put, a mysterious substratum with an enormous and very doubtfully remembered life history, decorated with transient qualities but getting its character from some simple attribute which it always carries around with it. What we find is an active experience, very vaguely delimited from its antecedents and successors. It is a peculiarly linked succession of acts of experience with a singular unity, so that each act integrates the antecedent acts. The actual entity is a succession of acts of experience. An act of experience is primarily a taking account of other actual entities. This taking account of other actual entities is analyzable, but it is a certain real togetherness issuing in a certain vivid intensity which we call self-value. The entity rises out of a constitutive activity

analyzable into elements which are not actual entities. This view opposes the materialistic view of nature introduced by Descartes.

33. The actual entity is dipolar. It is perceptivity which turns of itself into conceptual analysis. But the intensity of being does not necessarily lie equally between the two poles. One or the other may be negligible.

34. Each actual entity arises from its taking account of the whole past. It cannot have any intensity of being unless the important part of the past is favorable to its existence at a particular intensity.

35. The primary aspect of the physical world is to be conceived in terms of extension. The notion of extension is the primary description of how an actual entity is an organism and how it takes account of all other entities. Extension is extremely abstract, because extension only partly represents my relation to the physical object. It is an abstract statement of certain aspects of the relationship. Descartes looked on extension as an attribute of the extended things. Whitehead looks on extension as one very abstract side in the relationship of things. Descartes thought of extension in terms of geometry. He also had another principal attribute: endurance. But time is also an extensive quantity. There is something common to space and time; this is extension. Nowadays we do not consider space and time as so sharply distinguished. The first element in the connection between time and space is the primary abstract organic relation of being extended. This is compatible with a static universe. The incompleteness supervenes upon the morphological extensiveness.

NOTE

1. [See Victor Lowe, "Whitehead's Gifford Lectures," *Southern Journal of Philosophy* 7/4 (Winter, 1969–70), 332–333.]

Appendix 4

THE METAPHYSICAL SCHEME OF MARCH 1927

(These propositions were dictated to Whitehead's "Seminary in Logic 20" on March 4, 1927. This version is collated from the notes of Paul Weiss and George P. Conger.)

1. A proposition is a complex unity which is analyzable into many component elements.

2. An extended proposition is analyzable into component propositions logically antecedent to given proposition, and a bond of unity.

3. A non-extended proposition is not capable of such an analysis, though there may be propositions among its components. There are also non-propositional elements among the components and they are not capable of such analysis. ("The man *whom I saw yesterday* has gone away" is such a subordinate proposition.)

4. A basic proposition is a particular sort of non-extended proposition, which is not analyzable into components which include other propositions. Example: "That is red." Natural to call it an atomic proposition, but in a slightly different sense.

How do there come to be complex entities in the universe? Propositions are a particular sort of complex entity. How what is many can also be one requires some general assertion which lies outside of logic altogether.

5. The source of all types of complex units is to be sought in their derivation from the individual unification of the universe in each actual entity. An actual entity is an individual unification of the universe with its own particular individuality. Nothing is left out, but relevance. You can find every entity in each actual entity. The character of the universe as actual is this progressive individualization of itself.

6. Every other type of complex unit is derivate from that type. The complex unity of the actual entity discloses among its components subordinate types of complex unity. In abstracting certain components from the finished actual entity, you leave out the individual unity of the actual entity. These merely abstract types of unity are derivate types, to be explained by their relevance and occurrence in the actual entity.

7. An actual entity is an act of experience, whose past history has relevance as it determines it. You are always new, only integrating your past. (Descartes: God sustains the universe by perpetually creating it.) There is nothing in the universe which cannot be found in a sufficiently adequate analysis of an immediate act of experience. Nothing to be known beyond that, and anyhow we don't know it.

8. This is the real crux of metaphysics: there is great difficulty, enormous difficulty in stating with actual precision all the elements that make up an act of experience. All must oversimplify. Our own knowledge of what our experience is is always dim and fitful. I am not maintaining that every entity includes its own adequate self-analysis. Such self-analysis never can observe accurately. You never can know what you are unless you have thought of it before. What is new is dimly and inaccurately observed. In practice it is the imagination which disciplines reason. This requires an imaginative leap towards a scheme of the sorts of components to be found in experience. We discipline it by (1) antecedent knowledge, (2) logical coherence, (3) esthetic congruence (dim, vague), (4) partial verification.

The appeal is to future acts of experience rendered more adequate by their inheritance of this conceptual hypothesis. Not one-tenth of scientific hypotheses ever get printed. Imaginative leap.

9. An act of experience or actual entity, or actual occasion in the temporal world, is only:

(1) A synthesis of perceptivity of other acts of experience, together forming the actual universe. Its perception of how the other acts of experience, the rest of the actual universe, is synthesized into the one entity which is the act of experience in question.

(2) The emotional or esthetic intensity which is the primordial individual fact constituting the meaning or outcome of this unity. It is an esthetic intensity which is an enjoyment of being that synthesis.

(3) The conceptual functioning whereby what might be enters into a synthesis with what is, and is thereby analytical of it by reason of the yes and no types of analytical unity. Concept meets percept. If of the yes type, there is a certain unity and identity of relationship to the percept. If of the no type, there is a certain diversity.

(4) There is the additional self-creative action [activity?] of the self-judgment of the act of experience upon the complex stages of the non-temporal constitution of the actual entity. The entity is analyzable into layers, each of which presupposes one another logically. The new element is the self-judgment on what is logically antecedent in the entity, so that the esthetic emphasis of the earlier stages is controlled and adjusted. What is made important depends

on that. In this way there is control and adjustment of what is put forward or led back. The occasion begins as an emotional intensity which is then reconstituted by an act of self-judgment.

(5) There is the emergence of the final actual occasion providing a new creative character for the universe whereby creative passage is conditioned beyond the act in question. This doesn't sit in judgment on itself or know itself.

10. What is it to be actual? To allow creative passage beyond itself. Perceptivity is not the inclusion of other acts *simpliciter* but their inclusion under limitation of certain predicates and the exclusion of other predicates.

11. The act of perceptivity or act of experience includes some acts merely as exemplifying certain predicates and as excluding others which they might exemplify for that experience but don't. "Predicate" is used here for logical reasons. Santayana calls them "essences," Plato "ideas." They are "first cousin to Platonic ideas" and Aristotelian qualities; they are eternal objects. These predicates as functioning in perceptivity are relational between the perceived and the percipient.

12. The perceived is objectified for the percipient. It is held up and enters into the constitution of the percipient as exemplifying those predicates for the percipient. The perceived acts are many and complex. They are objectified as exhibiting their interdependence in the unity and solidarity of the world. By the relation of the predicate the objectification includes the synthesis of many objectified acts into an objective unity, for the predicates bind the one with the many. Thus, to give an example, *that* is objectified for me under the predicate of a cylindrical box.

Thus for the percipients there are two types of relational functioning on the part of predicates:

(1) There is the relationship between perceived and percipient.
(2) There is the relationship between diverse other perceived acts of experience whereby they are objectified in the unity of complex entity. That is done by the bond of the predicate which extends over the whole, expressing the union of many entities. In our example, the millions of molecules in the box are given to me under one predicate.

13. When consciousness supervenes there is yet another mode of functioning on the part of predicates: the synthesis of various objective unit entities with predicates which might not be theirs or may be

theirs. This synthesis of conceptual functioning with perceptual functioning issues in yes or no forms.

14. In the rudimentary stages of conceptual functioning the yes form entirely dominates. You vaguely know that you are perceiving. The no form emerges when the imagination which produces the conceptual functioning gives rise to an independent activity whereby predicates irrelevant in perception become relevant for conception. Only a high-grade intelligence can make errors. Practical absence of no form is the stage of unconscious instinct. Consciousness emerges with the emergence of unverified propositions.

15. Consciousness is the enjoyment of the distinction between the verified and the nonverified. If you haven't the distinction in your mind, how can you be conscious it is red? Predicates are the nonactual elements in the universe whereby factual or hypothetical objectification is effected. "Predicate" is not a good term.

16. Universals, essences, eternal objects, qualities, or ideas are those elements in the universe whereby objectification and its conceptual analysis are effected. They are eternal because they are in each entity, but impartially with respect to various entities. Each one in its abstract nature doesn't tell you about the how of its relation to the various entities.

17. The finished act of experience passes into objectification within acts beyond itself. It is never objectified for itself in the state of being finished *qua* finished. It always passes beyond itself. As a finished entity it thereby passes beyond itself and is only to be found in the objectifications of itself in other entities.

18. It is always in the stage of building up and is never finished completely for it passes beyond itself. The objectification of its next act is self-judgment.

19. A proposition is an intermediate universal.

(1) It is not a pure essence which is neither true nor false. There are no eternal objects in isolation from the actual world. Every eternal object has a meaning with respect to its possible functioning in the actual world, but gives us no information about itself. By a pure rational consideration of ideas you can't construct the actual world. A pure essence is merely *for* the universe in its various modes of functioning. It doesn't tell us how it functions in any particular instance.

(2) A proposition is not a particular since it is not an element in the conceptual functioning of just one particular act of experience. My belief in a proposition is a particular belief and my act of judging is particular. The proposition itself is not a particular; it has an

impartial relevance to all of us. It has a certain type of universal relevance.

(3) When you analyze a proposition it includes acts of experience among its components. A proposition about the actual world is itself the universal which expresses the hypothetical objectification of any set of acts from any one act of another set.

20. "Caesar crossed the Rubicon" is a proposition which expresses the hypothetical objective form of the act of objectification of one set of acts of experience—that set implicated in Caesar's crossing. There are certain predicates which bind together that set of acts of experience as one object or one fact for us. This is an objectification of that set for us by a certain complex predicate. Then these predicates objectify the Caesar set of acts as an element in the perceptive synthesis of any subsequent act of experience. Of course, the particular relevance of a particular set of objectifications is left undetermined. The percipient adds on further perspectives to this act of experience. It depends on whether you're Italian, etc., as to what perspective you add on.

Does determining and conditioning the perspective of Caesar's crossing the Rubicon set any condition which limits the objectification of that act in any subsequent act of experience? It may be so trivially relevant that it is in the background for any definite physical analysis. But a sufficiently accurate self-analysis can find effect of a shower of sand in Andromeda. Even the most remote things give us something that we can analyze. We must allow for fantastic difference in degree of objectification by new scientific measurements.

21. A proposition contains two subjects which have different functions.

(a) The logical subject whose objectification is topic proposed, that should be verified in perception. It is that particular set of actual entities. The topic proposed in the conceptual functioning of the proposition lies behind it.

(b) The percipient subject for whom the objectification is or is not a valid element in its experience, with due addition of perspective and relevance depending on the subject. There is always the question for whom, or for what, the proposition is. It is valid for a given percipient subject if it happens in its conceptual functioning to bring it forward. There is also the other question as to what the proposition is about. "Caesar crossed the Rubicon" is a hypothetical objectification of a certain set of actual entities, and these are only valid for subsequent entities.

22. The percipient subject is any one of a set of acts of experience. Part of the content of a logical proposition is the identification of the logical subjects from the standpoint of any one of the percipient subjects. A proposition is written out from the standpoint of where we are now to bring out its logical subjects, but finally it should get you to that state of mind where you point. A proposition is *for* any one of its percipient subjects and it is about its logical subject. It is not relevant to a past but only to a future act. That "Caesar crossed the Rubicon" is not *for* Romulus and Remus. We balk [at] this by divesting a proposition of its temporal relevance. Caesar crossing the Rubicon is an impartial fact which has its history in each of us at this moment and for our successors. But a rustic on the bank looking at Caesar didn't see the proposition. [cf. PR 196]

In fictional propositions such as in *Alice in Wonderland* you are dealing with a complicated imaginative history of many individuals who have seen printed pages. Otherwise there is no Alice. A proposition about Caesar is the objectification of those words which make up Caesar for the percipient subject. Unless you specify for whom your proposition is dealing, you run into a contradiction in terms between the future and the past. Propositions are only *for* those who come afterwards. They are only effective for those who think of them clearly.

Some propositions, like those of arithmetic, are for all subjects because they are about any act of experience, and exist for all acts of experience. But in general we ought to date most propositions.

Propositions have the passive totality of the universe in their background.

Prehension is more general than ingression, for it is the *general* way in which things come together as objectified for an entity.

Appendix 5

THE METAPHYSICAL PRINCIPLES OF OCTOBER, 1927

(These eight metaphysical principles were presented by Whitehead in his classroom lectures at Harvard, October 1 and 4, 1927. They are excerpted from notes taken by Professor Edwin L. Marvin, formerly of the University of Montana. A typescript of the entire set of notes for 1927–28 is available at the Center for Process Studies.)

1. That the actual world is a process and that this process is the becoming of actual entities.

2. That in the becoming of an actual entity, the *potential* unity of many entities acquires the actual unity of the one entity—the whole process is the many becoming one, and the one is what becomes.

3. That the potentiality for acquiring real unity with other entities is the one general metaphysical character attaching to *all* entities, *actual or nonactual*—i.e., it belongs to the nature of a "Being" that it is a potential for a "Becoming."

4. That there are two primordial genera of entities: (a) eternal objects and (b) actual entities, and that all other entities are derivative complexes involving entities from both of these genera.

5. That an eternal object can only be described in terms of its potentiality for "ingression" into the becoming of actual entities and that its analysis only discloses other eternal objects.

6. That two descriptions are required for an actual entity: (a) one of them analytic of its potentiality for its "objectification" in the becoming of other actual entities and (b) the other analytic of the process that constitutes its own becoming.

7. That *how* the actual entity *becomes* constitutes *what* the actual entity *is*, so that the two descriptions of an actual entity are not independent. All *explanation* of an actual entity exhibits its process as the reason for its potentiality, and all *description* exhibits the realized objectifications of that actual entity as a partial analysis of its own process.

8. That every condition to which the process of becoming conforms in any particular instance has its *reason* in the character of some actual entity whose objectification is one of the components entering

into the particular instance in question (the ontological principle—
or principle of extrinsic reference).

Actual entities are the only *reasons;* to search for a reason is to
search for an actual entity.

Appendix 6

The Prospectus for the Gifford Lectures
University of Edinburgh, June, 1928

(Reprinted from *The Southern Journal of Philosophy* 7/4 [Winter, 1969], 335–336)

Lecture I. Speculative Philosophy

Its Method and Importance; Conditions to be Satisfied; Dogmatism, Empiricism, Rationalism; Role of Imagination in Observation; The Scheme as a Matrix; Dangers of Commonsense; Schools of Philosophy; Scientific and Religious Application; Summary.

Lecture II. The Scheme of Interpretation

Influence of the Notion of "Faculties" upon Metaphysics; Actual Entities; Prehensions; Descartes and Locke; Creativity; The Community of Occasions; Categories of Existence; Categories of Explanation; Categoreal Obligations; Actual Entities *Become,* but do not *Change;* Objective Immortality; Being and Becoming; Enduring Objects; Time; Atomism and Continuity.

Lecture III. Fact and Form

The Platonic Tradition; Eternal Objects; Ideal Realisation; The Ontological Principle; Positive and Negative Prehensions; Inadequacy of Language; No Formulated Axiomatic Certainties; Brute Fact and Givenness; Decision; Potentiality; Intolerance, the Mark of Actuality; Dipolarity; Universal and Particular; Locke and The Philosophy of Organism.

Lecture IV. The Extensive Continuum

"Contemporary" means "Causally Independent"; The Contemporary Continuum; Sense-Data and Sense-Perception; The Objective Datum; Real Potentiality; Epochal Theory of Time; Newton's Scholium; The Philosophy of Organism and Descartes; The Actual World as Datum; The Animal Body; Objectification and the Sensationalist Doctrine; Enduring Stuff; The Physical Field and Quanta; Unison of Becoming.

LECTURE V. THE ORDER OF NATURE

Order and Givenness; Process as Elimination of Indetermination; Subjective Aim; Lure for Feeling; Subject and Superject; Societies of Actual Entities; Evolution of Laws of Nature; Values; Milton and The Timaeus; Intensity, Triviality, Vagueness, Narrowness, Width; The Actual World as a Medium.

LECTURE VI. THE LURE FOR FEELING

Conceptual Prehensions; Valuation; Propositions; Judging Subjects, Logical Subjects, Predicates; Propositions as Lures for Feeling; Inadequacy of Verbal Enunciation; Metaphysical Propositions; Probability; Suppressed Premiss in Induction. Summary of This Part: Process; Flux; Permanence; Macroscopic and Microscopic Process.

LECTURE VII. GENERAL THEORY OF PREHENSIONS

Divisibility of Actual Entities into Prehensions; Genetic Division and Co-ordinate Division; Factors of a Prehension; Subject, Subjective Aim, Superject; Subjective Form; Categoreal Obligations; Physical Prehensions not definable by universals; Three Types of Primary Prehensions, viz., Simple Physical Feelings, Conceptual Feelings, Transmuted Feelings; Simple Physical Feelings as Causal; Reproduction; Conceptual Feelings as Valuations; Hume's Principle; Conceptual Valuation and Conceptual Reversion; Transmutation.

LECTURE VIII. PROPOSITIONAL AND INTELLECTUAL PREHENSIONS

The Genesis of Propositional Feelings; Perceptive Feelings; Imaginative Feelings; Comparative Feelings; Intellectual Feelings; Physical Purposes; Consciousness.

LECTURE IX. PREHENSIONS AND THE EXTENSIVE CONTINUUM

Extensive Connection; Inclusion, Tangential and Non-Tangential; External Connection; Abstractive Classes; Points; Segments; Definition of Straight Lines; Flat Loci; Projection and Presentational Immediacy.

LECTURE X. FINAL INTERPRETATION

The Multifariousness of the World; Flux and Permanence; Order, Impulse, Tedium; The Ultimate Evil; Primordial and Consequent Natures of God; The Temporal World as Intermediate Stage of Self-Creation; Manifoldness and Unity.

Index of Proper Names

General Index

Citation Index

This index provides a listing of the texts cited from Whitehead's writings, indicating in the middle column the page of this book (EWM) on which each is cited. For purposes of conversion, the left-hand column lists the references as cited in the body of the text, while the right-hand column provides convient conversions where more than one pagination exists. Thus, *An Enquiry Concerning the Principles of Natural Knowledge* (PNK, 1919) and *The Concept of Nature* (CN, 1920) are published only in their original Cambridge University Press paginations, and are therefore cited just once. *Science and the Modern World* (SMW, 1925), *Religion in the Making* (RM, 1926), and *Process and Reality* (PR, 1929) are cited left according to their Free Press (FP) and Meridian (Mer) editions, which in the case of the last named is the corrected edition of 1978 (CPR). The conversion column on the right lists the corresponding standard Macmillan editions, using the 1926 second edition for *Science and the Modern World*. *Adventures of Ideas* (AI, 1933) is cited in the text according to the Macmillan edition, so that is listed in the left-hand column, with the corresponding Free Press (FP) edition in the right-hand column. Finally, *The Interpretation of Science*, (IS, 1961) is listed according to the Bobbs-Merrill edition.

SMW FP	EWM	SMW
151f	45	218
151f	50	218
152	14	219
152	15	219
152	34	219
152	41	218
152	168	218
155f	33	223f
157	72	226
158	13	227
158	67	227
158	72	227
158	173	228
158f	13	228
159	73	229
159	75	229
160	70	231
160	75	230f
160	122	231
160	158	231
161	13	233
161	35	232
161	66	232
161	114	232
161	118	232
162	35	233
162f	73	233
162f	75	234
162	94	234
163	70	235
163	76	234f
163	76	234
163	76	235
163	77	235
163	77	235
163	77	235
163	85	235
163	87	235
164	72	236
164	75	236
164	77	236
164f	109	237
165	77	237
165	79	237
165	85	238
165	86	238
165	111	238
165f	35	239
166	81	239

SMW FP	EWM	SMW
166	82	240
167f	83	241f
168	82	243
168	82	242
168	83	243
168	83	243
169	84	244
169f	84	245
170	14	246
170	73	245
170	85	245
170	112	246
170	131	246
170f	123	246f
171	73	248
172	10	248
172	92	248
173	102	248
174	117	251
174	121	251
175	121	252
175	121	252
175	125	251
176	110	254
176	118	253
176	122	253
176	122	253
176	122	254
176	123	254
176	123	254
177	13	255
177	96	255
177	110	255
177	116	256f
177	119	255
177	163	256
177	248	255
178	86	256
178	105	257
178	105	257
178	105	257
178	110	256
178	115	257
178	115	256
178f	117	257
178f	117	257
178	118	256
178	121	257
178	126	257

CPR	EWM	PR
7	164	10f
7	183	11
12f	141	18f
12f	182	18f
12f	183	18f
12f	252	18f
18	229	27
18f	117	28
21f	240	31f
21f	261	31f
22	229	32
23f	75	35
25	94	38
25f	157	38
27	243	41
28	208	41
29	194	44
29	195	43
29	208	43
31	76	46
31	141	46
31	229	46
31f	74	46–48
32	141	47
32	229	47
33f	110	50
35	13	52
39	161	62
40	117	64
40	186	64
40	221	64
41	75	66
41	163	66
41	192	66
41	200	66
41f	208	66
45	65	72
46	183	73f
47	208	74
48	143	76
48	192	76
50	200	80
52	173	82
53	193	83
58	183	91.21
58	200	91
60	195	94
61	183	96.9
62f	200	97f

CPR	EWM	PR
63	200	98
64	183	100.31
64	200	100
65	155	101
65	186	102
65	188	101
65	254	101
67	200	105
68	64	106
68	177	106
68	233	105
68f	250	107
68f	52	105–07
68f	53	105–07
68f	153	106f
68f	209	106f
68f	233	105–07
68n4	65	106n4
69	130	107
69	153	107
69	190	107
69	240	108
69	244	108
72	20	114
73	130	114
73	130	114
73	241	114
76	58	118
80	130	124
80	241	124
81f	195	126
83	65	128
83	185	127
83	188	127
83	199	127
83	208	128
83f	203	128
84	204	128
84	204	129
84.21– 89.2	209	129.7– 136.15
85	159	130
85	203	130
85	204	130
85	204	130
86	205	131
86	205	131
86f	256	132f

CPR	EWM	PR
211	201	322
211	201	322
211	232	322
211f	244	321f
212	162	324
212	202	323
212	202	323
212	203	323
212	208n 11	324
213	202	325
213	254	325
214f	156	327f
215	65	327
215	196	328
219f	65	336
220	244	337
221	214	337f
221	215	338
221	217	338
221	255	337f
222	183	340
222	208	339
222	208	340
222	216	339
222	222	339
223	216	341
223	217	341
224	108	343
224	223	342
224	223	342
224	224	343
224	235	343
224f	235	343
224f	260	343f
225	237	344
227	239	347
227	260	347
231	233	352f
233	208	356
235	239	360
235	260	359f
236	121	361
236	218	361
239	208	366
240	215	367
241f	242	369
242	220	370
244	243	374
245	196	374

CPR	EWM	PR
247–55	220	378–90
247	221	378
247	235	377
248	47	380
248	154	380
248	183	379
248	222	380
248	242	379
248	257	380
249	224	380
249f	280	381f
250	236	382
250	237	382
250	237	382
251.44–252.13	236	385.5–24
252.18–25	236	385.31–386.2
253	221	387
253	221	387
253f	243	388
254f	223	389
256	140	391
256	141	391
256	192	391
256	219	391
256	232	392
256	243	391
257	202	393
257	232	392f
258	225	394
259	202	396
260f	220	398
261	219	399
266f	141	407f
267	48	408
276	225	421
277–79	20	423–26
277ff	220	424ff
277	223	424
277	257	424
278	183	424
278	242	424f
283	154	434
286	178	438
286	239	438
286	244	438
287f	239	440f
290f	74	445